W9-CZH-993

Program Smarter, Not Harder

Other McGraw-Hill Titles of Interest

In order to receive additional information on these or any other McGraw-Hill titles, in the United States please call 1-800-822-8158. In other countries, contact your local McGraw-Hill representative.

Program Smarter, Not Harder

Get Mission-Critical Projects Right the First Time

Jay Johnson

Rod Skoglund

Joe Wisniewski

McGraw-Hill, Inc.

New York San Francisco Washington, D.C. Auckland Bogotá
Caracas Lisbon London Madrid Mexico City Milan
Montreal New Delhi San Juan Singapore
Sydney Tokyo Toronto

Library of Congress Cataloging-in-Publication Data

Johnson, Jay, 1957–
    Program smarter, not harder : get mission-critical projects right
the first time / by Jay Johnson, Rod Skoglund, and Joe Wisniewski.
        p.   cm.
    Includes index
    ISBN 0-07-021232-5 (h)
    1. Computer software—Development. I. Skoglund, Rod.
II. Wisniewski, Joe, 1955–   . III. Title.
QA76.76.D47J653   1995
005.1—dc20   94-39990
                                                                  CIP

    2 3 4 5 6 7 8 9   DOC/DOC   9 9 8 7 6 5

ISBN 0-07-021232-5

*The sponsoring editor for this book was Jennifer Holt DiGiovanna, and
the executive editor was Robert E. Ostrander. The manuscript editor was
John C. Baker, and the production supervisor was Katherine G. Brown.
This book was set in ITC Century Light. It was composed by TAB Books.*

*Printed and bound by R. R. Donnelley & Sons Company,
Crawfordsville, Indiana.*

Dedications

To my loving wife and family—Kathy, Eric, David, Mark, and Lara.
RLS

To Dad and all my girls—Clara, Carol, Dawn, Lovisa, Martha, Larissa, Karen, and Jana—who think I can write, and to Dr. Lynn Beus who told me to be a writer.
JMJ

To my parents, Bob and Mary, who instilled in me my spirit of independence and self-determination; to Jeannette, Eric, Felicia, and Rebekah, without whom none of this really matters and without whose loving support none of this would be possible.

To R.R., R.L. and Jack R.—your words, heart and lives supply me with daily motivation to not only do, but excel.

To those who have supported me in my many careers and in one way or another have helped me to strike out on my own, of which this book is a direct consequence; to Brad Churchwell, George Goldsmith, Ed Heitmann, Doc Schraut, Mike Parks, Nancy, Mike Bogrees, and John McFadden for having faith in me and giving me an opportunity; to Dick Griswold for being a second dad and to Dan and Debi for "moving me out of" unproductive career choices.
JRW

Dedications

Contents

Part 2   Smart Software Design

Part 3 Quality—A Practical Perspective

Acknowledgments

We are grateful to our wives—Carol, Kathy, and Jeannette—for their patience, love, and support through the many long nights we stayed up writing. Their help in editing and improving our manuscript proved invaluable. Thanks also to our children—Larissa, Karen, Jana, Eric, David, Mark, Lara, Eric, Felicia, and Rebekah—for trying to stay quiet and well-behaved while their dads wrote.

We also express our gratitude to Carol Johnson and Rosie Cooper for their patience and expert help in editing the manuscript. Thanks for all the free English lessons!

We offer our sincere thanks to Jennifer DiGiovanna at McGraw-Hill, Inc., Margot Maley at Waterside Productions, and our friends at Honeywell, without whom this project would never have gotten off the ground.

Special thanks go to Bruce Bennett, Ruth Fragale, Jane Furze, Chuck Macon, Tom Phinney, and Ian Close for contributing some excellent ideas about software requirements, tools, testing, software quality, and life in general.

Introduction

The phrase *software crisis* was coined in the late 1960s, and little about the general state of large software projects has changed since. Despite improved technology and considerable research into software development processes, the crisis is worse than ever. Most mission-critical projects are in serious trouble. Mission-critical systems, which are designed to handle crucial aspects of running a company or to control a vital process in real time, can involve millions of lines of code and staggering financial commitments. In addition, the average mission-critical system developed today is much more important and complex than those of a quarter-century ago, so failures are costlier and more difficult to fix than almost anyone could have imagined when the software industry was in its infancy.

Despite huge investments of time, talent, and money, three-fourths of all large mission-critical projects are never delivered or are never fully usable (Gibbs, 1994). The actual delivery date (if there is one) for most systems is far beyond the promised date, with budget overruns to match. None of this should come as a surprise to software developers and project managers with more than a few years of experience—you probably have seen project failure firsthand.

In an attempt to stem the tide of project failure, software development organizations focus primarily on improving the way that code is written. New tools and programming techniques are introduced continually, and desperate managers try everything from fuzzy logic to automatic code generators. While it's true that better programming languages and other software tools offer hope, the software crisis rages on in spite of them.

Some enlightened managers have focused on improving the software development process as a whole, introducing improvements such as software metrics, requirements analysis methodologies, advanced project planning techniques, and teaming strategies. These efforts often receive little support and fade away when a project reaches *crunch time*.

It doesn't have to be this way. During our combined experience of over 30 years in developing mission-critical systems, we've learned what it takes to make a project succeed. Some software development shops focus on technology, while others focus on overall process improvement. The key to success is to build a solid process that is based on support from the best technology. Tools and methodologies must support the process, or the process will fail. By the same token, the most powerful software technology is truly effective only when it is part of a good process. An integrated, effective combination of a solid process and good technology will greatly improve the chances for success in any mission-critical software development effort.

Key pillars supporting a good process include: effective requirements management and analysis, reusable component libraries, object-oriented methodologies, prototyping, quality assurance, and advanced tools and environments. A well-designed process, supported by these components, forms the foundation of programming *smarter, not harder*.

Is This Book for You?

In many companies, there are software developers and managers who know that, for their organization to be competitive in the global marketplace, the way that they produce software must undergo a significant overhaul. They realize that, in place of their chaotic, ineffective software development process, there must be a process strong enough to support industrial-strength software development, yet flexible enough to thrive on changes in technology and customer requirements. They also know that powerful technologies—such as object-oriented software development, software reuse, and client/server architectures—must become part of the way that they work. If you're one of them, this book is for you.

Even if you're relatively new to the software development profession or still are preparing to enter the field, this book could make a very useful addition to your library. It offers an introduction to what effective software processes and technology are all about, as well as an overview of some of the real-world battles that you'll need to fight to develop high-quality software on schedule.

Content Summary

In the three parts that comprise this book, we explain how the newest software technology can improve productivity and reliability and how to develop a practical and effective software process.

Part one: The foundations of system development

Here, we introduce you to the essential concepts behind successful software development.

Chapter 1: High-powered processes. We begin by examining the attributes of a high-powered process and lay a foundation for defining an effective process that will be built upon throughout the book. In the beginning of the software business, programs were small and algorithms were simple by today's standards, so no one cared much about how programs were developed, only that they worked. As the size of programs grew, experts began to come up with methods of organizing functionality and data. With these methods came the idea that the development of software could be reduced to a *process*. Most companies still are a long way from an effective software process, although some have made considerable progress.

Chapter 2: Intelligent requirements. The software crisis often is thought of as a coding crisis, but it could be described more accurately as a requirements-specification crisis. The software-development process must be focused on one thing: turning the user's requirements into high-quality software. Requirements define what the system must do, how it will respond to inputs from the external world, and the environment in which it will perform its tasks. Many times these requirements are vague, misunderstood and undocumented. We will discuss what it takes to define requirements that will minimize the impact of requirements changes that occur during the later stages of development.

Chapter 3: A methodology survey. This chapter takes a look at the different methodologies that are in use today and how they impact the software-development process. These methodologies generally fall into two categories: object-oriented and structured. In this chapter, we explore the advantages and disadvantages of these two philosophies.

Chapter 4: Object-oriented technology. Object-oriented technology is a major thread carried throughout the book. In this chapter, we will describe this technology and examine the benefits and risks of its use. Object-oriented methods and tools offer a number of advantages over their structured counterparts, including improved quality, reduced cycle time, and lower costs. None of this comes without significant up-front costs. These costs include not only new tools and retraining but also support from both management and developers to make a fundamental change in the way software is developed.

Chapter 5: Team strategies. Most successful software development is done by skilled teams. Team strategies therefore are an important part of ensuring the success of any software development project. When used correctly, teaming can reduce conflict and improve communication. On the other side of the coin, unproductive or conflicting teams can cripple a project. In this chapter, we introduce the strategies needed to build and maintain effective, well-integrated teams.

Part two: Smart software design

Part Two looks at the design issues that face software organizations today.

Chapter 6: The art and science of prototyping. In an interactive development model, the art and science of prototyping takes on great significance. Prototyping often is the only way to uncover the users' real requirements and to determine what can and can't be successfully implemented. In this chapter, we explore the ins and outs of effective prototyping strategies.

Chapter 7: Software reuse. Software reuse is a key element in the future success of any company that is involved in software development. It is becoming more and more difficult to redesign, recode, and retest the same basic software element every time that a new project comes along and also continue to stay competitive in the market. Code reuse is not enough. The ideal reusable component will include the requirements, design, code and tests that are associated with the element. Reusing low-level routines is good, but it too is not enough. Reuse must be expanded to entire systems that, when integrated with other systems, can be used to build more complex products with limited resources.

Chapter 8: Concurrent programming. The users' requirements for execution speed and multiuser capability have forced software systems to use concurrent programming techniques. These techniques allow systems to make more efficient use of the microprocessor and handle events in real time. We will introduce you to the concepts behind concurrency as well as some of the major issues involved with its use.

Chapter 9: Object-oriented programming. The details of object-oriented design and implementation, including encapsulation, inheritance, and polymorphism, are explored in chapter 9. We show how a set of requirements can be translated into an object-oriented design and also address the practical issues involved in developing object-oriented software.

Chapter 10: Tools and environments. An overview of some of the latest tools and environments is provided to show how technology can support a process and result in higher programmer productivity. Some of the technologies that are discussed in this chapter include graphical-user-interface builders, programming languages, and client/server architectures. This thread is continued throughout the book as we address concepts such as requirements analysis, object-oriented programming, automated testing, error handling, and configuration management.

Part three: Quality—a practical perspective

Part Three introduces the reader to the quality-assurance side of software development. We discuss how changes can be made that improve the quality of not only the finished product but the process as well.

Chapter 11: Guidelines for software quality. Here we provide an introduction to the Software Engineering Institutes Capability Maturity Model and discuss how it can be used to improve the development process. We also expand on software inspections and the notion of a software quality assurance organization, both of which have been proven to significantly reduce development costs and improve software quality.

Chapter 12: Configuration management. Configuration management plays an important role in the quality of the software products that we produce. It helps us to manage the many changes to the product that are made by many different people. These changes can occur during initial development or to fix a bug that is found after it has been released. This can affect the requirements, design, code, and testing phases of the project, and several phases often are affected by the same change. We explain why configuration management is important and how it impacts the software development process.

Chapter 13: Automated testing. Testing, often a labor-intensive undertaking, can be streamlined significantly through the use of automated tools. Fully automated testing is not quite a reality, but by using the latest tools and methodologies, testing cycle times can be greatly decreased, with no loss of test coverage. Chapter 13 addresses the role of automated testing in an effective process and explores various types of testing tools.

Chapter 14: Error handling. A mission-critical system needs to keep running in spite of any problems encountered. Intelligent error handling is one of the keys to a truly fault-tolerant system. Despite changing technology, little seems to have changed in the way that most systems handle errors. In this chapter, we offer some new and better ideas to prevent embarrassing software crashes.

Whether you're a grizzled veteran of the software wars, still in college, or somewhere in between, our hope is that the ideas that we present here will help keep the raging software crisis from consuming your project, or your career.

Portions of chapter 14 appeared previously in an *Embedded Systems Programming* article by Jay Johnson, titled "Handling Exceptions in Ada and C++."

Reference

Gibbs, W. Wayt. (1994). "Softwares Chronic Crisis." *Scientific American*, 271(3), 86–95.

The Foundations of System Development

1

High-Powered Processes

Webster defines *process* as "a continuing development involving many changes" and "a particular method of doing something, generally involving a number of steps or operations."

Process, as it relates to software and systems development, is getting more and more attention as a necessary element of successful software and systems development. There is even some debate within the software engineering industry as to whether some of the vast resources expended on process are ultimately worth the expense.

However, Atkinson, et al. (1994) states, "It should be emphasized that having a well-defined software development process will greatly enhance the probability of successful technology use. Having no process will almost guarantee failure." This is a strong claim.

Rettig and Simons (1993, 45) "documents a process for software development designed and successfully used . . .." They go on to describe how "the department realized that seat-of-the-pants management techniques would not be successful." Finally, "[a] good manager can remove many obstacles before they appear by providing one of the most fundamental resources any project can have: a clearly defined plan and process definition." This article clearly describes a successfully implemented software process that with sufficient "real-world" details could be used as a template for another project. The appendix contains a similar "sample software process" that has been defined using past experiences (lessons-learned), good and bad.

Software is, in essence, a product. It must be produced, quality-controlled, packaged, sold at a profit, and shipped in a timely fashion much like anything else in the marketplace. In the beginning (30 years ago), software was simply written as one would write an essay. Programs were small and algorithms were simple by today's standards, so no one cared much about how programs were developed, only that the program worked. As the size of programs grew, experts began to come up with ways of organizing functionality and data. By the late 1970s, "structured" methods were widely adopted.

With these methods came the idea that the development of software could be reduced to a "process." Requirements could be fed into one end of the process, and validated software would scroll out the other end. By the mid-1980s, most project managers still didn't care what went on between requirements and results but were willing to train software developers in structured methods and to buy some CASE tools for them to use.

The software process incorporated these structured methods. It mapped them to what was thought to be a clear understanding of how software development needed to occur, including linear requirements, design, code, test, and integration models. As the size of projects began to grow, it became clear that this model was woefully insufficient due to the incorrect assumption that the software requirements analysis phase could be "completed" before latter phases were started.

Object-oriented (OO) techniques have attempted to deal with this need for a more iterative approach to software development. These "OO techniques" often perform better in the all-too-real world of changing software requirements. The reasons are many:

- OO techniques focus on mapping a "type of solution" to the "type of problem" that is attempting to be solved. The "real world" is comprised of "things" or objects. What better requirements model to use than one that is similar to the real-world model?

- OO technology, being based on these standalone objects, naturally supports an iterative development approach: analyze and design a few objects, then code and test them. Then go back and modify as it becomes clear that the requirements, as stated, misrepresent the system to some degree. Continue to iterate on those objects and incorporate more objects via the iterative development life cycle.

- OO methods have pioneered the concept and technique of system event analysis. To be able to assess the effects of changing requirements on a system, one has to be able to know how a system reacts to system events in the first place.

- Finally, through this iterative nature, OO and prototyping form a natural alliance. Part of the iterative life cycle can be activities that quickly give the customer an initial view of the system and those system requirements.

With these development methodologies (which will be addressed in chapter 3) changing, the software development process also will change. Some encouraging attempts have been made at standardizing software processes. The US Department of Defense has developed Mil-Std-2167 and 2167A that attempt to standardize some of the software development process. The Federal Aviation Administration (FAA), along with private aerospace companies and other institutions, has developed DO178A and DO178B. There also is International Standards Organization (ISO) 9000, a standard process that has been accepted by the European Economic Community. As a rule, ISO 9000 must be used by all software vendors hoping to do business in Europe. ISO 9000 is essentially the lowest common denominator of good processes and as such leaves a lot of leeway for adapting to specific situations.

Despite all of these efforts, the process that any one company uses is unique from any other and involves far more details than have been described up till now. How much does the implemented process vary from one organization to another? Some have volumes of process "gospel" that is strictly followed, and others have very little process.

How well do these different approaches work? Because most software projects are in trouble, you'd be tempted to say that neither of the approaches work.

The justification for software process will be discussed and immediately be followed by the methods and goals of process. These issues lay the foundation by discussing the necessity of process and the path to be followed when defining an effective process. If a good software process is a potential cure, then what are the symptoms of the illness? Warning signs that the current process is in trouble will be discussed along with what to do when there is no process or even in the case when there is too much process. (Yes, that is possible!)

Formalized software process is new business to most organizations. Therefore, the "process of defining the process" is something that interests most of them. For some organizations, implementing software process is a revolutionary concept. For others that accept change easily, implementation of formalized software processes quickly becomes an evolutionary concept.

A tremendous amount of tools and software development environments have arrived on the software scene. This topic plays such an important role in current software development that an entire chapter is devoted to a discussion of its role. The relationship between tools and process, however, warrants discussion of some very specific issues. Some believe that the tool should drive the process, while others support the converse.

Software development costs, like all other system costs, are undergoing and will continue to undergo ever-increasing scrutiny. Software process is here to stay; however, as with any other aspect of systems and software development, it must be done right or it can help to ensure failure.

Justification for Process

Not very long ago, most process-oriented articles were relegated to just the software engineering world and to a much lesser degree in the so-called commercial software world. This is not the case anymore. Effective software process has a place in all types of software development where a product is being generated to customer specifications.

Software process modeling and implementation are not cheap; therefore, like any other cost, its need or potential benefit must be measurable in economic terms and result either directly or indirectly in lower costs or higher profits.

Any discussion of justification of process must include an analysis of the costs involved in implementation of that process. Much of the process costs are borne very early on in the project life cycle. As a result, these software process costs are even more difficult to justify than "normal" product-related costs. These costs are incurred at such an early stage of the project, and the benefits due to these costs therefore are not readily recognizable and therefore less justifiable. The argument for incurring these costs, especially in an organization that has not done formal process, can be a very difficult one to present and win. That argument usually goes something like this:

> [Old Stodgy Project Manager]: "Jim, I don't understand this line item that you've requested for software process. It's almost half of what the project is going to spend on the entire design phase! I can't remember any project that I've been on that spent that much on process. I remember getting the work done without it. We got the product developed and delivered. Why the heck do we need it now?"

> [Software Manager—Process Advocate]: "Sure, if you consider missing the original delivery date by 11 months, overrunning budget by 40%, never coming close to delivering original spec-ed functionality, and working off problem reports for another year "getting the work done without it.""

Note: Don't try this tactic if you're a junior engineer!

As with any "revolutionary" organizational change, there must be strong management support for the change. Implementing a new software process is going to cost money up front. After all, the processes need to be in place *before* that corresponding stage of development occurs. This would seem all too obvious, but again, the experienced developer probably also has seen the following situation or something similar to it (see Figure 1.1):

> [Same-Old Stodgy Project Manager]: "Jim, I don't understand this line item that you've requested for software process. It's almost half of what the project is going to spend on the entire design phase! Look, there is no way that I can justify

Figure 1.1 Initial salvos being fired in a "process battle."

bringing on that many people that early in the program. Why the big hurry? This process stuff can't be that big of a deal. Just do this process-stuff at the beginning of each phase, and we can get it done then as we go, instead of all at once up-front.

[Software Manager—Process Advocate]: "Do you know what is going to happen if we do that? We are not going to have time to react if the new process and the new tools don't quite interface the way that we think they will. On top of that, you also are implying that my developers are going to be part-time process people then. They are not going to have the time to do that, and you know what will win out when process is pitted against short-term deadlines. That kind of policy is doomed to failure."

Once the justification for process has been accepted as valid, it really is just the beginning. All we really have done up to this point is to acknowledge the fact that business could be done better, perhaps much better. The question now becomes, "What exactly needs to be done to improve matters?"

Attributes of a Good Process

Software process is just the path to the goal, the delivered product. This path can be rocky and virtually impassable, or it can be a smooth, paved road. The attributes of the process will determine this. These attributes are:

- Timeliness of the process is critical
- Process is a "process"
- Must become second nature to all on the project
- A "better" process is better than the "best" process
- Encourage creativity, don't stifle it
- A process is not a process until it is repeatable
- A method of ensuring high levels of "software quality," usually through independent auditing procedures, is necessary. *Note*: This usually is achieved through the implementation of an independent software quality assurance (SQA) function. Much more will be said about SQA later.
- Process oversight function must be in place
- Upper management commitment

Timeliness of the process is critical

If it were possible to design the "perfect process," it still would not be effective if the relevant parts of the process are not in place when needed. This is a pitfall that is encountered by many organizations when attempting to implement software processes for the first time or when making major modifications to an existing process. As would be expected, this is difficult to accomplish. This situation occurs because the up-front investment in process definition is invariably underestimated, both in terms of funding and manpower.

What very often occurs is that the process effort is underestimated and underprioritized. As a result, system and software engineers are performing requirements analysis before the process for this phase of the project is defined. Once this occurs, the entire process definition effort will be behind for the rest of the project. If this situation occurs, the best realistic solution is to simplify the process as much as possible by doing the following:

- Make the process as absolutely tool-independent as possible.
- Determine the minimum level of customer acceptance of documents in terms of format and content.
- Try to allow the individual groups as much leeway as is possible when it comes to methodology choices. Don't force any single method on the de-

velopers. At this point, a strictly common method might not be the best solution as it would be if the process were in place.

These suggestions might seem to fly in the face of what we are trying to accomplish with process. You must recognize, however, that, if the process is not in-place when it is needed by the developers, the only other real option is to constantly "pull the rug out" from underneath the developers by changing tools, documentation formats, and even deliverable products. This is not an acceptable solution.

Process is a "process"

Good software process is not merely the path to the goal of a successful product but is the establishment of an ever-changing curricula of improvement practices. After the implementation of the process, it might become apparent that some aspect of that process needs to be modified. The process must be malleable enough to not only provide a framework to incorporate a possible modification, but to encourage constant re-evaluation and improvements to the process.

Conradi (1993, 26) states, "Software processes . . . need to continuously evolve in order to cope with different kinds of changes or customizations both in the organization and in the technologies used to support software production activities." Conradi is correct. Like any other aspect of a software organization or any organization for that matter, any and all aspects of the organization must be able to adapt to changes. If a method for accepting change is not part and parcel of that organizational construct, that construct will become obsolete (perhaps along with the organization, also).

Keep in mind that any improvements to the process that affect work currently being performed must be thought out very carefully. As mentioned in the previous section, changes to the way that developers are performing their work can have an extremely deleterious effect on the development team.

When changes are made to the process, the overall effect of those changes must be considered. A process might be changed for the better, but the ultimate effect might be a tremendous amount of rework to previously completed activities, unanticipated downstream effects to other aspects of the process and a drop in employee morale.

Usually, a more prudent approach to process improvement is to make minor modifications as you go, then make needed major changes at the end of the project, in preparation for the next project. When areas for major improvement are identified, they must be recorded immediately and catalogued in some fashion. At the conclusion of the project, it is imperative that several "What We Did Right/What We Did Wrong" meetings take place.

Process needs to become second nature to all on the project

In addition to the process being continually analyzed and improved, involvement with and attention to the process needs to become second nature to everyone on the project.

A warning sign that a project is in trouble is when an inordinate amount of time is spent by groups within the project trying to substantiate reasons why some aspect of the process should not apply to them. It then is obvious that the process has not been accepted. This usually is not because of incompetent engineers or software developers who like to argue. (This is very often the impression however.) To one degree or another, groups don't go along with process because the activities dictated by the process are not viewed as value-added activities. This is why it is critical that, when a software process is being developed, valueless activities be struck from the process. If not, it is very possible that some value-added activities will be ignored along with the valueless activities. Here is a quote that, if heard, should raise red flags in this area, "Well, yes, I know that this is the process, but our software is unique and must be developed in ways that are just not accommodated by the process."

The following could be elements of a project's software process that some might argue are "valueless":

- Formal reviews/inspections of all produced elements, such as requirements documents, design elements, code, test, etc.
- Configuration of any element prior to its being reviewed
- Conforming to coding standards
- Requirement to have interface documents between software subsystems that interact
- Any attention paid to software reuse such as common software teams
- Conforming to design standards that require a specific design methodology

In short, there must be buy-in from all staff, especially management. (Management support and buy-in is addressed specifically in the next section.) There undoubtedly will be some disagreements about the specifics of the process that is implemented. Unanimous initial acceptance is rarely possible concerning any decision. However, support for the process (which includes the method for changing the process) is absolutely necessary for success of the process and ultimately the project.

If pockets of resistance develop and grow, "process battles" will develop. If this is allowed to occur and continue (by either direct management involvement or tacit management approval), irreparable damage can be done. Invariably, when "process battles" occur, the skirmishes become personal.

I was directly involved in this kind of situation. I was a member of a small group on a large project. I was actively involved to one degree or another on process teams due to the interest in "process" by our immediate manager. Unfortunately, however, my manager and another manager "staked out" conflicting positions on many process issues and became highly vitriolic defending those positions. (Each took their positions feeling that their positions were right and justified.) These antagonistic positions taken by these managers were adopted by the staffs of these two managers. This did not have to happen. It was completely unnecessary and seriously damaged our process definition efforts.

Joe Wisniewski

The positions taken by these two managers and the resultant conflict was neither planned nor desired. Both managers truly believed in their individual positions. One felt that process was being ignored or at least wasn't getting anywhere near the attention that it deserved and would result in serious problems to the entire program. The other truly felt that the proposed process was composed of non-value-added activities and would negatively impact his group and the entire project.

This is not to say a severe difference of opinion must thwart the process or the process definition effort. Differences of opinion, even severe differences of opinion, are desirable. However, if the differences are severe and they linger past the point that the process is defined, these differences will be counterproductive. Once the process has been defined, it must be committed to by all. There should be opportunities within the process for improvement. Whether it be before the process is defined initially or during certain process modification efforts, these severe differences of opinion must be either solved or simply internalized. "Process battles" that continue throughout the program can destroy that program.

This is what is meant by the process needing to become second nature. To get to the goal of the deliverable product, you have to "watch your step" along the path to that goal (the process). The process that is in place needs to be applied and changed, as appropriate. Upon first glance, these might appear to be conflicting goals. On one hand, follow the process; however, on the other, change it as necessary. Upon further analysis, however, there is no conflict. Implement the process as defined, give it an honest chance to work, and if there are problems with it, go through the procedures necessary to improve the process.

For this to work, however, everyone involved with the project needs to feel that they can comment on aspects of the process that they feel need to be changed, but only after a true honest effort to implement the process. This is not to say that every change requested will be accommodated. The optimal process for a given project and organization cannot be achieved without the input of those who use the process the most, the actual developers. Support personnel, such as aides and secretaries, also must have input into process definition and improvement. Very often, these personnel are impacted when valueless documentation aspects of the process exist. When all personnel are cognizant of how all of their activities interact with and are defined by the process, then the process acquires the "second nature" aspect that is necessary for project success.

Every standard should have provisions for deviations from that standard. Valid deviations are just that. Differentiating between valid reasons for deviations from a standard and simple noncompliance can be a difficult task. This issue of deviations from the standard process raises another issue relevant to the pursuit of good process. That is the issue of buy-in to the process and the role of "benevolent dictators." More will be said of this later.

A "better" process is better than the "best" process

Why would you want to settle for something less than the best? Because the "best process" simply does not exist. The process itself needs to be malleable enough to change as the organization and tools change. As both the demands and our capabilities increase, the process needs to keep pace. The cost tradeoff, however, might not be worth some specific improvement to the process. This is an especially difficult concept for developers who are new to the industry to accept. The best possible product at all costs is simply not the best policy.

In addition to being cost-ineffective, even if the "best process" exists, it might be that the organization might be too immature to proceed to the "best process" level before traversing intermediate levels of improvement. One of the major underlying themes of this book is that object-oriented practices will ultimately help an organization to deliver a better product more efficiently. Many organizations are not currently capable of fully adopting complicated object-oriented methodologies immediately without experienced personnel and comprehensive training. For example, consider an organization that attempts to deliver a large business system to be developed in C++. It will fail miserably without staff successfully experienced and trained in C++ (not just C!) and object-oriented techniques.

The topic of software process improvement is methodology independent. A good process can be implemented that incorporates any valid development methodology. In this regard, this chapter is mainly method independent. This is largely due to the fact that the choice of a "more modern" method will not improve the quality of the product (and could very well decrease it) if the overall process is inadequate.

This phenomenon is seen time and time again within organizations that have a tendency to look for the "quick fix." Frequently "over-zealous method advocates" will claim that the solution for all the organization problems lies in the adoption of a new method, such as object-orientation. What is overlooked is that, if the process is not in place to handle the new method, the new method will fail as surely as previous methods have failed. Yourdon (1994, 94) states, "A primitive DP organization . . . does not need OO to improve; it needs much more basic things, such as the ability to estimate the size of its projects and a rational process for deciding when it must refuse to accept budget or schedule constraints imposed upon the project." Well said!

Booch (1994) takes a slightly different approach to this problem of method and process. He describes how a "well-implemented" object-oriented methodology can have an impact on and help direct the development of the process that is used. He introduces the concepts of micro and macro development processes that reflect iterative and incremental aspects of development.

The micro object-oriented development process encompasses the iterative aspects of the classic object-oriented paradigm. They are:

- Class specification, object interface definition, and object implementation
- Class and object identification
- Class and object semantics identification
- Class and object relationship identification

These activities typically constitute elements of a repeatable cycle that operates within what Booch calls the macro object-oriented development process. The elements of the macro development paradigm are:

- Establish core requirements (conceptualization)
- Develop a model of the desired behavior (analysis)
- Create an architecture (design)
- Evolve the implementation (evolution)
- Manage post-delivery evolution (maintenance)

This macro development paradigm encompasses the incremental aspects of development. Despite this more interactive approach to process and method, the basic premise still holds true. Unless the process is managed and implemented, the method just won't matter.

This is exactly what the Software Engineering Institute (SEI) posits with its Capability Maturity Model (CMM). The SEI and its CMM will be discussed in much more detail in chapter 11, but the SEI has defined five levels of software capability maturity at which an organization operates. Refer to Table 1.1 (Finklestein 1992; Milligan 1994) for a summary of the CMM.

Note: That is, unless you subscribe to the very well-written tongue-in-cheek analysis of the three additional subbasement levels of the CMM in Finklestein (1992)! In addition to the levels 1 through 5, levels 0, –1, and –2 are added to the extended immaturity model.

TABLE 1.1 Software Process Maturity Model

Level	Characteristic	Key problem areas	
Optimizing (5)	Process Change Management Technology Innovation Defect Prevention	Automation	PRODUCTIVITY AND QUALITY
Managed (4)	Quality Management Quantitative Process Measurement and Analysis	Changing technology Problem analysis Problem prevention	
Defined (3)	Qualitative Process Measurement and Analysis Peer Reviews Intergroup Coordination Integrated Software Management Training Program Organization Process Definition Organization Process Focus	Process measurement Process analysis Quantitative quality plans	
Repeatable (2)	Process Dependent on Individuals Software Configuration Management Software Quality Management Software Subcontractor Management Software Project Planning Requirements Management	Training Technical practices Process focus	
Initial (1)	Ad hoc/chaotic	Project management Project planning Configuration management Software quality assurance	RISK

The vast majority of organizations (over 70% according to SEI assessment results) are assessed at level 1 (initial level) when initially rated. As you can see, organizations that are assessed at the "initial" level are mostly *ad hoc* or chaotic organizations. They consistently have many problem areas. Projects that are completed are done so strictly due to individual heroics. Project management and planning is inconsistent or even nonexistent. Configuration management occurs sometime in the midst of the project, if it is done at all. There usually is no quality assurance function. If by some chance this function does exist, it has no teeth and must go along with all software development decisions.

Organizations that choose to move up the maturity model scale do so incrementally, a level at a time. It simply is not possible to do so in any other manner. Organizations then can progress from the chaotic level to the repeatable, defined, managed, and optimizing levels. The vast majority of projects organizations will never progress past the repeatable or defined level. (For an interesting overview discussion of the CMM and how software measures can be used in the model, see Carleton, Park, and Goethert 1994.) As stated before, much more will be said about the CMM in chapter 11.

Encourage creativity, don't stifle it

Software development is no doubt a "technical" activity. Euphemistically, technical activities such as this are described as "left-brain" activities. However, there is little doubt that successful and effective software development projects also require a vast degree of so-called "right-brain" skills. Maybe good software developers are "frustrated artists" from another life!

Solving problems in software requires a great deal of creativity. One criticism often leveled at "software process activities" is that they stifle creativity. This is extremely misleading. This attitude usually is borne of a "hacker's" mentality, because "creativity" is mistakenly equated with undocumented classroom-style programs or hack-it-out kinds of projects. This doesn't mean that university-level software programming is bereft of undocumented programming assignments. Activities that are attributed to this stifling of creativity (such as adherence to programming standards, standard design documentation and methodologies, and documentation activities) are not emphasized in academia, in general, as they are in the business world.

Whether or not one's creative juices are being stifled is not really the issue. There are numerous opportunities to express one's skills when developing software. Expressing this creativity is mistakenly identified as a "coding phase" construct, when in fact creativity probably is needed in all phases of software development.

There is even more to be said concerning creativity and software development, however. It is this inherent creativity that makes software system development different and perhaps more complex than other technical disciplines. Perhaps it is the failing of software reuse activities that leads to this complexity. For example, there is a tremendous amount of creativity that goes into the development of a house. However, when that house becomes one of many very similar or identical tract homes, there is very little additional creativity involved in the process.

This rarely happens with software, however. Even within so-called "well-constructed" systems, minor changes or upgrades require a "creative effort" to implement. Whether it be fixes or modifications to an already fielded system or the development of a new system, a creative process occurs to determine the best possible design decisions.

Certainly this creativity needs to be managed; otherwise, this unbridled creativity becomes massive chaos. Software process procedures, whether good or bad, will not stifle creativity, at least that kind of creativity necessary to developing a good product.

A process is not a process unless it is repeatable

To be effective, any "process activity" first must be repeatable. It is not coincidental that the "repeatable level" is the second level in the SEI CMM. By definition, a process must be repeatable, else the process becomes essentially a "one-shot" event.

For the process to be repeatable and effective, however, other characteristics also must be present. Ultimately, the process must not depend upon individuals; however, to some extent, individuals should depend on the process. This is not to say that the developers are slaves to a bad process. The process must constantly be open to improvements so that the developers are not slaves to a bad process. However, individuals must begin to learn to operate from within the process.

Active SQA involvement is essential

Most customers require medium- to large-scale projects to have an SQA function. This function usually is required to have a management reporting ladder that is independent of the software or engineering function. Unfortunately, in most cases, actual SQA involvement goes downhill from there. Active and effective SQA involvement is an absolute requirement by SEI for progression beyond a level of an SEI Level 1 organization, as it should be. (Note Table 1.1.)

Why is an active and effective SQA organization necessary for an effective software process? Sometimes it is just necessary to have an informed, capable, independent organization ensuring that the process is being followed.

For example, all projects undergo schedule pressures. As a result, project management prioritizes the remaining activities to ensure a quality product is developed. With the involvement of an independent SQA organization, those remaining tasks can be prioritized in such a way that the long-term product quality is not sacrificed for short-term schedule gains.

The SQA department can be of great help to the software development organization when the project has a lot of junior software developers that have not been exposed to a lot of formal software process. An informed SQA department can be of immeasurable help by becoming actively involved with these junior developers with appropriate guidance as to adherence to process and quality standards.

If the concept of an SQA organization is such a good one, then why does the SQA function seem to disappear from most projects? One reason is, when a project undergoes cost pressures, staff members that are not directly generating the product are susceptible to being eliminated. These people are viewed as adding less value to the project than the coders, designers, and testers. Typically, the customer, who required the SQA function, is given a choice between support functions such as SQA or "getting the job done." Usually a skeleton, overworked SQA staff is left to finish up the project.

What can be done then to keep SQA not only involved but an active element of a project? We offer the following suggestions:

- Appropriately staff and train all SQA staff before the project starts.

- Ensure that there are formal reviews and inspections AND that SQA is actively involved in these activities.

- Develop a symbiotic relationship between SQA and the development groups early on in the project so that they are treated as an important part of the project.

- Ensure that the SQA group is given high visibility by management within the project and within the organization.

If these occur, then it is much more likely that SQA will be an active, involved, and respected organization on a project. As such, there is much less chance that it will be considered an "expendable" overhead cost late in the project.

This can be a viewpoint that often is shared throughout a project. For the most part the customer sees the value of SQA and usually is very supportive and, as stated earlier, requires active SQA involvement; that is, unless SQA involvement means schedule slips. The engineering or software management department has less enthusiastic support of SQA. Their support usually is tenuous, at best. It usually is not overtly negative however. Program management's support for SQA varies. It usually starts off positive but usually will correlate with how the project is performing to schedule. Because practically all projects miss their original delivery date, project management support of SQA is not very high toward the end of a project. Programmers view SQA with disdain. They just get in the way of getting the job done. Of course, SQA views their own contribution on an ever-increasing scale. Henry and Blasewitz (1994) present a graphical representation of these varying views of the relative contributions of SQA. (See Figure 1.2.)

Another reason that there are problems with SQA has to do with the skills necessary for a very good SQA department member. The SQA department needs to be able to effectively critique how well the project is abiding by the spirit and intent of the process. The SQA staff must be able to fully understand all aspects of the software development process and the methodologies used in the development. To be able to most effectively critique a coder, you pretty much need to be a good coder. This follows for all phases of development. You can have an SQA department that is useful without being experts in all phases of software development; however, to be able to do the best possible job, you need very skilled people in those positions. The problem is that most projects cannot afford to have that skilled of an individual in a support function and not "on the project."

SQA is important to product quality. Unfortunately, this usually is not the majority opinion of the staff on the project.

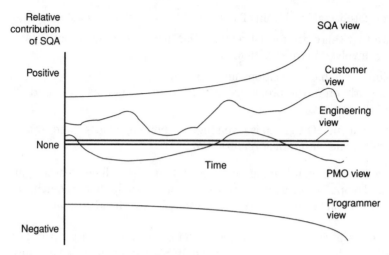

Figure 1.2   Relative contribution of SQA. (Joel Henry)

Saradhi (1992, 21) states very appropriately, "[H]ardware technology has seen fantastic progress, whereas, the software technology . . . is still at its infancy . . .. [I]n one way, software is oxygen for the life of the computer system. So, for the health of the application software . . . the quality of software put into the . . . computer hardware is a deciding factor. I strongly feel that software quality shall not be an additional attribute, rather it must be synonymous with software as such."

SQA is a necessity that most projects need to not only learn to deal with but to take advantage of to improve the quality of the product. Without the quality, there really is no effective product.

Process oversight function must be in place

As stated on several occasions, the process needs to be constantly critiqued, then adjusted when appropriate. A mechanism needs to be in place to accomplish this. Most projects have a management team that is responsible for this oversight function. This team must be empowered to make lasting decisions necessary to keep the project on track and the process in place.

The responsibilities of the team are to:

- Help with the definition of the overall process
- Coordinate tool purchase decisions with the process definition
- Manage any modifications to the process
- Mediate process-related disputes from project groups
- Help to coordinate necessary training to facilitate implementing the process
- Do whatever is necessary to make the process work and get the product out

Henry and Blasewitz (1994) provide an interesting viewpoint concerning the last two sections: the relevance of an SQA organization and the role of a process oversight team. Their conclusion is that the role of SQA has changed over time and can best be "implemented" through a process oversight team that oversees the determination and implementation of the software process. Although the perspectives concerning SQA that they provide in this discussion (SQA from the viewpoint of SQA, program management, engineering, software developers, and customer representatives) offer differing viewpoints, this conclusion is flawed.

To maintain its effectiveness, the SQA function must have organizational autonomy. However, a process oversight team must directly represent all or most of the development groups that comprise the project. Realistically, you could never expect an organization to allow a group (SQA/process oversight) that is not directly affiliated with the project to determine its software development process. The lack of accountability directly to the project would be politically unacceptable to the management of the project. Their only direct input to the process definition and modification efforts are through the process management team.

One of the biggest temptations that the process management team will encounter usually will occur about midway to two-thirds of the way through the project. Inevitably one or more of the groups on the project will begin to encounter severe schedule difficulties. To meet schedule milestones, process-imposed tasks that are viewed as non-value-added will mysteriously appear. The dialogue typically goes something like this:

> [Manager of Section in Trouble]: "Look, I told you guys that all of this process stuff was going to get us in trouble. Yea, I know I agreed to it at the beginning of the project, but what do you want, process or product? And I guarantee you that if you are going to make us go through this process stuff, then we'll let upper management know that the reasons we are going to miss scheduled deliveries is because of process."

> [Process Mgmt. Team Leader]: "The purpose of the process is to help us develop and deliver a better product than we have in the past. How could these activities have changed from being absolutely necessary a few months ago, to a waste of time now? We have been through several replans, and what we have left to do HAS to be done."

The real problem that the process management team leader has on his hands now is that, if parts of the project are "allowed" to bypass certain tasks under the impression that they will get back on schedule, the rest of the project will follow suit. What happens when this section does not follow the process? Short-term gains are realized; however, in the long-term, more time and money are spent getting the product out.

We believe that, despite the "bad rap" that SQA can receive, it is a necessary and critical aspect of a successful software process. Likewise, a process oversight team is mandatory but is accountable for an entirely different set of responsibilities.

The following sections contain some examples of "late-in-the-game cost-savers" that ultimately result in higher product costs, delayed product delivery, or just a poorer quality product.

Short-cutting the testing phase. When a project goes over budget, it usually is very apparent by the testing phase (assuming some kind of waterfall development approach) that the project or the section is in trouble. Module or unit testing (depending on the phraseology used) usually gets reduced in scope. The reasons that are given at the time are that a lot of the "unit testing," as it is called, is a waste of time anyway. It would be more efficient to just eliminate the unit testing and perform all testing during the integration phase.

There is no argument here that sometimes small parts of unit testing can be deferred. What is conveniently ignored, however, is that, during integration, the developers will not have access to anywhere near the amount or quality of debugging aids. Fixing a bug in integration is almost always more costly than eliminating that bug during unit testing. So, if everyone knows this, why is this kind of decision repeatedly made? Because it moves the problem further down the timeline and perhaps under someone else's accountability. There is no other way to say it.

Elimination or large-scale curtailment of documentation. In one form or another, this probably is the most frequently occurring short-term cost-saving device that ends up costing more than it saves. When a project incurs schedule and cost overruns, the scope of documentation is reduced or eliminated. Some of the documents that typically are affected are requirements documents, design documents, user manuals, code documentation, and test plans.

However, is money or time really saved? When the inevitable system and software changes occur, it becomes a very difficult task to implement these changes because the requirement is not documented well, the design construct can't be found anywhere in the design documentation, the impacts of the change are unpredictable because the code is documented so poorly, and no one has any idea of what tests need to be rerun because the testing documentation is out-of-date.

Elimination of online help. Many projects promise the golden Cadillac but end up delivering the Chevy Nova. Online help often is another one of the casualties of the "cost overrun" war. Everyone agrees that it is absolutely necessary during system specification; however, when it comes to cutting out functionality, it is one of the first to go.

Inappropriate concurrent development. This is a very common shortcut and also is one of the most dangerous. As certain aspects of early program development begin to slip, there can be a tendency to begin other "downstream" activities before earlier "dependent" phases are done. In and of itself, concurrency is not a bad development construct. What causes problems, and usually serious problems, is when development activities are begun before necessary and essential dependencies are complete.

Certain sections of code cannot be developed until necessary interfaces are developed. When schedule pressures are felt, however, development is begun before it should. It is clear what happens next. This early development is truly "shot-in-the-dark" development. Most of this code ends up being redone when those necessary interfaces eventually are developed. This situation brings to mind the often-seen cartoon of a manager with a staff of programmers ready to start coding. The manager tells the staff to start coding and that he will find out what it is that they need to do later.

Do not confuse this "inappropriate" use of task concurrency with that which represents activity concurrency that is not only "appropriate" but is inherent in all but the most nontrivial of software projects. Davis and Sitaram (1994) discuss, in a succinct and relevant manner, how projects that are to be successful projects are never, at any single point in time, involved in just a single phase of the project. The oversimplifying assumptions of the waterfall development method are exposed in a very thorough discussion. This topic will be addressed in much more detail in chapter 6.

It does no good to implement a process unless there is a mechanism in place to monitor that process and work with the development teams and SQA to ensure that the correct process is implemented. Some kind of process management team that has representation from most of the project is a good way to do this. It is absolutely critical, however, that, just as the process needs to be fully supported by upper management, so too must this process oversight team have the full support of upper management and be empowered to make lasting decisions.

Eliminate the reviews. When it gets to crunch time, elimination of reviews is a classic perceived timesaver. Reviews should be occurring for all phases of the development: requirement reviews, design reviews, code reviews, and test plan/test case/test procedure reviews. For any review to be effective, all functions that interface with the element to be reviewed should be involved in that review. If the designers who should be involved in these reviews are behind schedule and "coding like crazy," reviews will not be a task that gets a high priority relative to their "main" task.

As with the other "short-cuts" that have been discussed, this one also is very short-sighted. When interface functions don't take the time to review relevant segments of the system to ensure that the expected interface exists, code rewrites are inevitable. Dismissing reviews results in rework that ultimately costs more in the long-run.

Upper management commitment

Unless those who hold the true power in the organization are committed to the process, it will fail. In a sense, that is all that needs to be said. Commitment is easy when the project is on schedule and under budget. True commitment occurs when times get difficult, when it appears easier to succumb to short term gains and to question the process. There is little else that will demoralize a project faster and ensure failure than for upper management to buckle when the going gets a little tough.

Warning Signs that the Process Is in Trouble

Many have laid the foundation for the need for strong process in software development. Boundy (1993) observantly describes the symptoms of the "project in trouble" illness that require the healing power of good process. These are early warning signs that the "patient might be terminal." Do any of these sound vaguely familiar to you?

Degrading quality of the software

You know that the quality of your software is degrading when one bug fix results in several "fatal improvements" that just seem more difficult to fix than they should be. Another major telltale sign of degrading software is, while bringing someone new onto the project, it seems to take a lot of time to explain all of the "special circumstances" that caused the code to be written in a certain manner.

There are other signs that your software is de-evolving into a lower life form:

- Has a single data type change caused days and days worth of changes and fixes?
- Has a single hardware address change caused a multitude of changes to seemingly unrelated code?
- Does a misspelling of a word in an error message cause multiple changes in the code?
- Does the reordering of the fields cause massive changes to the code everywhere that those fields are referenced (absolute references everywhere instead of field-by-field service routines)?

What do you do when this starts happening? There is no clear-cut answer. In many circumstances, a redesign certainly might be warranted. In other cases, living with the current design and installing patches as needed might be the appropriate solution. There are some general software quality checkpoints that should be heeded:

- Single changes to code cause unknown and indeterminable system behavior.

- It is not possible to determine the tests to rerun based on changes to the code.

- It is not possible to describe system behavior or system design without looking at the code.

- Design and coding activities occur without at least initial commitments to requirements stability.

- For a system that has real-time requirements, timing studies before coding is mandatory.

- Minor changes to code consistently resulting in modifications to requirements documentation.

- Checkpointed versions of the code cannot be re-created.

Occurrences of these checkpoints indicate serious problems with not only the quality of the software but most certainly also with the software development process.

Constant and expected "replans"

If deadlines are being missed, especially early on in the schedule, and even more importantly, if everyone is sliding schedules out, rough times are very likely ahead. Even more fatal is when deadlines are being missed and there is no sense of urgency about it. This says that everyone knows the schedule was unrealistic from the start. Chances of timely completion of the project are extremely slim.

Accurate software scheduling is one of the areas at which most organizations perform poorly. One reason for this is that most organizations don't do an effective job at collecting and utilizing relevant metrics. This is just another symptom of the problem of every new project starting over from a clean slate (new management, new process, new technology, etc.). Without a quantitative history of cause and effect, the planning managers have no better information as to how to plan and schedule than someone who knows nothing of the organization!

What is most disturbing about the constant "replans" that most software programs encounter is how readily they are accepted and even expected. They can be demoralizing to the software developers. The developers eventually might ignore the schedules completely due to the constant revisions.

Replans become necessary when project milestones are missed and it is clear that more milestones and/or the final product delivery will be missed. Replans change the dates of interim milestones and might or might not slip the final delivery date.

Whether or not the final delivery date is slipped on the replan is much more of a political and human nature issue. While the customer might be tolerant of agreeing to slips in interim milestones, it might be political suicide to suggest that the final delivery date be slipped. Human nature takes over at this point. Typically the program manager will agree that the final delivery will not slip, knowing full well that it will take a miracle of biblical proportions for that delivery date to be met. Miracles, at least of this type, simply don't happen.

Regardless of the type of replan that is being discussed, lots of interim milestone slips will result in missed delivery dates. Constant replans are the result of poor plans and poor planning ability. The fact of the matter is that replans rarely, if ever, get a program "back on schedule." After all, when a program is planned out, a given set of activities are scheduled that will result in the product being delivered. "Extra" activities are not scheduled in that they can be cut out later "if there isn't enough time." Therefore, if milestones are missed and more work has to be done in a set period of time, some tasks don't get done, some tasks don't get done as well, the Mongolian horde approach is used, or the final delivery date is missed. Many times all of these occur.

Abounding tribal knowledge

Tribal knowledge is a phrase used to denote undocumented information that is known to but a few select individuals. There also is an implication that the owners of this tribal knowledge (the high chieftains) have an advantage over others that are not privy to this information.

It is not always true that the existence of tribal knowledge is indicative of project problems, but an excessive amount can be an indicator of concern. Tribal knowledge manifests itself when aspects of the project are changing so rapidly that "there is just not time to document it all," or so one is told. When requirements are changing so rapidly that to get the "true meaning" of those requirements one has to have them translated, trouble might be looming.

Tribal knowledge can exist anywhere on a project. Here are some examples:

- The very specific tricks to using a buggy toolset
- The traceability between hardware and software requirements documents and system and software specifications
- Where files and directories that represent different configurations of software are located
- The current list of problems that exist with the software
- The requirements that are incorrect and need to be rewritten to match the software

One specific area in which tribal knowledge seems to breed is in the area of testing and in the use of test beds for flight critical software. Very often, various kinds of hardware, hardware/software deliverables, and software simulations are melded together into a test bed that (hopefully) closely emulates the operational environment. These kinds of scenarios are rife with tribal knowledge, usually due to the fact that hardware and software simulations typically are not tested to the extent that deliverable hardware and software is and as such is prone to be "buggy." Not only does it very often take "black magic" to reboot a test bench, but that magic changes daily. This inevitably leads to delays, inefficiency, and frustration.

This is just one aspect of the project where pockets of tribal knowledge exist. In reality, all areas of the project are vulnerable to be ruled by tribal law when process is lacking. During the coding phase, if there is an ill-defined process, a select group of coders will understand how all of the coding tools interact, what special login scripts are necessary, what the quirks of the debugger are and how to get around them, what the "unique" aspects of the compiler are, etc.

Likewise, the design phase is not impervious to this phenomenon. A select number of the software designers are aware of how the design interfaces with the requirements and how up-to-date the design documentation is and how relevant that design really is with respect to the code.

Historically, requirements analysis has had this reputation. In some organizations, the "systems group" is responsible for analysis of the customer specification and will very often be responsible for generation of systems and hardware and software requirements documents. These requirements documents then will get "thrown over the wall" to the software group for implementation. The systems "tribe" truly is the keeper of the "knowledge" of what the customer really wants. Few project scenarios are as potentially dangerous as this.

These are examples of the "high chieftains," and it is not uncommon for many of these individuals to occupy highly regarded positions on the project. They are truly the experts, but they inevitably are trying to manage a far greater number of tasks than is humanly possible to handle. As a result, they very often are behind on much of their work. These individuals very often are the ones that see the project through to its conclusion, whatever that might be. In a positive sense, these very often are the individuals that are responsible for a successful conclusion of a project. In a negative sense, these sometimes are the individuals that have a difficult time incorporating their skills into a project where process is implemented well.

Once abounding tribal knowledge occurs there is not much to be done about it. More importantly, how does one avoid this type of situation? Remember, we are talking about inappropriate tribal knowledge. Long-lived projects naturally will have experts, due simply to longevity with the project.

This is desirable, not detrimental. Many deleterious tribal knowledge situations can be prevented by:

- Keeping documentation up-to-date. New staff on the project don't need to be "hand-held" to get the basics of the system.

- Practice "good-coding" principles so that design and code can be understood as easily as possible, again without a lot of one-on-one guidance.

- Do what is necessary to keep good people on a project therefore keeping a "few good individuals" from having to become the remaining key individuals on the project.

- Keep from getting into "end-of-project" panic situations where the previous situations occur.

A plethora of indispensable individuals on the project

This is somewhat related to the previous topic of tribal knowledge. Many projects are staffed with lots of "experts" or "can't do without" people. Again, in and of itself, this is not a major problem. The problem occurs when any single individual cannot leave a program without potentially dooming the project.

This is a concern for several reasons. Why is this person so indispensable? Unfortunately, too many times it is that the code (if this individual is responsible for development of code) has become so complex that the learning curve is just too steep for someone new to come up to speed. Other times, it is simply that there is a paucity of documentation available for the work that a given individual is responsible for and, again, the learning curve is just too costly for someone new to traverse.

When essential people are stuck on a project indefinitely, it might not reflect favorably on those individuals or the project. What also can happen is that individuals can be unhappily tied to a project for an extended period of time, making some of the more productive people in the organization unavailable for work on new development projects.

These are some of the symptoms that a project is in trouble. What are the cures? Good software process activities attempt to put in place proactive remedies to these all-too-common problems.

"Over Process" or "All Things in Moderation"

We've discussed in some detail what happens to projects and organizations that lack the appropriate amount and quality of process. It might be hard to believe, but there are situations where process overshadows the actual development work that must be accomplished on a project. In some cases, the commitment to process totally overshadows the development of the project.

This can be a very difficult problem to solve, especially for immature organizations. As stated earlier, holding out for the "best process" might just not be feasible. When the "best possible" process that can be realistically implemented by a project or organization is defined, it is time to begin development. It's very difficult to know when that point is reached however.

Getting out the product that the customer expects within schedule and cost constraints is all that really matters. It is possible to overwork the process issue. How can this happen? While it is true that some organizations are extremely cost-conscious and, in some cases, process is a casualty in the budget wars, an equally strong force in the workplace is the concept and implementation of teams and teaming in support of process. We feel that this is such an important issue that an entire chapter will be devoted to it. (See chapter 5.) If the scope and role of these teams is lost, then the teams can become self-serving ends in and of themselves. These teams can forget that they exist to solve a problem. When the problem is solved, the team should be "dis-solved."

It is possible to "overdo" a good thing, and this certainly can be the case with any "new management" philosophy. Teaming and its resultant effect on process is no exception. When determining the specifics of system and software process, by definition, this process will be in effect across the entire project. It follows that, for rules to be in effect for an entire project, everyone working on the project must agree unanimously to those rules. The implementation of this simple premise or assumption can doom a project. If this seems to be a rather far-reaching statement, continue reading.

Although the concept of unanimous approval seems to appeal to certain inalienable democratic ideals, there are arguments to be made against this method of management or business decision-making. Software process teams that are run so that the only decisions that can be made are those unanimously agreed upon can run into trouble. What can happen is one or more of the following:

- Highly controversial issues that must have unanimous approval end up being implemented as group A can do process A, group B can do process B, etc. That is, when there are highly controversial issues being decided upon, it is very likely that the involved parties will never agree willingly to a single solution.

- The implemented process ends up being a least-common denominator of all of the varying opinions and inputs. As a result, the process is so vague that, again, anything is acceptable.

- Deadlock occurs and no decisions are made.

These kinds of teaming dynamics are some of the causes of over-process. When a compromise is not possible, it sometimes is necessary for a "benevolent dictator" to step in and make decisions that "keep the ball rolling."

Another aspect of over-process (or perhaps uncontrolled process) is related to how teams are implemented in an organization. This aspect, however, is not related to the gridlock that can occur among teams, but more to the propensity for unnecessary overlapping of teams, both within a project and then within an organization. Let's address overlapping teams within a project first.

This can very easily occur and often does occur. For example, it is common for a project to have a team chartered with determining the best requirements analysis methodology to implement as part of the overall process. It is important for the project to have a consistent requirements analysis approach because differing approaches often will have differing forms of documentation. If the customer is concerned about requirements documentation, he normally will find it unacceptable for one part of a project to have a requirements document that is of one form and another segment of the project to deliver a requirements document that reads completely differently.

It also is very common for a project in its early stages to still be investigating tools (via a tools team) to be used on the project. It is best to purchase or build a toolset that will play together for all of the phases of the project. Don't purchase one tool for requirements, another for design, and another for coding and testing only to find out that they don't interact well together, if at all. It would be common for this team to be deciding upon a consistent toolset that crosses all of the software life cycle phases.

While trying to determine the optimal requirements method for the project, the aforementioned requirements team certainly should be considering the tools that are available to support this method. What do you think is going to happen if the requirements team and the tools team don't work together closely? The tools team might come up with one toolset to be used across the entire project and the requirements method group might come up with an entirely different tool recommendation for the requirements phase. This scenario is very common.

It is important for any and all teams that are convened to understand the common processes within which the project (and the teams) should be operating. As pointed out in this section, "over-process" or uncontrolled process can occur as a result of unbridled team efforts.

Now consider the fact that there are or will likely be teams assigned to work on methodologies for each phase of the development. Again, the potential for uncontrolled process becomes even greater. If that were not enough, many companies have organizational-level process teams that are working on many of these same issues, but from a company-wide viewpoint.

Team coordination across the differing levels of an organization takes company and project management that is committed to making process work. If not managed effectively, however, it is easy to see how management and the project staffs can get frustrated when dealing with process issues. It can seem like all that the project is doing is bouncing among process "nondecisions," when these aforementioned process issues are not managed effectively.

The unfortunate result is that process can very easily get a bad name. It is not because the process was necessarily bad (which of course it could be), but the amount of money and time that is spent when teams are not managed appropriately will evoke bad memories for managers when it comes time for the next project.

Keeping a team focused is another crucial aspect of teaming and process. As stated earlier, a team should exist to solve a problem and, when that occurs, there is no reason for the team to continue to exist. Unfortunately, this simple common-sense concept can be totally forgotten with some teams. Typically, such a team will become undirected, unsure of why it exists, and what problems it is chartered to solve. Perhaps an example of such an undirected team will serve as an illustration.

Here is an example of a process-related team "gone awry":

> This process team would meet twice a week. Early on, the goals were relatively well-defined and some successes were achieved. After a while, however, the team meetings typically would begin with "What do we want to talk about today?" To further illustrate the misdirection of this team, one member took it upon himself to perform a task that he thought would be of great benefit to the team. He spent two weeks using a data-flow diagramming tool to graphically describe the process of defining the process. In some academic setting, this might have been viewed as a useful activity, but here it was akin to a batter stopping in the middle of a pitch to study the laws of physics involved in hitting a baseball. It was time to leave this team.
>
> Joe Wisniewski

It is very easy to lose focus. Process does not exist for the sake of process. It exists to help ensure development of a quality product through the development of quality organizations.

When the Process Is Nowhere to Be Found

All children, on Christmas morning, learn that Santa never brings all of the toys that they want. Today's corporate "belt-tightening" strategies often result in difficult budget cuts. In many organizations, "overhead" costs are the primary candidates for these initial cuts. Many times support for software process development is reduced and sometimes even eliminated.

Despite voluminous information extolling the virtues of software process modeling and implementation, personal experiences with the "process" of management frequently are negative. This often is due to previous experiences with "process" where tremendous amounts of money have been wasted so that management always views process as a waste of money. So what do you as a software developer do if there is no project-level software process in place?

If a project involves more than 20 developers or so, it is almost inconceivable that there would be no process at all. More likely, there are general ideas of what kinds of documents will have to be generated and what they will look like. There is some idea of what tools might or might not be used to generate customer documents and internal documentation. Most importantly, there usually is no official process in place to ensure consistency in the development of the actual product among all of the developers or the development groups. Let's try and address the situation of a small to medium-sized project because this probably is the most common and the one that you, as a developer, will encounter most often.

One individual can make an impact on doing things right. We have all been involved in projects, large and small, where we have been able to positively impact major process changes from within. These changes, however, typically were not implemented from a top-down approach. They were implemented across the program by first instituting the changes within very small groups, then succeeding with this "new" aspect of the process, then "proselytizing" this improved process to other parts of the project.

This approach might be frustrating because it usually is slow, but it probably is the only way to effect change when there is no consensus process in place.

Whenever process is deficient, it usually is because there is an explicit dictate against it. It might be viewed as an overhead cost for which the immediate benefits are not readily identifiable, or it can simply be that no one knows quite what to do. It is next to impossible for a single individual (read as developer) to have any kind of direct effect on the "top-down" implementation of process. Any changes that you can influence will have to work up from your level, unless the program or organization is sufficiently small or you are high enough up the management or lead scale.

An additional point should be made. When discussing topics such as process, some of the "solutions" discussed might not scale up to larger projects or, if they do, to scale up to these larger products, these solutions must be modified. Keep this in mind. This certainly might be one of the reasons why one hears about "large project failures." Solutions that were adequate for small and even medium-sized projects are just not sufficient or appropriate for large projects. Most of the problems large projects have are related to coordination of communication (or a lack thereof).

Is it possible that process isn't affordable for organizations, in the long run? Is it possible that, through implementing such a good software process, the amount of money to be made by an organization will decrease "too much" and the developers will become so efficient that many developers will end up becoming unemployed? Despite these and other like conclusions in Scott (1992), we believe the answers to these questions to be a resounding, "nay."

There is another side to the issue, that is, the "cost of quality." It is possible that an over-commitment to quality can result in negative returns on quality investment. Admittedly, this would truly be a rare situation. However, this can happen on a micro-scale. For example, suppose there is a line manager who is a "process advocate" on a project. It is possible that his or her attention can be focused on process to such a degree that the "real work" never gets done.

All projects have finite resources within which to operate. It certainly is possible that some elements of the process become overbearing and onerous to the point of diminishing returns on quality. There always has to be some trade-off between level of quality and the cost necessary to achieve that quality.

Reduction of overall costs (including process costs) will not result in an organization losing business or a net reduction in developers, all else being equal. There are enough organizations doing a less than adequate job in software development that there is work to be had, depending on the sector, of course. As to the argument concerning process improvements resulting in loss of employment for developers, competitive pressures among organizations ultimately will force out inefficient organizations. Maintaining inefficient organizations to "prop up" projects assumes a never-ending supply of cost-blind projects, which is a specious argument, at best.

Process Evolution and Process Revolution

A good repeatable process is necessary for consistently successful projects. There probably are very few project managers that would disagree with this assessment. Ideally, the goal is to get a sound, effective process in place that "works" for an organization.

Once that occurs, does that mean that this is the end of money or effort spent on process? Of course not. In this regard, the process is no different than any other product that the organization builds. It is not perfect the first time that it is released. There will be aspects of the product that are not "correct" and need improvement. As mentioned previously, Conradi (1993) does an excellent job describing this necessary evolutionary aspect of implementing a software process.

The organization needs to constantly evaluate the state of its process and determine where minor modifications should be made. This is all part of the self-evaluation process that SEI and most successful organizations have determined is necessary for advanced process status. Once again, this can occur only if the mindset within management is such that self-evaluation is deemed to be an effective and desirable management activity.

We are not espousing, however, the concept that a project that is in the midst of development activities should constantly alter its processes, just for the sake of changing, in the hopes of improving. We recommend that, during all of the phases of the project, everyone working on the project should constantly evaluate what works and what doesn't. This process of self-evaluation, once embedded within the ranks, will quickly move the organization to increasingly higher levels of productivity and quality.

Rettig and Simons (1993, 54) not only support this concept of continuous self-evaluation but have made it an active, constituent element of their process. "At the end of each stage, the team sets aside time to reflect on the previous few months. Did any modules take far more or less effort than planned? Why? What can be done to avoid such miscalculations in the future?" This is more than a passive, after-the-program analysis of the software process. This is proactive, management-led involvement in process refinement.

This method of analysis goes much further beyond standard post-project self-assessment. The goal of this mid-process analysis is to analyze, recognize, and implement modifications to the process in "real-time." In addition to the immediate benefits of this kind of approach, the authors go on to describe how this mid-process analysis allows developers to be critiqued in a positive, nonthreatening manner. It allows the team to "focus on how the programmer could have been better supported, how planning could have improved our original time estimates, or how the process should change to improve performance in the future."

If an organization does not feel the need to make incremental changes and improvements to the process, it ultimately might find it necessary to make a "revolutionary" move to improve the process. However, if that organization is undergoing these same "revolutionary" process awakenings every two or three years, then something is desperately wrong. Usually some basic errors were made in some process decisions that became noticeably apparent during one or more projects but could have been fixed incrementally along the way.

This revolutionary approach will likely increase costs, certainly in terms of dollars. It also will cost the organization in terms of lost opportunities, such as missing the chance to capture and implement improvements through involvement of the entire development team.

This active involvement is the second nature that was spoken of previously. The process needs to become second nature along with the consistent self-evaluation of the process. The continuing advent of new and improved languages and programming environments (such as Ada 95, C++, Graphical User Interfaces, etc.) practically guarantee necessary modifications to the process as new tools become available. Even if it were possible to have implemented the perfect process, improvements to languages, tools, and environments in just a few short years invalidates that "celestial" position.

Constantine (1992) puts it best when he says, "If your process isn't changing, if it isn't a subject of discussion and debate, it probably isn't being used. A good process is organic, embodied in the habits and conversations of the team."

Process and Tools

As high-powered processes are molded into the fabric of an organization, it is inevitable that the issue of tools must be addressed. Tools and development environments will be dealt with in much more detail in chapter 10, but it is critical at this juncture to discuss the crucial relationship that exists between software processes and those tools or environments.

In many organizations, debate rages as to which should be defined first: the process or the tools. One view is that the process is paramount and tool decisions should be made *only* after decisions have been made as to how the organization's processes will be defined. The contrasting viewpoint is that, because there are only a limited amount of tools available, the appropriate toolset first should be chosen for an organization and only then should issues related to process be investigated. Let's examine both positions.

Process first

One side of the argument makes the case that the organization shouldn't be constrained by the tools that are available. It kind of goes like this:

> After all, this organization is not going to adopt a process just because it's all that the available tools will support. Tools don't make the process. Tools are just that: tools. If we have to make the tools to fit the process, then so be it.

This, it seems, in and of itself is not a totally unreasonable position. After all, tools don't do the engineering work (despite what we sometimes are led to believe by overzealous vendors). Also, why should the starting point be the tools? Organizations have unique needs. Those needs should be addressed first and foremost without regards for the available toolset. If the process or set of processes that are developed are so far out of bed with toolsets that are available, then the organization probably will consider just making the tools inhouse.

Tools first

Let's now explore the other position. Usually the argument goes a lot like this:

> It is clear that tool XYZ is being used by everyone who is serious about object-oriented development. After all, look how integrated it is. They really have developed their object-oriented requirements analysis (OORA) tool. It has a graphical

front-end that we would be foolish to pass up. Then they have integrated the analysis tool with the design tool that also does the code generation. Our code costs will go down dramatically. Look at all of the automatic documentation generation that it does! On top of it all, they have a training department that will help us define our process if we need help. What more could we ask for!

This is the position tool vendors just love. "Regardless of your organization's goals, this product can do it for you." This philosophy actually can be seen in action when an organization is just beginning to implement any kind of formal software processes. Tool vendors can be persuasive. This is not a knock on tool vendors, per se. Usually the solution to this problem is a compromise of these two opposing positions.

The real solution

Be wary of any solution that has no tolerance for compromise, especially in this case. Neither process nor the toolset can be chosen without fully considering the impacts of one on the other. A process cannot be fully defined without considering what tools are available to implement that process. In addition, defining the process based solely on tools can be extremely shortsighted.

Summary

In this chapter, we have spoken a lot about different aspects of process, including:

- Definition of what is good process
- Benefits or goals of good process
- Justification for its use
- Warning signs associated with bad process or no process
- What happens when process is done badly
- What happens when there is no process
- Making process evolutionary instead of revolutionary
- Relationship between process and tools

The most important aspects of this entire discussion have had a lot to do with commitment—commitment to improvement in product quality. Software process has been accepted, for the most part, from an academic standpoint. It is the real-world trial-and-error of implementing these software processes that has been difficult.

The SEI has been of immeasurable benefit to those organizations that have tried implementing formalized software processes according to their guidelines and suggestions.

It is our firm belief that appropriate improvements to software process will be accepted by the developers because most developers want to deliver a better product. The discipline that most aspects of software process improvement espouse will help to make that developer a better employee, a better software developer, and ultimately a more marketable commodity. Software process improvements offer opportunities for the organization, the project, the developers, and the customer.

References

Atkinson, Shane, Ralph Ganska, John Grotzky, Jack Rubinstein and Jim Van Buren. March 1994. *Requirements Analysis and Design Technology Report.* Software Technology Support Center (STSC). Hill Air Force Base, Utah.

Booch, Grady. 1994. *Object-Oriented Analysis and Design with Applications. 2nd Edition.* Redwood City, California: Benjamin/Cummings.

Boundy, David. 1993. "Software Cancer: The Seven Early Warning Signs." *ACM Software Engineering Notes* 18 (2): 19.

Carleton, Anita, Dr. Robert E. Park and Wolfhart B. Goethert. 1994. *The SEI Core Measures: Background Information and Recommendations for Use and Implementation.* Crosstalk. The Defense Software Engineering Report. Software Technology Support Center (STSC). Hill Air Force Base, Utah. May 1994.

Conradi, Reider. 1993. "A Conceptual Framework for Evolving Software Processes." *ACM Software Engineering Notes* 18 (4): 26–35.

Constantine, L. 1992. "Decisions, decisions." *Computer Language.*

Davis, Alan M. and Pradip Sitaram. 1994. "A Concurrent Process Model of Software Development." *ACM Software Engineering Notes* 19 (2): 39–51.

Finkelstein, Anthony. 1992. "A Software Process Immaturity Model." *ACM Software Engineering Notes* 17 (4): 22–23.

Henry, Joel and Bob Blasewitz. 1994. "Do we really need SQA to produce quality software? No! Well maybe. It depends. Yes!" *ACM Software Engineering Notes* 19 (2): 63–64.

Milligan, James R. 1994. *Transitioning Automation for Process Enactment.* 1994. Crosstalk: The Defense Software Engineering Report. Software Technology Support Center (STSC). Hill Air Force Base, Utah. May 1994.

Rettig, Marc and Gary Simons. 1993. "A Project Planning and Development Process for Small Teams." *Communications of the ACM* 36 (10): 45–55.

Saradhi, Motamarri. 1992. "Software Engineering From a Practical Perspective." *ACM Software Engineering Notes* 17 (3): 21–26.

Scott, Gregory J. 1992. "Can Software Engineering Afford to Improve the Process?" *ACM Software Engineering Notes* 17 (2): 39–42.

Steward, Donald V. 1993. "A Simple Straightforward Method for Software Development." *ACM Software Engineering Notes* 18 (4): 36–43.

Yourdon, Edward. 1994. *Object-Oriented Systems Design.* Englewood Cliffs, New Jersey: Prentice Hall.

2

Intelligent Requirements

creationism n. The (false) belief that large, innovative designs can be completely specified in advance, then painlessly magicked out of the void by the normal efforts of a team of normally talented programmers. In fact, experience has shown repeatedly that good designs arise only from evolutionary, exploratory, interaction between one (or at most a handful) of exceptionally able designers and an active user population—and that the first try at a big new idea is always wrong. Unfortunately, because these truths don't fit the planning models beloved of management, they are generally ignored.

RAYMOND (1993) (Figure 2.1)

The software development profession exists solely because computer users are willing to pay for the development of the software that they need. These users can range from a horde of PC owners to a consortium of chemical companies, and their software needs can be anything from real-time process monitoring to artificial intelligence. The formal descriptions of these needs are called *requirements*—the raw materials of the software development mill. These might (and should) be in a formalized format (i.e., a controlled document) but sometimes are nothing more than an amorphous mass of information referred to in the trade as *tribal knowledge*. The acquisition and updating of this information often is neglected or treated as a "black art," with requirements appearing and disappearing out of thin air. There seems to be little attention paid to organized requirements management. As Boddie (1987) explains in his book entitled *Crunch Time*, most software is based on "truly wretched" requirements, if requirements exist at all. He describes software development as a "ritual dance of successive approximation."

Figure 2.1 The fallacy of spontaneous generation.

I've worked several projects where there was never what could even loosely be called a set of requirements. Vague ramblings and tribal knowledge had to suffice until costly formal software release attempts made clear what the customer wanted; then most of the code had to be rewritten. In my experience, teams sometimes are a lot better off to try writing their own requirements and get direct approval from the customer than to wait for requirements to filter down through correct channels.

Jay Johnson

Requirements often are ignored, but they won't go away. Developers might not know what users want, and users themselves might not be able to express it. To be successful, however, your development team must deliver a system that fulfills customers' needs.

Facing the Risks

The lack of effective requirements management is one of the major factors keeping most software development organizations from being successful (Humphrey 1990). Barry Boem, in his classic *Software Engineering Economics*, explains that, without sufficiently detailed and accurate requirements, it's impossible to estimate the size and cost of a project (Boem 1981). It should be obvious, then, that a great place to begin building a good process is with better requirements management.

Any successful attempt at process improvement must first and foremost address the most important risks to project success. On many projects, a lack of complete and accurate requirements is behind many of the primary risk factors, such as unrealistic schedules, inappropriate staffing, incorrect technology, etc. Requirements also are the basis for estimating the size, response time, cost, schedule, and staffing of a software product. For example, 6 of the top 10 most serious software development risk factors identified by noted software-engineering writer and lecturer Capers Jones (Jones 1994) are directly related to requirements management.

Memory and processing power

If a requirements specification is sufficiently detailed, depending upon the customers' performance needs, you might see requirements such as:

```
Trace Anchor AB00197: The error-handling system shall be capable of
updating the status of <customer-defined constant 01> records per
second

Trace Anchor AB02133: The error-handling system shall be capable of
storing and retrieving at least 100,000 status records.
```

With requirements such as these, it's possible to plan for the correct level of performance and storage capacity.

Level of effort

Any real chance of coming up with a reasonable schedule or staffing and resource plans is based on high-quality requirements, because they are the only source of information concerning the total amount of work involved in the project. On the other hand, the lack of a complete requirements specification or disregard for requirements is a major culprit in the proliferation of unrealistic schedules.

> When it comes to unrealistic schedules, what I've seen in my experience is that project management's disregard for, or failure to understand, the total amount of work defined by the requirements is equally as detrimental as poorly defined requirements. In other words, even when we know the risks, managers often refuse to face them.
>
> Jay Johnson

Technology transfer

Requirements also help to determine the technology and training needed for a project. A good requirements specification will specify the hardware needed for execution, as well as performance that the user expects. A customer might require a specific technology to be used (i.e., a relational database, a client-server architecture, or a GUI builder), although this most often is left to derived requirements or design. This information will be invaluable in developing a plan for technology transfer.

Go or no go

Faced with a core set of requirements (including prototypes) detailing the customers' needs, we can determine not only the level of effort needed but whether or not the effort is worth the development cost and the risk that there will be insufficient demand for the product. It also might be the case that, due to contradictory needs, the customers' requirements simply can't be met. It's far better to know that the project won't be worth the effort early on rather than after resources have been committed to develop the product.

If We Build It, They Will Come

Knowledge is the raw material of a software project. The two most important types of knowledge on virtually any project are: technical (includes design and analysis methodologies and tools) and problem domain (knowledge of the customers' business). Both of these are necessary, but knowledge of the problem domain is a rare and precious commodity on many projects. Knowledge of what users really want often is the single most important factor in the failure or success of a software project. It's also one of the most neglected factors.

The causes of requirements neglect are many and varied. Here are a few of the more common:

- Users' needs cannot be completely known until after a system is built, so it's almost never possible to fully specify a system at the beginning. Even if it were possible, by the time the system was delivered, users' needs would have changed.

- Even when requirements are stated up front, they probably will change at least several times during development and certainly will change immediately after deployment. (Davis and Hsia 1994)

- Booch (1994) points out that in "industrial strength" systems, "the problems that we try to solve in software often involve elements of inescapable complexity, in which we find a myriad of competing, perhaps even contradictory requirements." This complexity, according to Booch, arises from four sources: "The complexity of the problem domain, the difficulty of managing the developmental process, the flexibility possible through software, and the problems of characterizing the behavior of discrete systems."

- Users in general have little knowledge of the trade-offs involved in implementing requirements in software, such as conflicting needs, schedule pressures, performance considerations, and implementation constraints.

- Ninety-three percent of all communication is nonverbal (Arthur 1992), so it's likely requirements will be misunderstood as they are gathered and refined.

- Responsibilities for gathering and refining requirements often are not clear. Which departments are responsible for digging up detailed requirements for what functionality? Who chooses which ones have the highest priority for implementation?

A lack of real requirements leads to the development of software that is developer-driven rather than customer-focused. The prevailing philosophy seems to be to build what developers think customers want, rather than working closely with customers to find out what they really need.

The Requirements Chase

Good requirements are the foundation of high-quality mission-critical systems. Effective design, implementation, verification, and maintenance are impossible without them (see Figure 2.2).

There is only one proven way to get good requirements. Representatives of the development team, who understand what the end-users of the product do for a living, need to work with representative customers to collect all the facts about what the system should do. The requirements gathered from customers then need to be filtered and refined so that they can be implemented and understood, don't conflict with each other, and provide the users with what they really need, not what they think they want.

The only way to build software that does what it's supposed to do is by thoroughly understanding the users' world. At least a select few of all the developers on a software team must have an intimate understanding of how the product being developed will affect end-users' lives. Sometimes called *system architects* or *system analysts*, these individuals must do some diligent detective work with representative users to gather the right requirements.

Once requirements are gathered, they must be filtered and refined until they are consistent and understandable enough to proceed with design and

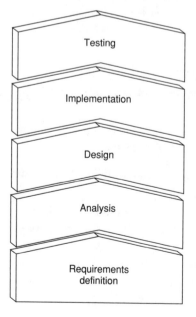

Testing

Implementation

Design

Analysis

Requirements
definition

Figure 2.2 Good requirements provide a solid foundation for development.

implementation. The result of all this collecting and filtering should be some kind of formal representation. This could be a document, a prototype, a database, some combination of these, or some other organized representation. An organized set of requirements is variously called a *specification*, *requirements document*, *design intent document* (Walz, Elam, and Curtis 1993), *users' manual, functional specification*, or any one of at least a dozen other names.

No matter what they're called or how they're represented, developers need to trust the correctness of their requirements, understand them, and be able to implement them. Good requirements are consistent and complete. As a general rule, only those features that are necessary for the user to do his or her job are eligible for real "requirements" status. To be useful, requirements also must be traceable, at the right level of detail, and testable.

Correct

The goal of a requirements specification must be to exactly communicate what end-users need. If requirements are represented in the form of a document, something as small as a missing or misplaced punctuation mark or a single incorrect word can cause serious problems later (Parrington and Roper 1989).

Consider the changes in meaning a few misplaced hyphens can cause:

A. The node calculating status shall be determined by the master node processor.
B. The node-calculating status shall be determined by the master node-processor.
C. The node calculating-status shall be determined by the master-node processor.
D. The node-calculating-status shall be determined by the master-node-processor.

Now look at how ambiguous language really can be:

> There shall be an overview object for every status object, descriptor object, or storage object.

On the surface, this requirement looks fairly precise. On closer examination, however, you might (and should) wonder if it means:

- There is one and only one overview object, and it suffices for all status, descriptor, and storage objects in the system.

- There is a unique overview object for each status, a unique overview object for each descriptor, and a unique overview object for each storage object.

- There is at least one overview object for each of the three objects: status, descriptor, and storage. There is at least one of the three objects—status, descriptor, and storage—for each overview object.

Actually, the answer is "none of the above." The writer really meant that there should be one specific overview object related to every group of three objects consisting of a status object, a descriptor object, and a storage object.

The worst enemies of correctness, however, are ambiguous, imprecise phrases such as "enough time," "sufficient resources," and the ever-popular "appropriate error message." Good, implementable requirements detail exactly the "how much," "how often," "when," "what," and "where" of each specified product feature. To assure this precision, requirements must be refined via reviews, inspections, and prototypes throughout the development process.

Understandable

Correctness greatly increases understandability; however, in addition, all terms used in requirements, such as acronyms, must be explicitly defined. A glossary of terms must be included in the requirements specification. Ideally the specification also should include diagrams and appropriate language to increase readability. Because a requirements specification might be looked upon as a contractually binding document, it makes sense to use precise words such as "shall" or "must" to indicate that a sentence or paragraph is a requirement rather than a "nice to have" feature or a helpful piece of information, as in the following examples:

- Requirement Trace anchor AB0130: "The system shall be accessible only to users with valid passwords."

- Design Goal (nice to have feature) Trace anchor AB0100: "The system will be accessible only to users with valid passwords."

- Informational Text: "The system provides support for user-level security."

Implementable

Those who study the topic of requirements engineering often have maintained that requirements must describe only the "what" (an abstract view), not the "how" (implementation). Unfortunately, despite what some ivory-tower dwellers say, you have to have some idea of how something will be done before you sign up to do it, and sometimes the "how" needs to be specified in a requirement, especially if:

- Those who define the requirements have insight into the most practical, or the only possible, means of implementation.

- The customer requires a specific language (such as the federal government requires Ada), requires a specific operating environment (for its specific features or to be compatible with existing and future systems), or requires specific hardware and/or detailed hardware-software interactions (common in real-time embedded systems).

The idea that requirements should be expressed only in abstract terms simply does not always work in the real world (Siddiqi 1994). At the abstract level, conflicting requirements often go undetected. When the "how" of implementation is considered, however, conflicts often surface. The details of implementation must be considered for all requirements, but it's not always advisable to put these details into a user-focused requirements document. An internal requirements document or a design document usually is the right place for implementation details.

Consistent

It is common for requirements to conflict at some level. For example, on the same system, some requirements call for open data sharing while others specify strict data protection. The truth is that customers often want everything and want it immediately. They need to be educated through presentations, prototypes, users guides, and one-to-one conversation that they can have anything they want, but not everything.

> Several years ago, the team on which I worked was handed an impressive two-volume requirements specification. We were to assume that these tomes (which actually came from the "systems" group) had just been handed down from on high and therefore were a flawless representation of what the users wanted. None of the mere software developers were allowed to speak directly to either the "systems" engineers or the potential users but instead had to channel all communication through a management team, which knew little about software implementation or customer requirements.
>
> As we read and analyzed the requirements, it became clear that the systems engineers who wrote the document knew little about software and that few of them knew what the others had written. Several major conflicting requirements soon surfaced, and it became obvious that at best fewer than half of the "users' wants" could be implemented. After six months of awkward bargaining involving nontechnical management, the requirements finally were pared down to one large volume. We then labored for two years in implementation; however, after users began beta testing, we discovered to everyone's sorrow that the requirements were so wrong that much of the system would need to be redone.
>
> Jay Johnson

Requirements must be filtered and refined before they're of much use, but too many filtering layers between the developers and end users leads to inconsistent requirements. On the other hand, too little filtering leads to requirements that are certain to be implemented incorrectly, if they are implemented at all.

Complete

It pays big dividends to do a thorough job of ferreting out and filtering requirements early in the project. A solid core of requirements provides developers with a base from which to develop prototypes and refine the product specification. Conversely, finding out about a missing requirement late in the game (for instance, when the customer does his acceptance testing) can be disastrous (Glass 1979).

Usually, *complete* means *currently complete*. With developers, users, and managers constantly pushing and pulling on the requirements specification, change is inevitable. The impact of each change must be understood, and the schedule, resources, and staff must be updated accordingly. The first step is to determine the "core" requirements. The key is to manage the change via prototyping, reviews, formal channels and procedures.

It sometimes seems that customers endlessly demand changes and additional requirements. On the other side, however, it's almost inevitable that, at some point in the project (the earlier the better), developers will revolt, realizing that all of the requirements cannot be met by the deadline for the current release. With the success of the project at stake, negotiations then commence between customers, managers, and developers. The ideal result of this negotiation is a reduced (or "down-scoped") set of requirements that can be met by a reasonable date and still meet the customer's basic needs. In the worst of cases, the whole process will be a waste of time and put the project even farther behind schedule.

For any number of legitimate reasons, there might not be enough information available from the customer, a tool vendor, a subcontractor, etc., to completely specify a requirement. In these cases, dutifully record any assumptions made and flag all missing information to be filled in later. Verification and completeness is crucial, but it certainly doesn't pay to hold up the project over a few incomplete requirements.

Necessary

Both customers and inexperienced developers have a tendency to add "nice-to-have" features into the requirements soup. Make sure there's no "gold plating" in the product, and that you're giving customers what they really need, not what their managers (or your managers) think they need.

At the right level of detail

One of the major decisions to be made in generating a requirements document is the level of detail. For example, "I/O port validity information shall be maintained" probably is at the right level of detail, depending upon the level of abstraction of the requirements as a whole.

A corresponding, more-detailed requirement might state: "A data-validity flag shall be maintained for each I/O port." This requirement probably is too detailed, because it forces developers to create "flags" when they could accomplish the same thing by a real-time check of the port, etc.

The most-detailed representation of this requirement would specify what each bit in the flag represented and would be far too detailed, unless there were specific hardware considerations driving the requirement.

The level of detail in requirements is a crucial consideration and, as such, can be quite controversial, especially when you realize that working from requirements written at the wrong level of detail can seriously hurt a project and limit requirements reusability (see chapter 7).

If a requirement is not detailed enough, it essentially is useless because it doesn't give designers the information that they need. If it's too detailed, designers are shackled and changes are extremely difficult to make once the design is begun in earnest.

Those who define requirements must walk a tightrope between the general and the specific. (See Figure 2.3.) The key to walking the tightrope is an understanding of the level of abstraction that the user needs.

For example, the owner of an automated parking garage might want to know only the net amount of money collected per month. He wants to see this in the form of a report containing only the total receipts and total expenses. Details such as the number of cars parked each day, the make and model of each car in the garage, and how the information is stored may be of no interest.

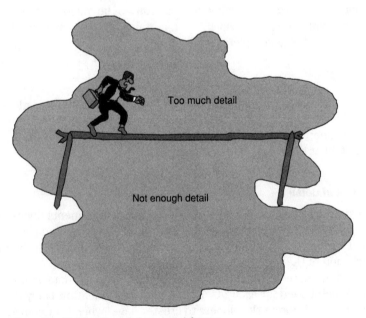

Figure 2.3 Walking the requirements tightrope.

Traceable

Every requirement that is implemented in software needs to correspond to a specific user need. These needs should be recorded in a document the user writes, or in interviews, memos, meeting minutes, etc., and the requirements written by the development team should refer back (or "trace") to them. Traceability is proof that the product was developed as the customer requested, even though the delivered system might not be exactly what the customer wants.

The pursuit of traceability is the reason some teams walk the requirements tightrope by developing two requirements documents. One is high-level, based directly on the customers' expressed needs. The other, a detailed software requirements specification, contains not only users' expressed needs but implementation considerations, or *derived requirements*, as well.

This introduces the problem of keeping the detailed set of requirements accurately mapped to the less-detailed set to make sure nothing gets lost in the shuffle. Traceability can be a sticky problem not only between different requirements documents but also between a requirement specification and a design document, source code, or a test plan.

Generally, traceability is achieved by the use of unique identifiers, or *anchors*, embedded into each requirement, as in the following example:

Trace anchor APG0001. The exit gate shall open only when a PDC is inserted into the exit-gate card reader.

The design, source code, and test cases then must refer back to the appropriate trace anchors to prove that the users' needs are being met.

Testable

If a requirement is specified correctly and is at the right level of detail for the abstraction, it can be tested. For example, a test case could easily be written for:

> If at least one 2MB block of disk space is available on the user's default server, the list will be stored on the user's default server in a file named list.dat.

It could be much harder to test this requirement:

> If sufficient disk space is available, the list will be stored.

Ensuring their testability improves the quality of requirements, because correctness and detail are prerequisites for writing a test case (Boem 1981). To ensure testability and quality, some processes specify that a complete set of test cases must be included in each requirement. While this practice makes it easier to develop a test plan, much of the effort in writing detailed test cases before implementation will be wasted. This is largely due to the changes that must be made to facilitate design and implementation and the fact that generally not enough details are known about the test bed to write executable test cases until deep into implementation.

Test cases, when included with requirements, should be written at a high level. Included test cases should not detail how the test will be done, only what should be done for the test in general terms. These cases will be useful for proving the testability and correctness of requirements and can serve as the basis for future test plans.

Inspections

Errors in requirements definition are 20 times more expensive to repair than coding errors (Glass 1979). Yet there are many good tools for debugging code, and only one good tool for debugging requirements: inspections.

It's far more economical (Schulmeyer 1990) to find errors during requirements inspection than during debugging, and inspecting and reinspecting requirements are virtually the only ways (aside from prototyping) to uncover errors, inadequacies, gold plating, etc. Inspection is facilitated by means of an *inspection checklist* (see chapter 11 for more details) that consists essentially of questions based on the same points detailed earlier in this section:

- Is each requirement correct?
- Are the requirements understandable?
- Can each requirement be implemented?
- Are the requirements consistent (no contradictions)?
- Are the requirements complete?
- Is each requirement necessary?
- Are the requirements at the right level of detail?
- Is each requirement identified by a unique trace anchor?
- Is each requirement testable?

This list provides a good starting point but is by no means complete. Each organization should add questions to address project-specific, customer-specific, and company-specific issues.

Try one on for size

Prototyping can be a powerful tool, allowing customers to try features out to determine what will work for them. Prototyping can be expensive in time and money, however, and developers often need to know a considerable amount about what a system is supposed to do before they can develop the prototype. Prototyping is most useful for fine-tuning requirements after the core system is fully understood.

Innovative ways of determining true customer needs include prototyped mock-ups of possible enhancements or new products and inviting customers to try them out and inviting customers to work inhouse with the engineers developing a system. All of this should result in a meaningful document containing requirements represented both pictorially as well as textually or in accurate updates to existing documents. Some organizations bring in customers to use a prototyped system in a room with video cameras and/or two-way mirrors. The user-reaction to the new system then can be recorded and analyzed.

Some systems (embedded real-time software, for example) do not lend themselves well to protyping to determine requirements, because the user interface is minimal. In these cases, a simulator developed to give requirements feedback to users can be useful. Some level of simulation is needed to debug embedded systems, but providing users with a graphical representation of requirements in action generally is not practical (refer to chapter 6).

A prototype is not only useful in ferreting out the details of requirements, it actually might be part of the requirements. Often the best way to express and manage user-interface requirements is by means of a prototype of the user interface. If the prototype is well-maintained, it can help both users and developers understand the requirements.

The Source

There are essentially three types of projects when it comes to requirements gathering: those being developed for inhouse use, those with a limited number of external customers, and those that are entirely market driven with potentially millions of users. The sources for requirements are similar in all three cases, but how requirements are gathered can be quite different.

When a project is being developed for inhouse use or is targeted to a limited number of customers, representative users from each customer organization can work directly with developers. Requirements documents then can be developed jointly and reviewed by all concerned. This doesn't guarantee good requirements, but it gives developers a fighting chance. In this case, methods such as presentations, interviews, and prototyping work well for requirements definition.

To develop software for the masses, software organizations typically rely on knowledge of competing products, previous versions of the product, and innovations from developers. User groups, conferences, big customers, and sometimes representative users working closely with developers also can provide valuable requirements feedback.

Even if a software organization does a pretty good job of collecting and implementing requirements, it seems there always are enough left over for another version. Because users' wants are nearly infinite in market-driven software and development time and resources are limited, one version often quickly follows another for the life of the product.

Ideally, most of your requirements will be reused from a well-maintained repository (see chapter 7). In reality, however, almost all requirements are written from scratch. Because reusability isn't planned from the beginning across all projects, almost all requirements, designs, code, and test suites are much too project-specific to be reused.

Internal Filters

Unfortunately, on many large mission-critical projects, direct contact with customers is rare for most developers. Documents from users, as well as user interaction with other members of your organization, must suffice. Users aren't always the best source for detailed requirements, however, because they usually know little about implementation considerations. Interviewing end users yields valuable insights, along with some impractical and conflicting ideas.

User-generated requirements often come in to developers through internal filters. These filters help refine requirements but also can obscure real user needs, because whenever a requirement is evaluated, meaning can be added, lost, or changed. Requirements tend to drift into a software development team through systems architects, maintenance/support, or marketing.

Systems architects

Also known as *analysts* or *systems engineers*, systems architects often have the primary responsibility of translating users' needs into software requirements. Ideally, they understand the customer's business as well as the customer does and will work with him to write flawless requirements to fit all of his current and future needs. In reality, this is never the case because no human being alive has sufficient knowledge for this task. On a new project, the best that you can hope for initially are some intelligent guesses about the future and a hazy interpretation of the present from this source.

On many projects, a requirements specification generated by systems architects is the only link between developers and customers. On these projects, managers, developers, and customers must work closely with the architects to get the requirements right. If there is an honest working relationship between these four parties, the project has a good chance for success. Major conflicts here, however, can doom an otherwise well-conceived project.

Maintenance/support

Every product upgrade, new version, or revision starts out by fixing problems with the previous version, then adds enhancements. Both bugs and user-requested enhancements generally are channeled through maintenance-team members—sometimes via irate phone calls late at night. Some forward-thinking companies maintain complex databases of user requests that can be used to generate changes to requirements documents. In the case of a new product that replaces an old one, existing support data can be vital in producing a new requirements document.

Marketing

Marketeers try (with limited success) to present product proposals that have enough functionality to be enticing to potential users and to managers who control the development money, yet are within reach of the engineering teams who must develop the software. In some organizations, the marketeers make functionality commitments to big customers that the engineers cannot possibly accomplish in the promised amount of time. Because marketing people might know little about what it takes to produce software and definitely have an unclear picture of the resulting design dependencies, they are prone to make bad decisions about what can be done by the engineering department. A marketing representative often will be part of the development team, sometimes even helping to write the requirements documents, but this doesn't always prevent signing up to implement conflicting or unclear requirements.

Marketing reps can provide the users' perspective better than any of the other internal filters. As a requirements channel, however, there's a lot to be desired. When marketeers contribute requirements, check for gold plating. Ask questions such as "Does the customer really need this feature?" or "Is it necessary in this version?"

If possible, you should try to get answers directly from customers. Unfortunately, if you don't have a good understanding of the customer's business, management-level negotiations, or company priorities, you could do much more harm than good by contacting end-users directly. This depends entirely on the type of project that you're involved in (market-driven, inhouse, etc.) and the relationship that your company has with its customers.

When All Else Fails

What can you do if your project seems to have no real requirements from any source? The first step in getting a decent problem definition is to read everything written that has anything to do with the product you're trying to produce.

There might be no real documents; however, if the new product is either based on or is an enhancement to an old product, there probably is some helpful code lying around. Study the code, and get your hands on any memos, e-mail, informal papers, presentation slides, sales brochures, etc., that might be available, Study these, and take your persistent questions to the authors of the documents that you read (assuming they still are with the company). If your team has an architect or two, they also are prime sources for knowledge. Even if they don't know the answers, they probably know someone who does. If you've read and outlined everything that you can about a topic, you probably will be in a position to understand an answer when you get one.

Even if your management doesn't see the need for requirements, the knowledge that you gather should at least end up in an informal document. You, and hopefully some of your fellow workers, can use this document as a much-needed link to your customers.

The best advice is: no matter what your circumstances are, never develop any software (especially a mission-critical system) without a good requirement specification and customer/management buy-in to it. Working without requirements is like walking a tightrope without a net. Like a net, a requirements specification isn't much good if it's full of gaping holes.

Solid Requirements

The last set of carved-in-stone requirements came down from Mount Sinai, and soon, even those had to be rewritten. Since then, most requirements specifications have been in a constant state of flux. Customers' needs change as the world changes, and software can never be changed quite fast enough to keep up with them.

Unfortunately, managers and customers generally expect project phases—such as requirements analysis, design, implementation, and testing—to be completed by specific dates. To complete these phases as planned, requirements are assumed to be frozen solid. When development proceeds and requirements prove to be slush, things start to fall apart. The result often is that a project must be kludged together or completely redone from square one.

A much better approach is to plan "increments" in which an agreed-upon amount of development will take place. The number of increments in a project might increase or decrease during a project. The products delivered to the customers consist of "releases" or "versions," each of which has increasing functionality. In the first few versions, only the customers' most important needs should be met. In later releases, the customers' wants and wishes can be added.

Changes, though inevitable, need to be worked into the requirements specification through formal channels involving screening and negotiation by developers, management, and customers. Customers will constantly want "tiny changes" or "small improvements." Even one of these, implemented at the wrong time, can set a project back several months. New wants and wishes must be constantly evaluated under the closest scrutiny. It is absolutely necessary to inform the powers that be (the end-users' management or your own managers) of the cost and schedule impact of every enhancement.

Here are some questions to ask when choosing whether or not to implement a requirement in a specific release:

- Do the end-users really require a specific feature (is it a need, want, or wish)? To find out, ask the question "What would happen if this feature were not implemented in this release?"

- What impact will this have on future releases?

- What impact will it have on the rest of the system or on the implementability of other requirements?

- How difficult will it be to implement?

- Can the implementation of a requirement be reused from somewhere else, or is it available off-the-shelf?

- What impact does it have on the current-defined model or the implemented system?

- What is the system-resource impact on developmental or users' platforms?

- What will be the schedule impact?

Requirements specifications often are created like metamorphic rocks. All of the requirements gathered must be subjected to heat and pressure from developers and users as well as managers of both users and developers. In the end, most requirements are a compromise between what users want and what developers can deliver (see Figure 2.4).

Are You Listening?

Whether requirements come directly from customers or through an internal filter, developers need to communicate to get requirements clarified. It's a mistake to take any requirement for granted, no matter where it comes from. Before you base part of a design or a prototype on a requirement, find out why the requirement is necessary and what it really means.

The best way to do this is to talk to the customer using "active listening" statements that involve a summary of what the customer says:

> Customer: "These reports just pile up anyway; maybe we don't need this much information."

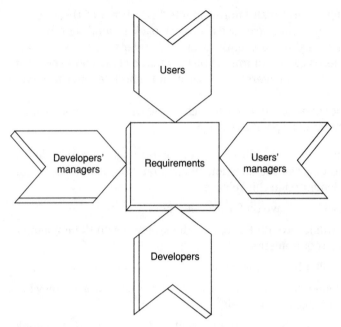

Figure 2.4   Requirements-building forces.

Programmer: "Does this mean you don't really need to generate a daily report?"

Customer: "We've already trained our data-entry people, so I don't think we want to rock the boat."

Programmer: "Do you mean that you don't want this to impact the user interface?"

Communication channels such as in-person meetings and electronic mail and forums, as well as formal documents, should be used constantly for as long as requirements are generated and filtered (probably for the life of the product).

Tools

Up until a few years ago, there weren't many good tools to help with requirements management. Now, however, some CASE tools (discussed in detail in chapter 10) support requirements traceability as well as analysis. A good place to begin looking for requirements-management tools is the "Requirements Analysis and Design Technology Report" (Ganska et al. 1993)

A database can be helpful in organizing requirements and querying them according to criteria such as priority and difficulty, and an electronic forum or e-mail system is highly useful in keeping the requirements channels open. All team members need to review and understand the requirements specification, so requirements ideally should reside on a combination electronic forum/e-mail/database system such as Lotus Notes. This type of tool supports browsing, reporting, and updating of requirements, as well as requirements reusability (see chapter 7).

Good tools, according to Thompson (1994), will facilitate different views into a requirements specification, such as:

- A list of all high-priority requirements that have a low probability of being implemented successfully

- A report on all requirements pertaining to the user interface

- A prioritized list of all database-related requirements

This capability is useful throughout the development effort and helps make the requirements specification a living, useful document.

Examples

In the following sections, we provide two simplified examples of requirements gathering: a software-bug tracking system and a parking-garage control system. These examples represent two major categories of software development projects: hosted data management utilities and an embedded control system. The methods of gathering requirements in each of these examples are somewhat different but really amount to the same thing: finding out what the user really wants and what you can deliver. We will refer to both of these sample projects throughout the remainder of the book.

Example 1: Software bug tracking

Many projects start with a manager making a simple statement:

> Our customer service people need a system for reporting and tracking the bugs that users find in our software. How soon do you think you can get one online for them?

Obviously, your boss is making a number of assumptions here, one of which is that you can read his mind. Even if you could read his mind, you wouldn't get all the details that you're going to need for this project.

In situations such as this, your best bet is to assume nothing. Above all, don't smile and say "I'll have it for you right away!" Instead, ask some intelligent questions, then say you'll get back to him by the end of the day with some ideas.

Questions.   Here are some of the questions that you probably will want to ask:

- Will both customer support people and developers use the system?
- What kind of notification will we provide for the requesting customer?
- What kind of query/reporting facility do we need?
- How will the system interface with the software quality assurance systems?
- How will the system interface with our configuration management system?
- What about regression testing?
- Will the system track repair reports as well as trouble reports?
- What kind of priorities will be associated with the software trouble reports?
- Will closed-out trouble and repair reports be archived?
- Will there be a many-to-many relationship between software trouble-reports and software repair reports?
- What level of security is appropriate for the system?

If your boss is like most, he won't have answers to all of these questions. You'll have to draw upon your own knowledge, interview some experts, and track down some clues. You'll need to round up the usual suspects: SQA, testing, the "tool builder" bunch, customer support, as well as various project managers.

Scenarios.   With answers in hand, the next thing that you probably will want to do is write some simple "use cases" or "scenarios," such as the following.

Scenario 1.   A user finds a bug to be fixed in a released version of software and e-mails information about the bug to customer service. A customer service representative then fills out a software trouble report (STR). A trouble report consists of an automatically determined number, a description of the problem, a priority, a date, and a status of either repaired or unrepaired.

Scenario 2.   As developers work on the next release of the system, they can check the bug-tracking facility, find an error there that pertains to their code, fix the error, and fill out a software repair report (SRR). An SRR consists of the number of the corresponding trouble report, an automatically defined number, a description of the repair, the names of all files updated to carry out the repair, and a date. Many repairs can correspond to the same bug, and many bugs might be fixed by one repair.

Scenario 3.   A software manager queries the STR/SRR database to generate a report of all STRs with a status of "unresolved" and a priority of greater than 3 (1 being the highest, 5 the lowest).

The requirements specification. Once you get the "usual suspects" to review your scenarios and incorporate their corrections, you're ready to crank out requirements such as these:

Trace anchor STRS0001. The STR/SRR system shall be open only to users with a valid password.

Trace anchor STRS0002. An STR shall consist of the following information, which customer support personnel shall enter into the system in response to customer complaints.

- A description of the problem.
- A priority code between 1 and 5 (1 is highest, 5 is the lowest). (These will correspond to the "Failure Criticality Index," as explained in chapter 13.)
- The date of creation for this STR in *mm/dd/yy* format.
- A status of either repaired or unrepaired.
- The name of the customer who reported the bug.
- The name of the customer-support person who entered the report.
- The name of the software product to which the STR applies.
- The version of the software product to which the STR applies.
- The name of the hardware platform on which the customer was using the software product.

Trace anchor STRS0003. A 6-digit STR-identification number shall be automatically generated and displayed when an STR is entered.

Trace anchor STRS0004. It shall be possible for many SRRs to correspond to the same STR, and many STRs can be fixed by a single SRR.

Trace anchor STRS0005. An SRR shall consist of the following information, which a developer shall enter into the system in response to one or more STRs:

- The STR number of each of the corresponding trouble report(s).
- An automatically defined number.
- A textual description of the repair.
- The names of all files that were updated to carry out the repair.
- The date of creation for this SRR in *mm/dd/yy* format.
- A field for SQA approval.
- The name of the subsystem to which this SRR applies.

Trace anchor STRS0006. A 6-digit SRR-identification number shall be automatically generated and displayed when an STR is entered.

Trace anchor STRS0007. All files changed or deleted in connection with an SRR shall be accessed only via the check-in and check-out procedures of the standard configuration management system.

Trace anchor STRS0008. All files added in connection with an SRR shall be placed under configuration in the standard configuration management system.

Trace anchor STRS0009. SRRs shall be written only for STRs that have been approved by a representative of the SQA organization.

Trace anchor STRS0010. Only SRRs that have been approved by a representative of the SQA organization shall be considered completed.

Trace anchor STRS0011. The system shall, on demand, produce a report containing all of the stored information concerning unresolved STRs that are at a user-input priority level.

Trace anchor STRS0012. The system shall, on demand, produce a report containing all of the stored information concerning STRs and corresponding SRRs that pertain to a specific software product, version, platform, and subsystem.

Trace anchor STRS0013. All STRs and SRRs entered shall be archived for a period of up to one year.

This is by no means a complete set of requirements, but it does provide a good starting point for reviews and prototypes. After representatives of all interested departments review the requirements, you probably will need to do some more detective work to determine exactly what capabilities (i.e., report generation, concurrency, etc.) that the system really needs to have.

While refining the requirements for this system, it would be wise to prototype the user interface, then let all interested parties try it out and provide feedback. Once the prototype passes muster, you can get the requirements reviewed and updated. As you develop the system, the requirements will change; however, at this point, you should have a basic core from which to work.

Armed with a good set of requirements, you can provide your customer with a good estimate of the time and effort needed to complete the project, an idea of whether or not the project can or should be done, as well as what tools and resources will be needed for the project.

Example 2: An automated parking garage

This example is a slightly new twist on the old park-and-pay idea. Here are the original requirements that you get from the customer:

I want the whole thing automated—no parking attendants. People just drive up to the gate, put in their cards, and park their cars. Parking time will be tracked automatically. The best part is, I'll automatically make money and get financial reports!

The third degree.   These are better than the requirements some developers get, but they're worthless until you ask some questions to clear things up:

Are different types of parking spaces tracked differently (i.e., motorcycle, compact, handicapped, reserved)? *No, don't worry about that right now.*

Do you mean that you might want to add this later? *Yes. (Of course, you'll need to point out that if a feature isn't part of the original requirements, it will cost extra to add it "a la carté.")*

What do you want done if the lot is full? *Light up a sign and lock the gate shut!*

So you want more cards and accounts distributed than there are parking places in the garage? *Of course! Can't make money otherwise!*

Do you want to eventually accept all major credit cards, not just parking debit cards? *Probably some day.*

Is parking sold by the day, hour, or minute, or by some other arrangement? *It will have to be by the minute.*

What's the minimum that a driver needs in his account before he can get into the garage? *Enough for a day's parking.*

How often should reports be generated? *Once a day, with weekly and monthly summaries. E-mail them to me.*

What information should appear on a report? *Total receipts, expenses, the bottom line.*

What kind of receipt should the driver receive? *I don't care, whatever's fair.*

To make implementation possible, a few derived requirements need to be added, such as an exit gate, card readers at both gates, receipt-printing capability, and the lot being open only to valid card-holders. We also need to add a requirement that the account information be stored on a database server, just in case someone gets the idea that a box of 3" × 5" cards would work better.

How to use it.   The next step is to write a general use case to sort out the customers' needs. The following paragraphs demonstrate a sample usage of the product, assuming that all will go as planned.

The parking garage is open only to drivers with valid parking-debit cards. When a customer drives up to the entrance gate, the driver puts a parking debit card into a slot in a card reader mounted near the gate. The card reader is connected to a database server where each customer has an account corresponding to the account number encoded on the customer's card. If there are parking spaces left in the garage and if the driver's account has sufficient funds for at least a full day of parking, the gate opens and a timer begins. The customer then can drive into the garage and park in any available space.

When a customer leaves the garage, he or she must exit through another gate. To open the exit gate, the patron must insert a valid card into a card reader mounted near the exit gate. The timer stops at this point and an amount equal to the number of minutes elapsed since the card was inserted in the entrance card reader multiplied by the current per-minute cost of parking is deducted from the customer's account. A printed receipt then is dispensed to the customer, and the gate is opened. The cost per minute can be changed at any time by the owner (although if he is wise, he will give ample notice to his customers).

The requirements specification. Here's the first iteration of the specification, ready for the customer's approval:

Trace anchor APG0001. The parking garage shall be open only to drivers with valid parking-debit cards (PDCs). *Note*: In the future, the owner might also want to open the garage to responsible holders of major credit cards.

Trace anchor APG0002. A unique, encoded number on each PDC shall correspond to a unique account number for each card holder. The account number shall be printed on each daily management report.

Trace anchor APG0003. An account, indexed by account number, shall be kept on a database server for each card-holding customer.

Trace anchor APG0004. Each account shall hold the current balance, as well as a one-year transaction history for one customer.

Trace anchor APG0005. The account also shall contain the name, address, and phone number of the customer. These shall be displayed on each customer receipt.

Trace anchor APG0006. A valid PDC is defined as one that corresponds to an account that contains funds sufficient for at least one day's parking.

Trace anchor APG0007. There shall be a single entrance gate and a single exit gate. *Note*: The customer might add more gates in the future.

Trace anchor APG0008. The number of available parking spaces shall be tracked constantly, incrementing by one for each car that enters and decrementing by one for each car that leaves. The number of available spaces shall be displayed on a sign outside the parking garage.

Trace anchor APG0009. The entrance gate shall open only when a valid PDC is inserted into a card reader near the gate and there is at least one available parking space in the garage.

Trace anchor APG0010. If there are no spaces available, a lighted sign ("parking status sign"), which is visible from the street, shall display the message "Lot Full."

Trace anchor APG0011. The exit gate shall open only when a PDC is inserted into the exit-gate card reader.

Trace anchor APG0012. As a customer exits, a receipt detailing parking time, charges, and an account balance shall be dispensed to him.

Trace anchor APG0013. The amount of money deducted from a customer's account at the exit gate is calculated as the elapsed time between the insertion of a valid PDC into the entrance-gate card reader and the insertion of the same card into the exit-gate card reader multiplied by a per-minute charge, with seconds truncated.

Trace anchor APG0014. If there is not enough money in a customer's account to pay the amount due, the customer shall be allowed to exit the lot but shall automatically be billed by mail for any amount due beyond what is in the customer's account.

Trace anchor APG0015. The per-minute charge can be changed at any time by the parking-garage owner or manager (although if he is wise, he will give ample notice to his customers).

Trace anchor APG0016. A lighted sign, visible from the street, shall display the current per-minute parking charge.

Trace anchor APG0017. A report containing all information from all customer accounts shall be e-mailed to the parking garage manager at 6:00 PM each day.

Trace anchor APG0018. A report containing all parking transactions, as well as the total fees collected and spaces used, shall be automatically e-mailed to the parking garage manager at 6:00 PM each day.

Change in the wind. Of course, the customer will want you to make changes to the system as soon as it is delivered, if not sooner. Some of the probable changes might be as follows:

- Handle all vehicles, with special parking for motorcycles and trucks, and a weight and height limit for trucks.
- Provide reserved parking spaces, handicapped spaces, time-limit spaces, and compact and full-size vehicle spaces.

- Provide a report of parking-lot activity for a customer.
- Produce an end-of-the-month report to the owner and manager of all activity in the parking garage.
- Use all major credit cards, not just the debit card.
- Add four new pairs of entrance and exit gates.
- The government requires twice as many handicapped parking spaces.

The Real World

The customer generally is concerned only about how the system works, not how it doesn't. Unfortunately, things go wrong with even the best systems. Users provide the wrong input, memory allocation fails, and logic errors can crop up. Good systems need to be able to recover from these problems by means of error-handling code. Derived requirements for error handling can be included in the requirements specification or added into the requirements analysis, the design, or implementation depending upon your defined process and/or your common sense.

The requirements that we've defined so far ignore a number of real-world considerations in addition to error handling, such as user-interface specifics, database management systems, existing libraries, and the operating environment. These can be added during requirements analysis or design.

Constitutional Amendments

After the customer officially accepts this initial specification, it becomes the constitution of the project. It needs to be protected via reviews, analysis, and negotiation, but it can be amended through a (hopefully) well-defined process. A requirements specification is precious but must be made accessible and understandable to everyone on your team. It must be protected from unauthorized changes, but it must be a living, useful document. Something probably is wrong with your software development process if developers aren't constantly referring to and discussing changes to the requirements specification.

Learning Through Requirements

One often-overlooked benefit of a good requirements specification is its usefulness in helping developers get up to speed on a project. If you're new to a project and the requirements specification is accurate and up to date, you can simply study it and get your questions answered, and you soon will be ready to start contributing your own ideas.

Keep a list of "domain experts" on each category of requirement and work with them to build up your knowledge, as well as to iron out problems with the requirements. Once you write down a question, give yourself a day to discover the answer before asking an expert (you'll learn more this way). Keep your notes organized by topic.

Take advantage of requirements reviews, inspections, walkthroughs, and design meetings by taking notes to build your store of knowledge—and to ask intelligent questions. These could be the only chances that you will have to fix problems with the requirements before it's too late to save the project.

Requirements Analysis

Once a core set of requirements has been ferreted out and adequately filtered, it's time for developers to start the on-going process of analyzing requirements. Object-oriented requirements analysis, which often is done in parallel with requirements gathering and filtering, consists of dividing requirements into objects and modeling the interactions between the objects. Chapter 4 will explore requirements analysis, as well as design and implementation.

Summary

Effective requirements management is the foundation of quality, on-time software. A requirements specification is an organized representation of all of the things that a software system must do to meet users' needs and wants. In spite of the importance of requirements, they often are neglected. Good requirements are correct, understandable, implementable, consistent, complete, necessary, at the right level of detail, traceable, and testable.

There are a number of methods for gathering requirements, including interviewing and giving presentations to users and building prototypes for users to evaluate. After requirements come in from users, they often must pass through internal filters, including architects, marketeers, and maintenance programmers. Tools are available to facilitate the organization, modification, understandability, and protection of requirements, but there is no substitute for actively listening to customers and asking questions.

Because even the best requirements can be subject to change, intelligent requirements management for the life of the project is the key to success. Up-to-date requirements are essential in predicting the level of effort and the resources needed to complete the project on schedule and can be used to get new team members up-to-speed.

Whatever form requirements take or wherever they come from, they represent the main link between the real world and the solution that programmers struggle to implement in software. Requirements invariably are unstable, incomplete, and inaccurate; however, like clues in a murder case, they're all a software developer has to go on.

References

Arthur, Lowell Jay. 1992. *Rapid evolutionary development; requirements, prototyping, and software evolution.* New York: John Wiley and Sons.

Boem, Barry. 1981. *Software engineering economics.* Englewood Cliffs, New Jersey: Prentice Hall.

Booch, Grady. 1994. *Object-oriented analysis and design with applications (second edition).* Redwood City, Cal.: The Benjamin/Cummings Publishing Company.

Cox, Brad J. 1987. *Object-oriented programming, an evolutionary approach.* Reading, Massachusetts: Addison-Wesley Publishing Company.

Davis, Alan M. and Hsia, Pei. 1994. "Giving voice to requirements engineering." *IEEE Software.* March v11 n2 p12(3).

Ganska, Ralph et al. 1993. *Requirements analysis and design technology report.* Software Technology Support Center (STSC) Hill Air Force Base, Utah.

Glass, R. L. 1979. *Software reliability guidebook.* Englewood Cliffs, New Jersey: Prentice Hall.

Humphrey, Watts. 1990. "Software process maturity." Proceedings of the CASE World Conference, Andover MA: Digital Consulting, October.

Jones, Capers. 1994. *Assessment and control of software risks.* Englewood Cliffs, New Jersey: Prentice Hall.

Siddiqi, Jawed. 1994. "Challenging the universal truths of requirements engineering." *IEEE Software.* March v11 n2 p18(2).

Parrington, Norman and Roper, Mark. 1989. *Understanding software testing.* New York: John Wiley and Sons.

Pohl, Ira. 1993. *Object-oriented programming using C++.* Redwood City, Cal.: The Benjamin/Cummings Publishing Company.

Raymond, Eric. 1993. *The new hacker's dictionary.* Cambridge, Massachusetts: MIT Press.

Rettig, Marc and Simons, Gary. 1993. "A project planning and development process for small teams." *Communications of the ACM.* October v36 n10.

Rumbaugh, James; Blaha, Michael; Premerlaini, William; Eddy, Frederick; Lorensen, William. 1991. *Object-oriented modeling and design.* Englewood Cliffs, New Jersey: Prentice Hall.

Schulmeyer, G. Gordon. 1990. *Zero-defect software.* New York: McGraw-Hill.

Thompson, Jess. 1994. "What you need to manage requirements." *IEEE Software.* March v11 n2 p115(4).

Walz, Diane B., Joyce J. Elam and Bill Curtis. 1993. "Inside a software design team: knowledge acquisition, sharing, and integration." *Communications of the ACM.* October v36 n10 p62(14).

Weiner, Richard S. and Pinson, Lewis. J. 1988. *An introduction to object-oriented programming and C++.* Reading, Massachusetts: Addison-Wesley Publishing Company.

Winblad, Ann et al. 1990. *Object-oriented software.* Reading, Massachusetts: Addison-Wesley Publishing Company.

Yourdon, Edward. 1993. *Decline and fall of the American programmer.* Englewood Cliffs, New Jersey: Prentice Hall.

3

A Methodology Survey

One of the main threads that continually will reappear throughout this book is the role of object-oriented methodologies and techniques in helping to solve the so-called *software crisis*. We feel strongly that object-oriented techniques offer the best opportunity, from a methodology standpoint, for software success.

OO is hardly the only methodology out there, however. CASE vendors and the careers of many a methodologist have been "made" from non-OO methods such as structured and information techniques.

This chapter compares and contrasts the most popular methodologies that have flourished over the years. The various structured methods will be discussed in great detail. In general, these methodologies are characterized by the emphasis placed on the functionality in the system. This class of methodologies has been, and probably still is, the most popular of all approaches. *Structured*, however, is a rather broad term and encompasses a wide variety of variants of functional methodologies, some of which might be new to you. We will mention and describe some of these functional methodologies.

Information engineering methodologies also are addressed. As opposed to structured techniques, the primary focus of information engineering methodologies is the role that data plays in the system.

Object-oriented methodologies are the most modern of methodologies. OO attempts to preach encapsulation, where functionality and data together are viewed as an inseparable entity. This methodology has given rise to object-oriented programming (which is discussed in chapter 9) and languages such as C++, Objective-C, OOCOBOL (which is discussed in chapter

4), Ada 95, and Smalltalk along with object-oriented design (OOD) and object-oriented analysis (OOA) techniques.

Structured Methodologies

Structured methodologies, often referred to as *functional technologies*, have been and still are the most popular of all software analysis and design techniques. The term *structured* often is used rather loosely, usually referring to anything that is not "object-oriented." This and the next section hopefully will clarify this misidentification, because this omits information on data methodologies.

As with most new software technologies, structured techniques first arrived on the software scene in the form of structured programming followed by structured design, then structured analysis techniques and methodologies.

The same technology development scenario has been true of object-orientation. OO programming arrived on the scene first, followed by OO design (OOD). OO analysis (OOA) or OORA (object-oriented requirements analysis) still is considered to be maturing and is just beginning to gain some level of confidence and acceptance in the software community.

Some of the more commonly known structured techniques are those of Demarco (Demarco, 1978), Gane and Sarson (Gane and Sarson, 1977), Yourdon and Constantine (Yourdon and Constantine, 1979), Myers (Myers, 1978), and Page-Jones (Page-Jones, 1988). As these gained acceptance, CASE tools soon followed. Structured techniques have been around since the late 1970s and will likely continue to have an acceptance and following into the next century.

Booch (1994) relates that structured techniques were directly affected by popular languages of the late 1970s era, such as FORTRAN and COBOL. As a matter of fact, many universities, at that time, taught structured techniques as part of the classes devoted specifically to one of these languages.

Description of structured techniques

Just as the kinds of methodologies have evolved from structured and information techniques to object-oriented techniques, there has been an evolution within the class of techniques known as structured techniques. Structured methods have evolved from their beginnings in the 1970s to what they presently are.

As such, attempting to describe *exactly* what structured techniques are would be an impossible task. In general, however, structured techniques can be thought of as *algorithmic decomposition*.

All structured techniques, in one form or another, are described in terms of algorithmic decomposition. The problem space is decomposed by functionality. This decomposition is represented, in many of the methods, by the commonly recognized structure chart. The problem space is decomposed until the functionality that is represented at the lowest levels of the decomposition can't be distilled any further.

This decomposition representation (structure chart) has undergone growth, development, and sophistication over the years. The structure charts used with CASE tools today have the capability of representing data flows between the levels of the chart. They also can contain symbology to represent selection and iteration constructs. Very often, structure charts can be viewed as a kind of system "calling tree."

As structured techniques have undergone changes, the "tools of the trade" have changed. Structured methods moved from the structure charts and have incorporated another representation technique called *data flow diagrams* (DFDs). DFDs offered a method to manage the decomposition of increasingly more complex systems that structured techniques were being required to address. Another important aspect of DFDs is the recognition that, in addition to *function*, *data* plays an important role in software analysis and design techniques. (*Function* still is the driving force in most, if not all, structured techniques.)

DFDs allowed a bit more attention to be paid to the data involved in the system. As CASE tools got onto the DFD bandwagon, additional tools were developed that helped form the changing view of structured techniques: "balancing" tools whereby the data flows into and out of all process bubbles on a "higher" level DFD would have to "match" those on a DFD that represented a decomposed process/function bubble. Data dictionary tools arose concurrently whereby all data flows would have to be defined and also decomposed to lower-level data flows, where appropriate.

Other structured techniques now have incorporated state transition diagrams (STDs) to "beef up" the model. You can see quite readily that the structured techniques CASE tools market has been a very competitive one. Over the years, many methodologists have aligned themselves with CASE vendors to lend credibility to the CASE tools and help sell the product; for example, Grady Booch with Rational.

Shortcomings of structured techniques

Structured techniques can go only so far, as currently modeled. DFDs attempt to address both data as well as function. Although the data is being "addressed," structured techniques do not address the issue of *ownership* of the data. Simple modifications to data elements can cause havoc in a system that "uses" this data everywhere. In short, issues such as data abstraction and data encapsulation simply are omitted.

Inclusion of state transition diagrams in some structured techniques has been a positive. Some systems (especially control systems) exhibit a high degree of state behavior. STDs do an excellent job of modeling this behavior.

Structure charts allow a system to be decomposed along functional lines. DFDs allow better identification of the flow of data throughout the system. STDs allow state-related behavior to be modeled. None of these aspects of the model easily allow representation of the system behavior to system events. Also, the timing of data flows, if important, can't easily be represented in DFDs. System concurrency (multiple-tasking systems) can hardly be addressed at all in structured techniques.

These shortcomings have provided the motivation for movement toward what now are known as object-oriented techniques. Before we discuss OO, however, we'll address another type of methodology that arose at roughly the same time that structured techniques did: data or information methodologies. Much more information concerning OO technologies is covered in chapter 4. In addition, Figures 4.2, 4.3, 4.4, and 4.5 pictorially represent structure charts, DFDs, flowcharts, and STDs.

Information (Data) Methodologies

Some structured methodologies have been known to support some forms of data analysis, such as inclusion of entity-relationship diagrams (ERDs). However, for most, if not all, structured methodologies have the "functional" viewpoint as their focus. This is why, as stated previously, structured methods are known as functional methods.

There are methodologies that have data as their main focal point. These methodologies are known appropriately as *data* or *information methodologies*. We will focus on two information methodologies: Warnier-Orr (Warnier, 1974 and Warnier, 1981) and Jackson (Jackson, 1975 and Jackson, 1981). Pressman (1987) presents an outline and discussion of these two information methodologies that are discussed here.

Warnier-Orr method

The Warnier-Orr method also is known as Data Structure Systems Development (DSSD). The highlights of this method are as follows:

- Information is organized into a hierarchical format, which is known as an *information hierarchy*.
- Processing that must be performed on the information then is depicted (much like a DFD).
- The model assesses the *application context* (that is, how data moves between producers and consumers of the data), then application functions and results are assessed and modeled.

Jackson method

The Jackson method is summarized as follows:

1. Entity Action Step: Entities and actions taken upon or by the entities are identified.

2. Entity Structure Step: Actions that affect each entity are sequenced in temporal order and represented by Jackson diagrams, which are similar to structure charts.

3. Initial Model Setup: Entities and actions are represented as a process model; connections between the model and the real world are defined.

4. Function Step: Functions that correspond to defined actions are specified.

5. System Timing Step: Process scheduling characteristics are assessed and specified.

6. Implementation Step: Hardware and software are specified as a design.

In many ways, the Jackson method is quite powerful and, in some ways, goes beyond structured techniques in terms of thoroughness of analysis of the problem. There still are shortcomings, however, not only in the Jackson method but also in information methods in general.

Object-Oriented Methodologies

We have discussed the two prevailing classes of software development methods. Both groups of methods have helped formalize software development and have been the result of years of continuing development and improvement. As mentioned and as will be discussed in further detail in the next section, there are shortcomings and limitations with these methods.

Many of the methodologists who have labored in the structured and information methods "fields" over the years have progressed into the world of object-orientation. This section will serve as an introduction and a summary for chapter 4.

Basics of object-orientation

There is no question that OO has become more than just a passing fad. As already mentioned, OOP and OOD have become relatively well-entrenched in the software development business. OOA is quickly maturing to provide analysis coverage of the software development life cycle.

Yourdon (1994) (and many others) have summarized the unique characteristics and features of OO as follows:

- *Abstraction.* Defines the view that is presented to users of an object or class. Different users of an object can have different views of the object depending upon what the needs of that user are.

- *Encapsulation.* This is perhaps one of the most unique and important identifiers of OO that exist. An object (along with defining data or attributes) is encapsulated along with the functions that can be performed on that object or its data.

- *Reuse.* If objects are encapsulated well without any system-specific or any other kind of corruption, then it should be obvious that analysis, design, code, and test reuse becomes an extremely exciting possibility.

- *Specialization (or inheritance).* This occurs when an object inherits attributes or functionality from a parent object or class, often called a *superclass.*

- *Object communication.* The form of communication that occurs between objects with an OO system. User objects can send messages to another object only if the user object knows of the service object and the message is a request of a service that the service object can provide.

- *Polymorphism.* This concept, which is similar to inheritance, occurs when an operation can apply to several different objects (of different types or classes). There are two basic types of polymorphism: one where operations are inherited by every object and polymorphism where different objects have different operations with the same name.

Benefits of OO

OO claims to be able to handle more complex systems better than other methodologies. However, as is the case with any construct or method or process, the method (even OO) will not do the job on its own.

OO can do a better job at modeling the system that is being designed within the OO system. It follows that, if the software model allows the software to better model the real world situation that the software is trying to solve, then that system will be better understood and more easily modifiable.

As described in the definition of encapsulation and reuse, reuse could be the biggest potential benefit of OO. (Refer to chapter 7.) This goes far beyond code reuse. If the analysis and design is performed in a similar "encapsulated" fashion, these elements of the software system should be reused. Carrying this analysis one step further, the unit-level testing elements also should be able to be reusable. The problem with this benefit is that reuse, in general, has not ever been a major concern with most organizations. The concept of reuse must be institutionalized within an organization, regardless of the development methodology chosen.

If coupled with an iterative life cycle along with prototyping, object-orientation can get a system "in the customer's hands" sooner than normally is the case with structured development coupled with the waterfall method. This can only be a positive.

Problems with older methodologies

Yourdon (1994, 24–25) describes problems that have arisen with the older methodologies, mostly in terms of robustness and failings when it comes to very complex systems. This is especially true of the methods that explicitly separate data from function. When this occurs and the data model and the function model are developed separately, model mismatches are bound to occur when it comes time to merge the two models.

There is no question that vastly more complex systems are being built today than were being built in the early days of structural and informational methodologies. Concurrency also has been a driver for this complexity increase as well as the proliferation of distributed-types of systems, such as client-server systems. In many ways, this has been one of driving forces for the emergence of object-orientation and presents an argument for discarding or at least performing major modifications to current methodologies.

Should functional methodologies be discarded or merely upgraded? OO proponents feel that for today's more complex systems, functional decomposition methods are fatally flawed and ultimately will have to be discarded.

Methodology Mixing

As new methodologies are selected, it usually is the case that the new methodology is merged into the current process that an organization practices, as mentioned in chapter 1. As such, it rarely is the case that an organization will replace an old methodology with a new one throughout the entire life cycle. What is much more likely to occur is that certain elements of the new methodology will be inserted into the organization's software development process. Is this an efficient technique for migrating to a new process? The answer is not clear.

On one hand, it probably makes sense to gradually attempt to implement a new methodology step-by-step. After all, if the choice ends up being the wrong one, then the impact obviously is less than if a new method was implemented that was propagated across the entire process. There are problems with this approach, however; and the problems can be severe.

When migrating to an object-oriented methodology, the first step usually appears in the usage of an object-oriented programming language (OOPL). Typically, this is the time when the developers are just learning the new language and getting used to the new constructs. Good training is critical even at this step. Old habits will need to be modified. The power of the OOPL will need to be exploited. Some problems can occur at this step, but what typically happens is that the developers use the new language but will be designing in the old mindset. This is due to the fact that, in this example, OO has not been propagated to the design or even to the analysis activities, which again is the standard technical progression of a methodology within the life cycle phases.

The real potential payoffs occur (and also potential problems begin to surface) when the new methodology is used in the design phase. The real power of the OOP language can be exploited by designing the system in such a manner to take advantage of the OOP.

Although this certainly is a benefit of OOD, there are some problems that occur at this point of adopting an OO methodology. Few organizations, when adopting an OO methodology, instantly migrate to OOD and OOA at the same time. For many reasons, many of which are prudent, OOD is implemented first, while retaining non-OO analysis methods. What this implies, however, is that a "methodology jump" must occur when considering the design.

Much has been written about this issue because OOA is beginning to mature and becomes a more viable option. Many methodologists now propose that OOA has matured to the point where a full migration to OOA and OOD can "safely" occur. When requirements are written in a "functional" manner and an OO design approach is used, there will be problems. Keeping in mind that any OO approach requires a totally different mindset than a functional one, there will have to be some sort of "leap of faith" to determine the design. What happens, or should happen, is that some level of informal "re-analysis" occurs. The requirements are "reviewed" from an object-oriented standpoint and thus provide a common basis for the design.

The politics of methodology. There is another reason why a new methodology, at best, can be phased in only little by little with the resultant mixing of methodologies. One must never underestimate the role of "politics" in decisions like this. Much of the same political dynamics that occur with process change also occurs with a methodology shift. This is especially true if an organization has previously had a certain methodology in place for a long period of time. In such a situation, there certainly are individuals within the organization that will have built up empires around the old methodology.

There will likely be members of the technical staff that do inhouse training in the "old" methodology. A new methodology very often will be met with disdain and outright hauteur by individuals that feel threatened by it.

Other potential political roadblocks to a new methodology can be in the CASE tools that might have become established like concrete within the organization. This is especially true if the organization has a large investment with a given CASE vendor.

These political issues more than likely will force at least some of the remnants of the old methodology to remain beyond its expected time frame. A mixed methodology might be the only way that a new methodology can get a foothold within an organization.

Growing pains of CASE

One of the biggest reasons that methodology mixing occurs is due to a concept called "CASE lag." Effective and bug-free CASE tools take many years to appear after a methodology appears. Such is the case, for example, with object-oriented analysis.

The analysis phase (and possibly testing) is the last phase that is affected by a new methodology. The CASE tools that are developed are done so in such a manner by the vendors to support the phase that the new methodology affects first. When speaking of a flavor of OO as the new methodology, the languages are supported first, with compilers to support the OOP. Next is the design phase and last is the analysis phase.

Because it usually is necessary to have some form of good CASE support for all phases, it should be clear that until the method has been around for a long time, there will be methodology mixing across the different phases. There is just no way around it unless an organization is willing to risk development in a phase that has immature CASE tools.

Choosing a Methodology

When choosing a methodology for an organization, one criterion that must be examined is the ability of the development team to adapt to, learn, and implement the new methodology. This issue is not as much one of the "intelligence" of the development staff as it is the amount of time available to learn the methodology well enough to implement the new methodology appropriately.

Part of the ability to learn a new methodology has to do with willingness to learn. Methodology wars, as with process wars, can be as much a deterrent to the acceptance of a new methodology as the educational aspects of learning the new technology.

For example, if an organization has determined that it is going to move from one type of functional decomposition method to a different method, the learning curve likely will not be very steep. However, if an organization decides to take the OO plunge, it likely will be a long time before the developers are "good" OO designers. (Again, refer to chapter 4 for a much more detailed view of this topic.)

Availability of CASE support

Another key element to choosing an appropriate methodology is the availability of CASE support. It usually takes at least several years after the introduction of a new methodology before the CASE tools start to "catch up." This can be a big problem if a relatively new methodology is chosen.

This trend is starting to change, however. Many of the methodologists are beginning to work actively with the CASE vendors to get the CASE tool support "to market" as soon as possible. An additional benefit is that the methodology obviously will be implemented in the CASE tool very accurately because the methodologist is closely involved.

Even for the established functional methodologies, there are a wide variety of CASE tools in terms of price, quality, and supported platforms. Close attention must be paid when making a CASE decision.

Will the Method Save You?

Patrick Loy (1993) puts this entire discussion about methods in the appropriate light. Simply adopting OO will not automatically usher in salvation to the software crisis. Hardly. Loy confirms experiences that we have seen time and time again. If a shop is able to implement structured techniques well, then it is likely that they will be able to implement object-oriented techniques well. Conversely (and more importantly), organizations that are unable to implement structured techniques will *not* be able to implement object-oriented techniques well.

> Managers and other software professionals who are serious about improving the way their shops do business will recognize that there is no silver bullet to be found. The search for the perfect method or CASE tool is a futile one. New methods and tools might help, but they are unlikely to solve the root problems.
>
> Loy (1993, 33)

Often throughout this book, we will speak about many software development concepts that are necessary to developing software right the first time: good software process, prototyping, iterative life cycle development methods, object-oriented technology, CASE tools, and others. The methodology chosen, as with the other software development concepts, does not stand on its own as an "automatic solution" to all of one's software woes.

Summary

Choice of methodology is a critical decision on a software project. Structured methods have been around for a long time and have done well for many years. Some information technologies, although somewhat less popular than functional methods, have been very good methods and have even provided a basis for some of the OO methodologies.

Software systems are getting more complicated. More sophisticated languages are being developed as are new methodologies. Right now, OO technologies are becoming very popular. OOPLs and OOD have become fairly well established. OOA is coming into its own and is gaining more and more acceptance.

As organizations incrementally transition to newer methodologies, especially OO, it is likely that methodology mixing will occur. Although this might be the best decision to make at the time, there are problems with this approach.

When changing to a new OO methodology, if necessary, care should be taken to ensure that CASE tool support is available.

Finally, as it has been said before, and will be said again, there are no magical solutions, and the method is no exception. This is no substitute for the skills of the technical and management staff associated with a successful software project.

References

Boehm, Barry W. 1981. *Software Engineering Economics*. Englewood Cliffs, New Jersey: Prentice Hall

Booch, Grady. 1994. *Object-Oriented Analysis and Design With Applications*. Redwood City, California: Benjamin/Cummings Publishing Company, Inc.

Demarco, Tom. 1978. *Structured Analysis and System Specification*. Englewood Cliffs, New Jersey: Yourdon Press/Prentice Hall.

Gane, Chris and Trish Sarson. 1977. *Structured System Analysis: Tools and Techniques*. Englewood Cliffs, New Jersey: Prentice Hall.

Holt, Richard and Dennis deChampeaux. 1992. *OOPS Messenger*. 3 (2): 9–10.

Jackson, M.A. 1975. *Principles of Program Design*. Academic Press.

Jackson, M.A. 1983. *System Development*. Englewood Cliffs, New Jersey: Prentice Hall.

Loy, Patrick. 1993. "The Method Won't Save You (But It Can Help)." *Software Engineering Notes of the ACM* 18 (1): 30–34.

Myers, G. 1978. *Composite/Structured Design*. New York, New York: Van Nostrand Reinhold.

Page-Jones, M. 1988. *The Practical Guide to Structured Systems Design*. Englewood Cliffs, New Jersey: Yourdon Press.

Pressman, Roger S. 1987. *Software Engineering: A Practitioners Approach*. New York, New York: McGraw-Hill.

Rozman, I., J. Gyorkos and K. Rizman. 1992. "Understandability of the Software Engineering Method as an Important Factor for Selecting a CASE Tool." *Software Engineering Notes of the ACM* 17 (3): 43–46.

Warnier, J.D. 1974. *Logical Construction of Programs*. New York, New York: Van Nostrand Reinhold.

Warnier, J.D. 1981. *Logical Construction of Systems*. New York, New York: Van Nostrand Reinhold.

Yourdon, Edward. 1993. *Decline and Fall of the American Programmer*. Englewood Cliffs, New Jersey: Yourdon Press.

Yourdon, Edward. 1994. *Object-Oriented Systems Design—An Integrated Approach*. Englewood Cliffs, New Jersey: Yourdon Press.

Yourdon, Edward and L. Constantine. 1979. *Structured Design*. Englewood Cliffs, New Jersey: Prentice Hall.

4

Object-Oriented Technology

Pick up any computer- or software-related magazine in any bookstore, and it is rare if there isn't an article that is related in some way to object-oriented (OO) technology. Is OO technology just a fad that will pass with time? Is it a necessary or at least a desired technology? Is it necessary to use OO to get mission-critical systems right the first time?

OO might not be absolutely necessary for a software system to be a *success* (depending upon how one defines *success*); however, as systems become more and more complex, the chances of success, no matter how defined, will decrease if OO is not part of the project plan.

System complexity is continually increasing. There are an increasing number of horror stories of complex systems that have had serious software/system problems. It is clear that the current way of doing things is not cutting it anymore, and OO might very well offer some solutions to dealing with system complexity.

Certainly, if OO is worthwhile, there must be benefits that arise from its use. Some of the benefits that will be discussed are: coordinated efforts for effective reuse, more easily modifiable systems, reduction of risks during the project development, reduced development cycle, and the introduction of scenario or system event analysis.

Along with the benefits, there also must be some costs or risks. There are those who would claim that there are throughput or performance risks associated with OO. It is necessary, when embarking upon OO, that a mindset shift occur from functional (or algorithmic) methods to OO methods. If this paradigm shift does not occur, there are certain risks of attempting OO. This is no different than attempting anything new without being adequately prepared for the new venture. There are certain risks in regards to CASE. Some feel that object-oriented requirements analysis (OORA) is not as developed as object-oriented design (OOD). Along the same lines, CASE is not as developed in some of the areas of OO technology. Working with the wrong CASE tool can cause problems. Lack of appropriate training in OO as well as the language that the project is going to be implemented in are risks that also must be addressed.

Perhaps the most difficult step that is associated with embarking upon OO is just getting started. After deciding to implement a project using OO technology, there must be full and complete management support and adequate and timely training and education. A definite paradigm shift must occur or else it is likely that efforts to perform "OO-activities" will fail. Appropriate CASE decisions must be made to support the choice of OO method because there are many CASE tools to choose from. One must ensure that an adequate software process is in place to support the CASE tool and choice of method. Finally, OO inherently allows and strongly supports reuse activities that must be taken advantage of.

OO has made in-roads into the "engineering world" with some success. To be truly successful, OO technology must demonstrate its applicability in the business/commercial world. To a degree, this has been accomplished with the development of C++. There certainly is a fair amount of business-related code written in C along with current C development. The migration to C++ certainly is an "in-road" of OO into the business world. This will be accomplished additionally by the release of object-oriented COBOL, denoted as OOCOBOL. Additionally, OO and reengineering efforts must prove to be compatible concepts to deal with all of the legacy business code that is written, again mostly in COBOL. Finally, the similarities and the relationship between entity-relationship (ER) technology and OO technology will be discussed.

There is an ever-growing number of OO methods being developed. Choosing the appropriate method can prove difficult. We will compare the major OO methods that will help to determine which method is appropriate.

OO and Complexity

If there is a single driving force that has led to the birth, development, phenomenal growth, and acceptance of OO, it is the need to address complexity. Software systems that are being developed are becoming increasingly complex. The NASA space shuttle, stock trading programs, air traffic control systems, and military command and control systems are all examples of complex systems. The increasing complexity of systems such as these have stretched "functional" development methods beyond their capacity.

"Real world systems" that exhibit a given inherent level of complexity cannot be accurately represented by a software system that is any less complex. In the past, this complexity has been managed, barely, by strict adherence to functional or algorithmic decomposition methods. These decomposition methods had been applied successfully to both the analysis and the design phases of the software development cycle. However, these methods have failed to address the critical issues of *data abstraction* (the process by which data, represented by an object, presents its visibility and use to the user in a well-defined, concise manner), *information hiding* (the process or concept of hiding irrelevant information concerning an object such as implementation details of the object from the user), and *concurrency* (the characteristic of a system that implies multiple tasking or events occurring "at the same time"). This inability of functional methods to address these concepts is at least partially responsible for the failure to keep up with this "ever-growing" complexity. The inherent increasing complexity of systems has resulted in systems that have been canceled or have resulted in sometimes disastrous circumstances. Table 4.1 lists some of these projects.

TABLE 4.1   Examples of Complex Software System Failures

Project	Description/Problem
Denver Airport Baggage Handling System	Airport delayed in opening; tens of millions spent on backup system when primary system could not be fixed.
P-3 Orion Update IV avionics upgrade project	Scrapped military project due to hardware/software schedule failures.
Air Force C17 military transport project	Massive cost and schedule overruns resulting in large-scale cutbacks in order. For more info. refer to GAO Report IMTEC-92-48.
Navy A12 Aircraft	According to SECDEF, main contractor could not determine when project would be completed, how much it would cost and even if the project could be done.
Clementine space probe	Error in real-time software caused maneuvering thrusters to fire inadvertently causing scrapping of a mission.
Air Traffic Control (ATC) Advanced Automation System (AAS)	Attempt to upgrade antiquated air traffic control system is 5 years late and $1B over budget.
American Airlines/Marriott/Hilton/Budget system consolidation project	Attempt to merge airline/hotel/auto rental systems resulted in system cancellation and loss to American Airlines of $165M.
California DMV system consolidation cancellation	Attempt to merge driver and registration systems resulted in $44.3M loss and cancellation of project.

If one believes that the form of the solution (software system) should approximate the form of the problem (real world domain that is being modeled by the software system), then it is clear that algorithmic decomposition methods don't perform this approximation anywhere nearly as well as OO methods do.

Benefits of OO

OO would not be worth the necessary investment if the purported benefits could be achieved with methods and processes that already exist and are proven. In addition, OO must have an impressive return on that investment. In some ways, the potential benefits hoped for from OO are no different than benefits desired from any other new methodology or practice:

- Reduced product development time
- Better product (less errors)
- More easily modifiable product

There are some very specific potential benefits that OO purports to be able to deliver. Booch (1994) and Kamath, Smilan, and Smith (1993) contribute examples of such benefits:

- Encourages the reuse of software components
- Leads to systems that are more resilient to change
- Reduces development risk

There is not much more to be said about the need for systems that are developed cheaper, better, or faster. The potential benefits that OO can uniquely bring to a project are worth addressing further.

Reuse of software components

Regardless of the software methodology or language being used, reuse has always been a stated priority. Unfortunately, very few software organizations have made any meaningful headway in this area. (We feel this is such an important area that we have devoted an entire chapter to this topic.)

Proponents of OO technology claim that software component reuse (across all phases of the development) is enhanced when OO is employed. To determine whether or not this premise is true, Lewis, et al. (1991) embarked on a scientifically controlled experiment.

In this experiment, independent subjects/students were divided into four groups. Half implemented the project in Pascal, and the other half in C++. In addition, a portion of each group were encouraged to implement reuse, whereas the remaining portion were prohibited from implementing reuse.

The goal of the experiment was to answer the following questions with respect to the impact of an OO method versus a procedural method:

- Does the OO paradigm promote higher productivity than the procedural or functional method? (For purposes of comparing and contrasting object-oriented and "structured" analysis and design methods, the terms *functional, structured, algorithmic,* and *procedural* will all be used synonymously when referring to these methods.)
- Does reuse promote higher productivity than no reuse?
- Does the OO method promote higher productivity than the procedural method when programmers do not reuse?
- Does the OO method promote higher productivity than the procedural method when programmers reuse?
- Does the OO method provide incentives to reuse above those of the procedural method?

The results of this experiment were quite interesting.

- The OO method substantially improves productivity, although a significant part of this improvement is due to the effect of reuse. (Questions 1,3,4)
- Software reuse improves productivity no matter which language paradigm is used. (Question 2)
- Language differences are far more important when programmers reuse than when they do not. (Questions 3,4)
- The OO method has a particular affinity to the reuse process. (Question 5)

It is clear that this is just one study and far-reaching conclusions can't be implied from a single study. However, there can be no argument that, if components that are candidates for reuse are generated and reused, there certainly will be some costs savings realized.

The real benefits of reuse will occur when reusable classes are developed in which requirements, design, code, and test elements comprise the entire reusable component. Refer to chapter 7 for more information.

Easily modifiable systems

Perhaps the basic premise that underlines the purpose and benefits of OO systems is that these systems are easily modifiable. OO systems are constructed by assembling objects that interact with each other via message-passing. Everything that is indigenous to the object is contained within the programming construct that represents the object.

The best method to determine whether OO systems are more easily modifiable than functional systems is to consider the kinds of "typical" changes that occur to a system and identify how a well-constructed OO system reacts to these changes.

Adding functionality and data to a system. This might be the most common cause for system updates. The system simply doesn't do what it is supposed to. Systems that are not constructed in an "OO mindset" typically will be constructed with heterogeneous data structures that are visible and able to be modified from anywhere in the program. FORTRAN has COMMON blocks (which are made even worse with the EQUIVALENCE concept). Ada has package specifications that can easily be abused into a repository for common data (i.e., the common data package). C/C++ has "include" files.

Certainly, these are all valid constructs to use within a program. Use of these constructs for storage of heterogeneous data can lead to problems when adding functionality or data to a system. In addition, making these constructs available for uncontrolled modification throughout the program leads to additional problems.

Once data structures are set up that contain heterogeneous data, it becomes more and more tempting to use these data structures as a "dumping ground" for any new data that needs to be added. This causes maintenance problems because there is no intuitive way to know where in the system specific data is stored. To make matters worse, if the position of data elements in a data structure is referenced often elsewhere in the code, inserting new data elements will force references to those elements to change. This causes major headaches for developers and maintainers.

Once the data starts getting spread out over the system, it is very easy for the functionality to follow in the same manner. New data typically isn't added to a system unless there is a reason to access and/or modify it. Thus, if data is added to a system, then functionality (functions and procedures or operations) also will be added. One can see how real problems now can start occurring due not only to propagation of new data but also to functionality within a system.

Analogously, if functions and/or data are deleted from a system, some of the same problems can occur. If data is removed from a system, this might cause data access routines that use exact storage locations to no longer function.

Through the concepts of encapsulation and information hiding, OO systems attempt to solve this problem. The data and the associated functionality, in general, constitute an "object." If it discovered that a piece of data (attribute) has to be added to the system, it typically is added to the data structure within the object that it is an attribute of. Per the previous discussion, there typically will be functionality added to the object to allow access (read) to that attribute of the object and the ability to modify (write) to that attribute of the object.

If new data and functionality is handled in this fashion, it is much easier to control data and functionality growth to a system.

Attempting to reduce module complexity. Very often, you will find routines or subprograms that begin to grow beyond the bounds of comprehension. (This usually happens, by the way, due to routines attempting to do more than what originally was intended for them to perform.) To reduce this complexity, routines are "broken up" into smaller pieces.

Unfortunately, if it isn't clear what the original subprogram's intent is, attempts to make meaningful subdivisions of such a module will be haphazard at best. Very often, attempting to split a routine is not simple. Often data will have to be shared among the newly created routines. How should the data be shared? Should it be shared via parameter passing? Should that data be put into a common-storage area for both routines to access? What if the data originally was in a common storage area? Will passing the data as a parameter *and* having it in common storage cause problems?

OO systems that are well-designed have very little "common" data. All of the data and functionality that is associated with or, perhaps more appropriately, defines an object (very often a homogeneous data structure) is self-contained. When new functionality is added, that functionality should be able to be defined as a new combination of existing operations (or methods, in OO parlance), or new methods will need to be defined that operate on the object.

It should be intuitively obvious that OO systems have a tendency to have a lot of simple routines that typically don't get very complex. One can see how much easier it is for a maintainer to work with such a system.

There is a drawback to this approach, though. Systems that are comprised of many simple operations have more "calling overhead" than systems that are designed in a "functional" manner. This drawback can be largely mitigated, however, and will be discussed later in this chapter in the section entitled "Risks of OO."

Much more will be said about the details of OO programming (OOP) in chapter 9.

Reduction of development risks

For OO to be taken seriously as a modern methodology, it must demonstrate that it is an active player in overall risk reduction for a project that employs it. In actuality, OO does play a role in project risk reduction, but it must be a part of other methodology improvements—specifically prototyping and iterative life cycle methods.

It is a fallacy to design a system with the assumption that work progresses linearly through each of the life cycle phases with work commencing on a phase only after the previous phase is complete, such as in conservative implementations of the waterfall life cycle method. System development rarely, if ever, follows such a linear path. This is mostly due to the fact that requirements are never "potted" to allow such a linear approach to development. There are system and software analysis methods that certainly attempt to do a better job at quantifying and documenting the requirements, as presented. However, that really is what the problem is. Therefore, to be successful, development methodologies must recognize and accommodate this.

Through previously discussed "ease of modifiability," the use of iterative/spiral-like life cycle development methodologies and prototyping, OO systems can reduce risk. Early views of the system are analyzed through prototyping. Requirements and associated functionality can be delivered in a phased-release approach via a spirallike development method. Perhaps most importantly, however, is the specific method by which OO helps with requirement ambiguity. OORA helps to organize and categorize the system/software requirements by keeping the objects (nouns in a specification) grouped with the associated functionality (verbs in a specification) required of that object. The development risk then can be minimized by implementing a few objects, getting an early view of the system through prototyping, then iteratively implementing more and more objects. If necessary, objects that already are implemented can be augmented as appropriate.

It will be much easier to gauge schedule progression as parts of the system are implemented through a "design a little, code a little, test a little" methodology. In plain English, if the customer then is able to see what is expected sooner than later, any serious problems with expectations can be addressed sooner, not later. Addressing problems sooner versus later saves time and money and reduces risk.

Reduced development cycle

It is purported that OO development will result in reduced development cycle. This benefit will not be realized initially when implementing OO technology, however. Development time likely will increase due to the methodology learning curve, new language learning curve (or appropriate OO use of an existing language that has some OO support), time to learn and use new CASE toolsets, and the overall costs associated with the software process changes that are incorporated to adapt to an OO methodology. Also, development of reusable objects might have an adverse effect early on in the development of the first OO system. However, the sooner those reusable objects are identified and used, the more quickly the benefits will be realized.

As mentioned in other related chapters, it isn't just the OO method that will be responsible for reduction in development time. Appropriate adjustments must be made to the overall software process, the life cycle method (moving away from waterfall methods and toward iterative models), and the effective use of prototyping. All of these concepts are interrelated and are necessary aspects of any serious attempts to reduce the development life cycle.

Introduction of scenario or system event analysis

A very important aspect of all self-respecting OO methods is the concept of system event analysis. This is an aspect of software analysis and design that, although touched on in early functional methodologies, was never developed to the degree that OO methods have.

From the early days of OO method development, it was clear that system event analysis was not to be just a by-product of OO technology but a main component of OO technology. In general, objects and classes communicate with each other via messages. Typical OO static analysis techniques result in the definition of objects, classes, and methods that are associated with the classes. This certainly is not the entire picture though. It is just a snapshot of the system, per se. Things get interesting though when one considers the dynamic aspects of the system—that is, how the objects and classes interact with each other via the messages. You might ask how you determine what messages are to be sent from object to object. The starting point is the system events as specified in the specification document. Object message passing is the mechanism that an OO system uses to react to system events. It is simply a representation of how the job gets done.

It is the system event analysis that expresses the requirements of the software. In a very real sense, the "dynamics" of the system are best represented in system events. The mechanics of analyzing the dynamics of a system are accomplished through object message diagrams, class interaction diagrams, and other similar descriptions. In many ways, this dynamic analysis is representative of "shall" requirements that are represented in most textual and requirements documents.

Consider other graphical methods that are used to represent software systems: structure charts (Figure 4.1), data flow diagrams or DFDs (Figure 4.2), flowcharts (Figure 4.3), and state transition diagrams or STDs (Figure 4.4).

Structure charts adequately describe the hierarchy of software modules. DFDs describe only what data is passed between modules (remember data flows are *not* messages). Flowcharts, which are good for giving a "micro" logic-oriented view of one aspect of a system, don't do an adequate job of representing high-level system interactions. STDs do an adequate job of reflecting state transitions due to system events; however, they show the effect on only one aspect of the system. (STDs are used in several of the OO methodologies because they support a limited event analysis view of the system.)

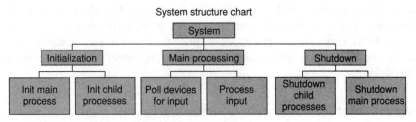

Figure 4.1 An example of a structure chart.

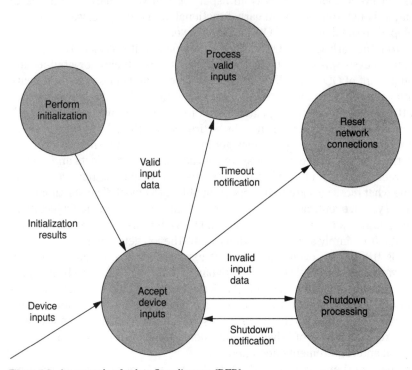

Figure 4.2 An example of a data flow diagram (DFD).

The impact of system event analysis cannot be underestimated. None of the other system representation formats allows a potential user, developer, or maintenance programmer to easily take a look at the system and answer the question, "How does the system react when . . . occurs?"

Risks of OO

As one would expect, whenever there are benefits to be had from an activity there also are risks. These risks can be enumerated in the following categories, again some of which are contributed by Booch (1994):

- Performance or throughput risks
- OO mindset risks
- CASE risks
- Training risks
- Language risks (inappropriate use of a language)
- General startup risks

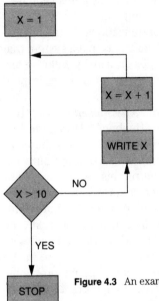

Figure 4.3 An example of a flowchart.

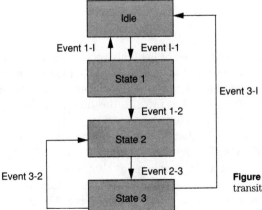

Figure 4.4 Standard state/event state transition diagram (STD).

Performance or throughput risks

There is a misconception that OO technology is inappropriate for real-time embedded systems. OO systems have a tendency to be more "layered" than other "functional" systems. This layering typically translates to more function and procedure "calls" than historically has been the case. These additional calls, if not optimized in some fashion, will result in additional processing time that often is blamed for real-time systems that have difficulties meeting timing deadlines.

The overall consensus feeling on this matter is that all systems should be designed (read specifically as design phase, *not* implementation) without attention to low-level timing details. Low-level optimizations should be considered later, in the coding cycle. The fact of the matter is that a system that is optimized for space or speed early on in the design usually will lose any benefits that are gained from the explicit optimizations due to a corrupted high-level design that most optimizations drive.

Another aspect of performance considerations that deserves attention has to do with the concept of "the most bang for the buck." During design, there certainly will be some occurrences where it is tempting to immediately optimize. Much time and effort might be spent on this optimization only to find that very little execution time is spent on this particular area of the code. It usually is much more fruitful to determine where the bottlenecks are and optimize where the gain will be the highest for the time spent.

This issue of performance is a concept that will occur with OO real-time systems due to the aforementioned additional "layering" that typically occurs with OO. Some low-level optimizations can be performed late in the coding when and where certain functions are having timing problems. Sometimes when these optimizations are unsuccessful in correcting potential timing problems, OO gets the blame. Typically, however, any attempt at performing optimizations much earlier in the life cycle would have resulted in even more problems.

OO mindset risks

When embarking upon OO for the first time, it is highly recommended that, if at all possible, the development teams engage in some sort of pilot project to test out the concepts that they have learned. (It is assumed that there will have been adequate and timely training prior to the time that the developers need to begin using the methodology.)

It can't be emphasized too strongly that OO is not functional or structured design by another name. CASE vendors, especially in the early days of OO, released OO tools that often were given a name that was a combination of OO and functional terminology. This was most certainly done to sell the tool with its current capabilities implying that their tool would be a good medium to perform a migration from structured methods to OO methods. While this certainly might be true, what this tactic also did was enforce the terribly mistaken impression that structured methods and OO weren't all that different from each other. When this occurs, developers then do not place a priority on establishing the new mindset that is required and trouble soon follows.

Let it be made very clear also, if it has not to this point, that OO is not a "silver bullet." There are no silver bullets! A poorly designed OO system still is a bad system and a well-designed structural/functional system still is just that, a well-designed system.

A pilot project will allow the developers to begin to struggle and, to quote a former colleague, "to burn-in new brain cells." It can be a painful experience, at first, but very quickly "OO habits" begin to take shape. When performing this migration, there typically is a common set of problems that result from a "functional mindset." It would be worthwhile to list these issues so as to be able to recognize them and more easily address them when they arise:

- Connecting lines between boxes on a diagram are no longer data-flow lines (from data-flow methodology). These connecting lines represent potential message paths or *lines of visibility*. Object A can communicate with Object B (through message passing) only if Object B is visible to Object A. This difference between *message paths* and *data-flow paths* is one of the most difficult concepts to leave behind when learning OO for the first time.

- It can be difficult determining how to represent an external device in an OO system and how to represent a software interface to an external device. Are they two separate "objects" or are they really the same concept?

- It can be difficult to determine whether an entity is an object or an attribute of an object. How does one decide?

- How is the concept of time implemented in an OO system? Should it be a "clock event" or perhaps a more passive construct?

- What exactly is a "relationship" between two classes? If the method being used implements the concepts of dependencies within a relationship, it very often is not easy to determine the "direction" of the dependency.

Tendencies to fall back into "old habits" must be resisted. After a while, however, like any other practiced talent, things begin to get easier. This is why it is important to be able to practice out these new concepts before having to work on the "real thing."

CASE risks

Some potential problems with CASE were mentioned in preceding sections (those having to do with CASE tools not performing as promised). Perhaps the greatest risk of all that is associated with CASE has to do with the fact that CASE tools are so aggressively marketed that unsuspecting potential customers very often develop a mindset that the toolset will implement the methodology for the developer.

Nothing could be further from the truth. A very good OO CASE tool might support object-oriented requirements analysis and design (OORA/OOD). It might support static and dynamic analysis concepts within OORA/OOD such as:

- Class and object definition including hierarchies of classes within a class structure
- Higher-level groupings of class hierarchies into subsystems
- Attribute definitions for classes and objects
- Object instantiation within classes
- Method identification
- System event analysis
- Textual specification generation
- Perhaps even some level of code generation

However, it is the developer that does the real work in the development of the system. CASE is a tool—nothing more and nothing less. As with any product in a free-market system, there is a wide range of products from very good to not so good. It is the responsibility of the potential purchaser to determine what constitutes a good tool and one that does not meet one's needs. (For more information on selecting a tool, refer to chapter 10.) Again, don't fall victim to the fallacy of thinking that CASE is going to do any of the real system development in lieu of the work performed by the developers.

Another more elementary risk with CASE, which certainly is not specific to OO, is that the CASE toolset might simply not do what you might think it does or what you might have heard that it does.

The vast majority of CASE vendors are very reputable and stand behind their products. Therefore, a thorough analysis of the toolset along with any competitors' products is an absolute requirement when purchasing a CASE toolset. Anything less than that is foolish and irresponsible.

Training risks

The importance of training was mentioned in a previous section when discussing the mindset shift that is necessary when delving into OO technology. In addition, more will be discussed later concerning the impact of training when starting up an OO project.

To summarize, however, the lack of appropriate and timely training will be fatal when embarking into OO technology. The training should cover both language-independent OO material as well as language-specific issues. The developers must understand the general concepts of OO, but this is not enough. The appropriate use of the language also must be addressed. If not, it is very possible that many of the general OO concepts taught to the developers will be lost on them. Without understanding how to specifically use the language and implement the newly learned techniques, the OO training might be useless.

When embarking on OO for the first time, it is critical to continue the training throughout the project. Effective use of experts (even external consultants) should be encouraged throughout the project. Training on the front-end of the project will not obviate the need for experts to help with problems, misunderstandings, and mistakes along the way.

The timing of training is as critical as whether or not there is training at all. Train too far ahead of work on a real project, and much will be forgotten. Train too late afterward, and there will not be enough time to learn the techniques. Train very late, and it might even be too late to use the techniques that are learned. (*Note*: Believe it or not, this actually occurs on many projects. When training is not given management support, a series of nondecisions often results in training that occurs literally "too late" to be of any use.)

Language risks

Part of the risks that are associated with the language that is to be used has been covered in the risks of inadequate training. If the appropriate use of the language isn't also developed and learned, the misuse of the language is inevitable.

Another risk that is associated with the use of an OO language is very similar to those that can occur when using OO technology for the first time. For some of the newer, more "modern" languages, it is possible that there is experience with use of the language, whether it is appropriate or inappropriate. This points out the importance of training to an even greater degree. In a situation where a new methodology and a new language both are instituted, the overall risk to a project is greatly increased. The situation isn't unmanageable, but special precautions, including the aforementioned training and expert consultation, are mandatory. In addition, management must understand that support and acceptance of the guidance of these experts are critical.

Summary of OO risks

In general, implementing anything new on a project increases risk on a project. Certainly, that risk can be managed as is the case for risks associated with OO. Very often, when implementing a new software methodology such as OO, there are other "new" aspects of a project that add risk to a project. This is especially true of real-time embedded systems.

As with any new technology, there are risks and activities that, when done well, have benefits. These same activities will inevitably have risks associated with them. Management of the risks by following the points mentioned here will greatly reduce that risk and help ensure success.

Getting Started with OO

Assuming that an organization has determined that OO is the "way to go," what happens next? Every member of the development team (including management) will be affected. Each has a role to play, and everyone must know what their roles are and how these roles will change as compared with the way that they had previously done business.

There are several key elements necessary to "getting off on the right OO foot." In general, when getting started in OO, there are several key elements that absolutely must be in place. If any of these are lacking, success is nearly impossible. For a successful OO project/organization:

- There must be full and active management support of OO.
- The staff (analysts, designers, programmers, testers, management, etc.) must be adequately trained in the appropriate use of OO.
- There must be an actual change in mindset away from "functional thought" to "OO thought."
- An OO method must be chosen.
- Appropriate tools (possibly including CASE) must be selected.
- There must be an adequately rigorous software process in place.
- Explicit support for reuse must be in place.

Management role in OO

It has been stated, and will be stated often, in this book that any change to the way that things are done in an organization needs explicit, active, top-level management support. This is the kind of support that is needed to introduce new methodologies, including OO.

Software development, and computer science in general, has had technologies that were billed as the long-awaited arrival of the definitive "silver bullet." The AI "over-enthusiasts" of the early 1980s were calling for an "expert system on every desktop" in only a few short years. Some of the newer languages (C++, Ada 95, and even OOCOBOL, which will be discussed later) have been touted by other "over-enthusiasts" as the "be-all/end-all" of software development. CASE, when introduced, suffered from some of the same "expectations."

Unfortunately, we have not learned from errors of the past and, in some circles, have subjected OO to the same unfair, unrealistically high expectations. As a result, many managers, perhaps due to those inflated expectations of the past, are very wary of lending their full support to OO. Without this support, however, OO will fail. However, management typically is wary of lending their full support and faith to anything due to the learned experiences with other proposed "silver bullets." So, what to do?

Yourdon (1994) suggests one possible approach to this problem. It might not be possible to garner widespread management support, but there might be one or more highly visible individuals that are willing to champion the cause. Sometimes there is a manager that is willing to risk his reputation by championing the "OO-cause" in the face of opposition or even hostility from other managers, even his or her superiors. Sometimes, however, this champion is all that the developers need to inspire their belief in OO and to turn that belief into results and proof.

Some managers refuse to even give OO a chance, either due to some bad experience in the past or just plain fear of leaving a "comfort zone." Some of these managers will actively fight the introduction of any new activity, including OO, to the project or the company.

If given a choice between getting full management support and that of only a few managers, you certainly would choose support from entire management staff. However, this rarely happens. While the single champion approach might be all that is available at the time, this kind of approach does have its problems.

If a single champion "carries the torch" so to speak, other managers are either watching and waiting to see if this manager drops the torch, or in some cases, they might be setting up obstacles for the champion to trip over. The single champion approach might be all that is available, but it might be a long, drawn-out effort to ultimately win the support of the rest of the management staff.

As is so often heard from the masses, without management support, it is next to impossible to change the way things are. Passive support is not enough. Active support is required.

Education/training

It is very tempting to preface the discussion of education/training with "This is one of the most important and necessary aspects when starting into OO." We have been saying this for just about every discussed aspect of OO. This is because each of these elements, as stated earlier, are critically essential. The need for appropriate and timely education and training is no less important than any of these other aspects. In Korson (1991), the need for appropriate training and education was one of the aspects of transitioning to OO technology that all of the panel members agreed was a high priority.

When starting out in OO, it is likely that only a very small percentage of the development staff will have had any real OO experience. Therefore, quality training is essential. The training must be of high quality and must be timely.

Where does one find good training? Personal experiences typically are the best way to go, at least at first. If there are highly skilled software developers that have undergone good OO training, get them involved in the decision-making process. Software training shops are popping up all around the country. Utilize the Internet to obtain references. Get a list of at least five training companies. Interview them thoroughly asking *very* detailed questions to assess their competence. Tailor the training course to meet specific needs.

One additional point concerning training should be noted. Many organizations, especially the large ones, have onsite technical training staffs that perform most of the inhouse training. Except for the rarest of cases, when embarking on OO for the first time, refrain from utilizing this method of OO training. Usually when an inhouse training staff has to perform some training on a topic that has not been done before, one or more of the training staff are sent away for a week to obtain necessary train-the-trainer education. This will *not* work for OO (as it doesn't for many other technical topics). To obtain good OO training, it needs to come from experienced people who do this for a living.

Selection of training and trainers should *not* be exclusively a management activity. Find every last experienced OO developer that you have and involve them in the selection/evaluation process. Upper-level management typically doesn't understand the criteria for selecting good trainers.

An aspect of training that is equally important to quality is timeliness. The phrase "just-in-time training" hits the nail on the head. One doesn't want the training to occur too soon before the developers are to use it and certainly not later than it is needed. The solution is to have the training some time before it is needed, then utilize onsite experts or training updates to solve problems that arise due to the inexperience in using the technique.

This leads us to the final aspect of education and training that is critical to an OO project. This is the need for ongoing training. There certainly will arise circumstances where the inclass training simply does not supply answers to questions that might be critical to the success of the project. Training, at least for a time, will be an ongoing effort. Experts will need to be around to offer guidance and overall direction to the OO effort. Make absolutely certain that, if "experts" are selected from inhouse, they truly are experts and will have the time to do the necessary mentoring. The fact of the matter is that this will never be the case, except in the most mature organizations. Good OO talent is rare. No group will be excited about farming out all of their expert's time to other's projects.

Training is not cheap. However, getting off on the wrong foot and losing confidence in OO technology can result in project failure, so the cost of short-shrifting on education is great.

Methodology

Just saying that one is going to transition to OO technology is not very specific. There are several well-defined and well-refined OO methodologies in the field. Some of the more well-known are Booch, Buhr, Coad/Yourdon, Rumbaugh, and Schlaer/Mellor. There also are methods from Colbert and Seidewitz that are slightly less well-known. Each has its own distinguishing characteristics. CASE support varies for each of the methods also.

How do you decide which method to employ? If used properly, any of the recognized methods will "work." (Later on in this section, there will be a brief review of the major methods that were just mentioned.) There are several main issues to address when deciding on the method to choose:

- Availability/affordability of a supporting CASE toolset.
- Inhouse experience with any of the methods.
- Will the transition mix structured methods and OO?

The method, or the CASE tool for that matter, will not analyze and design the system (despite what some slightly over-ambitious vendors might imply). It would be smart to utilize a method that is simple to understand, melds well with the process, and is able to represent most of the constructs that are desired. It makes no sense to purchase a CASE tool that has every "bell and whistle" notationally that you would ever want but will never use.

If the technical staff is highly trained in OO and the "right thing" is to use a more robust toolset and method, then by all means, do that. That is just the point; do what is right.

There are many who feel that OORA is not as mature as OOD. As a result, the migration to OO many times consists initially of a move from structured design methods to OO design concepts while keeping the structured analysis procedures in place. While an incremental approach might appear to be more appropriate and more risk-free than a wholesale overhaul of the entire analysis and design phases, there are risks with this approach.

If the requirements are represented in functional terms, there are many people that feel that a "leap of faith" is necessary to move to an OO design. Even more risky than this, however, is that the required "mindset paradigm shift" that is necessary will be sorely tested. What occurs in many cases is that, at least informally, the requirements are reanalyzed in OO terms and thus provide a much easier transition to OOD.

CASE support

Selecting an appropriate CASE toolset is a critically important decision. An OO method needs to be selected that has appropriate CASE support. There is more to be said about this however.

Not only should the CASE toolset support the method chosen, the toolset also must support the documentation requirements of the project. Very often, documentation requirements are driven by a specific customer and also by the way the contractor does business. Each company has its own form of documentation and perhaps even configuration management of those documents that is specific to the format of the documents.

The CASE toolset should be understandable and easy to use. This is much like "motherhood and apple pie," but one would be amazed at the toolsets that are released and sold that simply don't do the job. A good CASE toolset is supposed to augment the development process and free up the developers from mundane tasks that can and should be automated. Bad CASE toolsets can affect the development effort adversely by requiring more time than should be necessary to use the tool. In the worst case (no pun intended), a given design might not be able to be represented in the toolset, or heaven forbid, the design is changed to fit the toolset.

Rose from Rational is an effective and widely-used object-oriented CASE tool. Figure 4.5 shows an example of this tool in action. In Booch/Rose no-

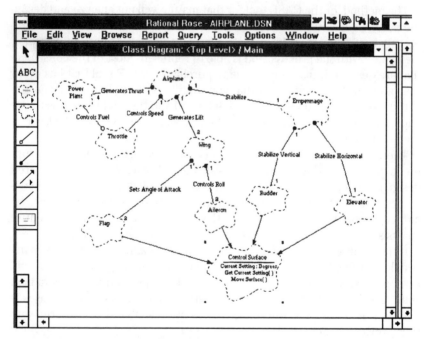

Figure 4.5 Rational Rose is an object-oriented CASE tool.

tation, a cloud symbol indicates a class, a line with a black dot on one end indicates a "contains" relationship, a line with a white dot on one end indicates a "uses" relationship, and an arrow indicates inheritance.

For more information on this, please refer to chapter 10.

Strong process

An OO project is no different than any other type of project as it relates to software process. A good, strong process is necessary for success. (Refer to chapter 1 to understand the importance of process to the success of a project.) In some ways, however, a strong process is even more necessary to the success of an OO project.

If you are transitioning to an OO technology, it is clear that there are many new aspects to be learned: new OO mindset, new tools, and perhaps a new software process. It is going to be infinitely easier to handle all of the "newness" associated with the OO technology if the process, or the framework of the project, is in place. Even if it is a new process, if it is based on past experiences with process and builds on it, then this will help. However, if there is no process at all or the existing process is radically different from anything that anyone has ever done, then this "overhead" could cause problems catching on to OO.

As an example, this would be akin to learning to write a new language but with the opposite hand! It is hard enough to learn a new language (with even perhaps a new alphabet), but learning the language along with the dexterity training that would be necessary is likely to take away from the language training.

Develop reuse plan

If you are serious about getting started on the right track in regards to OO, then reuse must be a "front-and-center" issue. Typically, reuse, if dealt with at all, is treated as a desired but not required side effect of good software development. Effective reuse will never be accomplished this way. Again, we feel that this is such an important topic that an entire chapter has been devoted to it.

There are three required elements of an effective reuse plan that warrant discussion at this time. There are other desired elements of an effectual reuse plan. Refer to chapter 7 for more information on this matter.

If any of these elements are missing, the result will be a plan that is impotent, at best.

Creation of reusable elements.   All developers must be prodded, cajoled, motivated, or threatened to always think in terms of reuse. Reuse will apply not only to code elements but also to design and even analysis and test elements.

Reuse on an OO project goes much further, however. Developers need to be thinking in terms of classes, which are reusable by nature. Specifically, starting with the initial activities, developers need to be thinking about:

- Generalization and specialization of the classes
- Essential methods associated with a class
- Reparented existing classes to a newly created super-class
- Splitting up a previously defined class into separate classes with a newly defined parent class

This is the essence of the reuse definition within OO systems. It is only after these kinds of issues become ingrained in the minds of the developers that reuse will become a viable opportunity.

Nelson Hazeltime in, Korson et al (1991) suggests that rewards be given to developers to create/submit elements to a reuse library. We wholeheartedly agree. This is what is meant by putting reuse "front and center." The mindset needs to be changed such that everyone is always looking for potential reuse opportunities.

Formation of a reuse development team. Having stated that everyone needs to be thinking "reuse" to truly be effective at this task, there must be a team that is chartered strictly to create and manage reuse. This is not in conflict with the previous point. Everyone on the project needs to be aware of reuse opportunities. Over time, a team that is chartered strictly with creating and managing the reuse components actually becomes more of a reuse "management" team instead of a reuse "creation" team. Typically it is not possible for the members of such a team to be aware of all of the reuse opportunities on a project. Over time, such a team will filter incoming reuse "submissions" and determine whether such an element should be "created" as the submitter suggests or perhaps will "retool" current elements to incorporate the recommendation.

Use of reusable elements. Creation of reusable elements is a waste of time if they are not used except for the creator/submitter. Again, as with the creation of reusable elements, the use of reusable elements needs to be rewarded. Therefore, the developers will be thinking not only in terms of what reusable elements can be created but also what elements can be reused.

To be able to effectively reuse already created elements, developers must be able to find candidate reusable elements readily. This is another task of the reuse team: to supply a method to easily query existing potential reuse elements from possibly a reuse database. Refer to chapter 7 for a much more thorough discussion of these topics.

OO and the Business/Commercial World

When discussing topics such as OO, software process improvements, software methodology, and similar issues, one assumes that we are speaking about the large engineering projects that use C, C++, Ada, Pascal, FORTRAN, etc. The majority of the software that has been written is not "engineering software," however. It is business-oriented software written in COBOL. Therefore it would stand to reason that, to get the most "bang for the buck," new technologies such as OO ought to address language and environment-related issues that affect the "COBOL world."

This section will address the following issues:

- Reengineering or reverse engineering of existing legacy COBOL code
- The relationship between entity-relationship diagrams (ERDs) and OO
- OOCOBOL: The proposed object-oriented standard for COBOL

Reengineering or reverse engineering of existing legacy COBOL code

Melymuka (1991) estimates that $30 billion is spent annually on software maintenance, which comprises 50% of most data processing budgets and 50% to 80% of the working hours of an estimated one million programmers. There is no question that these programmers and management face a formidable, if not impossible, task of understanding all of this software, both before and after the maintenance occurs. In addition, on the average, a Fortune 100 company maintains 35 million lines of code and adds over 10% per year in various forms of enhancements, bug fixes, and upgrades.

A tremendous amount of this software is data processing software written in COBOL. To be able to effectively perform necessary upgrades and maintenance, the software needs to be understood. If the original software is poorly documented or undocumented (which much of it is), any future maintenance is nearly impossible. To be able to understand this software and to enable upgrades to occur, there is no choice (except for total rewriting) but to reverse engineer the existing legacy code.

The advent of CASE has helped to automate this reverse engineering effort. Once the reverse engineering effort is complete, however, the developers typically have a picture or representation of the current system. It is at this point that the reengineering effort can begin. As stated previously, the reengineering occurs due to bug fixes, enhancements, and just general maintenance. Legacy code also can be reengineered to modularize poorly written code.

Structured modularization occurs when code is reengineered to conform within standard modularization guidelines:

- Single entry/exit points
- Removal of GO TO logic

- Appropriate use of sequence, alternation, and iteration
- Manageable-sized subprograms

Bringing the existing legacy code into the OO world, however, means that the reengineered code needs to go through object-oriented modularization. Reengineering existing COBOL code through object-oriented modularization is a difficult task. This difficulty is not inherent to COBOL, however. The difficulty in performing this transition is akin to the ongoing debates concerning generating an object-oriented design from a structured analysis paradigm. This has been a topic of many a conference discussion and paper with very little agreement reached.

If an OO modularization approach is considered, Newcomb (1993) offers some guidelines for this activity. In addition, Yourdon and others (Sneed 1992) have offered some proposed requirements for an OO reengineering process:

- Programs should be divided up into classes that correspond to the objects that are processed. Each class is an abstract data type encapsulating the attributes of and the actions on the object enclosed. There is one module per object.

- Classes are isolated against outside access.

- Classes should be designed so as not to exceed a specific size and complexity.

- Classes should be able to inherit data attributes from more than one superordinate class (i.e., they have multiple inheritance).

- Classes should be able to communicate with one another through message passing.

- Classes should have both private and public storage as well as private and public methods (operations).

- Classes should be adaptable to compile time parameters that allow attributes and methods to be altered or blended out. This makes it possible to have different variants or mutations of the same class, ensuring reusability.

Reengineering and reverse engineering activities must be given special attention as it relates to OO technology due to tremendous amount of legacy code that exists, which is practically all functional code. CASE tools, methods, and processes that address this issue will gain a high degree of attention in the data processing community now and in the foreseeable future.

Entity relationship model and OO

Those who have worked in the business or database world undoubtedly have been exposed to the entity-relationship (ER) model and entity-relationship diagrams (ERDs). Many of the concepts that exist in the OORA/OOD models have some commonality with the ER model. To attempt to show some of the similarities between the ER model and an OO model, Chen and Hung (1994) have described an integrated OORA and OOD method that emphasizes entity/class relationships and operation finding. Hopefully, this analysis will help those who have experience with the ER model to better migrate to a fuller understanding of the OO model.

The authors of this analysis identify areas that the OO model might be weak. They are (Chen and Hung 1994, 31):

- Neglect of the refinement of entity or class relationships. Most OO methods describe a methodology for defined class/entity relationships; however, some of these methods do not refine the relationships adequately.

- A lack of specific steps designed to identify operations and attributes of classes. Most of the OO methods have definitions and guidelines, but few have step-by-step identification procedures.

- Many of the OO models have a series of "submodel" representations that comprise that specific OO model. This can be very confusing. Usually there are object, information, state, and event submodels. The authors of this analysis feel that this is too complicated and offer a compromise.

- There is an overall weakness of OORA. This actually is not debated within the industry. There is recognition that OORA is a bit less well-developed than OOD. In some cases, due to this apparent relative weakness, structured methods are used for analysis. This approach, however, introduces a kind of mismatch where a "leap of faith" must be made when progressing from the analysis model to the design model. This, in general, is not very desirable.

This OORA/OOD definition process consists of three major steps with intervening sub-steps:

1. Construct the entity model
   ~Identify entities within the problem domain
   ~Establish the entity model based on relationships among entities

2. Construct the object model
   ~Identify classes
   ~Establish the relationship among classes
   ~Find the attributes
   ~Find the operations

3. Refine the object mode for implementation
   ~Establish message flows
   ~Build the OORA/OOD text document

Identify entities within the problem domain. To identify the entities, in general, prepare the systems information, then decompose the system into many problem domains. This concept is similar to the "contains" relationship as a composition attribute (Seidewitz and Stark 1992).

A question that often is asked is, "Well, what is an entity or what is an object?" Only your experience will yield a good feel for how to best go about this. If "it" is a representable "thing," then it certainly is a candidate. If it isn't a good object, as determined in later analysis, it can be removed later.

Establish the entity model based on relationship among entities. Chen and Hung (1994) use the concept of *relationship* as defined in data models to represent relationships in this model. As such, the types of relationships that will be identified will be categorized as: classification, aggregation, and association. Standard (entity relationship) ER diagrams will be used to depict these relationships.

Classification groups are entities that have common characteristics. So when depicting an ER diagram, the "box" that represents the classification of a group of entities will show only the classification entity, not the constituent entities within the classification entity.

Aggregation treats a collection of different entities as a single entity. This actually is identical to the aforementioned "composite class" as identified in Seidewitz and Stark (1992). In other words, this is the Whole-Part concept in the object model.

The other form of relationship is known as *association*. This is the "normal" kind of relationship when discussing object or class relationships. When an object or class explicitly needs the service or affects another object or class through the shipping of a message, this relationship is an association relationship.

Identifying classes. The entities that have been identified previously in the ERDs serve as the initial cut for the classes. The initial cut certainly will not be the final list of classes. Guidelines for refining the initial classes are proposed to be:

- Does each class represent a good abstraction in the system? If not, remove it or transform it into other classes.

- When finding attributes and operations, if there are any attributes or operations that cannot be allocated to any existing class, new classes should be added. Obviously, progressing through this mode is an iterative activity.

Establishing the relationships among classes. The authors feel that this is the aspect of OORA/OOD development that is omitted in most models. There are four types of class relationships:

- *Generalization-Specialization.* In the most simple sense, this is what is known as an Is-A relationship. Graphically, this type of relationship is represented as a hierarchy (single inheritance) or a type of lattice (multiple relationship). The specialization classes (as opposed to generalization class) inherit attributes and operations and can add its own attributes and operations.

- *Whole-Part.* The whole-part relationship correlates to the aggregation relationship in the ER diagrams. You also can view this as a parent-child relationship.

- *Use.* In general, the Use relationship is the most difficult to quantify and needs the most experience to address. The association relationship in the ERD corresponds to the Use relationship in the object model. It is helpful to add any additional textual information to clarify the relationship at this time. Directionality (implying control of the relationship) might or might not be easily inferred. This is where experience comes in handy.

- *Instance connections.* These are simply instantiations of objects from their parent classes.

Finding attributes. The best ways to identify attributes are to find some general attributes from problem domain knowledge, find attributes from I/O data, and examine system requirements (nouns) that might represent attributes (unless they already represent objects).

Attributes must describe the characteristics of data, can represent the common property of objects within a class or be some data that makes an object instantiated from a class unique, or simply is state data that is to be stored within the object and manipulated by operations within the object.

Finding operations. There are many suggested methods for finding operations. Some general guidelines are:

- Choose verbs as operations from the system specification.

- Define the constructor and destructor operations for each object when needed.

- Define the operations that access or update attribute values within a class.

- Define operations that arise as a result of the Use relationship.

This is where most of the "real work" occurs in an OO model—in the analysis of the "use" relationships. It also is the most difficult, naturally. It is at this point that event analysis occurs and scenarios are developed using the Use relationships.

Establishing message flows. All of the Use relationships then should be expanded into message flow diagrams, also known as object message diagrams. This is where the meat of the work occurs. System events are diagrammed, and the real requirements of the system are described.

It is clear that there certainly are some similarities between ERD models and the OO model. As OOCOBOL becomes a reality, we all might find out that the COBOL developers have a much easier time transforming to OO than the engineering world has, at least up till this point.

OOCOBOL: The proposed OO standard for COBOL

Walk into any coffee shop around America today and what discussion is one most likely to hear? The never-ending debate over the merits of the best OO programming language: Smalltalk, Eiffel, C++, Ada9X, CLOS, Objective-C, and OO Pascal. Well, move over boys. Soon, a new player will be entering the debate, COBOL. Actually, to be more precise, OOCOBOL.

When considering the totality of reengineered legacy code, new development, and just plain maintenance, more code is written in COBOL than any other language, by far. Therefore, according to the "most bang for the buck" principle, it would make sense that the oft-praised merits of OO would result in the most benefit if applied to the largest segment of code that exists.

The COBOL 97 standard, dubbed OOCOBOL, will have all of the expected OO constructs in an OO language. It certainly will not be a "weak sister" in this regard. Refer to Table 4.2 for a comparison of the standard OO programming languages (OOPLs) and the supported constructs.

Topper (1994) presents a summary, including Table 4.2, of the new OOCOBOL concepts and the keys to the success of OOCOBOL.

TABLE 4.2 Comparison of OOPL Constructs (Andrew Topper)

OOPL	Inheritance	Binding	Compiled/ Interpreted	Exception handling	Garbage collection
Ada	None	Static	C	Y	N
C++	Multiple	Dynamic	C	Y	N
CLOS	Multiple	Dynamic	C	N	N
Eiffel	Multiple	Dynamic	C	Y	Y
Objective-C	Single	Dynamic	C	N	N
OOCOBOL	Multiple	Dynamic	C	Y	Y
OO Pascal	Single	Dynamic	C	N	N
Smalltalk	Single	Dynamic	C & I	N	Y

New OOCOBOL concepts. One of the important concepts of OOCOBOL that will be in the standard is the concept of an object/class having an interface that consists only of the services available to that object/class, not the implementation to the service. In addition, OOCOBOL will support multiple inheritance.

Object factories will be supported along with static binding and type checking. An interesting (and potentially dangerous if misused or overused) concept will be a type called Universal, and objects of this type will not undergo any compile-time type checking.

The basic architectural structure of an OOCOBOL program will remain unchanged; that is, existing programs will compile with little or no changes. To support the new standard, the proposed changes are as follows:

- *Environment division.* A new section will be added. It will be called, what else, the Object Section. The classes and interfaces will be defined for the program here.

- *Data division.* Will be modified to support object definitions and the Linkage Section will be used to reference data passed between objects as messages.

- *Procedure division.* Will be able to include calls to objects, dynamic creation of objects, and even exception handling.

Keys to the success of OOCOBOL. There really are two classes (no pun intended) of keys to the success of OOCOBOL: those that are technically related and those that relate to proper utilization of the OO aspects of the language. (Remember, existing COBOL programs will compile under OOCOBOL.)

Class libraries will need to be built and developed, most likely by the vendors. OOCOBOL will need to interface with GUIs, DBMSs, and CASE environments that include analysis and design tools. As much will have to be done in developing the technical environments surrounding OOCOBOL as will have to be done in the development of the actual language.

Perhaps even more important to the acceptance of OOCOBOL will be the "appropriate" use of the language. This is not a problem that will not be unique to OOCOBOL. When C++ first was released and, in many circles, still now, C code is being written and submitted to a C++ compiler, and this is called C++ development. When developers design and code in Ada for the first time, especially without training, the resultant code is nothing more than "Adatran." The point being that simply writing code in a given language in no way guarantees effective use of the constructs of the language. OOCOBOL will be different in this regard.

Because there is more COBOL code and more COBOL programmers than any other language, inappropriate use of OOCOBOL (either in new development or reengineering legacy code) could be disastrous. Appropriate training beginning prior to the release of the final standard must occur to prepare the hordes of OO developers; not only technically, but in such a manner that the new standard is accepted.

Comparison of Current OO Methods

When deciding on an OO method to use when initiating an OO project, you should analyze all of the major OO methods to be complete. Very few projects actually do such a comparison. An OO method all too often is selected based on the best sales presentation by a CASE vendor that supports one of the OO methods or by which OO method a senior manager saw referenced in an article that he or she scanned over recently.

What follows is a comparison of many of the major OO methods. Most of this information was obtained from Colbert (1994). The methods that will be analyzed are:

- Booch
- Buhr
- Coad/Yourdon
- Colbert
- Rumbaugh
- Schlaer/Mellor

Development context

The context that a project is being developed in should have a lot to do with what OO method is selected. For example, not all projects are "start from scratch systems" (to be denoted in this analysis as Greenfield Development). The project can be a reengineered project where a current system is being modified to incorporate new requirements or some other modifications are being performed.

It might be that the system that is being developed will be a template for other systems. As such, there might be a lot of reusable components that will be generated from this project. It would be very desirable to be able to identify these components within the OO method.

On the other side of the reuse coin, perhaps there are a lot of reusable components that this project is going to use. It would be very desirable to identify within the OO model which components are native components and which ones will be brought into the system from a reuse library or other source. This is extremely useful information for management so as to be able to gauge the relative size of effort required to complete the project.

Table 4.3 identifies which methods are able to support each of these development contexts.

TABLE 4.3   OO Methods that Support Development Contexts (Ed
Colbert of Absolute Software Co., Inc., Los Angelos, California)

Method	Greenfield	Reengineering	With reuse	For reuse
Booch	*		*	*
Buhr	*			*
Coad/Yourdon	*			*
Colbert	*	*	*	*
Rumbaugh	*			*
Shlaer/Mellor	*			*

Coverage of software life cycle

One of the most important criteria in determining which OO method to choose is the life-cycle support that is supplied by that OO method. Deciding on an OO method without investigating its life-cycle coverage is very foolish. At best, you will fill in the gaps with "tribal knowledge" about general OO concepts. At worst, the entire process will fall apart.

It is interesting to note that none of the methods that were analyzed address OO testing. This is an area where much research is ongoing. Incorporation of OO testing techniques and philosophies into OO methods truly will allow fully reusable components to exist. OO testing is the area that is lacking.

Key features of object representation
during analysis and preliminary and detailed design

Tables 4.4, 4.5, and 4.6 identify which methods represent some of the more widely accepted key features of objects during the analysis phase and preliminary and detailed design. The information, as represented by these figures, should be thoroughly analyzed when selecting an OO method. It should be noted that the method with the "most checks" doesn't necessarily win. There might, and probably will, be much of a particular model that will not be used by the developers. This is especially true if this is the first OO project by an organization.

An organization must analyze exactly what aspects of a model are necessary, then weigh the benefits of each method against each other.

Concurrency

The last figure relating to the method analysis compares which methods support concurrency and which aspects of concurrency they represent. This was an area that the OO methods, in general, initially performed poorly. As one can see, however, all of the methods to one extent or another support some representation of concurrency in the models. Refer to Table 4.7.

TABLE 4.4   Key Features of an Object Represented During Requirements Analysis for Various OO Methods (Ed Colbert of Absolute Software Co., Inc., Los Angelos, California)

Method	Structure		Responsibilities				Qualities	
	Parts	Attributes	State	Behavior	Operations provided	Operations requested	Props	Constraints
Booch	X	X	X	X	X	X		X
Buhr	P		X	X		P		
Coad/ Yourdon*	X	X	X	X	X	X		X
Colbert		X	X	X	X	X		X
Rumbaugh*	X	X	X	X		X		X
Schlaer/ Mellor*	X	X	X	X				

P—Partially implemented.
*—Rumbaugh, Coad/Yourdon, and Schlaer/Mellor define the class. The objects are implicity represented.

TABLE 4.5   Key Features of an Object Represented During Preliminary Design for Various OO Methods (Ed Colbert of Absolute Software Co., Inc., Los Angelos, California)

Method	Structure		Responsibilities				Qualities	
	Parts	Attributes	State	Behavior	Operations provided	Operations requested	Props	Constraints
Booch	X	X	X	X	X	X		X
Buhr	P		X	X		P		
Coad/ Yourdon*	X	X	X	X	X	X		X
Colbert	X	X	X	X	X	X	X	X
Rumbaugh*	X	X	X	X		X		X
Schlaer/ Mellor*	X	X	X	X				

P—Partially implemented.
*—Rumbaugh, Coad/Yourdon, and Schlaer/Mellor define the class. The objects are implicitly represented.

Summary

Make no mistake about it, OO technology is here to stay. Organizations and projects that choose to begin to develop OO experience within their organization now will reap benefits. The benefits will be improved quality, reduced cycle time, and reduced costs.

TABLE 4.6   Key Features of an Object Represented During Detailed Design for Various OO Methods (Ed Colbert of Absolute Software Co., Inc., Los Angelos, California)

| Method | Structure | | Responsibilities | | | | Qualities | |
	Parts	Attributes	State	Behavior	Operations provided	Operations requested	Props	Constraints
Booch	X	X	X	X	X	X		X
Buhr	X		X	X	X	X		
Coad/ Yourdon*	X	X	X	X	X	X		X
Colbert	X	X	X	X	X	X	X	X
Rumbaugh*	X	X	X	X	X	X		X
Schlaer/ Mellor*	X	X	X	X	X	X		

*—Rumbaugh, Coad/Yourdon, and Schlaer/Mellor define the class. The objects are implicitly represented.

TABLE 4.7   OO Methods and Their Ability to Support Different Concurrency Concepts (Ed Colbert of Absolute Software Co., Inc., Los Angelos, California)

Method	Passive objects	Active objects	Internally concurrent	Mutual exclusion
Booch	*	*	*	*
Buhr	*	*	*	
Coad/Yourdon	*		*	
Colbert	*	*	*	*
Rumbaugh	?	?	*	*
Schlaer/Mellor	*		*	

As with any other new technology, there are risks associated with new ventures such as this. Most of the risks will translate into real costs when shortcuts are taken. Training and education must occur. Management support must be active and visible or else OO will not catch on. There are some throughput risks with OO; however, in most if not all cases, these risks can be managed and even mitigated. There absolutely must be a mindset shift to OO. OO is not a functional or algorithmic decomposition method. Thinking that OO is just structured analysis and design by another name is just a mistake and will doom OO to failure.

CASE will be a big player in OO. The right choice of an OO CASE toolset can help ensure success; the wrong choice could mean failure. However, keep in mind that, although CASE is a contributing factor to success or failure of OO, CASE will never be able to do the real analysis and design. It is only a tool.

Getting started on the right foot will make all the difference in an OO project. Basically doing what is necessary to enjoy the benefits and avoid the risks, as described in this chapter, will make or break an OO project.

If there is a single concept that typifies OO, it is reuse. Effective OO can't be accomplished without effective attention to reuse. If the system is developed without attention to reuse, then it is likely that the class definitions are not as they could be. Reuse should come naturally, especially if the organization is developing homogeneous products. It is in this kind of environment that reuse should flourish.

OO now is moving into to the area where there is the most amount of code written—the business/COBOL world. It makes sense that, to get the most benefit of OO, it should be applied to the single biggest collection of software that exists. OOCOBOL will be a true OO language with all of the standard OO constructs supported. If done right, the benefits could be astounding.

Finally, there are many OO methods out there to choose from. Most have some sort of CASE support. It is imperative that the "right" method be selected for an organization. The method must be understandable. The developers must be able to be trained in it. They must be able to take the general OO concepts, as taught, and be able to implement them in the development language of the project.

There is much to be said and learned about OO, and most importantly, there are many opportunities available—opportunities for success.

References

Booch, Grady. 1994. *Object-Oriented Analysis and Design with Applications*. 2nd Edition. Santa Clara, California: The Benjamin/Cummings Publishing Company, Inc.

Chen, Jen-Yen and Yu-Shiang Hung. 1994. "An Integrated Object-Oriented Analysis and Design Method Emphasizing Entity/Class Relationship and Operation Finding." *Journal of Systems Software*. (24):31–47.

Colbert, Ed. 1994. "Selecting the Right Object-Oriented Method." Presentation to the Phoenix Chapter of SigAda (ACM). 29 August, 1994.

Kamath, Yogeesh H., Ruth E. Smilan, and Jean G. Smith. 1993. "Reaping Benefits With Object-Oriented Technology." *AT&T Technical Journal*. Sept/Oct. 1993:14–24.

Korson, Tim, Nelson Hazeltime, Tim Hilgenberg, Reed Philip, and David Taylor. 1991. "Managing the Transition to Object-Oriented Technology." Panel Discussion presented at OOPSLA 6–11 October 1991. Phoenix, Arizona.

Lewis, John A., Sallie M. Henry, Dennis G. Kafura, and Robert S. Schulman. 1991. "An Empirical Study of the Object-Oriented Paradigm and Software Reuse." Paper presented at OOPSLA 6–11 October 1991, Phoenix, Arizona.

Melymuka, Kathleen. 1991. "Managing Maintenance: The 4000-pound Gorilla." *CIO*. 4(6):74–82.

Newcomb, Philip. 1993. "Automating the Modularization of Large COBOL Programs: Application of an Enabling Technology for Reengineering." Working Conference on Reverse Engineering. 21–23 May 1993, Baltimore, Maryland. 222–230.

Seidewitz, Ed and Mike Stark. 1992. "Object-Oriented Development" as presented to Commercial Flight Systems Group, Honeywell Inc. 3–7 February 1992. Phoenix, Arizona.

Sneed, Harry M. 1992. "Migration of Procedurally-Oriented COBOL programs in an Object-Oriented Architecture." Conference on Software Maintenance. 9–12 November 1992, Orlando, Florida. 105–116.

Tomic, Marijana. 1994. "A Possible Approach to Object-Oriented Reengineering of COBOL programs." *Software Engineering Notes*. 19(2):29–34.

Topper, Andrew. 1994. "Object-Oriented COBOL Standard." *Object*. 3(6):39–41.

Yourdon, Ed. 1994. *Object-Oriented Systems Design: An Integrated Approach*. Englewood Cliffs, New Jersey: Yourdon Press.

5

The Benefits of Teaming: If You Don't Manage the Team It Will Manage You

Yourdon (1992) states "Only in rare cases today do software engineers work entirely alone, on one-person projects; in most cases, people work in *teams*. Therefore, the productivity, and to some extent the degree of staff turnover, is related to the effectiveness of the team environment. Thus the world-class organizations are devoting significant effort today to the issue of building effective, harmonious, well-balanced teams."

If your project or organization is comprised of more than just a few individuals, then it is likely that you have been involved in "teaming" to one degree or another. Teaming has become not only one of the snappy "catch phrases" representative of company organizational behavior but a concept that likely will affect each and every software developer in years to come.

Within most organizations, teaming has been widely accepted as a method of increasing communication and improving the problem resolution process. Is teaming important to all software developers however? This question points out the changing role of the software developer today. Gone are the days when a software developer could count on spending most of his or her time writing code. Software developers must bring other skills "to the table." Communication skills, such as being able to work with a team, now have become an absolute must. Such is the justification for this chapter.

Is teaming all that different from other management strategies that have been tried in the past? Opinions vary.

Teaming—as well as prototyping, object-oriented technology, or spiral life cycle methods—isn't a magic solution for the software crisis. However, well-run, effective teams certainly can help most organizations develop critical projects right the first time. Unfortunately, teams that are run in this fashion are more the exception than the rule in most organizations.

What Is Teaming?

Teaming occurs on a project (or should occur on a project) when the cost expended (measured in terms of dollars, time, or opportunity cost) by the team is less than would be expended by all of the participants to accomplish the same goals individually. This might seem a rather simple point, but it can't be overemphasized. Very often teams are started with the best of cost-conscious intentions. However, these intentions can easily be forgotten, and the team begins to exist only for its own purposes. This issue of teams "overstaying their welcome" will be discussed in much greater detail later.

Teams are convened for one (or more) of several reasons:

- *To solve a common problem once and "reuse" the solution.* Usually, it is cheaper to solve a "common" problem once where all of the affected parties have input into the format of the solution.

- *To bring together varied expertise that is necessary to solve a problem.* Sometimes these teams are called "tiger teams," which are brought together to find a fast, experienced solution to a specific major problem.

- *To implement project-wide policies.* When project-wide policies are being implemented, it is necessary to include representation of all the groups that will be affected by any decisions made by the team. These teams typically are staffed with senior developers or managers.

- *To coordinate interface definition.* As software systems become more and more complex, it is imperative that interfaces are well defined and, even more importantly, well understood and documented. Systems that suffer total failure usually have problems with system or subsystem interfaces.

- *To solve problems that are multidisciplinary in nature.* An example of such a team is one consisting of system analysts, hardware designers, and software designers to perform up-front system analysis. A kind of "holistic" coordination is needed among the members of this kind of team. Requirements can't be allocated unless they are "implementable." Who better to determine whether the system can be implemented than a team of system, hardware, and software designers?

"Common problem-solving" teams

Often a team assembles when a problem arises that is likely to occur elsewhere on the project. This kind of team, when managed well, can greatly reduce overall cost on a project. Unfortunately, this opportunity is missed on most projects. Groups within a project often are more competitive than cooperative, and a degree of "provincialism" can creep in preventing the "spread of a solution" to other parts of the project.

An example of this kind of team is a common software team. If a project is of any size whatsoever, there could be a tremendous amount of potentially duplicative code. This common software team gathers requirements from the rest of the project and identifies common software that can be designed, coded, and tested just once and used by all. It isn't quite this simple, but it is a good start. Resources are not wasted because the individual groups don't have to redevelop software.

As stated earlier, none of the concepts associated with teaming or teaming itself is a "silver bullet." This also is true of "common problem-solving" teams. To solve a common problem, there usually is a common solution. This is where this kind of team can have difficulties. It can be difficult for a collection of representatives of various parts of a program to agree on a common solution for common problems. The reasons for this vary. Perhaps the problem being addressed is not identical among all of the represented groups. Each group might have a slightly different view of the problem. It is possible that a proposed solution to "the problem" might fit the needs of just one of the groups, but it might be overkill for another group and might not go far enough for still another group. These groups then might feel that it is just as well that they come up with their own unique solution "that meets their needs" instead of wasting time (as they would view it) investing in aspects of a solution that might be irrelevant to their needs.

Another very common reason that groups with common problems can have difficulties agreeing on common solutions often is stated as, "Well that solution might work for you, but our group has very unique needs and as a result that solution just won't work for us." This is where compromise comes into play.

Projects should take a proactive approach to solving these kinds of common problems early on in a project. How is this done?

For large projects where there are multiple project groups, a common software group must be convened at the earliest stages of the project. The common software group brainstorms what elements of functionality they will each implement. Areas of common functionality will appear immediately. The next step is to determine how "common" these areas of functionality are, agree on a common set of requirements, then have only one of the represented groups implement that functionality.

There are other areas of "commonness" that don't necessarily result in common software usage. Several project groups might have to interface to the same or similar devices. There might be inhouse expertise in another project group that one can learn from quickly instead of "starting from scratch" so-to-speak.

Let's say that a project is developing a product that is going to have a graphical user interface (GUI) front-end. That front-end is going to make underlying application calls to code that already is written in a language that does not readily interface with the GUI. There is another group that is doing roughly the same thing. Both groups should be collaborating from the very beginning.

Let's say another large project is being developed that will have to run on simulated hardware platforms. Every project group will have to test out its software on the simulated hardware. Each group is going to have to go through the inevitable problems that occur when testing on simulated hardware. All of the affected groups should be collaborating early on. Much time and effort can be saved in this and like efforts.

Utilizing teams in this fashion can be an effective method for arriving at solutions for common problems. A major benefit of initiating the kind of mindset on a project that common-problem solving teams instill is that a uniquely positive cooperative spirit can be fostered. Developers begin to look at every problem that they solve as one whose solution can be shared with others who might have the same problem or one similar enough to be able to gain from others' experiences. Various groups within the project will tend to interact more, and as a result, these varied groups will be more aware of what each is doing. A major benefit to this way of doing things is that this tends to benefit the definition and adherence to interfaces within the groups.

Expertise-driven teams

Sometimes it is necessary to bring together a team that draws upon various kinds and levels of expertise on a project to solve a technically challenging or unique problem.

For example, a system is being developed for a small investment firm that runs on a set of networked workstations. This investment firm wants to expand into some international markets but has little experience with both the international markets and the kinds of products that they will be dealing with in these new markets. This firm has never worked with workstations, just standalone or loosely networked PCs, and has never operated with concurrently accessed databases.

"Business as usual" is not going to be able to get this kind of mission-critical system right the first time for this customer. To be able to deliver the product that the customer expects and requires (assuming that the customer knows what is expected or required), it will be necessary to gather individuals with varied kinds of experience early on in the project (i.e., during system definition). It probably would be prudent to gather individuals who:

- Have had experience with this specific customer.
- Have had experience with this type of international investment product.
- Have had experience with international networking, especially real-time systems.

Without addressing the problem from all angles, the product simply will not be done right the first time. Remember, just because the customer got what he initially asked for does not mean that the job was done right.

Lets look at another example. A software company has been awarded a contract by the National Football League to write a software product to generate their schedule for next year. What kind of experience would you need on such a team or a project?

- Ability to understand all of the requirements of the players' union relating to games (including the total number of "non-Sunday" games allowed) and "hours worked" related issues.
- Ability to understand the best methods to minimize airline costs and minimize overall travel time.
- Familiarity with the schedules for the stadia involved to avoid possible conflicts with other events.
- Knowledge about team rivalries such that holiday weekends could feature such high-draw games.
- Technical expertise in general "operations research" modeling, which probably would be used to solve this kind of a problem.

Although some of these technical "issues" might very well be spelled out formally as requirements, this very unique system would need to bring together a team having widely varied talents to solve a complex logistical and technical problem.

Policy teams

As described in chapter 1, organizations are becoming very interested in software process. The implementation of one or more aspects of software process really is a kind of policy administration by the organization. A team very often is convened for this purpose of defining and implementing these new policies.

There are other policy teams that can exist on projects, most usually on large projects, such as:

- A team to come up with the standards for development of each of the phases in the life cycle.

- A team to decide on capital purchases of workstations/PCs and also tools that will be used.

- A myriad of management teams (most of which usually are worthless) to monitor activities and events such as schedule progression, expenditure monitoring, cost-savings and headcount reduction.

A software process team probably is the most important "policy team" that can be convened.

A project might have one process team that "sits" for the duration of the project, or there might be several process teams that are created, then dispersed as issues related to different phases of the project are dealt with and problems solved. In either case, these teams typically are responsible for determining the path that the project takes regarding software process. This kind of team typically determines what the rules and guidelines are for performing all of the actual activities related to the project. These team members often are euphemistically called the "software police."

Policy teams typically are staffed with low-level management and/or senior developers. Although policy teams can serve a very positive and even necessary role on the project, there are some drawbacks. These shortcomings are not unique to software process teams or to policy teams in general but do seem to occur rather often in these instances.

One of the major drawbacks with this policy team is its vulnerability to getting bogged down in "nondecisions." When implementing project-wide policies, the decision-making process that is implemented by the team usually is "decision by unanimity." As such, unless all parties immediately agree on some aspect of the policy being determined, the team can become hopelessly mired in debate. It often is very difficult to implement any kind of policy that all parties agree to that is anything more than the least common denominator of the contested issues.

"Bloody" battles often are fought on teams such as these. This usually is just the nature of trying to apply a single standard or a single set of standards across a project or organization that is comprised of many different individuals. Any successes that the team is to enjoy must be founded upon ground-based support for the team from upper management and an understanding by all that the team has been "empowered" to do what is necessary.

Software interface teams

One of the most important tasks that a team can play is in the role of determining and documenting interfaces. As stated previously, poor interface definition is one of the major factors in failed software systems. Before we look at the solutions that interface teams can implement, let's examine the problems first.

By the turn of the century, it is likely that every room in every new home built in the United States will contain microprocessor-based equipment controlled through a centralized monitoring and control system that will be accessible remotely via telephone. The software needed to control these systems will not be trivial. Software is becoming more and more a part of our daily lives. This software is interfacing with aspects of our lives that would not have been imagined a few short years ago. Increased inherent complexity usually will imply increased complexity of the interfaces.

Software development (as opposed to hardware development) is notorious for having consistently poorly defined interfaces with other software. I believe this is true due to the wide misconception that an error in hardware always is more expensive to fix than one in software. There is no arguing the fact that a hardware error has a "permanence" associated with it that software does not exhibit. The faulty reasoning, however, is embodied in the assumption that software always is easier and cheaper to fix than hardware. If the software interfaces aren't exactly right, then they can be fixed, or so the reasoning goes. Nothing is further from the truth.

Software interfaces must be well understood and documented with some form of interface contracts. If not, the results can be devastating. This is due to nothing more than human nature. If the interface is explicitly defined *in writing*, attention will be paid to it. It can be just that simple. Referencing the previous example, let's say that you are part of a project that is developing a home control system that is responsible for allowing control of a myriad of devices in the home (i.e., the VCR, lights anywhere in the home, oven, security system, alarm clocks, computer, etc.). Let's say that an initial protocol is set up between the control system and all of these "devices." This protocol (interface agreement), however, is not documented and is addressed initially early on in the project but is assumed to not change. When it comes time to start performing some testing on the interface between the control system and these external devices, it is found that the data protocol has been altered.

The effects of the change might be minor or it could cause major changes to the control system software. Although it is poor software development technique to allow the format of data at an interface to dictate data formats throughout a system, this does happen. This is one way that an error in interface definition can wreak havoc on a system. A mistaken data format is not the only manifestation of poor interface definition that causes problems. Wrong assumptions in terms of data content also can cause problems, sometime severe.

Let's assume that an airplane onboard navigation system needs to have a very important piece of information to perform its processing. It obtains this data from two different software systems (interfaces). These two systems obtain this data from different data sources, for redundancy reasons. Part of the interface contract with these two systems should have been the requirement that this critical piece of data be obtained from these two differing data sources. This critical piece of information was omitted from the interface contract. These systems, without requirements to the contrary, obtained this critical piece of data from the same source. The redundancy of the data has now been compromised. If the single source becomes unavailable, the data becomes unavailable. Catastrophic results could result from an error such as this. (An extremely thorough testing suite should catch this error, thankfully!)

In conclusion, interfaces are a critically important aspect of software/system development. These interfaces need to be rigorously managed and controlled.

Multidisciplinary teams

There have been many examples of multidisciplinary teams in industry. The apparent revitalization of the American automobile industry has been due, at least in part, to the realization that it is necessary for engineering, assembly, and maintenance personnel to collaborate on the designs of new automobiles. It makes no sense to design a vehicle that cannot be assembled or maintained due to unnecessary design complications. One group's problem is everyone's problem. Therefore, the solution that made the most sense was to get all of the parties that are involved in the production of the new car to address their concerns together.

This same process has been shown to be widely successful in the development of software. When an initial specification for a product is being analyzed, it is critical for the hardware designers, software designers, and specification/requirements analysis groups to work together to determine the requirements allocation and even some preliminary design constructs together. After all, it makes no sense to allocate requirements to a design that are not implementable. However, are the systems guys always able to make that call? Of course not. That is the job of the software designers. So why not get them involved in this "system work?"

Although this kind of thinking "makes sense," it wasn't until very recently that this "common sense" has been implemented. Standard project organizational concepts and the waterfall life cycle model have been the biggest reasons for this marked delineation of job responsibilities and lack of cooperative development. Standard project management would dictate that the software designers don't get involved until the "design phase." That just doesn't work.

In summary, a team attempting to solve a software-related problem is no different than, for example, a baseball team. Each is attempting to reach a goal. Each has individual members that have different roles on the team.

When they communicate well and understand each other's capabilities and responsibilities, the chances for success of this team are greatly enhanced.

Is Teaming Really All That New?

Is this teaming really all that new of a concept or is it just another rehashed management philosophy? First of all, what something is called is just not relevant. Some organizations have been teaming for a long time and are very successful at it. They might not call it teaming, but maybe instead of teams, they have work groups, clusters, or cells. The point is, when a problem surfaces that cannot be solved by a group that already exists, a group is formed to solve the problem. In the vast majority of the cases, the problem is not going to go away over time.

Teaming, as described previously, really is just an old concept with a few formalisms and "lessons learned" applied from experience. Tremendously successful nonsoftware-related projects have been accomplished that had to overcome huge obstacles. Certainly, teaming as we have described here had to have been practiced.

In a lot of ways, the basic concepts relating to teaming are not that new. The technologies involved today involve so much specialization that no one can be an expert on everything. So when there is a problem, get the right people together and get the problem solved.

Most projects that claim to "team" would do well to examine the incredible efforts to develop the first working prototype of the United States U-2 spy plane.

The project manager, Clarence "Kelly" Johnson, was given a scant eight months, commencing on December 9, 1954, to develop the first U-2 spy plane. Today, that would be about enough time to decode the customer specification into hardware and software requirements documents a similarly "brand-new" defense-related project!

Kelly Johnson and his development team of 80 hand-picked engineers were freed up from tyrannical paperwork requirements of technical specifications. Instead, his team was given performance specifications to meet. The lesson here is that the development team were allowed to do the job the way that they saw fit. They were told what the product ultimately had to do and were left to their own expertise to implement the requirements.

The development team decided on a perfect blend of conservatism and innovation. They utilized designs that already were proven and didn't create where creation was unnecessary. This left time and creative juices for areas where innovation was necessary, such as in weight reduction.

Johnson physically isolated his engineers away from other work at Lockheed so as to not be contaminated by business-as-usual themes.

On August 8, 1955, U-2 001 made its first official flight successfully. Note the date. Exactly on schedule *to the day.*

The U-2 team succeeded for many reasons, some of which certainly could only be voiced by those who participated on the team. The team was unbridled of unnecessary, nonvalued activities. The team was hand-picked not only for its technical ability but also for its necessary cohesiveness. The team was isolated from the business-as-usual surroundings. Most importantly, the team was given the freedom to do what they do best, unencumbered with overly-detailed requirements. They used proven technology where appropriate and innovated where necessary. Most incredibly, this was over 40 years ago. [*Note*: Most of the information on the U-2 noted here was obtained from Pocock (1989).]

Empowerment

A vital key to enabling the success of the team has to do with a concept called *empowerment*. Most often when a team is organized to solve a problem or set of problems, one will most always hear the following proclamation: "This team will be empowered to solve this problem with whatever resources are necessary." Is this an empowered team? Just stating that it is empowered doesn't make it so. If every decision that the team makes is subject to approval by management, then this team is *not* empowered at all.

We are exposed to empowerment every day. As you drive to work, you are empowered to make the right decisions in the automobile to get to work safely. If you make a judgment error, there is no one who is going to overrule any decision that you make (unless your spouse yanks the steering wheel out of your hands!). You simply will have to live (or die) with the consequences of your actions.

In our daily work lives, we make many empowered decisions every day. We decide which of several tasks to work on first. We are empowered (or empower ourselves, if you will) to decide when and if we go to lunch, etc. Again, if we have failed in correctly prioritizing our workload, then we will suffer the consequences of this behavior: missed deadlines, bad reviews, scorn of a supervisor, etc.

Very often, teams are not empowered, despite claims made by corporate or project management to the contrary. Why is this? There are many possible reasons why this phenomenon occurs. Some or all of the following may apply in differing quantities, depending on the project.

- *Lack of trust.* Despite claims to the contrary, management simply might not trust the conclusions and proposed plans of actions trumpeted by the team. Management might feel that the team is not capable of addressing the issues that the team has been chartered with, and management wants the veto option over any decision. (See Figure 5.1.)

- *Need for total control or inability to delegate effectively.* It simply might be the case that management not only doesn't trust a team to come up with the "correct" solution, but just the mere presence of a team being involved in making perhaps "important" decisions is just too threatening. It is true that this behavior is diminishing in today's organizations, but it still does exist.

- *"Bad" decisions made by the team.* It certainly is possible that the team simply has had a track record of making "bad" decisions. This often will occur because the team is uninformed of other higher priorities within which framework they must operate. Another possibility is that this team is simply staffed with the wrong people. This will be addressed shortly.

Apple Computer's Mike West quite clearly addresses this issue of restriction of empowerment. He states that the empowerment of employees (or team members) is very difficult for most organizations. Hardly any companies are even attempting it. Only the most successful companies trust in it (West 1990).

There is a reason for addressing this aspect of teaming; that is empowerment or the lack thereof on a team. Teaming, as has been expressly stated already, is an ever-increasingly visible aspect of most software development projects. It is important to understand the dynamics that exist in such organizations. Very often, members of teams become disillusioned when their efforts are swept away and decisions countermanded by upper manage-

Figure 5.1 Empowerment with a string attached.

ment, in effect "disempowering" the team. Teaming can be a very important positive aspect of a project, but one must be aware of the possible dynamics associated with actively participating on such a team.

To be fair to management, the concept of empowerment can be a difficult one to implement. After all, perhaps management has a good reason to not trust the decision-making ability of a team and therefore feels the need to oversee all decisions (i.e., micromanage) and retains the right to veto any decisions that they feel would be a detriment to the project or to the organization. After all, in most cases, project management has short-term corporate responsibilities (such as those of a fiscal nature) that members of a team might not be aware of or simply don't view with a high enough priority.

If every decision made by the team is micromanaged by management, however, sooner or later the team will become totally ineffective. The team will lose the respect of peers elsewhere on the project. Every decision that a represented group does not agree with will be challenged and brought up to upper management.

Common Reasons Why Teams Fail

There are many reasons that cause teams to fail. There usually is not one specific reason but a combination of fatal flaws.

Misguided or unguided teams

One of the basic premises of this chapter is that teaming is becoming very popular in organizations and therefore one must understand how to use teams for the betterment of the project. It actually is for this reason that some teams fail and then, as a result, sometimes projects fail. Because teaming has become a popular management construct, it sometimes is incorporated into the mechanics of a project without knowing exactly why it is there or what it is supposed to be doing while it is there.

Teams should be convened if and only if there is justification for the team's existence. As such, the team should be convened to solve a problem, then the team should be dissolved. This point cannot be overemphasized. Again, as simple as this concept might seem, it often is violated and can lead to an insidious waste of resources. Any efficiencies that the team initially might enjoy can easily be wasted away by a team that has outlived its purpose.

In the purest form of the term, there should never be a *standing team*, given what was stated in the previous paragraph. It is possible, however, that a team, such as a process management team, might be chartered to exist across the lifetime of a project. As such it is a "standing" team and an exception to the rule. Minimally, however, if this team has no business to conduct, then it simply should not meet.

If a team does not know when it has accomplished what it set out to do, then it is highly likely that the team does not really know what problems it is trying to solve. If it doesn't know what problems it is trying to solve, it will either solve nothing or try and solve problems that it isn't chartered to solve and maybe by chance will solve something relevant. This kind of scenario, as you can imagine, will just cause problems, not solve them.

Team staffed with the "wrong" people

Another major reason causing teams to fail occurs when the team is staffed with the "wrong" individuals. As stated earlier, teams can be organized for different reasons, trying to solve many different kinds of problems. As such, the "staffing" of the team can be critical to its success. Naturally, if the team is trying to solve a technically challenging problem, then individuals with the technical talent need to be present, as discussed previously. In addition, individuals that don't bring the technical talent to the table or don't bring any other specific talent that can't be found in another team member should consider leaving the team or at least be replaced. (See Figure 5.2.)

The appropriate staffing of a team might take a little while to get right. When staffing a team, there is one aspect that a team leader needs to be aware of and that is of the "professional team member." Sometimes it is difficult to staff teams due to schedule constraints and project responsibilities of potential team members. It often is necessary to solicit volunteers for teams. Within an organization, one often will encounter an individual that just loves to be a part of teams. This person isn't happy unless he is part of a team. This isn't necessarily a problem, in and of itself, but be aware that this really might not be the right individual for a specific team.

Figure 5.2 A team that is doomed to failure.

Again, just keep in mind that the team exists for a very well-defined purpose. Each member of the team needs to be a contributing member of the team, always moving toward accomplishing the stated goals of the team.

Besides being a good technical fit on the team, each member of the team should contribute in a positive manner to the progress of the team. This is not to say that there won't be differences of opinions and disagreements among the members of the team. In fact, if there are not differences of opinions, the team typically will not have all possible solutions to a given problem available for evaluation. There is a time for debate on the team, and there is a time for coming together to agree on and enact solutions. Each member of the team must put aside personal biases and contentions and support the team's decisions.

> It is important to note that a cohesive team cannot tolerate extremist mavericks. Some talented individuals cannot flourish in a team-oriented environment. If team cohesion is not to be eroded, management must recognize such a mismatch and address the problem before team goals are jeopardized.
>
> Hyman (1993)

A "misfit" can occur due to technical shortcomings or an inability of the individual to function effectively or professionally on the team. Often, the team member does not recognize that there is a problem, and the team leader might need to take action. If left unaddressed, problems such as this will result in a loss of efficiency of the team and could even push the team to dissolution or failure in its charter.

Teams unable to make decisions

The purpose of a team is to solve problems, or at least to solve problems quicker and cheaper than if the team did not exist. To be able to "solve" anything, the members of the team have to come to agreement on a solution. This issue of "coming to agreement" can be a very difficult problem for a team.

Software project teams often are run in such a way that it is felt that decisions should be arrived at by unanimous consent. Is this appropriate? After all, because this is a team whose members all want to do the right thing, when the "right" decision presents itself, it will be apparent that this is the right thing to do and everybody will agree. As one can imagine, this is not how software teams (or any other groups for that matter) operate. As a matter of fact, the exact opposite very often can be the case.

Teams can be comprised of technical leaders or even low-level management. A solution to a problem might benefit one group but might impose some restrictions on another group. Because most teams whose purpose is to make project-wide policy decisions are comprised of representation from all potentially affected groups on the project, most decisions will just not be unanimously supported. So how are any decisions reached at all? You might be surprised that these kinds of teams grapple with this very issue, sometimes for long periods at a time.

What ends up happening more often than not is that a least-common-denominator decision is the only thing that all of the groups can agree to. In essence, tough decisions simply are not made. This is quite unfortunate, but when unanimous approval is required or at least implied, this situation is inevitable. A "majority rules" format might be preferable to that of a unanimity-based decision structure. There is a problem with this format also. Decisions can begin to take on a "voting on ideological lines" format. Voting in this kind of team setting begins to take on the look of congressional partisan voting. This, as you can imagine, can have devastating effects on the cohesiveness of the team.

There is a way to at least partially remedy this situation. This is through the concept of a "benevolent dictator." We will discuss this shortly.

Too many teams doing the same thing

One last major cause for team failure occurs when there are simply too many teams such that the same problem is being solved by one or more teams at the same time. This is not to say that a certain degree of overlap among teams is necessarily a bad thing. However, as you probably can imagine, if several teams are trying to solve the same problem, there is likely a tremendous waste of resources occurring.

Obviously some coordination is necessary among teams. This is as common a problem within projects and organizations that are experienced at teaming as it is within projects that are just learning. Again, communication and awareness usually will solve this problem rather quickly within organizations that are experienced in this sort of thing. Charters for teams can change and as a result redundancy then might occur. Teams ought to be combined, charters altered, or teams disbanded when egregious overlap occurs.

Characteristics of a High-Performance Team

We've discussed in a fair amount of detail why teams fail. Approaching this topic from a positive viewpoint, what are the characteristics of a high-performance team?

A high-performance team must be narrowly focused. It's activities must be defined in such a way as to address these narrowly focused issues and only these issues. When the role of the team and its goals are not specific, focused, and narrow, the team never really will be sure when it has completed its tasks.

When the team has completed its tasks, it should disband. Managing teams in this manner has a very positive impact on a project, in general. One of the major contributing factors to the failure of projects is a lack of a sense of urgency along with the tendency of certain kinds of problems to never quite get solved completely. Teams that have a limited number of problems to address and successfully address these problems begin to instill this sense of urgency to the project and bring problems to resolution.

High-performance teams must have strong leadership that keeps the team focused. It is very easy for a team to lose focus and stray from its charter or the narrow set of problems that it is meant to address. The team must have a strong leader who is sympathetic to the concerns of the team members but keeps the team on track and constantly is making progress toward its goals. The team leader of a successful team is highly respected by the team. This leader recognizes that the team members, in many cases, are representing groups that might have divergent views on issues that the team addresses. As such, wide and varied opinions will be brought to the table as to how to solve some of these problems. In some cases, there will be strong disagreement as to the appropriate solution for some of these problems.

The team leader must have enough self-confidence to recognize one's own strengths and weaknesses. The leader must be able to look to the individual team members for answers that lie in their specific field of expertise. The team leader also must be able to keep the team working together through difficult issues.

The members of these high-performance teams must be high-performance individuals who "can work together to create high-quality software products" (Yourdon 1994). As mentioned previously, success might be unattainable for a team comprised of the wrong people. Yourdon (1994) goes on to say that "very few software projects today are the work of a single person; no matter how powerful the language or CASE tool, the trend toward large, complex systems inevitably involves the joint efforts of teams who must collaborate, coordinate, and communicate their ideas."

The specific composition of the team also is critical. Thomsett (1990) has generated a model that consists of the following eight roles:

- *Chairman.* This role is filled by what we have described as the team leader.

- *Shaper.* This is a chairman-wannabe. Usually an assertive individual, this person will attempt to shape or steer the outcome of group activities.

- *Plant.* This is the individual who usually is looking at the "big picture" and usually is addressing the big issues.

- *Monitor-evaluator.* This individual usually tries to enforce balance into discussions and constantly is evaluating possible outcomes.

- *Company worker.* This individual takes concepts and plans and turns them into practical procedures.

- *Team worker.* This individual is the consummate "team player" and constantly is involved in improving communications between the team members.

- *Resource Investigator.* This individual is the "network person" who makes all of the external contacts that the team needs.

- *Completer.* This individual makes sure that the team "covers all of the bases" and doesn't leave anything undone. This person usually also will maintain a sense of urgency with the other team members above and beyond what the chairman does.

Any of the characteristics that are attributed to the team must be found in most of the team participants. The team does need strong leadership, but the leader can impart only so much energy to keep the team functioning. The team itself must provide the vast majority of the sustaining energy for the team. One can think of the team leader as not actually imparting energy to keep the team running, but simply redirecting that energy periodically in appropriate directions.

As discussed in depth earlier, successful teams must be empowered to do the "right thing." There is no substitute for management support. It is absolutely essential for success of the team.

Disbanding the Team

This issue has been mentioned several times already but is so vital that it warrants its own discussion because this principle so often is misapplied or violated.

Teams are no different than any other entity that needs to accomplish tasks to be successful. However, to be able to accomplish those tasks, it needs to know what those tasks are. If there are too many tasks to be addressed, the chances for success drop significantly because progress is much more difficult to realize. If there are a small number of well-defined tasks and the team knows that, when these specific sets of tasks are accomplished, the team will have been successful, then disbands, there is a high degree of probability that the team will accomplish those tasks and thus be successful.

Remember that the members of the team, in almost all cases, have project-related responsibilities in addition to these team-related responsibilities. In most cases, these team-responsibilities cannot be of an "open-ended" nature. If the teams are run in such a manner that the goals of the team are nebulous and ill-defined and the team has no idea when it will get these problems solved, then it is likely that the "right" people will not want or be able to be involved with the team.

Teaming in an Object-Oriented Environment

One of the major threads of this book has to do with the role of object-oriented technologies in successful projects. If a project is making an attempt to implement object-oriented technologies, what impact, if any, does this have on the teaming environment, or vice versa?

If a project is implementing object-oriented technologies, especially for the first time, it is likely that there will be little object-oriented expertise amongst the project staff. In the initial planning stages of the project, just as the project is beginning, all of the current object-oriented experience that the organization has access to, probably along with outside object-oriented consulting, should be brought together on a team to plan out the project in regards to the impact of the object-oriented techniques on the project.

Although this is strictly something that will be discussed in chapters specifically related to object-oriented technologies, it is worth mentioning that, in general, each of the following issues will be impacted by the introduction of object-oriented technologies. Therefore, teams ought to be convened that address the following issues on an "OO project," if they weren't already going to be addressed by the project anyway.

- CASE tools—New OO CASE tools are being introduced all of the time. Care should be taken to address how the tool suite should be selected to support this new methodology. As discussed in chapter 1, the tool choice must be part of the overall process but not a totally independent driver of the process.

- Documents—It is likely that project documents such as requirements and design documentation will take on a completely new format, partially due to the impact of the OO CASE toolset but mostly due to OO. The organization and the customer might need some "training" to understand the new formats of the documents produced using this technology.

- Implementation of some type of prototyping—Many OO methods espouse some method of prototyping. Depending on the specific application and the past experience that the project or organization has had with prototyping, there might be a team called to specifically address the methods of prototyping in this OO environment. Refer to chapter 6 for a more thorough discussion of prototyping.

- Training—This certainly will be something that will need immediate and early attention in the project life cycle. Failure is guaranteed if one attempts to implement a new technology such as object-orientedness without full and adequate training. The specific kind of training that is necessary might need to be determined by a team however.

- Reuse/common software—Arguably one of the most important benefits of OO technology is in the area of reuse. This is due to concepts such as inheritance (single and multiple) and polymorphism that are integral to OO. Whether or not the project is utilizing an OO method, there should always be a concerted effort to address reuse and common software.

- Testing—Due to the code structure of OO systems, there might be some unique issues that arise in the area of testing. The project needs to fully understand the implications of OO technology on the area of testing. Therefore it would be prudent to address this issue.

Some of the aspects of teaming will not change with implementation of object-oriented techniques. You still will want to have a *process oversight team* that ensures that the approved process is being followed. Specialized technical problems will arise that will need a specialized "tiger team" to solve. At some point in the project, there might be a need to have a cost-reduction team that will look at ways for the project to reduce costs.

However, some of the teams will have a change of focus, and there might even be a need for new types of teams, as mentioned earlier. Because object-oriented techniques still are new to most organizations, it might be necessary to pay increased attention to training. This certainly could be addressed by a team. It is important to realize, however, that there will likely be two aspects of training that *must* be addressed: methodology training and language training. If an organization has decided to implement object-oriented techniques, then it hopefully will have decided to do this with an object-oriented language such as Smalltalk, C++, or Ada 95. (There will even be an ANSI standard for object-oriented COBOL, appropriately called OOCOBOL. Refer to chapter 4 for further discussion.) However, just usage of the "new" language will not guarantee success. This is a faulty assumption that many organizations make. Programming in a language does not guarantee that all of the facilities of the language will be used correctly. Therefore, language training that includes "appropriate" use of the language is mandatory.

However, in addition to the language training, there must be training available in the concepts of object-oriented techniques. There are many object-oriented techniques; once one is decided upon, the specifics of the technique need to be taught. This also is an aspect of the object-oriented migration that cannot be overplayed. Object-orientation is more than defining a class in C++ or "withing in" a package or deriving a new type in Ada and calling it inheritance. There is a definite mindset change that must occur, and it is not easy; however, there are benefits.

Most object-oriented techniques work well with nontraditional life cycles that include some aspects of prototyping. This definitely will affect any teams that are chartered to deal with requirements analysis and design definition and integration. This kind of team still will be interested in being able to implement and allocate all requirements into an architectural design but probably will want to go about its task a bit differently. It will not be necessary to force all requirements-related issues to resolution initially (as the waterfall method attempts to do), but to address the major requirements early that would most likely affect the architectural aspects of the design.

Any design teams that exist will (or at least should) address reuse as a high priority. One of the most important aspects (read as opportunities) of object-oriented techniques is the built-in capability to manage reuse through the inheritance and polymorphism constructs. Object-oriented techniques, by their very nature, encourage reuse through well-defined classes and objects. Any design team should have this as a high-priority item.

The discussion of object-oriented issues has become more and more common in the software literature. It will be essential that any testing teams are aware of new methods and concepts related to this burgeoning field.

In summary, object-oriented technologies are affecting just about all aspects of projects that have implemented them. Just about any process that investigates, analyzes, or manages aspects of the project, such as teams, also will be affected.

The Role of a "Benevolent Dictator" on a Team

We have discussed in some detail the need for strong effective leadership on a team. A necessarily important quality of a team leader relates to a specific role that a team leader sometimes is required to play. Previously, we discussed how an effective team is one that is able to focus on a limited number of issues and bring those issues to resolution. This is a noble goal, but the path to this goal can be rocky and sometimes can be filled with impassable obstacles—impassable perhaps for a team without a uniquely qualified leader, that is.

This is where an effective team leader is essential. As noted previously, the dynamics of many software teams are such that unanimous decisions are required for problem resolution. What happens when unanimity is unattainable? Either the team adopts a "majority rules" posture or the team leader needs to take the bull by the horns, so-to-speak, and make decisions.

One might argue that there shouldn't be a need for a "benevolent dictator." After all, a team can just implement a "majority rules" standard. This is just not that easy to always do. When highly volatile issues are being decided, which a project software standards team often does, leaving the resolution of an issue to a vote can be extremely divisive to the team and even to the project. Sometimes it might make more sense for the team leader to propose a solution to the team that is hopelessly deadlocked over an issue.

Typically, however, the role of the benevolent dictator isn't one of making decisions for the group but ensuring that the team is able to come to some decision somehow. The most difficult kind of decisions that a team leader in this role will have to make will be associated with issues that are very controversial and divisive. Very often, resolution of these kinds of issues can occur only with near unanimity when the "least common denominator" solution is proposed for some issue. Many times this is in actuality a nondecision, and it then might become the role of the benevolent dictator to "threaten edicts from the throne!"

Benefits to the Team Members

Any discussion of a matter such as teaming would be incomplete without discussing the benefits to the team members. We certainly have touched on the benefits to a project of teaming. Increased communication is inevitable when effective teaming occurs. Common problems can be solved with a reduction in overall resources spent. Policies can be implemented where all affected parties have some level of input into the decision-making process. Pro-active coordination of interfaces between groups can be accomplished. Functional groups that deal with different views of the same problem can gain insight from others' views of the same problem.

However, it is the benefit to the individual team members that often gets overlooked when discussing the "positives" of teaming. There probably is no better method to gain positive visibility throughout a project than being a member of an effective team. (For that matter, being a member of an ineffective team certainly should not only be a learning experience but also might afford one the opportunity to take a more active role on such a team and gain visibility.) As long as the potential team member is adequately capable, one can gain positive visibility that is certainly useful in today's volatile employment market.

There is another added benefit when one is involved in a "cross-functional" team. One can hardly help from becoming knowledgeable about the other groups on the project that the other team members represent. One cannot underestimate the value of this knowledge. You now have the potential of becoming one of the more knowledgeable individuals in your group about the other groups on the project and the project as a whole. Being knowledgeable about potential interfaces with other groups is a very valuable skill.

This *networking* can be a skill that can prove extremely valuable throughout a project and indeed throughout your career. Having made these contacts with others in other groups will help get questions answered more quickly than would otherwise be the case. You now are a resource to be used by others who have come to know you also. You now know the valuable resources and become a valuable resource to others. You will become a primary contact for other groups also.

Making the contacts and getting the visibility that teaming provides certainly has a positive impact on the self-image of the team member, and assuming that one is contributing positively to an effective team, any positive recognition that the team might enjoy certainly flows through to the individual team members.

Summary

A "catch word" that has made its rounds in organizations that relates to the organizational behavior of teams is *empowerment*. Many lay claim to understanding this overworked term, but few understand the full implications of empowerment. It is interesting to note that, for organizations that are very hierarchical in nature, true empowerment might exist only at the Olympian heights of these organizations. There is no one to overrule top management decisions (except the stockholders, of course). There are those that would claim that any attempt to implement empowerment strategies at any lower levels is simply not possible in such organizations. There always is a layer of management that can overturn a "lower-court decision."

It is becoming all too clear, however, that deeply nested hierarchical organizations might just not be competitive with organizations that are "lean and mean." If you take away layers of management, then this "vacuum" must be filled by empowerment. After all, in a simplistic sense, someone has to make the decisions. Effective teaming seems to be a way to fill this so-called void. However, it is necessary to go one step further in the analysis. All of the aspects of teaming that have been discussed are necessary for projects to be successful. There might be no other way to gain all of the benefits that have been discussed here.

All too often a team becomes an end unto itself. The charter of the team is ill-defined, if it is defined at all. As a result, not only is the team directionless, but without clearly defined goals for the team, it wanders aimlessly. Another contributing factor to misdirected teams very often has to do with the makeup of the teams. If the team is not comprised of the "right" people, it stands to reason that any goals that the team has will be more difficult to accomplish and the success of the team will be compromised. The observant reader will detect an interesting circularity here. Not only will the choice of inappropriate individuals hamper a team from achieving its goals, but a team whose goals are not very clear from the outset certainly will not be able to determine who should even be on the team in the first place.

The decision-making process in large organizations can be excruciatingly slow. Most large organizations are able to make decisions only when there is unanimous consent on the change to be made. This philosophy results in two kinds of closely related phenomena: changes come very slowly and the only changes that do occur are those that reflect a kind of "least common denominator" of change. Teams, which very often reflect the nature of the organization, often exhibit this same kind of behavior. Teams that consistently perform in this manner will never be productive.

A solution to the problem of indecisive teams is inclusion on the team of a "benevolent dictator." Reasonable debate on a team is healthy; inability to make decisions is not. Very often teams are faced with difficult decisions. There inevitably are varied and strongly held opinions among the members of the team. Teams often are run in such a manner that the decisions are made by unanimous decision only. This form of team government rarely works, and therefore the need for a decision maker exists.

For effective team management to occur, effective team management must exist. An organization that is "highly teamed" very often will find itself with multiple teams trying to solve the same problems. Management of the teams via well-defined charters and explicit communication between the teams is key to being successful.

Teaming is an organizational concept that is quite diverse and will undoubtedly have an effect on organizations that make a conscious effort to implement a teaming approach. It certainly can be argued that teaming (or the lack thereof) also will have a definite effect on those organizations that don't use it, and probably should.

In addition, as with almost all management and organizational philosophies, more is not necessarily better. Is it possible to team too much? The answer, of course, being that, if some organizational philosophy or construct outlives its purpose for existence, then that aspect of the organization is counter-productive to success.

References

Hyman, Risa B. 1993. *Creative chaos in high-performance teams: an experience report.* Communications of the ACM, 36(10), 56–60.

Hutchings, Tony, et. al. 1993. *Process improvement that lasts; an integrated training and consulting method.* Communications of the ACM, 36(10), 104–113.

Pocock, Chris. 1989. *Dragon Lady: The History of the U-2 Spyplane.* Shrewsbury, England: Airlife Publishing Ltd.

Yourdon, Ed. 1993. *Decline and Fall of the American Programmer.* Englewood Cliffs, New Jersey: Yourdon Press.

Yourdon, Ed. 1994. *Object-Oriented Systems Design.* Englewood Cliffs, New Jersey: Yourdon Press.

West, Mike. 1990. "Empowerment: Five Meditations on the Soul of Software Development." *American Programmer*, July–August 1990.

Thomsett, Rob. 1990. "Effective Project Teams: A Dilemma, a Model, a Solution." *American Programmer*, July–August 1990.

Smart Software Design

6

The Art and Science
of Prototyping

*Most currently recommended methods for defining business system
requirements are designed to establish a final, complete, consistent,
and correct set of requirements before the system is designed,
constructed, seen, or experienced by the user. Common and recurring
industry experience indicates that, despite the use of rigorous
techniques, in many cases users still reject applications as neither
correct nor complete upon completion. Consequently, expensive,
time-consuming, and divisive rework is required to harmonize the
original specification with the definitive test of actual operational
needs. In the worst case, rather than retrofit the delivered system, it is
abandoned. Developers might build and test against specifications, but
users accept or reject against current and actual operational realities.*

BOAR (1984)

Simply put, *prototyping* is an aspect of system development in which a
scaled-down working model of the final product is developed very early on
in the development cycle of that product. Boar (1984) aptly describes the
situation that necessitates the prototyping construct.

Note that a prototype applies to system development, not necessarily software
development alone. Very often, when contracts are awarded for new military
aircraft, a working prototype is built first. For example, on the YF
military fighter aircraft program, working prototypes were developed by the
two teams of defense contractors vying for the production contract prior to
the contract being awarded. These two prototypes did a "fly off" to determine
the best working prototype and thus the winner of the production contract.

Prototyping does apply, at least in the context of this discussion, specifically to software development. It often is a great idea to develop a prototype of any software to be delivered. We will discuss various important aspects of prototyping in this chapter, including whether it is a necessary aspect of "getting software right the first time." Also the form that the prototyping can take is important. It can be a "throw-away" version that is meant to be a simple proof-of-concept to a prototype that is ultimately fully integrated into the delivered product.

Is prototyping always appropriate? Some software systems have no user interface whatsoever. Does prototyping serve any useful purpose in cases such as this? If it is decided that a prototype is appropriate, there are certain characteristics (or goals) of the prototype that must be met. For a prototype to be effective, it must serve a specific purpose and must exhibit some specific characteristics.

When deciding upon a prototype, the "kind" of prototype also must be decided upon. This will depend a great deal upon the purpose of the prototype. The prototype might be just a simple throw-away version that bears little resemblance to the delivered system. The prototype might have been developed to determine the relative ease of interfacing several specific pieces of software. The purpose of the prototype might be to demonstrate the use of a new technology or tool suite. So the form of the prototype depends a great deal upon the reason for the existence of the prototype.

If prototyping is such a great idea, then why is it that so few projects or organizations "seem to" include prototyping as part of the normal software development activities? For years, the waterfall method has been accepted as "the" software life cycle methodology. Development of the software product progresses linearly from software requirements analysis through design, implementation, testing, and integration. This method, in its purest form, does not reflect the real iterative nature of software development. Life-cycle methods that are based on this iterative nature, such as the spiral method, are gaining some degree of popularity. Prototyping has no role in the pure waterfall method. However, it does fit very nicely in an iterative model. Prototyping is considered an essential aspect of most iterative software life cycle methodologies and has been proven to be very effective.

When Is Prototyping Appropriate?

Except for a few isolated cases, prototyping, in some fashion, usually is necessary for a successful project. Perhaps more accurately, whatever it is that prototyping brings to a successful project is necessary for getting the system "right" the first time.

As is mentioned several times in this book, ambiguous requirements are the norm. As such, specific steps must be taken, *early in the project*, to resolve these ambiguities prior to them becoming an implementation disaster. To be able to get the system right the first time, an effective feedback loop with the customer needs to be established so as to be able to elucidate these ambiguities. Effective prototyping provides the vehicle or framework for establishing this feedback loop. There are many more benefits to prototyping that will be discussed in short order.

Therefore, it should seem clear that prototyping is appropriate for most software projects. This is the case except for perhaps a few isolated examples. Not only is prototyping appropriate for the vast majority of software systems being built, but it also is essential. Doing without prototyping to "stay on schedule" is shortsighted and reflects the lack of "forward thinking" prevalent among much of software management today.

Are There Cases When Prototyping Is Inappropriate?

It stands to reason that no software development construct or method is going to be a panacea. Prototyping is no different. Despite all of the inherent positive aspects that prototyping purports to bring to modern software development efforts, which will be discussed in great detail, there are situations that *might* be inappropriate for prototyping, such as the following:

- A fully embedded-system project that has no user interface

- The requirements are very well understood

- The project is very small

- The project has multiple deliveries that begin relatively soon in the total life cycle

- The prototyping/tool environment is immature

- Neolithic software development environment, including lack of management support for prototyping

- The project is an add-on from a previously completed effort

These are examples where it *might* be inappropriate to perform prototyping, not to say that prototyping is always a bad idea in these circumstances, however. An embedded system that has no user interface does not fit the mold of a project that usually is prototyped. There is simply nothing for anyone to see.

If the requirements are very well understood and documented, then you might consider forgoing a prototype. This is extremely rare, however. There are very few projects that would not benefit from an "early look" at the contractor's interpretation of what the implementation of the requirements should look like.

A project that is very small in terms of size or effort might not need to be prototyped. In this case, if the delivered product would take roughly the same time to develop as the prototype, then certainly the effort that would be expended on a prototype would be a waste of time.

It might very well be the case that a project has multiple deliveries built into its schedule. As such, this already is a project that is part of a mature organization, and any explicit prototyping above and beyond the multiple deliveries already scheduled might be overkill.

Unfortunately, the development environment might be sufficiently immature to be able to handle prototyping. The tool environment might be insufficient to be able to deliver a prototype. Perhaps the tool environment is so new that no one has any experience with or knowledge of the toolset. Developing a rapid prototype might add more risk to the project. Note, however, that it is likely that, if a project has such a new toolset and no real experience with it, the risk attributed to the prototype might pale in comparison to the risk associated with the entire project. Indeed, prototypes (in this case, also known as a *pilot project*) can be written just to try out the tools and get the programmers up to speed on these tools.

Although a prototype usually is helpful in any life cycle that a project is being run under, the overall management of the project might be "set in its monolithic ways." These "ways" might not incorporate prototyping as part of them. Attempting to get a prototype underway and accepted as a needed part of the overall development effort might be fruitless. Such a project likely has or will have much larger problems.

It might not be necessary to consider a prototype if the project is an add-on to a previously completed project. It might be the case that some deferred functionality is being developed that *might* not need that additional functionality developed. For example, if a message-passing system is being developed, it might be the case that a few messages did not get implemented in a prior release of the product and were deferred. No part of the architecture will be changing due to this added functionality. A prototype might not be worth the effort.

These are examples where prototyping *might* not always be necessary. Even then, however, in most cases, prototyping probably would not hurt the development effort. Reiterating, these instances should be the rare exception to the rule. The benefits of prototyping, which will be discussed next, almost always will improve any system that is under development.

The Benefits of Prototyping

There are some basic reasons that prototyping is a good idea for most projects. As all programmers have seen, unfortunately, just because it is a good idea and makes sense does not mean that it will occur. There are benefits to prototyping, tangible and nontangible, that ultimately will need to be weighed against costs of prototyping.

Identification and elimination of risk areas

Perhaps one of the most important reasons for prototyping is to identify areas of potential risk to the project and get an "early look" at how serious those risks are by prototyping a first cut at those problem areas. In general, too many projects fail to perform adequate risk analysis and, as such, don't have any idea where the stumbling blocks are going to occur. When these stumbling blocks are identified and addressed, some potentially inexpensive solutions have undergone needless hyper-inflation because it took so long to identify this risk area.

For many projects today, one of the major risk areas is processing throughput. This risk is compounded in real-time systems where tasks must be complete within a fixed time frame. Amazingly enough, given this well-known risk area in these kinds of projects, ensuring that throughput demands can be met usually is given very little if any attention until the project is well underway.

Prototyping a real-time project, even with simulated data inputs, can go a long way toward managing this critical risk area. An early prototype will not unequivocally determine whether a project or a part of a project is going to have throughput problems, but it will do several positive things. First, it will identify this as a potential risk area that needs constant monitoring. It will at least raise awareness to the throughput issue. If the prototype or key elements of it then can be incorporated into an early release of the product, it then will give project management an initial view of the criticality of this risk area and, more importantly, the trending of this risk. As the system is further developed and begins to resemble the final product, it will be easy to determine if this is really a risk or not.

Gets customers onboard early

Prototyping allows the customer to get an early view of the system. The customer can easily recognize the progress of the product or lack thereof. When viewing an early prototype, an awareness of the implications of certain requirements is awakened within the customer. The project will be a disaster if the system is not prototyped and the delivered product is not what was expected. Refer to Figure 6.1.

> Yes, we like how this is going, but we didn't realize that these other requirements would require this kind of implementation. We will have to really consider whether these requirements are really necessary or not.

> "An awakened customer"

Figure 6.1 A missed opportunity for success.

The ultimate goal of any software development organization should be to keep the customer happy. Prototyping gets the customer onboard early to ensure that the project is progressing in the right direction. The development of the customer's product should be viewed as a team effort. A team consisting of the contractor and the customer.

There are some organizations that are reluctant to involve the customer at an early stage, or any stage for that matter, of the development project. This is an increasingly untenable position for contractors to take.

Customers typically don't know their own needs

It *is* the job of the contractor to read in, on, around, and through the customer specifications to determine what the real system requirements are. Very often, the customer knows only peripherally what is truly desired from the system. What better way to help the customer tangibly formulate what is desired from the system than to give the customer "a look" at the system as soon as possible. It just makes sense.

From a historical standpoint, Boar (1984) was one of the original pioneers who forged a path in the area of unknown user requirements through the use of prototyping. He had an interesting vision of prototyping. He recognized the inherent iterative nature of prototyping. Revisions to the prototype would be continuously implemented as long as refinements to the requirements would occur and if some of the components of the prototype needed to be further detailed.

Boar recognized that a critical aspect of the entire prototyping effort is the documentation of the prototype. Regardless of whether the prototype is "thrown away" or incorporated into future designs of the deliverable product, the actual prototype and the lessons learned from the prototyping effort must be documented.

A picture is worth a thousand words

Why is a picture so valuable? Because it can exhibit a level of understanding that goes beyond that which is attainable with words and language. In this sense, a prototype is like a "picture" of the delivered system. The user interface aspect of the prototype actually is a picture. What better way to convey an understanding of the requirements that are imposed on the system than to see a "picture" of the system.

This is precisely the failing of systems and software development processes that are not iterative in nature. The development of the end-product very often becomes an all-or-nothing proposition. No one really knows what the system is going to look like until it is done.

Method to test new technologies

Certainly a prototype is valuable in and of itself for purposes of demonstrating the feasibility of the delivered system. A successful prototype can be even more than that. It is inevitable with today's rapidly evolving technologies, and any project will be attempting to utilize some of these new technologies in the development of the product. New technologies can range from one or more of the following:

- Requirements and/or design CASE tools
- Testing philosophy
- Language compiler
- Software process activities
- Use of a new language (or use of the language for the first time)
- New hardware (processor, processor configurations, memory, buses, etc.
- New hardware architecture

Note: A large avionics mission-critical system actually implemented all of the new technologies at once, including the contractor writing the back-end of a compiler!

A prototype can be a real opportunity to "test-drive" one or more of these new technologies. When developing a prototype, many aspects of the new technologies will be used for the first time. Valuable "lessons learned," as they occur, can be communicated to the rest of the project to increase productivity. Problem areas with the new technologies can be identified early on, and these new technologies can be adjusted wherever possible to improve overall productivity.

It might be discovered that some tool or new technology that was committed to previously really does not make all that much sense to pursue. Perhaps the capabilities of the tool were oversold by the vendor. Finding out early is better than finding out later.

Arthur (1992) describes an interesting scenario that he went through when developing a prototype. He makes the point that the toolset and/or platform that the final product is delivered with should be what the prototype is developed with. However, that can change over time. He wrote a software metrics analyzer in COBOL. It satisfied the requirements. He learned so much from doing it that it was easier to do the next one in a Unix shell script, the next version in awk (a Unix utility), and the final versions in the Unix lexical analyzer.

This example addresses the issue that use of a tool, whether it be during a prototype effort or some other use, increases one's skills in the tool and ultimately can help determine what the appropriate platform should be. This is a lesson learned that comes from prototyping also.

Early interface verification

Many software systems that get "in trouble" do so because interfaces are ill-defined or not defined at all. In general, two types of interfaces are critical to the success of most software projects and need to be prototyped: software-to-software interfaces (to be known from now on just as *software interfaces*) and software-to-hardware interfaces (known as *hardware interfaces*). Because both are critically important to the success of the project, it stands to reason that both should be prototyped.

Most "modern" software development methodologies recognize that the aspects of a design that address interfaces are inherently more important than the rest of the design. Interfaces, to the degree possible, need to be addressed usually before any other aspects of the design are. Whether appropriate or not, details of design often are impacted by the interface decisions. It stands to reason, therefore, that interfaces would be an appropriate and even essential aspect of any prototype.

Hardware, as well as software, interfaces must be prototyped. It is true that some aspects of hardware interfaces often might not be completely defined at the time the prototype is developed. This should not hinder an attempt to prototype that interface, however. When developing the hardware interface, it usually is not necessary to fully design the interface with all of the supporting functionality. Typically, a prototype is seeking to demonstrate rudimentary handshaking and usually not much more than that. The lessons learned from this, if not the actual code itself, should be used in the delivered product.

It also is equally important to consider the potential software interfaces when developing a prototype. It has been stated on several occasions that the prototype is not meant to fully emulate the delivered system. It is necessary, however, to begin to validate some major software interfaces as a kind of "proof of concept," just as it was with the hardware interfaces. Prototyping of the software interfaces gives the developers an insight into some of the throughput requirements of the system, as data is moved around the system. As mentioned before, this is a critical requirement of a real-time system.

Interface definition rarely is given the attention that is necessary. Too often, one function or another "isn't far enough along yet" or hasn't had its own requirements fine-tuned to know what the interfaces should be. Effective prototyping must address the structural implications of a design, which very often is defined by the interfaces of the system.

Characteristics of an Effective Prototype

Regardless of the type of prototype being developed, there are some basic common characteristics that should be present in any prototype. Dichter (1993) has summarized some of the basic characteristics of an effective prototype, which have been expanded upon in the discussion that follows.

Miniature of deliverable system

In one way or another, the prototype must be a "miniature version" of the deliverable system. "Miniature" can take on one of several different connotations. *Miniature* can refer to the fact that only a fraction of the intended functionality is present in the prototype. The intent of this sort of prototype might be simply to demonstrate that a subset of the total functionality could be assembled. Other possible meanings of "miniature" as it relates to a prototype could be: utilizing a subset of the different kinds or amount of data to be processed, presenting a subset of the total user interface to be delivered, and providing access to only a subset of the different users that will be supported. For a system that interfaces with external devices, a typical prototype might support only a limited or representative number of device interfaces.

Quickly functional

A prototype often is characterized as being "rapid." The whole idea of a prototype is to get a quick view of the system developed, thus the term "rapid." This is because neither the client nor the contractor want to progress far along into system development only to find out that the product being developed is not what the client wants. If for any number of reasons it is not possible or is not very likely that the prototype can be developed quickly, then it should not be done at all.

Management often is not supportive of prototyping. If the developers have to perform a hard-sell to management on the concept of a prototype, then fail to produce a meaningful prototype rapidly, this could be devastating to the credibility of those developers. Getting management to pursue other "nonstandard" or "risky" activities, as far as management is concerned, then will be that much more difficult.

The moral to this story is: Don't put too much functionality in the prototype but enough for the prototype to be meaningful. Ensure that the goals of the prototype are well-defined and attainable. Make sure that whatever functionality is encompassed within the prototype will be demonstrated successfully.

Easily modifiable

A characteristic of a prototype that often is overlooked is that the prototype should be easily modifiable. In actuality, a prototype that is easily modifiable will make heroes of the developers. What typically will happen during a prototype demo is that the customers (hopefully!) will like some of what they see, will be somewhat dismayed with some of what they see, and will inevitably say something like: "Can you do this?" or "If you could just do this, it would be great!" A prototype that is easily modifiable and can easily and quickly incorporate these suggestions or modifications will turn a moderately successful prototype demo into a smashing success. Refer to Figure 6.2.

Figure 6.2   An effective, easy-to-modify prototype.

Should use a fourth-generation language

In support of the previous point, ease of modifiability, prototypes (that have a user interface, of course), should be generated with some form of fourth-generation language, or 4GL. This holds true even, if for some reason, the final deliverable product will not be developed using a 4GL. Today's graphic generators can generate code in a variety of languages, therefore usually supplying a ready interface to the host language.

Most importantly—and this is the biggest benefit of 4GLs—is that the user interface is easily modifiable. Buttons, panels, menus, and other graphical objects can be created, modified, moved, and deleted, usually within minutes. This is in stark contrast to user interfaces from just a few short years ago. Then, desired locations of graphical objects had to be "measured," usually by pixels and "coded" into a status file, which then was used by the graphics engine to generate the user interface. The process of generating a prototype, in essence, had to be prototyped itself, to get the actual desired locations of objects.

Approximate a solution

A prototype, to be effective, must offer more than just a cursory attempt at approximating a solution. On the other hand, it is not the purpose of the prototype to implement all of the intended functionality of the full-up system, but a meaningful solution. Such is the dilemma of the prototype developer.

First and foremost, the goals of the prototype need to be well understood. It isn't sufficient to just say "Well, let's do a prototype of the delivered system" and go off and start developing the prototype. It might be important to provide a sampling of all of the intended functionality of the system. For another prototype, it might be important to provide somewhat less functionality, but the functionality thread that is provided needs to be "deep." Another prototype might be developed with the intent of demonstrating only a limited subset of the intended functionality. However, what might be more important than demonstrating broad functionality is that the prototyped functionality uses real data and attempts to simulate intended throughput of the system.

Ensure that whatever the prototype ultimately demonstrates—whether it be breadth of functionality, depth of functionality, data throughput, or just general requirements coverage—that it "trends" toward the delivered product.

Should be used with live data

To the extent possible, the prototype should use "live data." In many cases, however, this is not possible, especially as it applies to embedded systems. Despite this possible restriction, however, every attempt should be made to use simulated data that resembles the live data, not only in regard to the type of data but also in terms of quantity of data.

Upon closer inspection, this last statement implies that a prototype should be comprised of enough functionality such that representative data or processing throughput should be tested. This points out one of the major failings of prototypes and projects, in general. Data throughput and processing throughput issues rarely are modeled or addressed till the end of the project. It is not uncommon for parts of flight-critical embedded systems, for example, to discover late in the development cycle, much to the dismay of management, that a subsystem needs twice the MIPS that have been allocated to it.

Note: MIPS is an acronym for millions of instructions per second. A given processor architecture has a maximum number of MIPS. Each major function of the embedded system typically is allocated some percentage of the total allowable MIPS. In addition, some percentage is always initially allocated to "growth" to allow for functions that overrun their allocated MIPS. Unfortunately, even with this growth factor, most embedded systems initially will overrun their total MIPS allotment and have a difficult time "fitting in the box."

How can this possibly happen? This is somewhat analogous to the builder of a water filtration plant finding out just before the plant is done that it can process only half of the water that it was intended to handle. See Figure 6.3.

Figure 6.3 The result of poor estimation.

The implication being made here is that a prototype that represents an embedded system or a system for which there is any possibility of data or processing or throughput constraints should address these constraints.

Different Types of Prototypes

Like Baskin-Robbins, there are many different "flavors" of prototyping. A common type of prototype is one that will be "thrown away" when complete. Its purpose is purely "proof-of-concept." There is no intention of reusing any of the code that was developed for the prototype in the final delivered product. Another form of prototype is one that is meant as a "proof-of-concept" but for which as much of the framework of the prototype is retained as is possible. Indeed, this concept of prototyped often is implemented as "phased" or multiple releases of the software.

Throw-away prototype

This type of prototype has always suffered from a bad image. The concept that software is to be "thrown away" is very difficult to sell to management. The reasons for this are simple. The effort expended on that code is quantifiable; however, the potential benefits usually are not quantifiable at all. This makes for a very difficult sell to management.

This method actually can be an effective technique for prototyping, however. Customers are always looking for "warm fuzzies" that their product will get built on-time and on-budget. A "proof of concept" prototype that demonstrates that a brand new toolset is viable or that the basic requirements are understood by the contractor and can be implemented certainly will be appreciated by any customer. To be able to do this, a prototype might have to be "hacked out" to get the prototype out quickly. In the long run, getting the prototype out quickly might be of a higher priority than developing the prototype using any reusable components. This "disposable" prototype might meet all of its goals but is just going to be difficult to justify to management.

Perhaps, a modified approach where some aspects of the prototype can be reused and incorporated into the "real product" might be a more acceptable approach. It just depends upon what issues the prototype is attempting to address. It might be necessary to garner customer support in a *very* short period of time. Reuse of the prototype just might not be a priority. This usually will be the exception, and management will be trying to get (in fact, demand) as much reuse as possible from the prototype.

Partial reuse prototype

What will be the case more often than not is that some level of reuse will have be extracted from the prototype. This reuse, however, can take many forms. It might be possible to reuse the architectural structure of the prototype. It certainly might be possible that some of the actual code can be reused or at least serve as a template for later versions of the code.

The benefits of prototyping have been discussed in great detail. Many of these benefits can be accomplished through a prototype that has some elements of reuse within it. Minimally, the lessons learned from prototyping—such as interface definition, new tool experience, user interface definition, and any other benefits—should be incorporated into the delivered product. Whether these lessons learned translate into direct reuse depends on the prototype, but almost always some kind of indirect reuse can be accomplished.

In some ways, the prototype itself can be viewed as the first preliminary release of the system. This approach, which is a vital part of many of the iterative software life cycle approaches, can develop into a process where the customer becomes a vital part of the development process. The system is continually prototyped and refined until the final deliverable product is complete.

Phased-release prototype

The standard waterfall life cycle approach, as defined earlier in the chapter, does not readily incorporate prototyping into the life cycle definition. Nontraditional life cycle approaches recognize the inherent benefits of an iterative approach to all elements of software development and thus usually are referred to as *iterative approaches*. Many organizations and projects are beginning to recognize that a software development approach that "schedules" a single release of the system, sometimes years after initial analysis work had begun, is not effective and actually is becoming unacceptable.

As such, an effective alternative takes the concept of a prototype one step further. Instead of a single "proof of concept" prototype, the system is prototyped continually and refined until the last of the customer requirements have been incorporated into the system. As previously stated, this concept is an integral part of non-waterfall/iterative approaches.

There are some drawbacks to this approach, however. There certainly is going to be "overhead" incurred when releasing multiple versions of a product. There are additional configuration management issues involved when releasing multiple versions of a product. There also might be documentation overhead involved when incurring multiple releases of a product.

The benefits, however, should outweigh the costs in almost all cases. The most basic benefit, which has been alluded to already, is that there is a much greater likelihood that the product will meet the customer requirements if the customer is able to view the "path" that the product is taking. From the developer's point of view, critical interfaces will likely have been prototyped and "potted" earlier than with other approaches.

The exact form that the prototype will take, whether it is a strict throw-away or is essentially part of a series of phased-releases, depends on more factors than can be outlined here. Any aspects of the system development can operate only within the parameters that are set by the customer and project management. It often is very difficult and even impossible to alter these constraints. In general, any prototype that meets its goals and derives benefits as described here will result in a better product.

This concept of a phased-release aspect of prototyping is what Yourdon (1993, pg. 105) refers to as "evolutionary prototyping." The prototype is merely a skeleton of the final system. Each release or version of the product moves closer and closer to the final desired version of the product.

Problems with Prototyping

There are several "problems" that can occur when prototyping. These include the apparent waste of resources, the possibility that the prototype is "all wrong," and incorporating the prototype into the delivered product.

Appearance of waste of resources

As discussed previously, if the prototype is entirely or even mostly of the throw-away variety or appears to be this way, then there might likely be problems selling this approach to management. If the organization is open to developing software with approaches other than the traditional waterfall approach, then this appearance of wasting resources to support the prototype should not be a very big issue. The problem will likely occur within organizations that are strict adherents to the waterfall approach. There will likely be reluctance to committing to any task that does not show on a schedule or project chart. Any such task will be viewed as being wasteful and unnecessary.

What if prototype is "all wrong?"

A fear that exists, as unfounded as it might be, is that it is not a good idea for the customer to get a look at the product too early; that is, before problems get ironed out. Some organizations feel that serious problems that are discovered by the customer, especially at an early stage in the project, will get the project off "on the wrong foot," so to speak. The customer "not seeing" the product is not going to get the project back on the right track faster than if the customer did not see the prototype. If it turns out that the customer is unhappy with the prototype, then in the long run, this is definitely a good thing. (That is, unless the project gets canceled, of course!) The ultimate goal is for the final product to be delivered as expected. Bumps along the way are to be expected.

A prototype that is all wrong is an opportunity to get the product right. It can be an indication that the communication process between the customer and the client is flawed and needs to be corrected. It also is an indication that there is a problem with undocumented or unclear requirements. These are problems, but they also are an opportunity to improve the software development process so as to build a better product.

This issue boils down to a common one that is often discussed throughout this book. Early and frequent interaction with the customer is critical to the success of any and all projects. Is a project successful if it meets the written requirements but yet is not reflective of the product that the customer wanted? Of course not. The successful system is that system that meets the customer's expectations. If the project is progressing along the wrong path, as demonstrated by an early prototype failure, it really is not a failure, but an opportunity for success.

Incorporating the prototype into the delivered product

A prototype, as stated previously, must be able to be developed quickly. To do this, design and coding standards typically are relaxed or even eliminated. This can cause a serious problem when it comes to incorporating all or part of the prototype into the delivered product. Prototype code typically will not be documented very well. Some design or coding standards relating to appropriate use of the language might not have been observed. When evaluating the appropriateness and the type of prototype, this issue also must be addressed. There will be costs associated with bringing this code "up to standard."

A case study

Hilal and Soltan (1992) performed a study that compared the results of a prototyping approach and a nonprototyping approach in the development of a knowledge-based system. It is interesting to note some of the problems or disadvantages, as noted by the "prototyping" team:

- The prototyping approach leads to a shallower knowledge domain. The quick feedback that a prototype affords tends to lead toward a particular type of solution. A global view of the solution is not easily attained using prototyping.

- The prototype reinforces the drive toward fast solutions in the user interface. The prototyping team felt that it missed the opportunity of having an intermediate solution on paper.

- Prototyping allows for too much flexibility, which makes the prototype difficult to control. (This could cause a real problem in terms of project management and system documentation.)

It is interesting to note that some of the very same aspects of prototyping that are considered benefits also can be considered as disadvantages. Especially interesting is the point about too much flexibility. Certainly the prototyping effort benefits from flexibility because perhaps the main reason for the prototype is to establish a "proof of concept" of the system. This very same flexibility can become a minor and even a major disadvantage over time.

The ability to quickly alter a prototype (which already has been mentioned as a benefit) could be a drawback if this flexibility is taken advantage of too often. If the prototype is being developed into the final deliverable product, the "prototype mindset" of quick responsive changes could wreak havoc with the development effort.

You must realize also that the prototype only represents a limited subset of functionality. Additional complex functionality that is not represented in the prototype certainly will complicate overall development efforts.

Relationship with the Life Cycle Approach Being Used

Prototyping is a good idea in most cases. What if the management style and development philosophy simply does not support prototyping, though? Creative developers have found ways to maneuver around these kinds of issues. If there is enough groundswell support for getting the customer involved in an early "peek" at the system, this can be accomplished, although like other issues, it might take some leadership and "selling" to get it done.

Most management teams recognize the need for accomplishing the goals of prototyping. They just don't want to call it prototyping, because there usually isn't a placeholder on any project chart for prototyping. With a degree of leadership among the troops, management usually can be convinced that performing an "internal demonstration of limited system functionality" would be beneficial to the project and allay the fears of upper management that nothing is getting done on the project. Once the demo begins to take a successful form, it then can be suggested that the customer be brought into the picture. (If it isn't clear to most of the readers by now, a possible subtitle of this book could have been "How to Train Management to Do the Right Thing!")

The waterfall approach, as described in Boehm, (1981), clearly does not support any kind of prototyping. When one is playing the "waterfall game," it is not possible to repeatedly ride the waterfall from top to bottom. Once one hits the end of the waterfall, one cannot go back. Software, even most tasks in life, simply are not developed in this manner. Development of "good" systems and software is an iterative activity.

So why is the waterfall approach so popular? It is because the waterfall approach is so simple. However, this simplicity causes many more problems than it solves. The spiral life cycle method, as an example of an iterative life cycle approach, much more closely reflects how software is developed. This is where prototyping is such a good match with iterative approaches. Each iteration through the spiral method can be supported by an iteration through a cycle of a prototype. Refer to Figures 6.4 and 6.5 for a comparison of the waterfall and spiral life cycle.

An addition has been made to the spiral model depiction in Figure 6.6. The option for the last iteration to feed back onto itself if it is determined that the final "implementation" doesn't quite fit the bill ought to be more explicitly depicted. Also, notice the very prominant role that prototyping plays in the spiral model.

The vast majority of software developers, and even some management, understands that a strict waterfall life cycle approach simply is inappropriate and is ignorant of reality. Far too many organizations still place an inappropriate amount of trust in its ability to help guide a software project. As prototyping becomes more prevalent, life cycle approaches such as the spiral model will gain increasing acceptance.

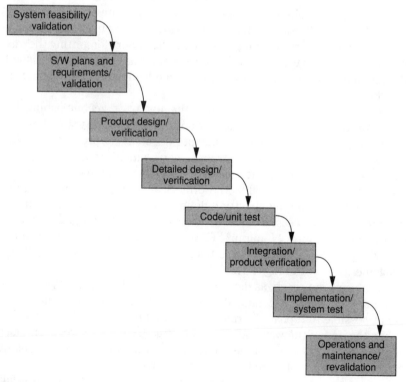

Figure 6.4 The waterfall life cycle approach.

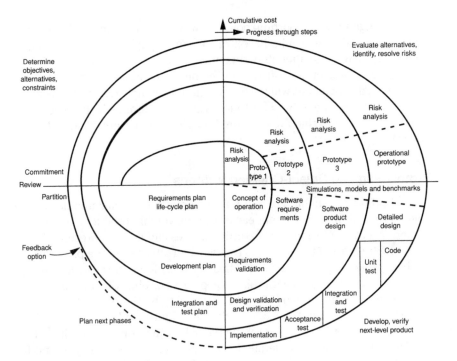

Figure 6.5 The spiral life cycle approach. (Boehm, 1981)

Why Isn't Prototyping Supported More?

We have discussed some of the reasons that prototyping doesn't occur in some projects. It is possible that the project is one where prototyping just does not make sense. The project management mindset might not support prototyping or make it very difficult to implement. There are other reasons that prototyping historically has not been supported. Unfortunately, these are somewhat management-related, again.

A prototyping effort will consume time and resources. If this is a one-shot prototype, instead of an iterative prototyping effort, then the cost of the prototype will be realized in the initial phases of the project. The expenditure of resources on the prototype will take resources away from other "early" efforts. Upper management of a project is very reluctant, understandably, to see early deadlines missed on a project. If deadlines are missed early on in a project, they will almost always be missed later on in the project.

If time is spent on a prototype, less time is spent on other activities. The "real design and coding" effort will get delayed. Standard analysis and design activities might be delayed, again to the consternation of management.

This brings up an important point, however. Prototyping isn't the only "new construct" that results in "extra" resource commitment early on in a project. It is well documented that most object-oriented methodologies "front-load" a project. As software development continues to mature along these lines, management will have to accommodate new resource allocation schemes. Management by milestones will never disappear, however, and shouldn't. The tasks that are measured that indicate progress must change, however.

Prototyping and Object-Oriented Methods

A good prototype should contain a representation of a fair number of the objects that ultimately will appear in the deliverable product. As inferred earlier, objects that represent external devices should be represented. It is likely the breadth of the methods that will be restricted in the prototype.

These objects can be the basis of higher class hierarchies, but it is imperative to not go overboard with this issue of class or object hierarchies in the prototype. Certainly a good class hierarchy can be the basis of a superior reuse effort if the prototype is to be developed into the final product. Keep in mind, however, that the prototype typically will not be addressing all requirements. Developing a detailed class hierarchy without accounting for all of the requirements could be devastating, especially to any proposed reuse goals. Yourdon (1994, pg. 67) aptly notes, "Reusability and prototyping are two sides of the same coin."

Initial determination of attributes should be undertaken. If the purpose of the prototype is to generate a relatively flat model without any single thread taken very deep, then only a limited number of methods should be identified along with only a limited look taken at relationships between objects.

Again, you should avoid the temptation to begin detailed class consolidation. Detailed relationships and message-passing between objects will likely not occur in the prototype. An overly detailed analysis and definition of all of the attributes that are associated with objects should not occur either. Detailed classification efforts might be a waste of time and might end up corrupting the model to the point that it might have to be scrapped entirely.

Another aspect of object-orientation and prototyping that is incredibly important is the opportunity for the development/prototyping team to hone its skills in object-oriented methods. It is highly likely that the number of individuals trained in object-oriented methods will be in the minority with even less experience in implementing projects successfully using object-oriented methods. A prototype could be a prime opportunity to begin to instill the OO mindset that is difficult to do when initially working with OO.

Summary

When considering all of the benefits that prototyping can bring to a project, it is somewhat amazing that this concept has not been accepted with open arms everywhere in the software development world. The main reason that it has not is due to the influence of the waterfall method throughout software project management. In a continuing effort to quantify and manage (some would say micro-manage) every activity in the software development life cycle, the iterative nature of software has been largely ignored. This has been to the detriment of software development, in general.

Prototyping reflects the true iterative nature of software development. For most projects, some form of prototyping is beneficial. In a very limited number of cases, prototyping should be analyzed to make sure that it is appropriate. The following are some examples of projects that might not necessarily need to be prototyped:

- A system that has no user interface
- A system where the requirements are very well documented and understood
- The project is very small
- The project has a series of deliveries that incrementally deliver intended functionality
- There is a very immature tool environment
- The project is founded on a very neolithic software development environment
- The project is an add-on from a prior successful project

The benefits of prototyping are well documented. Most or all of the following benefits can be realized from an effective prototype:

- Identification and elimination of risk areas
- Gets customers on-board early
- Customers typically don't know their own needs
- A prototype describes the product better than any documentation or review could
- It is a method to test out new technologies
- Early interface testing

There are some basic characteristics that ought to be present in any effective prototype:

- Miniature of the deliverable system
- Quickly functional
- Easily modifiable
- Should use a 4GL
- Approximate a solution
- Should be used with live data

Prototypes often are typified as being of the "throw-away" form. With this type of prototype, none of the code or design is used in the delivered product. Although there can be very good reasons for this type of prototype, it is almost always a very difficult "sell" to management. In general, some aspects of the prototype will have to be reused for the prototype to succeed politically within the organization. A prototype can be developed such that it actually can be viewed as a preliminary early release of the product. The prototype acts as initial cut and subsequent deliveries are continuous refinements of the prototype.

There can be some problems with prototyping. It is possible, that without full management support, prototyping might be viewed as a waste of time and resources. The prototype also might be "all wrong." In reality, this is not a problem. If the prototype is reflective of the true understanding of the requirements and that understanding is not in sync with the customer's expectations, then discovering this early in the project actually is a benefit. If the prototype is to be incorporated into the final product, then the prototype will very likely have to be altered markedly to bring the code "up to standard." It is likely that the prototype code was developed using relaxed development guidelines to get the prototype done quickly. The cost of this effort needs to be accounted for.

Prototyping is an "iterative" feature that works best within an iterative software life cycle. If a noniterative approach is being used, such as a pure waterfall method, it will be difficult to find a place for the prototype. There is just no allowance for iterative activities such as this. Due to this fact, organizations that have not progressed to iterative approaches will not be very supportive of prototyping.

Prototyping and object-oriented methods work well together. Initial class, object, and attribute definition can and should occur during the prototyping activities. Care should be taken however to not commit to a detailed class/subclass hierarchy at this point in time. All requirements certainly will not have been addressed in the prototype. An overly ambitious effort at designing this hierarchy could cause rework later.

Prototypes will result in a higher fidelity product for most projects. When done properly, the benefits will outweigh the costs and result in a satisfied customer.

References

Arthur, Lowell J. 1992. *Rapid Evolutionary Development*. New York, New York: Wiley and Sons.

Boar, Bernard. 1984. *Application Prototyping*. Reading, Massachusetts: Addison-Wesley.

Dichter, Carl. 1993. "Is it designed right? (Importance of rapid prototyping in software development)." *UNIX Review*. 11(6): 50–57.

Hilal, D.K. and H. Soltan. 1992. "To prototype or not to prototype? That is the question." *Software Engineering Journal*. November, 1992. 388–391.

Pressman, Roger. 1987. *Software Engineering—A Practitioner's Approach*. 2nd Edition. New York, New York: McGraw Hill.

Yourdon, Ed. 1993. *Decline and Fall of the American Programmer*. Englewood Cliffs, New Jersey: Yourdon Press.

Yourdon, Ed. 1994. *Object-Oriented Systems Design—An Integrated Approach*. Englewood Cliffs, New Jersey: Yourdon Press.

7

Software Reuse

In the words of poet/philosopher George Santayanna (1906), "Those who cannot remember the past are condemned to repeat it." In the software world, it might be more appropriate to say, "Those who don't reuse the past are condemned to redesign it." This might sound like good advice, and most people will agree with the statement, but reuse is not as simple as it sounds.

Effective software reuse allows companies to decrease costs, shorten schedules, and increase the quality of their products. Many companies are starting to realize this and believe that reuse is the key to their future success. Even the U.S. Department of Defense (DoD) has moved software reuse to the front burner. "The DoD realizes it could save $300 million each year if it improved software reuse by only one percent" (Anthes, 1993). Despite these cost advantages, many companies have been unsuccessful in their attempts to harness software reuse.

Software reuse is nothing new; we've talked about it for almost 50 years (Anthes, 1993). The software developer who builds up a set of software packages/subprograms and uses them instead of redesigning new code is using a form of software reuse. Many programming languages, development methodologies, and software tools have been designed with features that are intended to simplify software reuse. These advances have opened new doors and allowed software reuse to mature to the point where companies can take full advantage of software reuse and reap the rewards of its use.

Software development costs have skyrocketed. Because of this, companies are finding it increasingly difficult to justify the development of new projects that involve software. Some companies continue to develop software the old fashioned way, using brute force to develop and possibly redevelop all the software for the new project. Many companies try to utilize software reuse; some have succeeded, while others have failed.

How much longer can a company afford to pay several programmers to develop a stack or queue? In some cases, several stacks are developed (by different programmers) and used within the same application. What about the new tests and documentation associated with each new stack or queue? Can companies continue to redesign the tests and rewrite the documentation every time that they need to use a stack or queue? Does a company need to design a completely new "online help" system for each new application program that it develops? This repetitive effort increases costs and adds time to the schedule. In today's competitive market, where *downsizing* and *rightsizing* are common terms, companies must find ways to minimize both cost and schedule and, at the same time, improve product quality.

This chapter will begin by defining software reuse. The common definition of software reuse, simple code reuse, will be expanded. We will continue by examining how software reuse is affected by object-oriented techniques, as well as how it improves prototyping efforts. This chapter will continue by identifying some of the more common reasons for failures that were observed when a company tries to incorporate software reuse in its current development process. We will conclude by identifying some "keys to success" that everyone should consider if they want to effectively reuse software components.

What Is Software Reuse?

Software reuse is defined as the art of developing software that is used on two or more applications or projects. This sounds simple enough. Let's look a little closer and try to expand on this definition.

A good analogy comes from the hardware world. We have progressed from building things with diodes and transistors to using integrated circuits (ICs). Things continued to progress to where we are using entire boards to build more complex systems than would have been imagined just a few short years ago. We can look at software in a similar way. The individual lines of code are the "software diodes and transistors." Subprograms and packages are the "software ICs." Subsystems (such as an online help subsystem) can be thought of as the "software boards" that will be used to build more complex systems.

When most people think of software reuse, they actually are thinking of "code reuse." The code and unit test phase of an embedded-mode project represents only 24% to 32% of the overall development effort (Boehm, 1981). The code and unit test phase of an organic-mode and semidetached-mode project represents only 36% to 42% and 29% to 37%, respectively (Boehm 1981). These ranges are driven by the size of the project; the code and unit test phase represents a smaller portion of the effort for a larger project.

If you limit yourself to code reuse, the best that you can do is decrease the cost by 32%, 42%, or 37%, depending on the type and size of the project that you are developing. You also are limited on how much you can shorten the time that is required to develop the project (the "schedule"). This is unrealistic because it does not account for the work involved in identifying the code to be reused and putting all the pieces together, but it is not that far off. This is because the time that is required to identify the reused code and integrate it into the design is minor when compared to what it would take to develop the code from scratch. What about the analysis, design, and testing phases? Software reuse should cover these phases as well.

Historically speaking, new technologies have been incorporated into the coding phase first. They then are worked into the design phase, the analysis phase, and eventually the testing phase of the development life cycle. As an example, object-oriented techniques first were applied to the coding phase, then Object-Oriented Design (OOD) became the topic of the day. More recently, Object-Oriented Requirements Analysis (OORA) has been in the limelight. Applying object-oriented techniques to the testing phase also is getting some attention but still is in the early stages.

Software reuse is no different. Unofficially, we have reused code for many years now. In some cases, people have used "cut and paste" techniques to pull documentation from previous projects into the current one. Some companies have taken reuse several steps further and have had very positive results. The DoD has developed several software reuse libraries that are accessible to the public at little or no charge. Software reuse libraries also have been developed by tool vendors and are available at a wide range of prices.

If a company wants to survive the 1990s, it must successfully incorporate a software reuse strategy into its development process. Today's companies are achieving reusability levels ranging as high as 86% (Arthur, 1992).

Fujitsu introduced Kawasaki Steel to standardization and reuse in 1987. Within a few short years, Kawasaki Steel increased software productivity by 2.5 times (Arthur, 1992). Two transaction processing projects at AT&T Bell Laboratories have achieved reusability levels of 65% (Arthur, 1992). The sizes of these projects were 120 KLOC (thousand lines of code) and 210 KLOC. On a separate project of 1200 KLOC, AT&T Bell Laboratories achieved a reusability level of 86% (Arthur, 1992). These are just a few examples of the success stories. There have been many success stories, and more are identified each year. To see the benefits of reusability, let's look at an example.

Let's assume that two companies (Widgets-R-Us and American Widget) are bidding on a project that will require 100,000 lines of code. Widgets-R-Us is achieving a reusability level of 20%, while American Widget is achieving a reusability level of 80%. Therefore, Widgets-R-Us will need to base its bid on the development of 80,000 lines of code. American Widget's bid will be based on developing only 20,000 lines of code (Figure 7.1). This is based on reuse alone with all other factors remaining constant. These other fac-

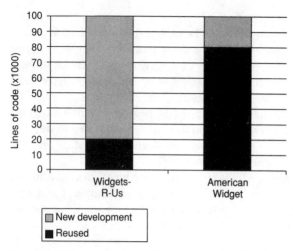

Figure 7.1 Differences between high- and low-reusability levels.

tors include the ability and experience of their staff, the experience that each company has in developing this type of product, and so on.

American Widget could develop the system for approximately one-fourth the cost of Widgets-R-Us. In addition, American Widget would be able to deliver a finished product in less time than Widgets-R-Us. Once again, this is based on reuse alone with all other factors remaining constant. The benefits are clear; American Widget will be able to submit a bid with a shorter schedule and a much lower price and will more than likely win the contract.

The majority of the software in American Widget's product is reused. The reused software is more thoroughly tested. This is due to the additional testing imposed on the initial development of the reusable software and the "in-use" testing that it receives from the customers of the previous applications that used the software. This means that the new product is less likely to have problems after it is delivered to the customer. Your customer will be more satisfied with your product and will feel that it is a high-quality product. This will give American Widget a good name in the industry and will have a direct impact on future contracts.

As with most things in life, software reuse is not free. There are some start-up and maintenance costs. The three main costs are described in the following paragraphs.

Initial investment or "up front" costs: This includes the purchase of reuse component libraries, training, purchase of tools to maintain the software (configuration management, browsers, etc.), and so on. These costs can be amortized over all the new projects that make use of reusability.

Cost of increased testing and quality assurance: Because reusable components are used on multiple projects, an error can be costly, so more extensive testing is required.

Different levels of test coverage: In the avionics world, as well as other disciplines, there are different levels of test coverage that are required based on the criticality level of the system being developed. The criticality level of the system is determined by the impact that the system would have on the airplane if it was inoperable. For example, a passenger entertainment system would be less critical than an engine controller. If the entertainment system fails, you have a few unhappy travelers. If an engine controller fails, the airplane won't take off until it was fixed or replaced. Therefore, by definition, a critical system requires more exhaustive testing than a noncritical system.

Assume that you plan to use a component in a critical system and a noncritical system. You must provide testing to satisfy the needs of the critical system. This more exhaustive testing also would meet the testing requirements of the noncritical system. This might seem to be an overkill for the noncritical system, but it increases the overall quality of the product.

Keep in mind that you will write only one set of tests that will satisfy both systems. You will not need to write one set of tests for the critical system and an additional set of tests for the noncritical system. A component that is used on several systems will be more thoroughly tested in the real world. Therefore, it will have fewer chances of creating problems when it is used on a new system.

The amount of testing that is required for a reusable component typically will be two to four times what is required for a nonreused component.

Maintenance costs: This includes the maintenance of libraries, browsers, and other facilities that help control the components and make it easier for software developers to find the best component for the job.

The definition of software reuse includes the analysis, design, coding and testing phases of the project. In the future, we might be able to expand our definition to include such things as user documentation, statements of work, cost and schedule projections, and so on. For now, let's focus on applying reuse to the main development phases of the project. Once you have successfully incorporated reuse into your development process, it should be relatively easy to apply reuse to these other project related work requirements.

The reusable software component

Let's define a *reusable software component*. From our previous discussion, you know that it should be more than just code. Figure 7.2 provides a pictorial representation of a reusable component. As you can see, it should include interface documentation requirements, any necessary specification and design requirements, code, test procedures, test cases, and test results. You might be wondering why all of the test documentation is included. This is what allows you to reduce the testing costs that are associated with the applications that reuse this component. After the component is initially de-

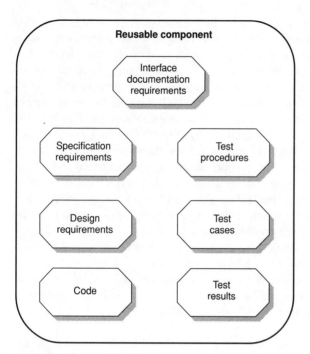

Figure 7.2 The reusable software component.

veloped, the tests already are written, executed, and evaluated, so any application that reuses the component can reuse the testing as well.

The elements that make up a reusable software component are as follows:

- Interface Documentation Requirements—This includes all the information that is required to support the library and browser tools.

- Specification Requirements—The information required for this element depends on the development process. It can include such things as an external class dependency diagram, system class dependency diagrams, initial text specifications for each class, event analysis information (e.g., object message diagrams), and so on (Seidewitz and Stark, 1992). Some low-level utility classes might not require this information as it might be considered implementation details associated with the user class.

- Design Requirements—Once again, the information for this element depends on the development process. It can include such things as a detailed textual specification for each class that includes preliminary design language (PDL), low-level structure diagrams, etc. (Seidewitz and Stark, 1992).

- Code—This element consists of the source code for each class within the component.

- Test Procedures—This element should describe the steps that are required to execute the tests associated with the component. It should include a description of the test tools and equipment that are required to execute the tests. This element also is dependent on the development process.

- Test Cases—This element should consist of the entire set of test cases that are required to test the component. The development process should define the contents of this element.

- Test Results—This element should include the results that were generated from the execution of the test cases. It should include an analysis of the results that indicates which tests passed (hopefully all of them) and which ones failed.

As you can see, the exact content of the reusable component is highly dependent on the development process. Therefore, it is important that the process is in place prior to completely defining the reusable component. Because the development process is not expected to remain static and is expected to mature over the years, you can expect the reusable components to change as well.

A reusable component will be written a little differently compared to its nonreusable counterpart. The design might need to be expanded to handle a slightly broader set of requirements and yet avoid becoming too complex (trying to be the end-all component). We'll discuss the complexity of reusable components later in this chapter. The testing might need to provide a more thorough, in-depth coverage than normally would be required for the initial application. Future applications might have different test coverage requirements; therefore, the application that initially develops a reusable component might take on some additional work to convert a nonreusable component to a reusable one.

Reuse and development tools

Computer Aided Software Engineering (CASE) tools have been maturing over the years. They are reaching the point where the analysis, design, coding, and testing can be done within the CASE tool. Software documentation often is produced directly from the CASE tool itself. This has allowed us to store all of the information that is associated with the component within the CASE tool. The stored information can be copied and reused on another project. The stored information must be under configuration control, possibly using a configuration management (CM) tool that will allow us to indicate where to get the specification information. The benefits of configuration management are explained in chapter 12.

Using good CM and CASE tools will allow us to identify similar requirements and reuse them in the current project. Once again, because these requirements are used on one or more other projects, they will be more fully tested. This is due to the additional testing required of a reusable component (on the initial development of the component) as well as the additional "in-use" testing from previous customers. We can have more confidence using these requirements as compared to redefining new ones. Of course, we will need to make sure that it is what the new customer wants.

Using object-oriented techniques, you define classes and objects (refer to chapter 4). This produces elements that are easy to recognize (as a reusable entity) and easier to extract from existing documentation (via a CASE tool). Object-oriented techniques package components such that the definition of a queue, for example, includes the type definition itself as well as the operations that can be performed on an object of this type. Good information hiding and data encapsulation will protect those who use the package. If you decide to change the underlying structure or algorithms that are used to perform the operations, the users will not be affected. They can continue to use the "package" without needing to make changes to conform to the new structure or algorithm change.

It is important to note that software reuse is not limited to the object-oriented methodology. You can apply it to structured methodology or any other analysis/design methodology as well.

The structured methodology is based on algorithmic decomposition. The products include structure charts, data flow diagrams, and state transition diagrams. The analysis and design focus on the procedures and functions and how they interact to fulfill the system requirements. You can design these procedures and functions such that they are reusable. You can even identify groups of procedures and functions, from the structure charts, that can form a single reusable entity. This is an oversimplification of structured methods, and creating reusable entities is more complex than what is described previously. Still, you can see how reuse also can be applied to a process that makes use of structured design techniques.

The object-oriented "packages" are defined with reuse in mind. They are simpler to identify, create, use, and reuse. They form the basic building blocks from which entire systems can be built. The reusable blocks also can be grouped to form a single reusable entity.

Software reuse can be merely copying text/code from one project and using it on the current one. The benefits will be much better if you have good CM practices in place. Good CM practices will allow you to not only extract the information but also to take advantage of "fixes" that are made when problems are found in an earlier project that uses the reusable component. Each new build or version of the application would extract the documentation/code from CM and use it to build the new version of the application. Any changes made as a result of testing or use of an older application that utilizes the reused software automatically will be incorporated into the new version of the new application.

Reuse and the development life cycle

The documents that you produce as you progress through the different phases of the project (analysis, design, coding, and testing) provide the details of how the complex application works and how it was defined and developed. This documentation is used to help maintain the application. It also is used when you need to incorporate new functionality or fix problems found during testing or out in the field. Therefore, it is important that reusable components span all the phases of the development life cycle as well.

If a CASE tool was used, you can identify small elements or entire subsystems that can be packaged together to allow you to use it on another project. The information that is stored (made accessible via CM) should include the analysis, design, and code. It also should include and test procedures, test cases, and test results.

Prototyping with software reuse

The typical prototype includes everything that is involved with a specific part of the application, such as the user interface. The prototype allows you to get that warm fuzzy feeling that what you have in mind will work (or that your customer will accept it). It usually has little, if any, functionality behind it. Let's look at an example and see how software reuse can help give you that added confidence that everything is going well.

Assume that you want to prototype the user interface to verify that what you have in mind agrees with what the customer has in mind. You design and code everything having to do with the screens, buttons, etc., but nothing will happen when you select one of the buttons.

Let's also assume that your application includes an online help facility that you plan to reuse from a previous application. Why not use the software from that other application instead of spending the time creating the dummy software that will be replaced later with the reused software? If you do, you actually will see something happen when you select the "help button," and so will your customer. Your prototype will be more complete, and you will get to prove a larger part of your design without the extra effort of designing the "online help" facility itself.

How would achieving 80% reuse impact your prototype effort? You would be able to provide prototypes that include a larger part of your design, giving yourself, and your customer, more confidence in the project as a whole.

Where do you start?

The simplest components to reuse are low-level utilities. Reusable subsystems are composed of many components, some of which are the low-level components. Therefore, it is a good idea to establish the low-level components first, then work on the reusable subsystems.

The first elements that should be considered for reuse are stacks, queues, and other low-level utility-type elements, such as character, string, numeric, and calendar utilities. These can be developed inhouse or obtained from one of the many reuse libraries that are available from the government, universities, and commercial vendors.

When developing or considering a subprogram or package for reuse, don't go overboard by either creating a component that is too general and complex or one that is too simplistic.

As an example, let's say that you need a first in-first out (FIFO) stack. You could develop a single stack package that could be used for all the different kinds of stacks (FIFO, last in-first out [LIFO], etc.), or you could develop one that can store only a specific, hard-coded element type (integer, character, etc.). A better choice would be to develop a FIFO stack package that could store a single element type but allow the user to specify which element type will be stored.

A program that handles all cases will end up being too slow and too cumbersome to use. The testing associated with this package will be difficult to write and execute and, therefore, is more likely to contain hidden errors that escape the testing and cause problems down the road.

If you try to develop a component that is too simplistic, you will end up with a large number of components in the reuse library that individually address all the different cases (e.g., FIFO Stack for characters, FIFO Stack for integers, FIFO Stack for . . .). The different FIFO Stacks would be based on the same design and have very similar test cases. What would happen if you find an error in the FIFO stack for characters? Would the error get fixed in the other FIFO stacks?

The "happy medium" would be to develop a FIFO stack that could handle a single type, defined by the individual application that is using the stack. You might end up using the stack several times—once for integers, once for characters, etc.—within the same application. You still could use a single set of test documentation to cover all uses of the stack (assuming that the test cases covered a wide range of different types).

If you are using object-oriented techniques, you can define superclasses and subclasses (refer to chapter 4). This allows you to group the common properties into the superclass, and the unique properties are defined within the subclass. The subclasses inherit the properties of the superclass. For example, cars and trucks are two types of vehicles. The superclass Vehicles defines properties that are common to both cars and trucks (color, type of transmission, etc.). The subclass Car defines the properties that are unique to cars (number of doors, seating capacity, etc.). The subclass Truck defines the properties that are unique to trucks (number of axles, capacity, etc.).

You can't stop there. To take full advantage of software reuse, you need to be able to reuse entire subsystems. Look at the online help example. This could include several queues, stacks, interrupt service routines, and so on. It is made up of many different, possibly reusable, components. Low-level utilities are nice and provide the framework for developing larger reusable subsystems, but the reusable subsystems will give you more bang for the buck.

How can you determine if a subsystem should be made into a reusable subsystem? The first thing that you should do is look at your company's primary products and identify commonalities between them. If you see something that is used on more than one application and is likely to be used on future applications, you should consider making it a reusable subsystem.

If a company's primary business is the development of software applications for personal computers, each application might include an online help system to make the application more user-friendly. The company might create a reusable online help subsystem that can be incorporated into its entire line of new products. When the company reuses the online help subsystem on a new application, it will save time and money because it won't need to redevelop that part of the system. Multiply that by the number of new applications that reuse the online help facility, and you have the potential for huge savings. In addition, if your customers are happy with the online help for one application, they will be more likely to consider the purchase of another of your applications. They will become comfortable with the new application in a short amount of time, because they already are familiar with a large part of the new application.

When a company identifies a subsystem (from an existing application) as a candidate for reuse, how can they convert it to a reusable component? One way would be to reverse engineer it by hand. You essentially would need to pull the design and requirements from the code. All the documentation and tests also would need to be developed. This might seem to go against the idea that the code should be driven by the design, but it will allow you to meet the process and reusable component requirements. You might be able to use the documentation from the original application.

What about the CASE tools? Can they provide any help? Several of the available CASE tool vendors have been working on both automatic code generation and reverse engineering capabilities. Automatic code generation will allow you to change the requirements and design and let the tools incorporate the changes into the code. The reverse engineering capabilities will allow you to take existing code and create the design and requirements associated with the code.

A few years ago, we performed an evaluation of several of the more popular CASE tools to determine which tool would meet the needs of our development process. Most claimed that they had both code generation and reverse engineering capabilities, but they would not be fully functional until a future release. At the time of the evaluation, none of the CASE tools could provide what we thought was the minimum functionality in those areas.

These CASE tools continue to evolve and mature. By now, they might be able to provide everything that you would ever want from both code generation and reverse engineering. You will want to look at these areas very closely when you are evaluating CASE tools for use within your company.

The Reuse Library

So now that you have all these wonderful, reusable components, how can you manage them so that they are accessible to anyone without impacting the individual development efforts? As you might have guessed from the section title, the answer is a reuse library. We have talked about it throughout this chapter, but we really haven't defined what it is.

A reuse library will contain reusable components in an area that is separated from the development libraries. The reuse library should be under configuration control, or at a minimum, the components in the library should be under configuration control (see chapter 12). The individual development groups must have access to the library so that they can use the components. A reuse group or organization should be formed and be responsible for the development and maintenance of the reuse library. We'll define this group and explain why it is necessary later in this chapter. For now it is enough to know that the individual development groups can focus on their individual project.

The reuse library can be contained within a CASE tool, if that is how your company manages its software. The reuse library should include browser tools that will simplify the job of the programmer that must find a reusable component that meets his or her requirements. This tool should allow the programmer to search through the library using key words or phrases that identify the type of component that they're looking for. Ideally, this tool will allow them to select one of the components found via the search and bring up a more detailed description of the component. If the browser tool and the reuse library are too difficult to use, the software developers will avoid using them. This will put a quick end to any hopes of establishing software reuse.

The reuse library can be organized in one of several ways. You can use a single reuse library structure, dual reuse library structure, or multiple reuse library structure. Whatever works best for the company and the development process. Let's take a look at these different organizational methods and see how they differ.

The single reuse library structure

The single reuse library structure is, as you might have guessed, one library that contains all of the reusable components. From the lowest-level utility to the most complex reusable subsystem, it's in there. Figure 7.3 shows how the individual development groups can utilize the reuse library as well as their own development library. The individual development libraries should contain the project's unique components. You also can see where the responsibilities exist between the individual development groups and the reuse group.

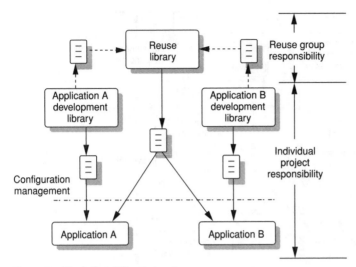

Figure 7.3 Single reuse library structure.

As shown in Figure 7.3, components can be promoted from the individual development libraries to the reuse library (shown using dashed lines). Note that the responsibility for performing the work associated with promoting these components lies with the reuse group. As we will explain later, the reuse group is responsible for any task that is associated with creating or maintaining components within the reuse library. This will eliminate problems from groups who do not want to use their budget and resources on the extra work associated with initial creation of a reusable component. As a matter of fact, it will help encourage its reuse because the development group won't need to perform the extra work at all; they will get "free" software (relative to their own project budget). They won't be able to use the excuse of "not on my nickel."

The dual reuse library structure

As the single reuse library continues to grow, you might find that it is becoming more and more difficult to control. The number of components within the reuse library might be getting out of hand. In addition, it might be increasingly difficult to maintain easy access to the components. One way to ease this management problem is to define two reuse libraries (Figure 7.4). One of these reuse libraries might be limited to low-level utility components. The other might contain reusable subsystems. You also could let one library contain the superclasses and the other library contain the subclasses.

By creating and maintaining dual reuse libraries, you can increase the number of reuse components that can be managed. You still will be able to maintain easy access to the individual components. When a software de-

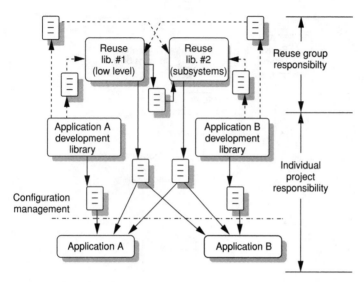

Figure 7.4 Dual reuse library structure.

veloper needs a low-level utility, such as a stack or queue, they can look in the low-level reuse library. They won't need to filter out all the reusable subsystems because these components will exist in a completely different library. The same is true for the software developer that wants to utilize a reusable subsystem. She or he won't need to filter out all the low-level components.

The reusable subsystems might incorporate reusable low-level components within their design. For this reason, the reusable subsystems library must have access to the reusable low-level library. This is not a problem. You can have one library dependent on the other. You should avoid defining the two libraries such that each one is dependent on the other (circular dependent libraries). This will definitely come back to haunt you. Some programming languages won't even allow you to define the libraries in this manner.

The multiple reuse library structure

You might find that two levels of reuse libraries still are not enough. You might continue to have problems managing the reuse libraries due to the continued growth. In this case, the first thing that you should do is to analyze the components within the libraries. You want to make sure that they are truly reused components or that they at least have a high potential for reuse. It is very easy to let a reuse library get out of control. Adding components to the library just for the sake of having a lot of reusable components is not going to help. In fact, it hurts.

The promotion of a component to a reusable component should be done cautiously. The aircraft engine controller software might make an excellent reusable subsystem for GE or Pratt & Whitney but not for Intel or Microsoft. Therefore, you must make sure that you choose your reuse components wisely.

Another thing to be careful of is a reuse library that is made up of components that are too simplistic. As mentioned before, this will tend to fill up the reuse library and make it harder to navigate. Once again, it is very important that you find the happy medium between components that are too simplistic and those that are overly complicated. A well-defined component that has the appropriate level of complexity can go a long way.

If you feel that your reuse libraries contain well-defined components and your growth problems still exist, you might want to consider a multiple reuse library structure (Figure 7.5). There are several ways in which you can break up the existing reuse libraries into multiple libraries.

Let's assume that you currently have two reuse libraries: one that contains low-level utility components and one that contains reusable subsystems. In the early stages of establishing software reuse, the low-level utilities will greatly outnumber the reusable subsystems. Therefore, your low-level library probably is where your greatest problem exists. In this case, you will need to rearrange the components into subgroups that eventually will become your individual reuse libraries.

As an example, one of your subgroups could be Structures. This subgroup could include such things as stacks, lists, trees, and so on. Another

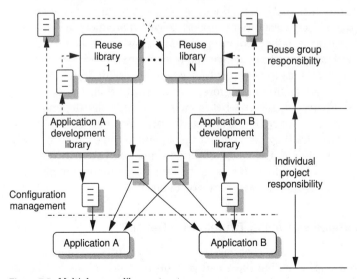

Figure 7.5 Multiple reuse library structure.

subgroup might be Tools. This subgroup could include character, string, numeric, and calendar utilities as well as sorting and searching utilities. "Software Components With Ada Structures, Tools, and Subsystems" by Grady Booch (1987) provides some excellent examples for grouping these low-level utilities.

Another option for breaking up the existing reuse libraries is to split up your reusable subsystems library. This generally is not an easy thing to do. A company's products typically are similar in nature. Once again, you can split up your subsystem library into a library of super classes and a library of subclasses.

If your company produces PC-based applications as well as real-time embedded systems, you could split your reusable subsystems library across these boundaries: one reusable subsystem library for PC-based applications and one for real-time embedded systems. Real-time embedded software typically is under more severe timing and memory restrictions. The designs for real-time embedded systems will focus on optimizing these characteristics. The designs for PC applications will focus on clean user interfaces and seamless integration with other PC applications. A component that is well designed for PC applications might not work as well for a real-time embedded system.

Which reuse library structure works the best?

All three of the library structures have their good points and their bad points. It is up to you to decide which one will work best for your company and development process. Although it is not impossible to switch from one library structure to another, it is not easy. Once reuse is established using one library structure, the products that you produce rely on the structure. To change, you must freeze the existing structure to support delivered products. When a new version of an existing product is developed, you can switch to the new library structure. It will take some time to completely switch to the new structure.

There are a few things to watch out for when you are defining the reuse library structure. As mentioned before, you must avoid circularly dependent libraries. Figure 7.6 shows what is meant by a circular dependent library structure. Remember that it is okay for one library to be dependent on another library, but they both cannot be dependent on each other.

You should try to keep the reuse libraries simple and easy to use. The tools that you buy or produce to access the reusable components must accommodate the reuse library structure you choose.

Why Are Companies Having Trouble with Reuse?

There are a lot of companies that have made valiant efforts at implementing a software reuse strategy but have had very little success. This can be attributed to a number of things.

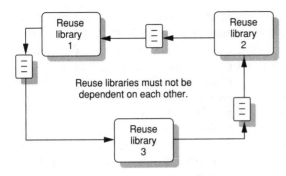

Figure 7.6 Circular dependent libraries.

Software developers are artists who take a lot of pride in their work. As artists, they do not want to use someone else's artwork. They prefer to design it themselves.

Most companies do not give the same amount of credit (in lines of code or other methods of measuring a software developer's productivity) for the use of reused software versus the development of new software. When software developers utilize reused software, they can be given less than 50% of the credit that they would receive if they developed the software themselves. This in itself discourages software developers from reusing software because it appears that they are less productive. It can even have an impact on their future employee evaluations and raises.

Software developers often feel that it is easier to develop software themselves than to search through reuse libraries to try to find something that will work. There is always a chance that they won't find anything and will end up designing it themselves anyway. The tools that are available to the software developer to search through the reuse libraries often are very crude and difficult to use. This just adds to the frustration when they are trying to find the component they need.

Today, many computer science classes taught at colleges, universities, and technical institutes indirectly discourage reuse. They are trying to encourage creativity, so they don't want the students "copying" someone else's work. It is important for the students to work through some of the common problems that they will encounter when designing systems. However, the importance of reuse also should be taught and encouraged.

Quite often, the price tag for developing the reuse library is applied to a current project, which already might be dealing with budget and schedule problems. The managers develop the attitude of "not on my nickel" and become defensive concerning "software reuse." This is very understandable given the schedule and budget pressures put on them. Eventually the reuse libraries are dropped in an effort to save the project. "Maybe we'll develop it next time is the often-heard battle cry."

As discussed before, a company's initial attempts at creating a reuse library result in components that are too complicated. Each component tries to meet all of the current and future needs of the component. The components become so complicated that they are untestable, too slow, and difficult to understand and use and therefore are not used. Even when software developers try to use these components, they spend a lot of time debugging and develop a bad attitude toward reusable software.

Some companies try to avoid this and end up with a reuse library that contains components that are too simplistic. The reuse library becomes extremely large, full of reams of components that do effectively the same thing. This makes it very difficult to navigate around the library and find the appropriate component for the job. The software developers become frustrated searching through all the different components and the interface documentation begins to look the same. This also tends to discourage software reuse.

Keys to Success

The key to successfully incorporating a reuse strategy in a company's current process is to provide solutions to the problems that were identified in the previous section. These are not easy problems, and the solutions might require some initial investment, both in cost and time. You won't be able to solve them all at once. You will need to plan them into the company's short- and long-term business plans and goals. You will need to monitor your progress so that you can make adjustments as needed.

The keys to successful software reuse are as follows:

- Establish a separate software reuse group or organization.
- Provide rewards for reusing software.
- Establish short- and long-term software reuse goals for the company.
- Provide good reuse library tools.
- Establish requirements for interface documentation associated with reusable components.
- Provide good configuration management tools for reusable components.
- Establish training courses on the identification, development, and use of reusable components.
- Establish a development process that will allow for and encourage software reuse.

Software reuse organization/group

Many companies try to put the responsibility of establishing and maintaining the software reuse library on a current development project. It makes sense that the best people to write the reusable components would be the programmers that currently are in the development trenches. The problem is that the project typically is under tight budget and schedule limitations that do not allow for the extra work that is associated with developing reusable components.

Developing reusable components requires more thought, documentation, and testing when compared to its nonreused counterpart. Upper management often assumes that "you are developing a queue anyway; just make it reusable." No additional time or money is allocated to the project. The project eventually will be looking for ways to reduce costs and make up schedules due to the typical problems encountered during a development life cycle. Software reuse, more often than not, is the first thing that gets cut in an effort to fix the organization's budget and schedule problems.

A separate group or organization, whose sole responsibility is the development and maintenance of the software reuse library, should be created. As Booch states, "An effective reuse program is best achieved by making specific individuals responsible for the reuse activity" (1994). This can help keep the focus on software reuse. In addition, it also will help future projects by allowing them to make use of the reusable components without putting forth the effort to create them.

This software reuse group should have the following responsibilities:

- Define the interface requirements that are associated with reusable components. This is very important to the success of software reuse as it will have a direct impact on the ease of finding the right reusable component for the job.

- Identify (with suggestions from current users) candidates for reusable components. As mentioned previously, the initial components should be low-level utilities such as stacks and queues. Larger, more complex subsystems can be identified by reviewing the software from existing applications and identifying common pieces of software. This software can be extracted from the older applications and expanded (documentation, code, testing, etc.) to create new reusable components that will be available for future use. Interface documentation will need to be written that conforms to the reusable interface requirements established by the group.

- Research available CASE, CM, browser tools, etc., and determine which ones should be used to implement the reuse library. Today, there are a number of good tools on the market. The company needs to find the tools that meet the requirements for the reuse library as well as the overall development process that is in place.

- The software reuse group would be responsible for producing the documentation (requirements analysis, design, code, as well as the test) associated with the reusable component.

- Develop and execute the tests that are associated with the reusable components. This also would require the analysis and resolution of software problem reports. These problem reports would be generated by the software reuse group (during reviews and testing) and the user groups.

- Research available component libraries. There are many component libraries available from the government, universities, and commercial vendors. Some are better than others. The companies might have different requirements and development processes. The component library that will be the best for one company might not be the best for another.

Provide rewards for reusing software

Many companies base employee reviews, at least in part, on the software developers' productivity. Many companies don't give the software developer the same credit when a reusable component is used instead of developing a new component. The assumption is made that reusable components don't take as much effort. While this might be true, the software developer is faced with the choice of getting more credit for developing a new component or less credit for using a reusable component.

If a company wants to build a library of reusable components, it should not discourage the software developers from using it. If the company gives at least equal credit for the use of reusable components, the software developer might look at reuse as a time saver. It will allow the software developer's productivity to be the same, independent of whether he or she reuses a component or develops it. Using a reusable component is much easier than developing a new one, especially when the reusable component comes complete with full documentation, code, and testing. The software developer will make an extra effort to reuse software, and the company's reusability goals will be within its grasp.

Another form of encouragement would be to offer monetary or recognition rewards to groups that meet or exceed the company's reusability goals for a project. Offer a special award to the person or group that reused the most software. Offer another award to the person or group that identifies reusable components that were used more frequently in other projects. The awards can be anything from a peer recognition plaque to a bonus or even a dinner for two at a special restaurant in the area.

Establish company-wide software reuse goals

A company must establish short- and long-term software reuse goals. You must be able to know where you are headed and if you are staying on course. An analysis should be performed to determine what the current reusability level is and what a good target level is for the next project as well as future projects. If your current reusability level is very low, you should start out simple. For example, try to achieve 20% software reuse on your first project. On the next project, try for 40%, and continue until you are satisfied with your current level of reuse. The target level that you choose should depend on the experience of your staff and the maturity of your development process and the homogeneity of your company's product lines.

High reusability levels will not happen overnight. You will need to spend some time setting up the underlying support structure, training your staff, and changing the mind set of your staff to accept reuse as a necessary part of development.

If you are not reaching a high enough level of reuse within four to eight years, you might end up playing catch-up with your competitors. This is not a comfortable position. You will be in a much better position if you can become proficient at reusing software before your competitor can react. Let them play catch-up with you.

Provide good reuse library tools

To make software reuse a reality, software developers must be able to access the information in a relatively easy way. The CASE, CM, and browser tools must be user-friendly. The tools must allow software developers to navigate through the different components within the reuse library and find the appropriate one that meets their specific requirements.

The tools must allow for changes to the components, while still allowing applications to access prior versions until the application is ready to move up to the latest and greatest version. The newer versions should identify why they were created and what changed from the previous version.

The tools must provide a user-friendly interface. If the tools are too cumbersome to use, software developers will be reluctant to use them and may begin to avoid software reuse altogether.

Establish reusable interface documentation requirements

The requirements for interface documentation that is associated with reusable components also are very important. They are the window into the component itself. This documentation should provide a good brief description of the component as well as how to use it. This goes hand-in-hand with the previous section.

The interface documentation is what software developers will read when they are looking for a specific component that meets a given set of requirements. If the documentation is not clear and consistent, the software developer will have trouble finding the right component for the job. They might end up selecting the wrong component or giving up and designing it themselves. If the documentation is not brief, the software developer will become frustrated, feeling that they are spending too much time reading the fine details of the component. Once again, they might give up and design the component themselves.

The detailed information that describes the component and how to use it will help the developer once he or she decides to use this particular component.

Provide good configuration management tools for reusable components

The CM tool will allow you to continue to upgrade or fix errors with a specific component without impacting the individual projects that are using it. Different projects might be at different stages of development and might not want to upgrade until a time that is convenient to their specific development schedule. The projects might be in the middle of debugging a specific problem and want to limit what is changing until they identify the exact problem. They might want the change to go into a specific build and not affect the current development. The project itself should be using the CM tool for the development of its nonreusable components as well (the justification for this can be found in chapter 12).

Establish reusable components training courses

A company must establish training courses on the identification, development, and use of reusable components. It is important that software developers understand the reuse strategy that is in place. The training will provide some consistency in how it is used. In addition, this training can get the software developers familiar with the browsers, interface requirements, etc., so that they can get up to speed on using the reuse library quicker and more efficiently.

Development process and software reuse

The development process and software reuse should go hand in hand. The company's development process must evolve to the point that software reuse is an integral part of the development. The development process should not make software reuse more difficult to use. The software reuse interface requirements must conform to the process requirements. It must meet all aspects of the requirements set forth by the documentation, standards, and traceability as defined within the process.

Summary

We've discovered that software reuse is much more than simple code reuse. It should address all phases of the development life cycle. When it is used correctly, software reuse will decrease costs, shorten development schedules, and improve the overall quality of your product. We've discussed how object-oriented techniques can affect software reuse and how software reuse can help your prototype efforts.

We used the hardware world as a comparison to get a better understanding of software reuse. Using this analogy, we derived the concepts of "software diodes and transistors" (the individual lines of code), "software ICs" (subprograms), and "software boards" (subsystems).

We looked at the differences between a company that is achieving a reusability level of 20% and one that is achieving 80%. The benefits were quite clear. The amount of work was considerably less for a company achieving a reusability level of 80%. The improved quality will translate into satisfied customers.

We also discussed some of the main costs that are associated with software reuse. The initial investment or "up front" costs should be amortized over all the new projects that make use of reusability. The increased testing that is associated with reusable components is offset by increased product quality and a decrease in the amount of tests that are required on a new project that reuses the software. The costs of maintaining the libraries also can be offset by the number of projects utilizing software reuse.

We looked at how Configuration Management (CM) and Computer Aided Software Engineering (CASE) tools have progressed to the point that software reuse can become a reality. The tools will allow us to implement software reuse more effectively.

We've provided some guidance on how to start developing a reuse library and where to begin reusing components. Starting out with low-level utilities, you can develop reusable packages and subprograms. You can continue by identifying reusable subsystems. We examined the appropriate level of detail for a reusable component and the impact of developing reusable components that are too complicated or too simplistic.

We examined some of the problems encountered when companies try to implement a software reuse strategy. We used the solutions to these problems to develop some keys to success. Following these keys will help ensure that a company will be successful when it incorporates software reuse into its development process.

Software development costs have skyrocketed. They will continue to increase unless something is done to offset them. A company that doesn't develop software reuse strategies and integrate them into its development process will find it difficult to succeed in the 1990s, let alone survive. Software reuse by itself cannot cure all the problems a company may face, but when combined with the other strategies detailed in other chapters, success becomes easier.

References

Anthes, Gary H. December 6, 1993. "Software Reuse Plans bring Paybacks." *Computerworld* 27 (49): 73 (2).

Arthur, Lowell J. 1992. *Rapid Evolutionary Development: Requirements, Prototyping, and Software Evolution.* New York, New York: John Wiley and Sons.

Boehm, Barry. 1981. *Software Engineering Economics*. Englewood Cliffs, New Jersey: Prentice Hall.

Booch, Grady. 1987. *Software Components With Ada: Structures, Tools, and Subsystems*. Menlo Park, California: The Benjamin/Cummings Publishing Company, Inc.

Booch, Grady. 1994. *Object-Oriented Analysis and Design with Applications*. Redwood City, California: The Benjamin/Cummings Publishing Company, Inc.

Bradford, Kain, J. February 1994. "Pragmatics of Reuse in the Enterprise." *Object Magazine*: 55–58.

Griss, M. L. December 1993. "Software Reuse: From Library to Factory." *IBM Systems Journal* 32 (4): 548 (19).

Horner, Ken. May 1993. "More to Reuse than Objects." *Software Magazine* 13 (7): 6 (2).

Prieto-Diaz, Ruben. May 1993. "Status Report: Software Reusability." *IEEE Software* 10 (3): 61 (6).

Rymer, John R. January 1993. "The Case for Reuse (Reusable Software)." *Distributed Computing Monitor* 8 (1): 2.

Santayanna, George. 1906. *The Life of Reason*. Vol. 1, chapter 12, 1906.

Seidewitz, Ed and Mike Stark. 1992. *Principles of Object-Oriented Software Development with Ada*. Rockville, Maryland: Millennium Systems, Inc.

Wasmund, M. December 1993. "Implementing Critical Success Factors in Software Reuse." *IBM Systems Journal* 32 (4): 595 (17).

Yourdon, Edward. 1993. *Decline & Fall of the American Programmer*. Englewood Cliffs, New Jersey: Yourdon Press.

8

Concurrent Programming

Early software system designs were based on a single execution path. High-order programming languages such as Pascal, FORTRAN, C, and COBOL also were based on this sequential view of programming. The real world, unfortunately, is full of asynchronous events that cannot be modeled using a single execution path model. The complexity of mission critical systems also have evolved such that the system is all but impossible to design without using some form of concurrent programming techniques.

The hardware on which the software was executing also continued to become more complex. The advances in hardware have provided the means to execute faster, store more data, run farther, and jump higher than ever before. Software design techniques that would take advantage of the advanced hardware and provide a better model of the real world had to be developed. Because of this, the methods used to model the real world have evolved into software systems that have several individual processes that run, or appear to run, simultaneously. The development of this type of software system is called *concurrent programming*.

Concurrent programming is a very complex skill. Management and developers must understand how concurrency works and what to watch out for to ensure a good solid design. Because concurrent programming is relatively new to most developers, the managers must become familiar with the issues involved in designing systems that are based on concurrent design. They must be able to ask the right questions and provide the right answers with respect to how to design and implement a concurrent system. The developers also must become familiar with the finer aspects of concurrent programming. They must know and understand concurrent programming issues and design techniques so that they can develop a reliable concurrent system.

The issues involved in designing concurrent systems are many. Even the simple idea of using (and abusing) data becomes more complicated when you must allow two separate processes to access the data. When designing concurrent systems, you must be concerned with such issues as deadlock, starvation, mutual exclusion, and race conditions, all of which will be explained later in this chapter. When you introduce concurrency in a system, you must focus on process abstraction and synchronization.

Concurrency is a topic that can fill, and in fact has filled, an entire book. This chapter will serve as an introduction to the concepts behind concurrency as well as some of the major issues involved with its use. The chapter will begin by providing a definition of concurrency. It will continue by discussing how object-oriented techniques can be used in concurrent systems. We will look at how concurrent systems are controlled and the different tasking models that have been used in the past. We will explore the various task communication methods and expand on the meaning of synchronization and mutual exclusion, both of which are important concurrent programming concepts. The dangers associated with concurrent programming will be identified and explained. The chapter concludes by describing some basic ways to identify the tasks within a system.

Definition of Concurrent Programming

"Concurrent systems are those in which two or more activities occur, or appear to occur, at the same time" (Shumate 1988). These activities can be thought of as tasks. Even the simplest software system has at least one task. The one task is the program itself. More complex systems require several tasks.

Let's look at an example. Assume that your company has a receptionist who is responsible for answering the phones, helping customers as they arrive, and filing company memos. Using the processing outlined in Figure 8.1, the receptionist will answer the phone, help a customer, file a memo, answer the phone, help a customer, file a memo, and so on. This processing style eventually will get you in trouble in the real world. If several customers enter at the same time, the last one will be forced to wait through several process cycles before getting any help. There is a good chance that they will just leave and chalk it up as a bad experience. Even worse, what would happen if the receptionist never received a phone call? The receptionist would be stuck waiting to answer the phone, because this step must be completed before moving to the next step of the process. No matter how many customers come in or how many memos needed to be filed, the receptionist will sit and wait for a phone call. Nothing gets done.

The processing shown in Figure 8.1 is known as *sequential processing*. A sequential process is one in which there is a series of operations where each operation is completed before the next one is executed. The series of operations within a process or task also is known as a *thread of control*.

If we use the processing shown in Figure 8.2, the receptionist would be able to perform any one of the tasks independent of which task was executed previously. This would allow them to help customers and file company memos even if no phone calls were received. By allowing individual tasks (Answer Phones, Help Customers, File Memos), you can assign priorities to ensure that things get done in the proper order. In our example, answering phones and helping customers should have a higher priority than filing memos. Even if the memos keep piling up, you don't want to ignore your customers.

The processing shown in Figure 8.2 is known as *parallel* or *concurrent processing*. *Parallel* or *concurrent programs* are programs in which there are several processes or tasks that are executed simultaneously. Each task represents a single thread of control. Therefore, a concurrent program is one in which there are multiple threads of control.

The human brain is an excellent example of a concurrency in action. While you are reading this book, your brain is telling your body to breathe. It determines when you need to turn the page and tells your hand to do it. If the phone rings, you will answer it. You might get sidetracked and end up performing several other tasks before returning to your reading. Your brain is truly capable of handling several tasks at the same time. While your brain is performing all these tasks, it still is capable of responding to any asynchronous interrupts (phone calls, door bell, etc.) that might occur.

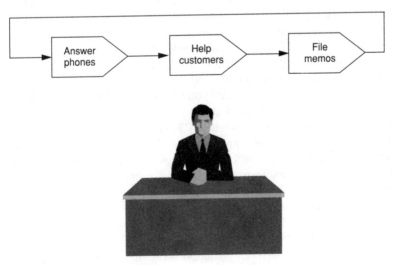

Figure 8.1 Sequential receptionist.

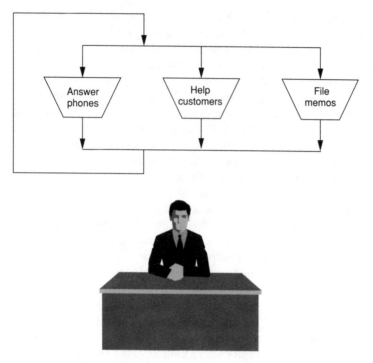

Figure 8.2 Parallel receptionist.

If your system is composed of two or more processors, you can implement true concurrency. If your system is composed of only a single processor, you still can give the appearance of concurrency by interleaving the execution of the threads of control from the various tasks. Although the single processor is limited to executing one instruction at a time, you can execute some instructions from one task, then switch and execute some instructions from a different task. You can continue until you have executed instructions from each task, at which time you would start all over again. Continue this until the program has completed its execution. Most PCs and workstations are based on a single microprocessor architecture. Business applications, which typically are targeted for PCs and workstations, will need to simulate concurrency using a single microprocessor. To get a better understanding of what this means, let's look at another example.

Consider a clothing store in the local mall. Five customers walk in at the same time. The single clerk skillfully moves from customer to customer, providing each with a little help, without neglecting the others. While one customer is in the dressing room trying on some new clothes, the clerk is waiting on another customer. After getting the general description of the style of clothes one customer is looking for, the clerk might ring up another customer's purchase before collecting clothes that meet the first customer's needs. In this case, the clerk is similar to the single processor that, through interleaved execution, is providing the appearance of concurrency. The clerk appears to be helping all the customers at the same time. Each individual customer represents a single task or process.

If you take the same situation with five clerks working in the store, you would have true concurrency. Each of the clerks represents a single processor that is dedicated to helping a specific customer. If you had only three clerks, you would need to distribute the workload (helping the five customers) among the available clerks. You would need to combine the processing shown in Figures 8.1 and 8.2.

From the previous discussion, concurrent systems can be defined as systems in which two or more processes or tasks are executed, or appear to be executed, at the same time. With this definition, we can look at how we can identify and design concurrent systems.

Object-Oriented Techniques with Concurrency

The object-oriented methodology is not the concurrency silver bullet. In fact, "concurrency is not orthogonal to OOP [object-oriented programming] at the lowest levels of abstraction. OOP or not, all the traditional problems in concurrent programming still remain." Lim and Johnson (1993) go on to say, "At the highest levels of abstraction, OOP can alleviate the concurrency problem for the majority of programmers by hiding the concurrency inside reusable abstractions."

Object-oriented programming deals with data abstraction, encapsulation, and inheritance (as discussed in chapter 4), while concurrency focuses upon process abstraction and synchronization. Using object-oriented techniques, objects represent a model or abstraction of a problem-domain or solution domain (real world) entity. In some cases, these objects represent a separate thread of control; this is known as a process abstraction. Booch (1994) refers to these objects as *active objects*. A model of a real world system consists of a set of cooperative objects, some of which are active (Booch 1994).

So how does the object-oriented paradigm address concurrency? In object-oriented designs, there are, in general, three approaches to concurrency, which are discussed in the following paragraphs.

Certain programming languages have incorporated concurrency as an intrinsic feature of the language itself. The Ada *task* provides the means to define a concurrent object. The interface to the task is defined in terms of *entry declarations* and/or *entrance procedures*. Entry declarations and entrance procedures define the points where two tasks can *rendezvous*.

The rendezvous is intrinsic to the Ada programming language. An Ada rendezvous occurs when two tasks combine into a single thread of execution and possibly exchange information. At this point, the two tasks are said to be *synchronized*.

An entrance procedure allows the task to be completely hidden from the caller; the caller won't even know that a task has been called. Ada has no need for a real-time executive and its services. This is due to the intrinsic nature of the rendezvous. Ada uses a hidden run-time system that underlies the Ada tasking model. The run-time system is not visible to the programmer. Therefore, the programmer can focus on the specific activities associated with the tasks.

The Ada tasking model allows the programmer to design the system without worrying about the underlying real-time executive that will be responsible for scheduling the individual tasks.

Ada is not the only programming language that addresses concurrency. Smalltalk provides the *Process* class, which can be used as a superclass for all the task objects. Other object-oriented programming languages include Actors, Orient 84/K, and ABCL/1. These languages also provide mechanisms for concurrency and synchronization.

We can develop a class library that implements several basic task structures. These classes can be used to define individual tasks within the system. This allows us to define reusable, concurrent objects. The advantages of reusable components are discussed in chapter 7. The AT&T task library for C++, which defines the classes Sched, Timer, Task, etc., is based on this concept. This approach does not require a programming language that addresses concurrency specifically. Therefore, no additional burdens are imposed on nonconcurrent systems that you are developing. Even so, it does give the appearance that concurrency is an intrinsic part of the programming language, via the reusable standard classes. This method also will work for COBOL, C, and other languages that do not provide direct support of concurrent programming.

There is one drawback to this approach: it is highly platform-dependent. However, given a set of well-defined reusable components, the library itself will be relatively portable.

We can use an interrupt-driven design to provide the illusion of concurrency. This requires that the designers have a certain amount of knowledge about the low-level features of the underlying hardware. You will need to understand how interrupts are handled by the processor, how to associate a software call to the specific interrupt line, etc.

The advances in operating systems also have encouraged object-oriented design. The more popular operating systems used today provide direct support for concurrency. Unix offers a *fork*, which is a system call that spawns a new process or task. Windows/NT and OS/2 also have provided multithreaded capabilities. These advances have created more opportunity, and demand, for the use of concurrency within object-oriented based systems.

Controlling Concurrent Processes

Controlling concurrent processes typically has been accomplished through the use of a real-time executive, typically based on the model of many tasks executing on a single processor. An executive program determines which task shall execute next based on the current state of the system.

The individual tasks within the system will be in one of many states. The state of the tasks will change during the execution of the program. The tasks can be running, blocked or suspended, ready, or terminated. A task that is running currently is executing on the processor. A blocked or suspended task does not have the necessary resources available for it to execute. A task that is ready has all the necessary resources available but is waiting for the processor. A terminated task has completed its execution and is no longer available or was abnormally shut down, possibly due to processing or execution error.

Using the example shown in Figure 8.2, when the receptionist is filing a memo, the state of the File Memos task is running. If there are no memos to be filed, the state of the File Memos task is blocked or suspended. When a memo becomes ready to be filed but the receptionist is busy helping a customer, the state of the File Memos task will change to ready. At the end of the business day, the receptionist locks the doors and goes home. This is analogous to the system being shut down. All three tasks will change to a state of terminated until the system is restarted the next morning. It is possible to define tasks that do not wait for the system to shut down before entering a state of terminated. You could define a task that, when the receptionist unlocks the door in the morning (restarts the system), will turn the lights on automatically. This is not something that you need to have running all day, so you design it such that it turns the lights on, then terminates.

A *context switch* is what happens when the real-time executive stops executing instructions for one task and begins executing instructions for another task. The stopped task changes its state from running to blocked or suspended, ready, or terminated. The started task switches its state from ready to running. Note that the started task had to be in the ready state for it to be selected by the real-time executive and placed in a running state. Care must be taken to ensure that the real-time executive is provided the opportunity to perform a context switch. In some programming languages, such as Ada, a delay statement can be used to pass control back to the real-time executive, which will reevaluate the state of the system and possibly perform a context switch.

When a context switch occurs, the real-time executive will look at the tasks that are in the ready state. Of these tasks, the executive will select the task with the highest priority (assuming that priorities have been assigned) and change it to the running state. Using Figure 8.2, assume that you assigned a high priority to the Help Customers task and a low priority to the

Filing Memos task. If there is a memo to be filed and a customer walks in (Help Customers and File Memos both in the ready state), the receptionist will help the customer before filing the memo. This is just one way that a scheduler, which uses context switching, can be designed.

Context switching is a relatively costly process. The low-level activities that occur during a context switch include saving of the processor state, including storing the registers for the task that has been in the running state. It also restores the processor state associated with the task that is transitioning to the running state.

Task priorities can be assigned to ensure that the appropriate task is selected during a context switch. This is not a problem when you are using a multiprocessor system in which each processor is not executing more than one task. However, in a uniprocessor system or a multiprocessor system where one or more processors are responsible for executing more than one task, you might need to assign priorities to the individual tasks. In the latter system, there are many different possibilities for interleaving the execution of the individual tasks. Some will work just fine. Other combinations might result in missed deadlines or even starvation or deadlock (which will be discussed later in this chapter). You must be careful when assigning the priorities, as the wrong choice also can lead to starvation or deadlock. Let's look at an example of a system that exhibits deadlock and starvation as a direct result of the priorities that were assigned to the individual tasks.

When I was working in Seattle on an embedded system, we designed a foreground-background structure to implement the system. We used the main procedure to start up all our tasks. We had a relatively large number of tasks, each with its own priority. The main procedure also was considered a task. The main procedure was used to perform our background processing and, as such, was assigned a low priority compared to the foreground tasks. In the lab, we discovered that all the tasks were not getting started. What appeared to be happening is that, as the tasks were started, they were in a ready state. The foreground tasks were at a higher priority than the main procedure. After enough of them were started, the main procedure was not allocated enough time. Some of the foreground tasks that were started ran into problems when they tried to communicate with another foreground task that was not started yet. It was a big mess.

Our first solution was to move our background processing into its own task and increase the priority of the main procedure. This allowed all of the tasks to get started, but it would remain in the running state and not allocate any processor time to the other tasks. We were executing in a loop of two or three machine code instructions that would check to see which task had the highest priority (the main procedure) and set its state to running. We went back to the drawing board.

Our second solution was to keep our background processing in the main procedure, which was assigned a low priority, and to define a separate task to start up the other tasks. The start-up task was given the highest priority. It was designed to start up all of the foreground tasks and terminate. This solution worked, and we saw our system run in the lab.

Rod Skoglund

The task lifetime can be a short moment in time, or it can exist continuously throughout the entire program execution. For example, a task that is designed to initialize a system will initialize the system and cease to exist. It will reach the end of its execution, and the state of the task will be terminated. Once a task is terminated, it cannot be restarted without restarting the system as a whole.

Task Interactions

Tasks can be classified by the type of interaction that they have with other tasks. The different types of tasks are:

- Independent
- Producer-consumer model (including intermediate tasks)
- Reader-writer model

A task that does not communicate with any other tasks is an *independent* task. Independent tasks can run at different rates. Because there is no dependency on other tasks, there is no dependency on the order in which the tasks are run. The three tasks in the receptionist example (Figure 8.2) can be considered independent tasks. None of the tasks rely on information obtained from another task. They can run independently without knowledge of the other tasks in the system.

The *producer-consumer model* of task interaction is one in which information is produced by one task and consumed by another. The task that is the source of the information is called the *producer*, and the task that is the target of the information is called the *consumer*.

A producer task gathers information that will be used by another task. These tasks might involve periodically reading a temperature sensor, accessing memory to collect a new message that has been received from an external system, etc.

A consumer task uses the information that is gathered by the producer task to perform its intended function. The task might store the information in a database, provide output to external device, etc. It might use the information in a calculation that produces new information, in which case the consumer task also is considered a producer task.

The producer-consumer tasks are limited in the amount of asynchronous action that they can maintain. They are tightly coupled by their interaction with each other. One way to decouple the producer and consumer tasks is to use *intermediate* tasks.

Intermediate tasks allow the programmer to control the degree of synchronization between the main tasks that perform the function of the system. The use of intermediate tasks helps decouple the producer and consumer tasks. We can classify intermediate tasks into three categories: buffer, transporter, and relay.

The intermediate tasks are distinguished by their method of passing the information between the producer task and the consumer task. The characteristics of the buffer task, which are shown in Figure 8.3, are that the producer task actively passes the information to the buffer and the consumer actively retrieves the information from the buffer. You can think of it as the producer calls the buffer (passing the information into the buffer), then the consumer calls the buffer (retrieving the information from the buffer).

The characteristics of the transporter task, which are shown in Figure 8.4, are that the transporter actively retrieves the information from the producer task, then actively passes the information to the consumer task. In this case, the transporter does all the calling.

The characteristics of the relay task, which are shown in Figure 8.5, can be one of two possible relationships. The first is where the producer ac-

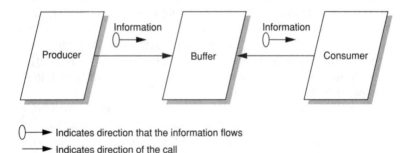

○━━► Indicates direction that the information flows

━━► Indicates direction of the call

Figure 8.3 Buffer task.

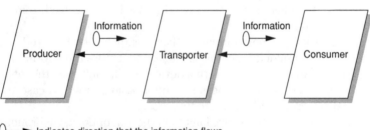

○━━► Indicates direction that the information flows

━━► Indicates direction of the call

Figure 8.4 Transporter task.

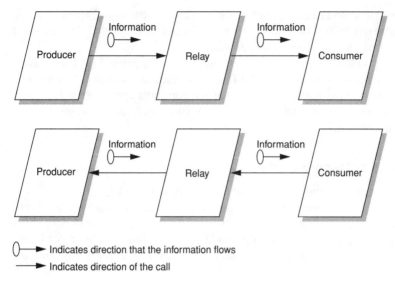

$\underset{\Large 0}{}{\longrightarrow}$ Indicates direction that the information flows

$\longrightarrow$ Indicates direction of the call

Figure 8.5 Relay task.

tively passes the information to the relay, which then actively passes it to the consumer. The second is where the relay actively retrieves the information from the producer while the consumer actively retrieves the information from the relay.

The *writer-reader model* introduces a new twist on task interaction. Can you have some tasks that manipulate the data (writer tasks) and other tasks that merely look at the data (reader tasks)? It does not make sense to limit the readers access when there is no chance for conflict with other tasks that are reading the shared information.

A *writer* task can update or change the state of shared information. You do not want any other task to interrupt the write operation until it is complete. If another task tries to read or write the shared information before the first write operation is complete, you run the chance of corrupting the data.

A *reader* task looks at the value or state of the shared information. Multiple read operations should not interfere with each other. The interaction between reader tasks is similar to independent tasks. They can access the information at different rates even if they both take a peek at it at the same time.

At any given point during the execution of the program, you can allow one writer or one or more readers to access the shared information. Note that you don't want a writer task and a reader task to access the information at the same time. If the write operation is an atomic operation and you are running on a single microprocessor (or if all the write/read operations are executed by a single microprocessor), you can allow multiple writers and readers. An atomic operation is a single, indivisible machine instruction. Typically, a single high-level instruction (assignment, if-then-else, case, etc.) is translated into several machine code instructions.

When you're using concurrent designs, you must define how the individual tasks can access the shared information without interfering with other tasks that need to access the information. You must synchronize the tasks and deal with the problems of mutual exclusion that are inherent in concurrent systems.

Methods of Synchronization

Once you understand how to define the individual tasks, you must determine how the concurrent objects will communicate or synchronize themselves with one another. As Booch (1994) states, "once you introduce [concurrency] into a system, you must consider how active objects synchronize their activities with one another as well as with objects that are purely sequential."

To understand synchronization, you first must understand what is meant by mutual exclusion. *Mutual exclusion* is nothing more than the mechanism by which a task is given exclusive access to a shared resource (Shumate 1988).

Methods of synchronization include semaphores, critical regions, monitors, and rendezvous. Each method has its good points as well as its bad points. Let's look at each method in more detail.

Semaphores

One of the earliest forms of synchronization was introduced by Dijkstra (1968) and is called the *semaphore*. A semaphore is an object that keeps track of the number of active objects (tasks) that are accessing a shared resource. The most common type of semaphore has only two states ("1"–"0," Open–Closed, Locked–Unlocked, etc.). This sometimes is referred to as a *binary semaphore* (Burns and Davies 1993). This type of semaphore will allow only one task to access the shared information at a time.

There are only two operations that are associated with a semaphore. The operations commonly are referred to as the P- and V-operations. The origin of the initials P and V are from the Dutch (Dijkstra's native language) words *Passeren* (to pass) and *Vrygeven* (to release). It is important that the P and V operations are indivisible; that is, they must not be interrupted at any time during the execution of the operation. If one task calls one of the operations, all of the other tasks must not be allowed to call that operation. Prior to using the shared resource, the task must call the P operation. When the task is done using the shared resource, it must call the V operation.

The best way to understand what a binary semaphore is and how it is used is to look at a simple, real-life example. Let's look at the bathroom on an airplane. The bathroom has a lock that controls a sign on the door. When the door is unlocked, the sign reads "Open," and when it is locked, it reads "In Use."

Figure 8.6 shows the normal operation of the bathroom. Initially the bathroom is empty, the door is unlocked, and the sign reads "Open." The first passenger enters the bathroom and locks the door. The sign now reads "In Use." The second passenger arrives and must wait until the first passenger is finished. When the first passenger is done, they will unlock the door (sign now reads "Open") and leave. The next person in line now is able to use the bathroom. This can go on forever, where no more than one passenger is allowed to enter at a time.

Everything sounds so simple, how could anything go wrong? Assume that the first passenger enters the bathroom, but does not lock the door (which still reads "Open"). This scenario is shown in Figure 8.7. The second passenger walks up, sees that the bathroom is open, and goes right on in. Besides being totally embarrassed, you now are faced with two people trying to use the bathroom at the same time. This is not a pretty picture. This also would happen if the first passenger locks the door, but the second passenger ignores the sign and smashes in anyway. The results are the same.

This can happen in software as well. If one task doesn't follow the protocol, you could end up with two tasks trying to access the data at the same

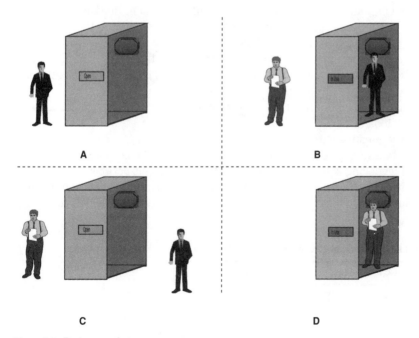

A

B

C

D

Figure 8.6 Basic semaphore.

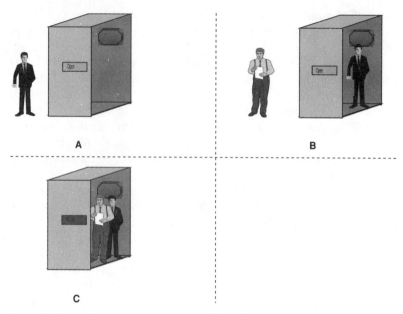

Figure 8.7 Semaphore—ignoring the protocol (part 1).

time. One might try to update (increment, decrement, initialize, etc.) the data at the same time that another task is trying to update the data. Let's look at the case where each task is trying to increment the shared data. Table 8.1 shows what the high-level language might look like.

Everything looks like it will work out. However, if we look at the machine code, we might find that the increment operation is not indivisible. Table 8.2 shows what the machine code associated with the increment actually might look like.

As you can see, the value of "Item" incremented only once even though both tasks tried to increment it. This shows the danger of assuming that high-level language statements are indivisible, atomic actions.

There is yet another example of where the semaphore fails when the protocol is not followed. Assume that a passenger enters the bathroom and

TABLE 8.1 High-Level View of Task Interactions

Step	Action of task 1	Value of data	Action of task 2
1	—	2	—
2	Item := Item + 1	3	—
3	—	4	Item := Item + 1

TABLE 8.2 Low-Level View of Task Interactions

Step	Action of task 1	Value of "item"	Action of task 2
1	—	2	—
2	Load item in register	2	—
3	—	2	Load item in register
4	Add one to the value in the register	2	—
5	—	2	Add one to the value in the register
6	Store value from register to Item	3	—
7	—	3	Store value from register to Item

locks the door (sign changes to "In Use"). The passenger leaves through the window instead of the door. Besides having the problem of negotiating the first step (which is a doozy), the bathroom will remain locked until someone else ignores the protocol and breaks it down. This scenario is shown in Figure 8.8.

Both failures show the importance of requiring that the tasks follow the protocol. You must rely on the integrity of the individual tasks.

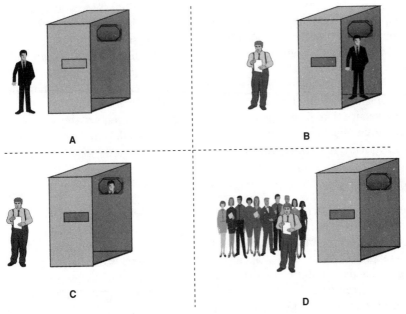

Figure 8.8 Semaphore—ignoring the protocol (part 2).

The other type of semaphore is called the *general* or *counting semaphore* (Burns and Davies 1993). The general semaphore can take an arbitrary nonnegative integer value. The semaphore keeps track of the number of times that it is entered and the number of times that it is exited. This type of semaphore is useful when implementing a producer-consumer model.

Assume that we are using a buffer as intermediate storage for the shared data (Figure 8.3). The consumer must not be allowed to retrieve the data from the buffer until the producer has stored the data in the buffer. The producer can store new information on the buffer, without the consumer retrieving it, until the buffer is full. Therefore, we cannot let a consumer retrieve information from an empty buffer, and we cannot let a producer store information onto a full buffer. The general semaphore can be used to ensure that these two hold true.

Critical regions

A *critical section* is a sequence of statements that must be treated as a single atomic action. In other words, this sequence of statements must be executed in mutual exclusion. You must never allow two or more tasks to enter a critical section at the same time. The code in the critical section accesses shared information that must be protected. The shared information could become corrupt if two tasks try to update it at the same time. Access to the shared information should be limited to the critical section.

A *critical region* is a critical section that is protected automatically by the compiler. The compiler recognizes the critical section and ensures that it is executed in mutual exclusion. This eliminates the problems that are associated with tasks that ignore protocols and programming errors. Examples of programming errors that might occur include forgetting to use the semaphore that is associated with the critical section, misplaced semaphore operations, and so on. The automated nature of critical regions makes them more secure than using semaphores. Critical regions require the support of a programming language that can offer the automated, compile-time checks to implement the critical region.

Monitors

Semaphores and critical regions work on separately defined, shared data. They cannot control access to the data. As we have seen before, a programming error can jeopardize the integrity of the data that is protected by a semaphore. A critical region can ensure mutual exclusion while it is working on the data, but it cannot protect it from access outside the region.

A *monitor* encapsulates the shared data structure and therefore the shared data itself. The monitor maintains complete control over data by limiting access to only those routines that the monitor has made accessible to the outside world. The shared data structure is defined within the monitor and is not known by the external tasks that might use the shared data. If the original data structure is an array and you (the designer of the monitor) decide to change it to a record structure, the external tasks would not know it had changed.

The data structure is not directly visible to the outside world and the data can be accessed only via the exported routines. Therefore, the programmer designing the external tasks cannot, either by mistake or malicious intent, compromise the integrity of the shared data. All the code that manipulates the data is located in one place.

Rendezvous

A *rendezvous* occurs when two asynchronous tasks are combined into a single thread of control (possibly exchanging information) at which time the tasks are said to be synchronized. The rendezvous addresses both synchronization and communication between tasks.

A rendezvous occurs when Task A calls Task B and Task B accepts the call. There are several ways to control this interaction between the tasks. The notion of rendezvous is incorporated in the Ada tasking model. This language provides a lot of flexibility to the programmer. It allows the programmer to define how the rendezvous will occur, which task (calling or called), if any, will wait for the other, and the direction that the information will be passed. This is accomplished by defining such protocols as selective waits, conditional guard statements, unconditional entry calls, conditional entry calls, and timed entry calls.

The code that is executed during the rendezvous sometimes is referred to as the *critical code*. It is a form of a critical region in that the compiler will ensure that one and only one rendezvous will be accepted at a time. The Ada compiler automatically creates buffers that will store the calls to the rendezvous and will create the code that will enqueue new calls and dequeue the next call when the current rendezvous is complete.

Hidden Dangers of Concurrency

There are many hidden dangers that are introduced when you design a concurrent system. These dangers can bring a system to its knees. They can remain hidden in a system that has worked for years and don't appear until you make a minor maintenance modification. (The code changes that were made might have absolutely nothing to do with the code associated with the tasks.) The shift in the object code that is produced might be all that it takes to uncover the problem. Understanding these dangers and using good concurrent design techniques will ensure that your system is safe. The three major problems to watch out for are: deadlock, starvation, and race conditions.

Deadlock occurs when two or more tasks are stuck waiting for a shared resource that will never become available. The example in the section "Semaphores" and Figure 8.8 is an example of deadlock. After the passenger exits through the window, all of the other passengers are stuck waiting for the bathroom, which will remain locked.

Starvation occurs when a task is not given execution time, even though it is ready, for an arbitrarily long time. This can be attributed to task prioritization or other tasks hogging a shared resource. Low-priority tasks can become starved if the processor is spending most of its available time servicing high-priority tasks. If the condition is bad enough, such that the low-priority tasks do not get any running time, the low-priority tasks will become deadlocked. If too many tasks are trying to access a specific shared resource, some of the tasks might become starved. Once again, if the situation becomes bad enough, you might end up with deadlocked tasks.

Assume that you are using a foreground-background design for the receptionist example shown in Figure 8.2. The Answer Phones and Help Customer tasks are considered foreground tasks, and the File Memos task will be the background task. If the receptionist gets memos at a rate of 10 per hour and one customer comes in and one phone call occurs every hour (on average), the receptionist won't have any problem keeping up on filing. What would happen if the receptionist had a day where there was an average of 40 customers and 40 phone calls per hour? Would all the memos get filed? The File Memos task might get some of the receptionist's time, but it wouldn't be enough to keep up with all the memos that are coming in. In this case, the File Memos task is getting starved.

The third dangerous situation to be aware of is a *race condition*. A race condition occurs when the results of program execution, with a given set of inputs, can be influenced by the relative speeds of two tasks (Shumate 1988). The situation shown in Table 8.2 shows an example of a race condition. The relative speeds of the processors associated with the two tasks will impact the value of the shared data "Item." This is because, at the machine code level, the increment operation is not an atomic action. The value of "Item," after being incremented by the two tasks, depends on the order in which the tasks increment "Item." If one task completes the increment operation before the other, the value of "Item" will be 4. If they both try to increment "Item" at the same time, the value of "Item" will be either 3 or 4, depending on how the machine code instructions are interleaved.

Task Identification

When designing a system, how do you know if you should use a concurrent design? Even more important, how do you identify the concurrent or active objects? It turns out that, as with most design issues, the answer depends on the preferences of the programmer who is responsible for designing the system. There is not a single correct way to define the tasks within a system. The definition of the tasks also is driven by the requirements imposed on the system and the environment in which the system will be run.

The environment in which the system will reside often will dictate the design of the concurrent system. The requirements imposed on the system by the external hardware and software systems will help define what types of concurrent objects are needed. Gomaa (1984) identified six criteria for identifying tasks within a system. These six are as follows:

- Input/output (I/O) dependencies—The interface with I/O devices is defined by the speed characteristics of the I/O device itself. Interfacing with these types of devices requires some sort of polling or interrupt mechanism to communicate with and control the device.

- Time-critical functions—Some system requirements might state that a given operation is executed at a fixed rate. A concurrent process must be used to allow the program execution to be interrupted so that the time-critical function can be executed.

- Computationally intensive functions—These functions typically are time-consuming and have a lower priority when compared to time-critical functions. By defining a process to control these functions, you are able to define the appropriate priority relative to the other tasks within the system.

- Functional cohesion—These are required to reduce excessive inter-process communication. The intermediate tasks identified earlier in this chapter are examples of functional cohesion.

- Temporal cohesion—A system might require that a set of activities occur together as a unified operation. When one function is executed, they all must be executed. A task can be used to group the activities together and ensure that they are all executed together.

- Periodic execution—This is a special case of temporal cohesion where the activities must be executed at a set rate. In many cases, the different activities are not related. An example would be if the system requires that several things happen at 10 Hz. You might be required to refresh some data, test a set of flags that might drive the state of the system, and update a relay—all performed at a 10-Hz rate. Once again, a task can be defined such that it is called at a 10-Hz rate and that all these activities are performed.

A system that is interrupt-driven also can help identify appropriate tasks within the system. You will need to define/design the interrupt service routines (ISR). In most cases, you want the ISR to be very short to allow other interrupts to occur and make sure that they are all handled. The ISR will need to retrieve any information from the shared data, signal the tasks that will process the data, reset the hardware interrupt, and become ready to accept the next interrupt. The ISRs are very hardware dependent and, therefore, are less likely to be as portable as other tasks that are defined.

As a final note, there is a classic concurrency problem known as the Dining Philosophers Problem (there are several variations on this theme). It provides a good, noncomputer-oriented look at solving a concurrency-related problem. It can be found in almost any book on concurrency. You can find a complete definition and solution in *Concurrent Programming* (Burns and Davies 1993).

There are many different ways to solve the problem. The different solutions help bring home the concepts behind concurrency as well as the issues involved in designing a concurrent system.

The Dining Philosophers problem, in a nutshell, is this: You have a set number of Chinese philosophers sitting at a round dining table. The table has some chopsticks sitting on the table along with a large bowl of rice. The number of chopsticks is the same as the number of philosophers. Between each set of two philosophers is a single chopstick (philosopher, chopstick, philosopher, chopstick, etc.). A philosopher must possess two chopsticks before he or she can eat, and he or she is only allowed to grab chopsticks that are adjacent to him or her. The philosophers are allowed to pick up or put down only one chopstick at a time.

As you can see from the problem statement, not all of the philosophers can eat at the same time. If they all pick up one chopstick, none of them will be able to eat (they need two, and their neighbor has the other one). This tends to bring home the idea of starvation and deadlock.

There is no single correct solution to this problem. I have seen this example used in several classes. The students came up with some very inventive solutions. When this problem is assigned in a class, you get the chance to see that there are several solutions. We'll leave it to the reader to try some different solutions to this problem.

Summary

Concurrent programming is a very powerful tool that allows us to model the real world and take advantage of the advanced hardware being designed today. The latest programming languages and operating systems provide mechanisms that simplify the design of concurrent systems. Concurrent systems are defined as systems in which two or more processes or tasks are executed, or appear to be executed, at the same time. Object-oriented techniques allow us to define reusable abstractions, and the majority of programmers can focus on designing the system without worrying about the concurrency issues. Concurrent processes can be controlled via prioritization and an understanding of the states that a task can be in. The task lifetime can be short, in which it executes its instructions and then terminates, or it can span the entire execution of the program.

We explored the different types of tasks and tasking models that are in use today. Tasks can be decoupled by using intermediate tasks to establish a communication path between the tasks. Mutual exclusion and synchronization must be addressed to allow the different tasks to share information. Designing concurrent systems is not without dangers. There are many conditions that must be addressed if the system is going to operate properly. Finally, we provided some basic ways to identify appropriate concurrent objects within a given system.

References

Booch, Grady. 1987. *Software Components With Ada: Structures, Tools, and Subsystems.* Menlo Park, California: The Benjamin/Cummings Publishing Company, Inc.

Booch, Grady. 1994. *Object-Oriented Analysis and Design with Applications.* Redwood City, California: The Benjamin/Cummings Publishing Company, Inc.

Burns, Alan and Goeff Davies. 1993. *Concurrent Programming.* Workingham, England: Addison-Wesley Publishing Company.

Dijkstra, E. W. 1968. *Cooperating Sequential Processes, in Programming Languages,* edited by F. Genuys, Academic Press, New York, pp. 43–112.

Gomaa, H. (1984). "A Software Design Method for Real-Time Systems." *Communications of ACM,* 12(10), 576–580.

Lim, J. and R. Johnson.1993. "The Heart of Object-Oriented Concurrent Programming." *SIGPLAN Notices* 24(4): 165.

Seidewitz, Ed and Mike Stark. 1992. *Principles of Object-Oriented Software Development with Ada.* Rockville, Maryland: Millennium Systems, Inc.

Shumate, Ken. 1988. *Understanding Concurrency in Ada.* New York, New York: Intertext Publications/Multiscience Press, Inc.

9

Object-Oriented Programming

> *It is likely that the popularity of object-oriented programming stems in part from the hope, as was the hope for many previous innovations in computer software development, that this new technique will be the key to increased productivity, improved reliability, fewer cavities, and a reduction in the national debt.*
>
> BUDD (1991)

A number of good books (Booch 1994 and Rumbaugh et al., 1991 for example) explain various object-oriented methodologies from a relatively theoretical point of view. What we offer in this chapter is an introduction to object-oriented programming, as well as some of the insights that we've gained from life in the object-technology trenches. Learning theories and notation is a good start, but it often takes ingenuity and compromise to make things work in the real world.

Objects

In the most basic sense, an object is a person, place, or thing. Indeed, candidate objects within a system often are determined by finding the nouns in the requirements and identifying the possible relationships between them.

In the object-oriented paradigm, an object, or class, generally is defined as an encapsulation of a data type and/or data store with all of the routines that operate on it. An object has specific states, such as "open," "closed," "on," or "off." An object also has behavior such as "start computation," "close connection," or "send message." Finally, an object has an identity that makes it unique within a class of related objects. For example, "books" is a class of objects, and within that class, a single book object might be uniquely identified by a number of attributes such as title, subject, author, and publisher.

The term "object" can have a dual meaning in object-oriented circles, because it can mean either one specific instance of an object within a class of objects or the class itself. In analyzing requirements, it is common practice to initially identify representative objects. These usually become classes as the analysis process proceeds.

Abstraction

Objects, as we know, model persons, places, or things in the real world. For example, an object could be a "customer." A customer, as a human being, has hair color, height, weight, hopes, dreams, loves, and many other attributes. In the system being designed, however, the developers probably are interested only in how much money a customer has, how much the customer has purchased in the past, whether or not the customer pays bills on time, and perhaps the customer's name, address, and telephone number so that he or she can be billed.

In other words, object-oriented system developers usually are not interested in a "real" object but instead are concerned only about an "abstraction" of a customer that fits into the design. These abstractions of entities in the real world often are called *abstract data types*. Here's an example of an abstract data type in pseudocode:

```
customer class
   attributes
      total amount purchased to date
      account balance
      total number of past-due billings
      string name
      string address
      string phone
   methods
      get name
      edit name
      get address
      edit address
      get phone
      edit phone
      total amount purchased to date
      account balance
      total number of past-due billings
      determine if this is a good customer
   end
```

The States of the Art

One way to look at the behavior of an object is through its states. An object changes states according to a set of events that can occur. For example, an object that models a switch might have two possible states: OFF and ON. If the current state of the switch is ON, the state can be changed to OFF by an event such as "turn switch off." Conversely, the state can be changed to ON by the "turn switch on" event. This simple example can be illustrated by means of a *state diagram* (Figure 9.1).

In the previous switching example, the state of the object could have been dependent on the value of only one attribute, but the state of an object often is an aggregation of its attributes. A complex object might have many attributes, and several of them might be combined to determine a state. For example, as Rumbaugh et al., (1991) explain, a bank can be in either a state of solvency or insolvency. The state of the bank depends upon whether the sum of its assets exceeds the sum of its liabilities. In the "customer" abstraction in the preceding section, whether a customer is in a "good" or "bad" state at any given moment is determined by a combination of monetary factors. A good customer buys a lot of merchandise, has a lot of money, and pays bills on time.

The analysis of a model through states and events is invaluable in designing complex control systems but is of questionable usefulness for data-centric systems such as those focused on interactions with a database. Many systems lie somewhere in between these two extremes, and in these cases, state analysis is a useful tool for parts of a given system and not for others.

Attributes

It's been explained previously that structured design is procedure-driven, and object-oriented design is focused primarily on data. The data that an object-oriented design centers on is contained in objects as *variables*, or *attributes*. In this sense, a class is like a C "struct" or a "record" in COBOL or Pascal. Of course, classes in C++ and other object-oriented languages also contain member routines that operate on the object and can change its state by manipulating its attributes. In a pure object-oriented system, attributes can be accessed only through defined operations within the class.

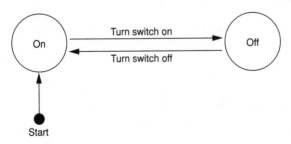

Figure 9.1 State transition diagram for a switch.

Class attributes can be almost infinitely complex, because they usually are classes themselves, as in the following C++ example:

```
#include "another_class.h"
#include "yet_another_class.h"
class someclass
{
    private:
        // attributes
        another_class        ac;
        yet_another_class    yac;
    public:
        // member functions — operations
        do_something_with_another_class();
        do_something_with_yet_another_class();
};
```

Methods in the Madness

The work an object does is accomplished by *routines* or *methods* that are made visible to other objects through a public interface. In general, methods are encapsulated into a class along with corresponding data elements, as in this example:

```
a_demo class
    attributes:
        data element A
        data element B
    methods:
        function A
        function B
end
```

Methods fall into four general categories:

- *Constructors*, which set the initial values of data elements in an object.
- *Destructors*, which delete an object of a specific class.
- *Selectors*, which retrieve values from the data elements within a class.
- *Modifiers*, which change data elements in the class.

All of these method types are illustrated in the following C++ example:

```
class transceiver
{
    public:
        transceiver( frequency_type tf,
                     frequency_type rf,
                     transmission_type *rq,
                     transmission_type *tq );      // constructor
            ~transceiver ();                       // destructor
            int send( transmission_type transmission );   // modifier
```

```
    transmission_type receive ();                               // modifier
    set_transmission_frequency( frequency_type *frequency ); // modifier
    set_receiving_frequency( frequency_type *frequency );    // modifier
    frequency_type* get_transmission_frequency ();           // selector
    frequency_type* get_receiving_frequency ();              // selector
private:
    frequency_type transmission_frequency;
    frequency_type receiving_frequency;
    transmission_type *receive_queue;
    transmission_type *transmit_queue;
};
```

Of the eight functions or methods in this example, five access specific data elements. The data elements are private and can be manipulated only through methods defined on the object interface. The "~transceiver" function is there to clean up the loose ends when a transceiver object goes out of scope. The C++ constructor in this class is called "transceiver," and it sets initial values for all of the data elements in the class.

Four functions modify data elements. The "send" function changes the transmit queue by adding a new element to it, and "receive" removes a message from the receive queue, thus modifying the queue.

Two functions retrieve or select data elements from the class without making modifications. The "get_send_frequency" and "get_receiving_frequency" functions return the current value of the frequencies.

Often objects and methods are obvious from the requirements. An object sometimes is described as something that can be kicked (a sign or a gate, for example), and a method is the thing that performs the kicking (open gate, reset sign). If the nouns in the requirements translate into objects and classes, the verbs often become methods.

Requirements can give us a good idea of the methods that we need, but we need to determine additional methods though scenarios and prototypes. Scenarios and prototypes also aid in determining which methods belong in which classes.

As the functional requirements of a system change, there's a temptation to add new methods into an existing object, even if the new method doesn't quite fit. If you constantly are adding methods and data elements to a class, it could be a sign that you need to redesign some classes.

Encapsulation

The whole object-oriented process drives toward one main goal: intelligently partitioned source code. All object-oriented languages facilitate the partitioning of a system into categories of objects. No matter how elegant a set of object diagrams and descriptions is, it has to be modeled using the class representation provided by a language. The primary reason for drawing diagrams and writing descriptions is to partition the source code into classes, packages, objects, or some other language-supported, object-oriented construct.

Constructs such as classes offer a level of organized information hiding unknown in structured languages. The implementation of all the methods in the class, as well as all data structures, are hidden within the class. Only those methods that are needed by other classes are visible through a strictly enforced interface.

A well-designed object in an object-oriented system is a self-contained, autonomous entity. Objects contain data and all of the routines necessary for operating on that data. This means that a well-designed object can easily execute within its own process.

If objects are well designed, then their work is well coordinated, and one object will not attempt to directly access data in another object (some languages enforce this at compilation). Objects interact with each other by activating routines within other objects to access and transform data.

Inheritance

Once a useful class of objects has been created, the first thing that the average developer would like to do is make changes to it. The usual copy-and-change-the-code paradigm leads both to reinventing the wheel and a proliferation of hard-to-maintain objects. What most developers would like is the ability to derive a new class directly from an old one, gaining some new functionality and keeping the capabilities of the old class.

This capability is implemented in object-oriented languages largely by means of *inheritance*. Inheritance allows a developer to take one or more existing library classes and derive a new class without copying or modifying the library. The new class has the functionality of the parent classes, plus any additional functionality that a programmer wants to add. The new class then can be added to the library, and additional new classes can be derived from it. Here's an example of inheritance in C++:

```
class basic_sign
{
    base_function_A();
    base_function_B();
    ...
};
class parking_sign : public basic_sign
{
    added_function_A();
    added_function_B();
    ...
};
```

In some cases, it is advantageous to create a new class by inheriting from two or more existing classes. Called *multiple inheritance*, this approach is not supported in all object-oriented languages and can cause considerable confusion when it comes to determining the origin or any given member function. It can be difficult to understand and maintain two or more inheritance hierarchies or to figure out where a function is defined. This is especially true if a function can take several different forms during execution (polymorphism). However, there are a few circumstances in which multiple inheritance is appropriate. The following example illustrates the basics of multiple inheritance in C++:

```
class telephone
{
    // telephone functions
    ...
};
class television
{
    // television functions
    ...
};
class videoconference : public television, public telephone
{
    // other functions not covered by television or telephone
    ...
};
```

Polymorphism

The idea that the same piece of code can execute in many different ways (called *polymorphism*) is almost as old as computer science itself. The first time that a programmer used a branch and a jump to a label, the concept that a program could run differently depending upon the data that it fetched was born. Later, "if-then-else" and "case" statements made it possible to create programs that made complex decisions during runtime. Programmers seemed to have all of the tools necessary to create flexible software. Then came object technology, bringing an entirely new meaning to adaptable, reusable software through polymorphism.

One of the beauties of inheritance is that a "hierarchy" of components can be created. Within this hierarchy, all of the components share the capabilities of those from which they inherited. This is roughly analogous to the role of genetics in biology. This means that *all* classes of the same parentage have abilities to respond to the same messages—in whatever way is necessary. For example, if child components C1 and C2 have the same parent, P1, both C1 and C2 can have the same methods as P1, except that these methods, as necessary, can execute differently, and additional methods can be added to the children.

The I/O requirements for a system can offer a more concrete example of this feature. Suppose we define a class called "broadcast." Its role in the system is to send data to the outside world. The data can be sent via different media, such as radio frequency, telephone, e-mail, print, etc. The pseudocode for the parent class might look something like this:

```
broadcast class
    send (data_block)
    ...
end
```

A child class now can be added for each medium required:

```
radio_frequency class inherits from broadcast
    send (data_block)
    ...
end
telephone class inherits from broadcast
    send (data_block)
    ...
end
email class inherits from broadcast
    send (data_block)
    ...
end
print class inherits from broadcast
    send (data_block)
    ...
end
```

Each of these media implements "send" differently and overwrites the "send" in the parent class.

Now, suppose you had a list of broadcasts. Each broadcast could be any one of the subclasses defined earlier. To send all of the broadcasts in the list, all that is necessary is to traverse the list and execute "send" for each broadcast. The system automatically will figure out which "send" to use. This is polymorphism based not on control structures such as case statements but on the very nature of an object. This makes it easier to write and debug code (providing a good object-oriented debugger is used), reducing the amount of logic that must be developed and understood. Polymorphism is extremely useful in modeling real-world objects, such as I/O devices.

Persistence

One of the major characteristics of an object-oriented system, or almost any nontrivial system, is the ability for entities that are created by the system to continue to exist on disk files after the program has finished execution. In an object-oriented system, this feature, called *persistence*, means that se-lected objects continue to exist until they're explicitly deleted, whether the process that they're in is executing or not. In the days when COBOL-74 ruled the Earth, persistence generally meant simply reading and writing files. In modern times, simpler systems still use this approach. In today's complex systems, persistence often is achieved through the use of a data-base management system.

A DBMS is not the only way to go, however. If a query language, report generator, and versioning and other advanced data management capabilities are not needed, other options make sense. A library that supports persistent data storage, such as the collection classes in the Microsoft Foundation Library, works very well in simpler cases. In some systems, all that might be needed are disk I/O capabilities such as those provided in C++ iostreams.

Analysis and Modeling

The raw material for the object model is in the requirements specification. Digging through the requirements specification to find information about objects, attributes, methods, persistence, inheritance, polymorphism, and relationships between objects and filling in the missing details is what requirements analysis is all about. The end product of requirements analysis is a good object model. The complete object model really consists of a static definition of objects and relationships along with a dynamic model of how the objects interact to fulfill customer requirements.

The static model

The *static model* is a detailed graphical and textual representation of all of the classes and objects in the system. It partitions the requirements into classes of objects that (ideally) have a one-to-one mapping to the customer's world. The object model is roughly the equivalent of structure charts and dataflow diagrams in a structured methodology. It also is similar (but certainly not identical) in concept to the entity relationship diagrams relational database architects use to partition a system into tables of records.

The initial key to success in the object-oriented paradigm is to identify the objects and classes of objects in the system. In a complex system, it can be extremely difficult to correctly divide the system into entities that both map to the real-world elements in the customer's domain, yet support the solution developers are creating in software.

This generally involves many iterations of definition and redefinition of the object model. The objects that are identified will form the basis of encapsulation, inheritance, and polymorphism in the model and eventually will lead to defining the relationships between objects. Initially, every noun, implied or explicit, in the requirements document is a candidate object.

The dynamic model

After an initial set of objects has been identified and while the relationships between objects are being determined, the object interactions needed to accomplish the tasks the customer has specified must be determined. This often is done via a set of "use-cases" or "scenarios" that map the customers' "problem space" to the developers' "solution space."

Our primary tools in developing the object model are a good set of requirements and some detailed scenarios that accurately portray how the system will be used. A scenario is a method-by-method representation and description of what happens when an external event, also known as a *message*, triggers a reaction in the system. An example of this is a driver entering his debit card into the card reader so the gate to the parking garage will open.

Through requirements and scenarios, we can flesh out the system with functions, or methods, for each object. A complete set of scenarios often is called an "object message analysis" or a "domain model" because it illustrates the behavior of objects in the users' domain. The scenarios illustrate this behavior by showing when and how each method must be invoked in every object.

As the model is being created and refined, the elements of implementation must be considered, such as prototyping, concurrent execution, network access, reusable-component libraries, etc. How well these elements work with the object model and how well the object model maps the customers' world often are what determine the success or failure of a project.

Examples

To demonstrate the object-oriented concepts that have been discussed so far, the requirements that were defined in chapter 2 will be examined in this section, along with the practical considerations that are involved in transforming the requirements into an object model. This process starts with identifying the objects and methods that are needed to fulfill the requirements, then determining the relationships between objects. A very simple notation is used for these examples.

Arrows indicate the relationships, a single object means there is only one object, and a stack of rectangles means a class of objects. In the scenarios, a labeled arrow means that the object pointed to by the arrow head is visible to the object on the opposite end in the sense that the label indicates. In terms of C++, a class would "#include" the header file for the class to which the arrow points:

```
#include "class_at_arrowhead.h"
class class_at_arrowtail ....
...
```

The Ada method of granting visibility is the "with" statement:

```
with class_at_arrowhead;
package class_at_arrowtail....
...
```

In the scenarios provided, the labels on the arrows indicate methods that exist in the class to which the arrow points. These methods are called by the class at the tail of the arrow.

Only a few of the many possible scenarios are illustrated in these examples—just enough to give a flavor of what analysis through scenarios is all about.

In our very simple notation (VSN), the objects/classes are represented as three-dimensional objects if they correspond to a physical object in the customer's domain. If the object exists only inside the system or the solution space, it is represented by a rectangle. A class of such objects is represented as a stack of rectangles.

The examples presented here are not complete. They are included only to illustrate some of the practical aspects of transforming requirements into a design. The trace anchor numbers in the examples refer to the examples in chapter 2.

An objective look at bug tracking

Transforming the bug tracking system example presented in chapter 2 into an object model involves first identifying the potential objects in the system, then determining the relationships between those objects and the methods that are needed for each object to accomplish its tasks.

An examination of the requirements yields the following list of candidate objects:

- Software trouble report (STR)
- Software repair report (SRR)
- Database
- A report on open STRs
- A report on all STRs and SRRs

The following four objects are included in the model but represent foreign systems with which the STR system must interface:

- Software quality assurance
- Customer support personnel
- Standard configuration management system
- Customer

Not all of these are real objects, and they will disappear when the three-way test is applied. One view of the static object model is shown in Figure 9.2. Included in the model are the relationships between these objects, as well as their attributes and methods can now be determined as we refine the model with scenarios like the following.

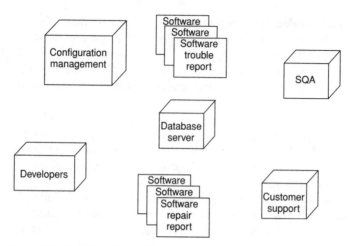

Figure 9.2 Candidate objects for the bug-tracking system.

Scenario

Assume that we already have entered an STR that has only one corresponding SRR and an SRR that corresponds to only one STR. To close out the SRR and the STR, we must do the following (Figure 9.3):

1. The developer must complete the required software repairs on the appropriate files and finish filling out the SRR, including the locations of the changed files.
2. The files must be stored into the configuration management system.
3. The SQA authority approves the SRR.
4. The SRR then is closed out, signaling that it has been completed.
5. The SQA authority approves the STR corresponding to the SRR.
6. The database server then automatically closes out the STR.

Relationships. In chapter 2, trace anchor STRS0004 gives some valuable clues about the relationship between STRs and SRRs. From this, we know that there is a many-to-many relationship between STRs and SRRs. We know that the database will consist of STRs and SRRs, which have the relationship illustrated by Figure 9.4. Other relationships that we can determine from chapter 2 are that developers, SQA, and customer support use the database.

Attributes. Some of the objects that were defined as pertaining to an STR are merely attributes because they don't have independent behavior. As stated in trace anchor STRS0002, the following are attributes contained in an STR:

- A unique STR number
- A description of the problem
- A priority code between 1 and 5 (1 is highest, 5 is the lowest)
- The date of creation for this STR in *mm/dd/yy* format
- A status of either repaired or unrepaired
- The name of the customer who reported the bug
- The name of the customer-support person who entered the report
- The name of the software product to which the STR applies
- The version of the software product to which the STR applies
- The name of the hardware platform on which the customer was using the software product

Some loose ends need to be tied up before we have the correct idea of what an STR is supposed to look like. To implement the relationship between SRRs and STRs as specified in requirement STRS0004, we need to add the following attribute: a list of corresponding SRRs. Because requirement STRS0011 specifies that the subsystem will appear on the report, we need to add an attribute to identify it: the name of the subsystem to which

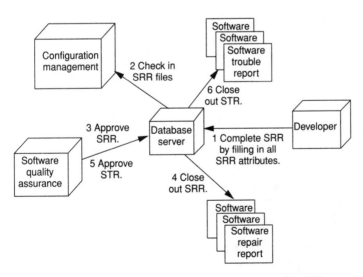

Figure 9.3 Scenario for closing out an SRR and the corresponding STR.

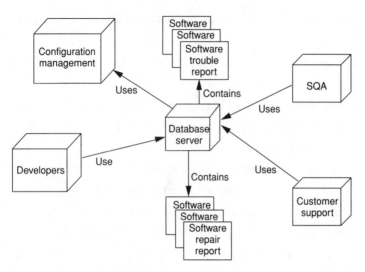

Figure 9.4 A static model for the bug-tracking system.

this STR applies. After these additions, the STR class of objects could be implemented like this:

```
software_trouble_report class
    attributes:
        STR number
        problem description
        priority code
        date of creation
        repair status
        name of reporting customer
        customer-support person
        software product name
        version
        hardware platform name
    methods:
        create
        remove
        edit description
        close out
        get STR number
        set priority
        get priority
        set date
        get date
        set status
        get status
        set customer name
        get customer name
        set customer-support name
        get customer-support name
        set product name
        get product name
        set version
```

```
        get version
        set hardware platform
        get hardware platform
end
```

Software repair reports. Just like an STR, the elements of a Software Repair Report (SRR), which were listed in the requirements in chapter 2, also are attributes of the SRR class, due to the fact that none of them have independent behavior:

- A unique six-digit identification number
- The STR number of each of the corresponding trouble reports
- A textual description of the repair
- The names of all files updated to carry out the repair
- The date of creation for this SRR in *mm/dd/yy* format
- A field for SQA approval
- The name of the subsystem to which this SRR applies

```
software_repair_report class
    attributes:
        SRR number
        STR numbers
        description
        updated files
        date
        SQA approval
        subsystem
    methods:
        create
        remove
        edit
        generate report
        close out
        get SRR number
        get STR number from list
        edit description
        add file name
        delete file name
        set date
        get date
        set subsystem
        get subsystem
        approve SRR
end
```

Files are mentioned in the requirements specification in chapter 2 but might or might not be objects in our system. Because we know the files will be stored in the standard configuration management system, files can be viewed as merely attributes of the CM system. In general, files have no independent behavior, although they have a state (open, closed, locked, etc.)

and can be uniquely identified by file name. Files also could be attributes of the Software Repair Report class.

The database. Because requirement STRS0013 states that we'll need to store data for up to a year after an STR is resolved, we know that data persistence is a major requirement. From this, we know a database will be needed. (We really didn't need formal requirements to figure this out, did we?) In addition, requirements STRS0011 and STRS0012 dictate the need for the system to produce a report of unresolved STRs at specified levels of criticality and a complete report of all STRs and SRRs pertaining to a specific product, version, platform, and subsystem.

We also know from STRS0011 and STRS0012 that reports of various database activities must be supported. Knowing that user's needs will expand in the future, we also could easily derive the requirement that a report-generation facility should be supported. This would be easy to do with a good database management system but extremely difficult without one.

Although it isn't mentioned explicitly in the requirements, we know from experience and conversations with customers that the system will be accessed simultaneously by many users, so a multiuser paradigm such as a client-server architecture is needed. Any database management system that we use therefore must support distributed access.

The verbs in the requirements are a good start toward identifying the methods needed in the system. Any nouns found in the requirements that obviously are contained within an object might not be objects themselves but be attributes of an object. This can be further determined, if necessary, by applying the three-way object test (state, behavior, and unique identity).

Abstracting reality. Our abstraction of the Software Quality Assurance is only the review and approval of an individual or a board of individuals, so SQA simply could be implemented using a category of user with a special password. Only users with the password would be allowed to fill in the SQA approval attribute.

From trace anchors STRS0007 and STRS0008, we determine that as we edit, add, or delete files in the process of completing an SRR, these files must be checked into and out of the standard configuration management system.

From trace anchors STRS0009 and STRS0010, we learn that an SQA representative must grant approval to all STRs before they can be considered closed and to all SRRs before they can be considered completed. We also learn that SRRs can be written only for STRs that have been approved by a representative of the SQA organization and that an SRR can be considered closed out only after SQA approval.

An objective automated parking garage

To see how some of the object-oriented ideas that have been presented so far might work to solve another real problem, here is an attempt at modeling the automated parking garage example presented in chapter 2. Our initial list of objects, gleaned from the requirements, is as follows:

- Customer/Driver
- Parking Debit Card
- Customer Account
- Transaction-history
- Entrance Gate
- Exit Gate
- Number of Parking spaces
- Available-spaces sign
- Parking Space
- Entrance Card reader
- Exit Card Reader
- Money
- Receipt
- Manager's report
- Cost-of-parking Sign
- Database server
- Cost of Parking

After applying the three-way object test, we determine that the objects in the system look something like those in Figure 9.5.

Scenarios

The scenario that is illustrated in Figure 9.6 shows the simple case of a driver using a valid parking debit card to enter the parking garage. The steps are as follows:

1. The driver enters a parking debit card into the entrance card reader.
2. The card then is checked for validity. To ensure the validity, steps 3 and 4 then are completed:
3. The current cost of parking is retrieved
4. The validity of the driver account is checked.

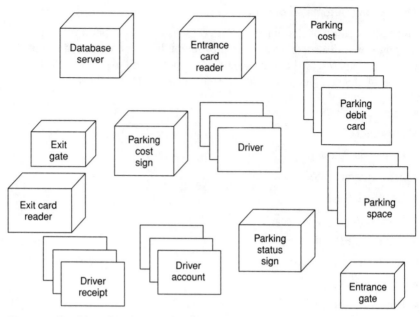

Figure 9.5 Candidate objects for the automated parking garage.

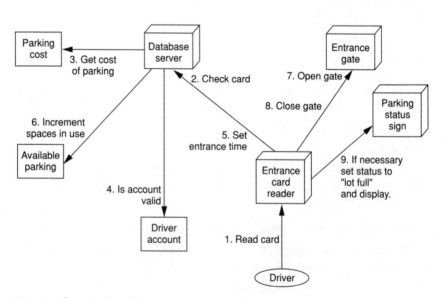

Figure 9.6 Scenario for a driver entering the automated parking garage.

5. Set the entrance time to the current time.

6. Because the account was valid, increment the number of parking spaces in use.

7. The gate then is opened.

8. Then the gate is closed (after the driver exits, of course).

9. If this was the last space in the lot, update the parking status sign to read "LOT FULL."

Ideally, a car won't stay parked in the garage forever—a customer's got to drive it out of the garage eventually. The scenario in Figure 9.7 shows what happens when a driver exits from the parking garage:

1. The driver enters a parking debit card into the exit card reader.

2. The entrance time is subtracted from the current time.

3. The cost of parking then is calculated.

4. The cost of parking is deducted from the customer account. If the driver doesn't have enough money in his or her account, drain the account down to zero and bill the driver for the remainder.

5. Print out a receipt for the customer.

6. The gate then is opened.

7. Close the gate after the driver exits.

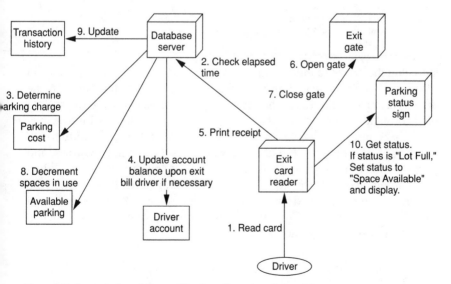

Figure 9.7 Scenario for a driver exiting from the automated parking garage.

8. Decrement the number of spaces in use.

9. If the lot was full before the driver exited, update the parking status sign to read "Space Available."

10. Update the parking history with this transaction.

Relationships

From this scenario, we can tell that there must be a relationship between each card reader and the database and that the database contains driver accounts. The entrance and exit card readers must send commands to open and close the entrance and exit gates, as well as updating the parking status sign. The parking space information also is contained in the database. These relationships are illustrated in Figure 9.8.

The database. By now we have defined some of the methods that are needed in the database. These include checking parking debit cards, printing receipts, and generating reports. From what we know, we can come up with a preliminary definition for the database object:

```
database server class
    attributes:
        available parking
        transaction history
        driver accounts
    methods:
        check parking debit card
        print receipt
          check elapsed time
        send customer account report
        send daily bottom-line report
end
```

Modeling the driver account. Requirements APG0001 through APG0006 in chapter 2 provide crucial information about the relationship between the driver (user) and the rest of the system. The driver is known to the system only through an account number, and the driver is abstracted into a customer account, which will be stored in a central database. In addition to a unique account number, the account will contain the name, address, and phone number of the driver, as well as a one-year transaction history. When the customer exits, an amount calculated according to the time spent in the parking garage multiplied by the current per-minute charge is deducted from his or her account. From these requirements, we can begin modeling the driver/customer abstraction:

```
driver account class
    attributes:
        account number
```

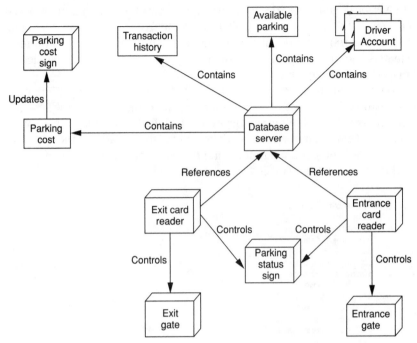

Figure 9.8 A static model for the automated parking garage.

```
        customer name
        address
        phone number
        account balance
        entrance time
        exit time
    methods:
        get account number
        get customer name
        get address
        get phone number
        get account balance
        update customer name
        update address
        update phone number
        add to account balance
        update account balance upon exit
        change account number
    end
```

Because a parking debit card is considered valid only if it corresponds to an account that contains funds sufficient for at least one day's parking, we know that we need a method to validate an account. Whether or not the customer has sufficient funds in his or her account, a receipt is always printed when the customer exits (APG0012).

In APG0017 and APG0018, we find requirements for two separate reports to be generated: one containing all information from all customer accounts and another reporting on all parking transactions as well as the total fees collected and spaces used. Both of the reports need to be automatically e-mailed at 6 PM each day

From trace anchor APG0014, we learn that, if there is not enough money in a customer's account to pay the amount due, the customer will be allowed to exit the lot but automatically will be billed by mail for any amount due beyond what is in the customer's account. After we add methods to validate the account, generate reports and receipts, record entrance time, and bill the customer, the following is the result:

```
driver account class
    attributes:
        account number
        customer name
        address
        phone number
        account balance
      entrance time
    methods:
        is account valid
        get account number
        get customer name
        get address
        get phone number
        get account balance
        update customer name
        update address
        update phone number
        add to account balance
        update account balance upon exit
        change account number
        bill customer by mail
        set entrance time
    end
```

In the future, there might be multiple entrance and exit gates. In that case, there would be a huge advantage to implementing the driver account as a concurrent class/object. A driver account object/task could be activated when a driver enters the garage and terminated when the driver exits and all necessary information has been stored for the account. For more information on concurrency, refer to chapter 8.

Knowing your history. From the requirements, we know that parking transaction information is needed for reports and that a record of parking activity must be kept for one year. From this, we know that we need to keep a persistent history of all of the parking transactions. This transaction history must be updated each time a driver leaves the garage. We also need a method for retrieving the whole history for use in reports. The requirement (trace anchor APG0004) indicates that a history should be stored with each account. When it comes to formatting reports and querying for specific transactions, it's much more efficient to store all transactions in one collection in the database.

```
transaction history class
    attributes:
        transaction list
    methods:
        get transaction history
        update transaction history
end
```

Parking spaces.   From APG008, it is clear that the abstraction for parking spaces in the system consists simply of a persistent running total of all spaces in the garage. We can create a single object called "available parking" and give it the intelligence to increment, decrement, and to provide a count of available parking spaces in the garage:

```
available_parking object
    attributes:
        count of available spaces
    methods:
        increment count of available spaces
        decrement count of available spaces
        get count of available spaces
end
```

In the future, the parking garage might be divided up in different types of spaces (i.e., motorcycle, handicapped, compact car, reserved, etc.). If that happened, this class would change significantly.

Parking cost.   From the requirements, we know that we need to keep track of the cost of parking. This cost is multiplied by the length of time that a car is in the garage to determine the total amount to be deducted from the driver's account upon exit:

```
parking_cost object
    attributes:
        cost of parking
    methods:
        get cost of parking
        change cost of parking
        determine parking charge
end
```

In the future, there might be different costs for different times of day, days of the week, discounts for having a minimum balance in an account, corporate discounts, etc. As things become more complicated, having "parking cost" as a separate object instead of an attribute in another object will make a lot of sense.

The pearly gates.   Trace anchor APG0007 explains that there initially will be a single entrance gate and a single exit gate with the possibility of more gates to be added later on. With no further information in the requirements, we assume that these gates are identical. A gate is a relatively simple thing and really has essentially two behaviors: open and close. The database server gets input from the card reader and, based on space available in the garage and the amount of money in the driver's account, instructs the gate to either remain closed or open up.

```
gate class
    attributes:
        status (can be "open" or "closed")
    methods:
        get status
        open gate
        close gate
end
```

If changes are made in the future and more than one entrance gate as well as multiple exit gates are needed, it would make sense to model the gates as concurrent objects.

Reading the cards.   According to APG0011 and APG0009, a card reader is connected to each gate. When the user enters the card, the information is checked by the database server (where the customer accounts reside).

The card reader must determine whether the correct type of card has been entered and that it can be read (i.e., it's not damaged, worn out, etc.). If the card that a driver enters cannot be read or is the wrong type of card (a library card, for instance), the reader status will be set to "error." Otherwise, the status will be set to "OK." Essentially all a card reader can do is check the card, read the information on the card, and supply it to another object:

```
card reader class
    attributes:
        reader status (can be either "OK" or "error")
        customer account number
    methods:
        check the card
        read the card
        get the customer account number read from the card
end
```

In an expanded parking garage system, multiple drivers could enter and/or exit at the same time through different gates. To support this, the card reader could be modeled as a concurrent object that is activated when a customer enters a card.

Signs of the times. In requirements APG0010, APG0015, and APG0016, two different signs are specified. One sign contains and displays the current per-minute parking rate, and the other contains and displays a status of "Lot Full" or "Space Available." The owner will want to change the per-minute charge at some point, so we need to build that capability in the sign:

```
parking garage status sign object
    attributes:
        lot status ("lot full" or "space available")
    methods:
        set lot status
        display current lot status
end

current parking garage status sign object
    attributes:
        current parking rate
    methods:
        set current parking rate
        display current parking rate
        get current parking rate
end
```

In real life, these two signs might have a lot in common. When two classes are similar, an inheritance subclass/superclass relationship often is advisable. In this case, the attributes and methods that the two sign classes had in common would be contained in a superclass called "sign." Both the parking garage status sign and the current parking rate sign then would inherit from the generalized sign class.

An implementation possibility here would be to combine the two signs into one that would display both pieces of information; however, because the two signs are logically different objects, it makes sense to keep them separate in our design.

Making a model work

It's important to stop iterating on the static and dynamic model alone and to bring the design into the process as soon as it is reasonable to do so. It's very easy to get stuck in the loop of constant model redefinition, and design/implementation considerations are the driving force in bringing the model "down to Earth."

In the examples presented, we're off to a good start in completing a detailed design, but we still are missing some important pieces in our model, including parameter definitions and pseudocode for each method. These will be added as the design merges into implementation.

An object model is a kind of map, and as explorers in the 16th century found out, a map is only the beginning. To make a map truly accurate, it is necessary to diligently explore and survey the area being mapped. We must find out not only how a system looks (static models consisting of class/object diagrams) but also how it works as well (user scenarios).

As we've seen, scenarios can be a powerful tool in defining the behavior of a system. Often, however, scenarios are not sufficient to provide a complete picture of what a system really will do. Some CASE tools offer a limited simulation capability, but to take a truly dynamic look at how a system behaves, prototyping still is the best tool.

One of the best ways to explore and improve a system is through a "vertical sampling" approach. This involves taking a scenario and prototyping it from user interface to the lowest-level utilities, making a "core sample" of what the system really will do. After taking several such cores into the cyber-strata, you'll have a much needed "reality check" to balance out the theoretical view of the object model. You also can get a pretty good idea of what must be done to make the various pieces of the system work together and what, if any, objects and methods are missing from the model.

Another part of prototyping is performance benchmarking. From the best object models, it's impossible to accurately predict whether the system that is defined will fit into the customer's timing and memory restrictions. This can be a major sticking point in the acceptance of a mission-critical system. One way to prevent major design overhauls late in the game is to write programs to stress test the parts of the system that you suspect. Some of the usual suspects are network access, number crunching, data sampling, and database, but study your model carefully because memory and processing hogs can be hiding in unlikely places.

Once you know the performance risks, a number of effective actions can be taken short of redesigning the object model. In the best of cases, simply using the automatic optimization options available on a modern compiler will solve the problem. Beyond this, there are many more aggressive approaches that you can take. For example, if the language and compiler that you're using supports inline routines, you can use this feature to improve execution time where the overhead for a call is roughly the size of the routine. Selective linkers and shareable libraries such as Microsoft dynamic link libraries can help relieve bloated source code, and storing the data and applications locally can prevent expensive server accesses across the network. Because copying blocks of data can be expensive in both memory and processing, using pointers and references to blocks of data can be very efficient.

Be aware of time and memory hogs and how they may be optimized, but proceed with caution before undertaking ambitious rewriting to gain efficiency. Without executable software and thorough timing/memory analysis, you might end up spending several weeks optimizing a routine that is executed so rarely that you save only a few microseconds over the useful life of the program.

Detailed Design/Implementation

Like prototyping, OO development is tightly iterative. Developers begin with an initial set of classes, then refine them, add to them, and merge, split, and delete them throughout the life of the project. Because of this relentless updating, a successful object-oriented design must be extremely flexible and resilient.

In the object-oriented paradigm, there often is little distinction between requirements analysis, design, and implementation. Because the development of an object-oriented system is a highly iterative process, a team often is involved in design, analysis, prototyping, and requirements gathering simultaneously. It is during detailed design/implementation, however, that issues of concurrent execution and networking most often are resolved.

Tasking/concurrency

Object and structured technology are quite different when it comes to flow of control because each object is autonomous and could be running in its own process. This model lends itself quite easily into the client server paradigm. An object-oriented system can easily be comprised of objects executing in parallel with each other, passing messages back and forth. This can be both a curse and a blessing. Once you progress from the standard structured call-and-return model, tracing program execution can be more complex, but errors might be more easily isolated. In addition, you'll have to start worrying about sharing data between tasks, deadlock, starvation, etc. (refer to chapter 8).

Developers who are new to the object paradigm often are pleasantly surprised at how easily objects fit into a multitasking model. Unless specified as synchronous, object methods are assumed to operate asynchronously. The details of concurrency, such as what tasks go on what server and how to implement the needed scheduling model, often are addressed in the coding stages.

Because the object paradigm lends itself so well to multitasking, several object-oriented languages such as Smalltalk and Ada provide built-in support for concurrency. For C++, concurrency is available through the AT&T task library, among others. On many projects, however, developers must rely only on the target operating environment (i.e., Microsoft Windows, IBM OS/2, UNIX etc.). Operating systems support a variety of multiprocessing facilities, including semaphores, event flags, process waits, and critical sections. Because some operating systems offer only a limited tasking model, it's wise to investigate how multitasking works on your target system very early on in the life of the project.

Networking concerns

The object-oriented model often seems to naturally progress into a client-server paradigm, but that doesn't do much to lessen the complexity of communication between processes across a network. Detailed design often is the time when networking inter-process communication (IPC) details are addressed.

As with most aspects of a mission-critical system, the devil is truly in the details. Some of the details that you'll need to work out are whether to use remote procedure calls, the CORBA standard, DDE/OLE, or some other means of communication across the network. For more information, refer to chapter 10.

Persistence/databases

In developing a new complex mission-critical system, there are only two realistic database-management options: object-oriented and relational. Each has strong and weak points when it comes to object-oriented systems. It doesn't take a lot of extra effort (beyond those usually required for third-party software) to fit an object-oriented DBMS into a data model, and the system can be effectively optimized for storage and access efficiency. Relational systems generally offer more features (especially when it comes to querying and reporting). Relational systems also are a more mature technology, offering better compatibility with other tools, support, and reliability. For more information on databases, refer to chapter 10.

Classic Programming

In the object paradigm, requirements analysis and design are very closely coupled, often overlapping to some extent. Even starting with a solid analysis, however, there usually are plenty of details to be worked out in design. Each of the classes in the design diagrams now becomes an encapsulated component.

The variable values are hidden and private and can be read or written only via methods. These classes, sometimes called *abstract data types*, represent the real-world entities in the problem domain. We might need to define some implementation-oriented classes beyond those in the design, and we certainly will use low-level classes (stacks, queues, strings, etc.) that are not explicitly diagrammed in the design. We will use utility classes for database access and screen I/O.

In some cases, we will instantiate templates; in others, we will use one of the defined subclasses of a more general class (i.e., "queues"), which is a parent to LIFO, FIFO, and priority queues. The three subclasses are related to the parent class but are template-instantiated because the range of types or subclasses that apply (i.e., the set of all integers) is too great to be practical for inheritance. In other cases, we must write a new class that inherits from an existing library class, then adds new methods and variables.

On the bumpy road from requirements analysis to the implementation of an object-oriented software product, a number of tasks must be completed as we advance from one iteration of the product to the next. Among these are defining new classes and deriving, instantiating, and otherwise using existing classes to create new classes to build a hierarchical library of reusable components.

A well-designed class inheritance hierarchy is the best thing that ever happened to software reuse. Classes build on each other, getting increasingly complex as the hierarchy progresses, yet the simpler classes still are available for further derivation. These advantages are important, but the biggest advantage is that new classes can be derived and added to the hierarchy without making changes to existing classes. This all sounds great, but it's not without risks. A mistake in a basic class definition can mushroom into a system-wide problem, especially if you factor in multiple inheritance and polymorphism.

As classes are identified in the requirements specification, wise software developers first will look for existing library classes that fit the requirements (refer to chapter 7 for more information). Classes such as those used for graphical user interfaces or data storage and retrieval are excellent candidates. Once a class is found that might be used in the design, a decision must be made about how to make it fit. A class can be instantiated directly as in this C++ example:

```
sign *parking_lot_status_sign = new sign(a,b,c...);
```

Similarly, a parameterized component can be specialized as in this Ada example:

```
package parking_lot_status_sign is new sign(a,b,c...);
```

Finally, a class can be derived from one or more other classes, with additional methods added or nonuseful methods ignored as in the previous inheritance examples.

Ideally, a new system will consist entirely of classes inherited and specialized from an existing class hierarchy. Usually, however, it's necessary to resort to more mundane approaches, such as including several reusable components from a library into an otherwise newly written class. A class that meets some of the required functionality but has too much excess baggage to make it useful simply might be copied and modified into a new class. In the worst of cases, a new class can be written completely from scratch, but this should always be a last resort.

Not the Holy Grail

Object technology is not a cure-all, and a poorly designed object-oriented system can be as big a mess as a poorly designed structured system. Debugging and testing can be more difficult than in the structured paradigm, and there's a lack of good development tools, although these continue to mature. De-pending on what kind of libraries are available in the development framework, object-oriented development can be extremely difficult. Success in object technology requires not only formal training but a paradigm shift away from procedure definition and toward an object/class-centric view. This shift is being made easier with the influx of client-server technology and graphical user interfaces, which contain objects such as buttons and scroll bars.

It can be much more difficult to trace the flow-of-control in an OO system; the complexity is in the interactions between objects, not in the methods themselves as in the structured paradigm. Thanks to encapsulation, however, problems can be more easily isolated to the responsible class (refer to chapter 13).

The key to making an object-oriented project work is a commitment at all levels of management to a new way of thinking about software. Without this, an object-oriented approach, or any new technology for that matter, is doomed to failure.

OO: More Teams

The heavy emphasis on reuse and the fact that the complexity is in the interactions between classes, as well as the iterative nature of the object paradigm, necessitates more and better communication between team members. In some ways, closer communication is needed. Class interfaces aid in this, but where reuse is concerned, there must be a meeting of the minds.

Early and well-defined object interfaces are the key to teamwork on an object-oriented system. It's not necessary for those working on one set of classes to know how the other parts of the system work, only the interface definitions that apply to them. The users of a class often help define the methods that are needed in external classes without knowing any implementation details. This is one of the major advantages of well-encapsulated objects. Of course, nothing ever goes exactly as planned, and a poorly specified interface can cause serious problems.

Interface contracts and standards are the key to coordinating the multi-team efforts. Very early on in the project, work must begin on solidifying the interfaces between subsystems. Standards for defining abstract data types, error handling, and parameter passing must be codified in a widely available document. This requires that interface architects have experience with the development tools and third-party libraries being used on the project. Because an interface is essentially a contract between two software entities, the persons involved in developing each software component or partition must commit to providing needed data and functionality to the other side. This commitment sometimes takes the form of a formal document detailing the interface, which is signed by all parties involved. Whether or not signatures are involved, each side must be informed early and often of the needs of the other side until the interface is solidly defined.

Metrics

The de-facto standard method for measuring programmer productivity is lines of code produced. In the best of cases, this is a silly measurement, but it is absolutely ridiculous when applied to the object paradigm. More reasonable measurements are the number of reusable components used or created.

In the best of cases, software developers on an object-oriented project don't spend much time writing new code. The best use of developers' time is in finding and understanding existing classes and integrating them into the solution. This is done by instantiating a template class from a library (framework), adding another level of inheritance (expanding an abstraction), or in some cases, copying and modifying the source code of an existing class. Finding code rather than writing it from scratch can reduce the amount of debugging and testing needed.

Maintenance

Due to the iterative nature of object-oriented development, all coding and design in an object-oriented system is a form of "maintenance." Fortunately, object-oriented programming makes maintenance easier because the modularity is much higher than in procedural/structured methods. The classes map more directly to the real world, so someone with a good understanding of the problem domain can easily understand the class hierarchies.

In a well-designed object-oriented system, it can be much easier to determine what needs to be changed, added, or deleted to enhance functionality or repair bugs. Testing newly added or changed code also can be easier because the effects of the changes can be isolated.

Objective Advice

The following is a list of advice that we offer in using object-oriented programming:

- Start with general classes, then inherit from and specialize them to get down to specific solutions.
- Look first at similarities, potential similarities, then differences when deriving new classes from existing classes.
- Several small teams of experts work better on OO projects than a horde of average programmers.
- The primary goal should be to implement a judicious mix of the most crucial classes and the classes most visible to the user.
- Write a new method instead of expanding a good one, especially if it already is in use by other classes.
- Keep methods short and classes simple.
- Get a small vertical slice working first, then expand the slice slowly.
- Partition a system along natural divisions. There are three main partitions in most systems: the infrastructure/utilities, the application, and the user interface.
- An object is the expert on what it means to be that object. Put the intelligence about the object in the object, not somewhere else.
- An object-oriented system should work like a corporation of capable and empowered people—very little "management" should be needed.
- A subclass (child) can be used anywhere that its superclass (parent) can be used.
- When it comes to class inheritance, hierarchies should be deep and narrow.
- Just as you shouldn't use a rifle to kill a mosquito, don't use inheritance everywhere. Use generics and templates where they make sense, and use multiple inheritance very sparingly.
- As you begin to develop an object model, you can never have too many classes and objects. Start out with everything as a candidate object, even if you're sure it's only an attribute.
- Coalesce these mini-objects into larger objects as necessary.
- Do all you can to map software closely to the real objects and classes in the problem domain.
- If something needs to act on an object, a good candidate for the actor is the object itself.

- Don't be afraid to break out of the paradigm when necessary, especially at the lowest level where performance can be critical.

- Make objects do one thing and do it well. Make each object into a tiny expert in its own domain. Look at a large system as a bunch of experts coordinated together.

- The complexity in OO systems is not in the methods themselves but in the magnitude of the interactions between objects.

- Use analogies and even role-playing in addition to scenarios, prototypes, and simulations to explain difficult interactions between objects.

- In the early stages of analysis, don't hesitate to split objects apart or to combine objects into larger entities.

- Design for other developers and the future, not yourself and the present.

Summary

The essence of object-oriented programming is transforming a set of requirements into a set of classes. An object-oriented system consists of related objects and classes of objects that work together to provide a solution that maps the customer's problem domain to software entities, such as C++ classes. An object is a self-contained, or "encapsulated," entity that usually models an entity in the customer's world. An object has state, can be uniquely identified, and has behavior. The behavior of an object is modeled in its methods, or executable routines. An object also contains attributes, or variables, that determine the state of the object.

We have seen how the key object-oriented concepts of abstraction, encapsulation, inheritance, polymorphism, and persistence can be used to develop a model of the objects in a system. A good object model must be based on solid requirements, and the requirements must be analyzed using scenarios, or examples of how the system responds to external events. In making an object model work, prototyping also can be an important key. In implementing a mission-critical system, available class libraries, network access, concurrency, and database management must all be integrated in with the object model.

Object technology demands different kinds of metrics, testing, maintenance, and perspective on writing code. Object technology is not a cure-all, but it can offer significant advantages if project managers are committed to sticking with it throughout the project life cycle.

References

Booch, Grady. 1994. *Object-Oriented Analysis and Design with Applications*. Second edition. Redwood City, California: The Benjamin/Cummings Publishing Company, Inc.

Bud, Timothy. 1991. *An Introduction to Object-Oriented Programming*. Reading, Massachusetts: Addison-Wesley Publishing Company, Inc.

Coad, Peter and Jill Nicola. 1993. *Object-Oriented Programming*. Englewood Cliffs, New Jersey: P. T. R. Prentice Hall, Inc.

Pohl, Ira. 1993. *Object-Oriented Programming Using C++*. Redwood City, California: The Benjamin/Cummings Publishing Company, Inc.

Rumbaugh, James et al. 1991. *Object-Oriented Modeling and Design*. Englewood Cliffs, N.J.: Prentice Hall, Inc.

Weiner, Richard S. and Lewis J. Pinson. 1988. *An Introduction to Object-Oriented Programing and C++*. Reading, Massachusetts: Addison-Wesley Publishing Company, Inc.

Winblad, Ann et al. 1990. *Object-Oriented Software*. Reading, Massachusetts: Addison-Wesley Publishing Company, Inc.

Yourdon, Edward. 1993. *Decline and Fall of the American Programmer*. Englewood Cliffs, New Jersey: Prentice Hall.

10

Tools and Environments

Man is a tool-using animal. Nowhere do you find him without tools.
Without tools, he is nothing, with tools he is all.
THOMAS CARLYLE (Evans 1978 702)

During the software-development stone age, intrepid geniuses wrote usable software with nothing but machine code. Later on, assembly language opened new programming vistas, and high-level language compilers gave programming productivity and software quality a much-needed shot-in-the-arm. Over the years, CASE tools, ever-more advanced operating environments, database management systems, and a plethora of other software gizmos have been added to the programmer's toolchest.

Some usable systems have been developed using a bare minimum of software tools, but there's no question that, with an integrated set of the best tools and training on their use, programmer productivity can increase significantly. The operating environment in which tools are used also can greatly affect productivity, because modern environments support graphical user interfaces, network access, and multitasking.

Today, progressive project managers want their developers to use the best tools. These commonly include tools for building graphical user interfaces; advanced compilers, linkers, and debuggers; CASE tools; database management systems; and multitasking operating systems. Managers and developers alike, however, often overlook the fact that no tool can be of much use unless it fits into a working process and is compatible with the environments and tools with which it will be used.

As well-equipped software developers sit in front of their computers, they have at their disposal advanced design tools, powerful languages, and client-server operating environments with virtually limitless capabilities. The most powerful of all tools are those that leverage development efforts through reuse (refer to chapter 7). An extensive library of components, a browser to access the library, and the ability to combine components together with new code to create more complex library classes can give software developers a huge advantage.

To equip these cyber-workbenches, some software vendors offer an impressive array of integrated tools. Microsoft, for example, offers the Microsoft foundation classes, an optimizing C++ compiler, a selective linker that produces dynamically shareable libraries, and a graphical user interface builder bundled together. Two of the new buzzwords for this kind of toolset are *software development framework* and *developers' workbench*.

In addition to any bundled programming environment, other tools must be added to develop any nontrivial system. If, for example, the system that you want to develop primarily will store and process large amounts of data, you'll need to add an appropriate database management system to your toolset. The system that you design also will need to execute in concert with an operating environment that is suited to supporting a database server. If the system that you're developing requires distributed access, you'll need to add in the tools that are needed to support network interfaces, and those tools will need to be compatible with (and ideally are built-into) the operating environment that you're using.

Toolsmiths

In every successful software development organization, the members of at least one team serve as "toolsmiths" (Brooks 1972). The toolsmiths are in charge of making tools that are useful to software developers. A toolsmith's main task should be to locate, evaluate, become expert in, and provide training in the tools on the market that are suitable to the needs of the software projects in the organization. These tools include compilers, database management systems, test coverage tools, configuration management systems, CASE tools, etc.

The toolsmith group also serves as a clearinghouse for tools that other teams create in the course of developing a project. Often, these tools need improvement and documentation before they can be truly useful to other teams. In a heads-up organization, the toolsmiths will provide this, along with cataloging and maintaining such tools.

Toolsmiths also must develop tools as requested by other teams. Such tools might include test-data generators, data reformatters, text conversion utilities, and other types of software scaffolding.

Successful toolsmith groups have access to online search facilities, where they can research the latest product abstracts and reviews. They also have support from management in their efforts to build better bug-swatters, as well as close working relationships with software development teams and product vendors.

The toolsmiths also need to work closely with the process and SQA teams (see chapter 11). The process team will need to incorporate tools into the process and make sure the tools are compatible with the process. SQA also should be involved in validating all third party software, including development tools and libraries.

Programming Languages

In one sense, a programming language can be considered a tool; however, as is so well demonstrated in various computer-language newsgroups on the Internet, languages also can approach the status of a religion. Those who have invested their professional lives in a specific programming language sometimes feel compelled to defend it and to downgrade other languages. Prejudice aside, programming languages are the single most important component in any software developer's toolbox.

Many volumes could be and have been written on the merits and weaknesses of the most popular languages, such as COBOL, C/C++, Ada, BASIC, and Smalltalk. When it comes to programming, however, the key tool-related success factor is how all the tools and environments fit together to fulfill the users' requirements, not what programming language is used. A language might be powerful and well-known; however, if it doesn't fit into the development environment or is not compatible with other important tools such as database management systems and GUI builders, it will only make things worse.

BASIC

It doesn't take a genius to see that BASIC, once viewed as a hobbyist's language, has become, in one flavor or another, a good language for implementing small- to medium-sized systems. Compare Microsoft Visual BASIC or Computer Associates' CA Realizer to the average BASIC of about a decade ago. Back then, BASIC had only rudimentary support for data structures and little in the way of control structures. The current incarnations of BASIC have become very popular because graphical user interface building capability is built into the language, along with relatively advanced control and data structures.

COBOL

The current default standard of object-oriented languages is C++. It definitely is a usable language but is far from perfect. Object orientation hasn't yet made major inroads into common business applications such as general ledger and payroll; however, with the eventual acceptance of the OOCOBOL standard (also known as COBOL 97, COBOL++, or "ADD 1 TO COBOL"), business application programmers needn't feel left out of the object revolution.

According to the current draft standard for COBOL 97, there are plans for the next generation of COBOL to include inheritance, polymorphism, dynamic binding, exception handling, and other advanced features. These will be grafted onto the venerable business language standard by 1997 (Micro Focus already has a working compiler). This is all pretty impressive considering that features such as parameter passing, local-variable definition, and dynamic data structures were unsupported in COBOL 74.

Ada

Ada has gained a reputation for being an ideal language for huge realtime embedded systems. Ada 95 now has full-fledged object-orientation support, as well as enhanced input/output and data processing support. Ada offers built-in build-tool, validation, and multitasking support, as well as low-level support and strong typing. Only time will tell whether or not Ada catches on outside of the realtime-embedded-systems world.

C/C++

C is essentially a low-level language with higher-level functions supplied by means of standard libraries. This makes it one of the most portable and flexible languages around. Using C, developers can write low-level device drivers, database applications, or virtually any other type of program as long as the correct set of libraries are included. Thanks to the strategy of library-based functionality, C runs on more platforms than any other language and is hugely popular among software engineers.

C++ has everything C has, plus support for object-oriented programming and other features such as improved I/O and parameter passing. As such, C++ is not a pure object-oriented language, yet it has become the de facto standard for object-oriented programming. C++ is a popular language because C programmers have a head-start in learning it and can write structured programs that have some object-oriented features. This eliminates the effort of making the transition to a completely new language to gain the benefits of object technology.

Smalltalk

Smalltalk was one of the first *pure* object-oriented languages, and has become the most popular. The first version was developed in the early 1970s, and subsequent versions have brought definite improvements to the language. Smalltalk is relatively easy to learn and is gaining popularity in fields as diverse as engineering and financial programming. It is both powerful and flexible due to the interpretive, late-binding nature of the language, and the fact that *everything* is an object in Smalltalk, including class definitions.

Fourth-generation languages

A *fourth-generation language* has not only a built-in GUI builder capability but a high-level scripting language and an integrated DBMS as well. 4GLs, such as Windows 4GL from Computer Associates or PowerBuilder from Powersoft, are great for a fairly narrow range of applications but lack the flexibility needed for others. If the application you're building is fairly standard and straightforward, a 4GL is ideal. For complex applications such as process control systems, 4GLs don't work as well. The most flexible 4GLs have not only a proprietary, scripting language but also can call routines that were written in other languages, such as C or COBOL, as well. In addition, code that was written in other languages can call functions defined in the 4GL.

When it comes to languages or virtually any other software tool, the best advice is to avoid becoming bigoted. Don't fall in love with any language or any other software tool. Get training and experience in as many in-demand languages and tools as possible, and use what best fits the needs of your customers and the resources of your company. There is no single language or tool that works well for everything. The most effective software developers are adept at using several languages and can work well in more than one operating environment.

Database Management Systems

If you're developing a new system, your only real database management system choices are relational or object-oriented. Relational technology definitely has the edge in maturity and variety of systems available because it has been in use for about 25 years, while OO has been available for only 3 to 4 years. Relational database management systems have the advantage of having been proven over the years in huge (1 gigabyte or more) databases with high-concurrency of access. The methodology is well-known, as is the standard relational query interface, SQL. Report generation is easy, but it's hard to optimize storage and performance or represent complex relationships. The best database management systems can be easily integrated with other tools such as GUI builders.

Most programmers already know that a relational database consists of tables of data that are interconnected by foreign keys. Object-oriented databases are another matter. As explained in chapter 9, database objects can represent highly complex real-world entities. The relationships between these objects are represented as webs of connections.

Both types of database have specific niches in the grand scheme of things. Relational databases generally work better for large numbers of simultaneous transactions such as airline reservations and ticketing. A relational DBMS also is best for standard business applications such as payroll and general ledger. Object technology works well for systems that require very complex data modeling, such as financial portfolio management, telecommunications, process control, computer-aided design, expert systems, and parts inventory.

There are a couple of general rules to use in choosing a database management system appropriate for your project. If you're using an object-oriented programming language and your project is committed to object technology, a good object-oriented database management system is your best option. If not, a solid relational DBMS is a much better choice.

In some departments in an enterprise, such as accounting, much of the needed data already has been reduced to tables and forms that translate easily into the relational paradigm. In these cases, relational technology is the obvious solution. The more multidimensional (keeping track of real-world objects as opposed to stacks of paper) your problem is, the better OO fits and the less appropriate relational technology is. The more complex the data, the more sense object technology makes.

Although the market is growing rapidly, object-oriented databases really haven't caught on in most standard business applications such as payroll and accounts receivable. A relational database management system works better for these applications because the data already exists in an essentially tabular format.

A good place to start your search for a good database management system is in the pages of *DBMS* magazine (published by Miller Freeman, Inc.). *DBMS* publishes an annual "Buyer's Guide" issue that provides information on hundreds of database management tools.

Editors

Any good tool set must include a reconfigurable editor with a built-in macro language. A point-and-click interface can be a big plus too. DEC's LSE, GNU's EMACS, and Underware's Brief are examples of this type of industrial-strength programmers' editor. Good editors are bundled with many language toolsets, including both Microsoft Visual C++ and Borland C++. The best editors are language sensitive. These tools highlight keywords, handle indentation, match parentheses and the beginning and ending of control structures, and otherwise check syntax as code is edited.

These editors allow the user to type in a keyword such as "if" and use a *hot key* that will put a template for an "if" statement into the code. Hot keys can bring up choices or further documentation for any language element. Some sophisticated editors also facilitate browsing for data and subprogram definitions. Using a good language-sensitive editor, programmers can initiate a software build, perform selective compiling and linking, or start a debugging session from within an editor.

GUI Builders

Graphical user interfaces, such as Microsoft Windows and X Windows/Motif, essentially have become the standard for any system involving human/computer interaction. Computer users have come to expect a sophisticated interface, putting pressure on programmers to constantly improve its power and flexibility. A well-designed graphical user interface can be a major selling point for almost any software product, but it doesn't come cheaply. Traditionally the lion's share—about 90% according to some studies (Bowman 1994)—of the effort involved in developing a large non-realtime software product has been spent on designing and implementing the user interface.

The use of software development workbenches, such as Microsoft's Visual C++ and Borland's Professional C++, are making the development of graphical user interfaces much easier. This type of workbench includes many tools, which (hopefully) are coordinated with each other. A typical workbench has a code editor; a graphical editor for designing forms, dialog boxes, icons, etc.; a symbolic debugger; libraries of reusable components; a component browser to locate specific components; a selective linker; and an optimizing compiler (Figure 10.1).

The most useful visual environments allow developers to select elements—such as buttons, edit controls, tool bars, scroll bars, etc.—from a "palette" of predefined components and drag and drop them onto the screen. Facilities also must be provided for a programmer to define his own components, or *controls*. A control is an onscreen graphical object through which an end-user can activate specific processing within a system. Simple examples are the OK/Cancel buttons on a Windows dialog box.

Good visual programming environments automatically will create all of the cookie-cutter code that is needed to access and update controls and will supply other tools to help update the system, taking care of some of the details of defining and registering changes. As new controls are defined, these tools also can assist in mapping them to variables and routines within the system.

GUI builders such as the App Studio, which is provided with Visual C++, can be quite useful but are basic tools that generally run in only one environment and might not provide the specific GUI features that complex applications need. There are a number of effective GUI builders around that run in nearly every major operating environment. The capabilities of tools

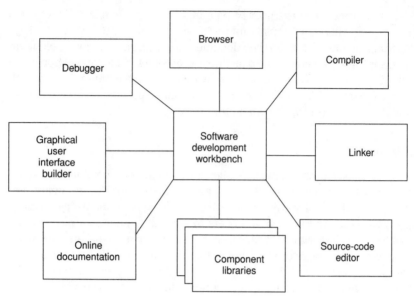

Figure 10.1 A software development workbench.

like Teleuse from Telesoft or Zinc Designer from Zinc might be much better suited to a specific application.

The term *graphical interface* is a bit misleading. In most cases, *graphical* does not mean impressionist art or detailed animation. It means that the user's environment can be controlled without a user having to type in text commands, and the user can use the keyboard only to type in text meaningful to his or her environment, such as a memo or a text description.

It also supports drawing/diagramming for the user. In an advanced graphical interface, the end user can draw diagrams on the screen, using a palette of predefined components. This system then can use components from a library to bring the graphical components to life.

In general, successful GUI-based programming proceeds as follows:

1. Chose graphical components and arrange them in the interface screen as desired.

2. Browse and retrieve supporting components from a class library, adding them into the application.

3. Write custom code as needed.

4. Incrementally compile and link.

5. Invoke the debugger to test the application.

6. Repeat 1 through 5 until the system is complete.

A good GUI builder also can give an interface a "dry run" after creating it, making sure everything scrolls and clicks along as planned. To make the interface come to life with real data, however, the current state of the art necessitates that the developer write much of the code that is needed to access and update controls and stored data.

All of this allows a new level of user-friendliness that is light years beyond the old text, command-line, function-key interface. Seasoned users still will want "accelerator" commands that allow them to save a few seconds by typing function, Ctrl, or Alt key combinations instead of pulling down a menu and selecting from it.

The following paragraphs contain a visual tool example using Microsoft Visual C++.

To start a new application, a programmer can select the AppWizard tool from the project menu. AppWizard provides a complete set of cookie-cutter code, which forms the basis for the application. This comes in handy, especially because it automatically sets up the half-dozen or so files that are needed at the beginning of the average application. When AppWizard is invoked, menus are presented that allow a developer to customize the application to use Object Linking and Embedding (OLE), be a multiple or single document interface, use Visual Basic controls, etc.

After the application shell has been constructed, a user-interface can be created using the AppStudio GUI builder that is included in the workbench. In the AppStudio, a developer literally can draw an interface, selecting controls such as menus, bitmap graphics, dialogs, forms, icons, buttons, scroll bars, etc., from a palette of resources, then dragging and dropping them directly onto the user interface (Figure 10.2).

As the interface is built, each control in it must be tied to the underlying program logic. This can be done using another tool in the Visual Workbench: the ClassWizard. Using this tool, corresponding member functions, variables, and messages can be bound to the interface. ClassWizard fills in the blanks that AppWizard creates, and helps bring the AppStudio-build interface to life. If ClassWizard is used to make all changes in the interface during development, it can help keep graphical components coordinated with the rest of the system.

The latest version of Borland C++ has essentially the same features as Microsoft's Visual C++. These two development frameworks work well for many developers (the authors included) and generally are considered the standards for object-oriented software development.

There's some strong competition emerging, however, with Smalltalk environments such as VisualWorks from ParcPlace Systems offering extensive libraries and high-level GUI programming. Programmers using Smalltalk-based environments often are more productive than C++ programmers, but system performance can be an issue. Smalltalk generally is not the best choice for low-level programming and time-critical systems; however, for

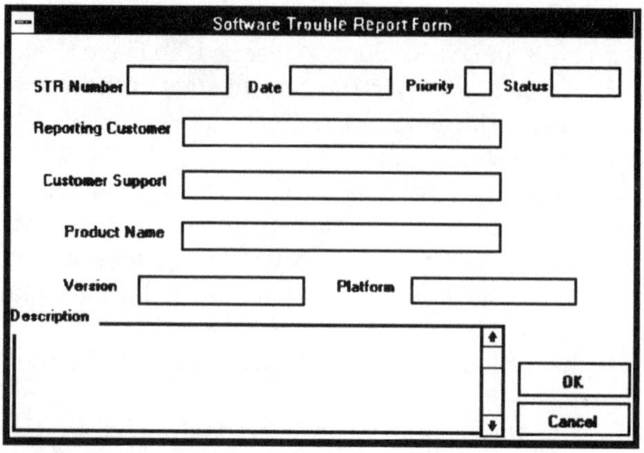

Figure 10.2 A simple data-entry dialog box for a defect-tracking system.

higher-level applications, an advanced Smalltalk environment is definitely worth considering.

CASE Tools

Software development is a complex, labor-intensive undertaking; therefore, attempts to automate portions of it via CASE tools can be only partially successful at best. CASE tool designers face huge challenges in providing features that will be useful to a variety of software development organizations.

CASE technology has been given a bad name and not entirely without good reason. CASE vendors have become notorious for over-promising and under-delivering. On top of that, CASE generally is thought of as a mainframe technology, and useful CASE tools haven't quite made it to other environments.

The lack of good CASE tools is only part of the problem, however. As Yourdon (1993) explains, most organizations don't have a sufficiently advanced software development process to take full advantage of CASE technology, even if the right tools were available.

The concept of using a software tool to graphically design software is a great idea; however, on the whole, CASE tools still are lacking, especially in client/server environments. CASE software is extremely complex, and the needs of CASE users vary widely. The notation supported in most CASE tools is not flexible enough, data dictionary technology is not mature enough, and effective requirements analysis features are lacking. Code generation and especially reverse engineering have a long way to go when it comes to most CASE tools.

> CASE vendors have made a number of exaggerated promises and delivered, on the whole, only mediocre products over the past 15 years. Of course, some

software development projects have found success with CASE, but on the whole, I have been vastly underwhelmed with how useful CASE tools are on large, mission-critical projects. As weak as CASE technology often is, projects generally are better off with some CASE tool than with no CASE tool.

I've yet to work with a truly effective CASE tool on a large project. I've worked with seven different CASE tools. Four supported structured methods, and three were object-oriented, but all were, at best, of limited value, primarily due to an immature process.

Jay Johnson

Partially because of the perceived inadequacy of CASE tools for client/ server environments, many programming teams are attempting to develop client/server software using fourth-generation languages, GUI builders, and visual programming workbenches, sans CASE support. Advanced GUI tools can work wonders, and this approach actually can work well for small applications. The truth of the matter, however, is that CASE technology, as inadequate as it might be, is an absolute necessity on a huge project.

Fortunately, CASE tools are slowly improving as the client/server paradigm catches on and client/server applications increase in size and importance. There are some good tools out there; the trick is finding them and fitting them into your process. CASE tools can be extremely expensive on a large (100+ programmers) project. The total cost can be well over $1 million (Semich 1994), but that's a bargain compared to project failure. The expense and learning curve needed to make CASE (or almost any other major software tools) work can amount to a huge commitment, so choosing the wrong tool can mean both financial and schedule disaster.

A good first step in finding the right CASE tool is to read the "Requirements Analysis and Design Technology Report," which is a regularly updated report that is available at no cost from the federal government. The report provides information on over 100 CASE tools ranging from EasyCASE Plus (Evergreen CASE Tools, Inc.) to Teamwork/OOA (Cadre Technologies, Inc.). It's available from the Software Technology Support Center, at the following address:

Software Technology Support Center
Ogden ALC/TISE
7278 4th street
Hill AFB, UT 84056-5205

In choosing a CASE tool, here are a few questions to ask:

Will it support your organization's software development process?
Each organization has a unique process (if they have one at all). Whether you're using a waterfall or spiral-based model, or something in between, the tool must fit in not only with what the process is today but also what it will be in the future, because a good process will change and evolve as the customers, technology, and business environment changes.

Does it support the methodologies that developers actually use in your company? Whether you're using a methodology designed by Booch, Coad/Yourdon, or Rumbaugh, et al., the tool that your organization's developers use must support a methodology that they know or are committed to learning. The methodology also must be appropriate for mapping the problem space.

Does it support a client/server architecture? Even if you're on a mainframe or stand-alone system, the odds are that you eventually will end up on a client/server system.

Is the user interface intuitive? If not, the tool will get in the developers' way, proving as much a hindrance, at least in the early stages of the project, as a help.

Does it support reverse engineering? This is a weak spot in nearly all CASE tools and is an essential feature for reengineering efforts. Reverse engineering is necessary to keep the design coordinated with the generated code. Ideally, a software engineering effort must come full circle, from design to code and back to design.

Does it support effective code generation in your organization's languages of choice? This might seem obvious, but watch out for nonstandard and version-related differences.

Can many developers easily work on the same design? This is a major sticking point with many tools, and it's tied to the fact that CASE repository technology often is not ready for prime time.

Are scenarios and use cases supported for requirements analysis? This is the only efficient way to keep requirements in synch with design and code.

Does it support popular document processors such as WordPerfect and Interleaf? The ability to easily incorporate design elements into documents, and vice versa, is important for generating documentation and keeping it in synch with design and requirements.

Can freeform diagrams be included in the design? This is especially important when it comes to detailed design.

What kind of support for configuration management does the tool offer? Versions of the design must be maintained, just as are source-code versions.

The surest way to ensure some success with CASE technology is to learn and practice a methodology (Booch, Rumbaugh, Coad/Yourdon, etc.), then find tools to make the methodology more efficient. Don't expect a CASE tool to be a panacea, but realize that there will be significant benefits in the long run if a wisely selected CASE tool fits into a good process and is compatible with the other tools being used on a project.

Compilers, Linkers, and Debuggers

The most productive programmers use tightly integrated tool sets, featuring a language-sensitive source-code editor, an incremental compiler/linker, and a good debugger/profiler. Any tool in the set should be accessible with just a couple of mouse clicks, and source code, data, and documentation can be dragged and dropped or cut and pasted between tools.

The best compilers can produce optimized code to rival that of even the most adept assembly-language programmers. Modern compiler/linkers can incrementally compile a system, automatically recompiling and relinking only those files that have been changed and those depending on them. Using modern linkers, libraries can be shared and dynamically linked.

Some of the best toolsets support library *parenting*, which allows libraries of shared/stable code to be linked-in by many users, each with his or her own personal development library. This allows any high-level changes to be made in the parent library, which is visible to all developers. Individual users also can make changes to their personal libraries without affecting the shared library system. As the personal libraries solidify, their components can be moved up to the shared libraries. This strategy can make partitioning and integration go more smoothly.

Sometime in history soon after the first line of code was written, programmers started looking for help in debugging code. Debugging tools have been around for a long time. A decade or so ago, they were barely usable or were of dubious benefit. Today, however, symbolic source-level debuggers have become powerful and indispensable. In a client/server environment, it's almost impossible to fix code without an advanced debugging tool. Fortunately, there are some good ones available to handle asynchronous, multitasking environments. A good debugger/profiler can not only help find logic errors but also can find performance bottlenecks and also can be used to show test coverage.

Environments

The environment in which an application executes often is thought of as simply an operating system. Today's applications, however, often execute in a complex bed of runtime software, including graphical display managers, message queues, database servers, and interprocess communication across networks. This goes far beyond the usual concept of an operating system simply scheduling tasks, handling text I/O, and managing memory. Today's advanced environments are best represented by client/server systems.

Operating systems

The days of the centralized mainframe surrounded by terminals or of the stand-alone desktop computer are fading away. Today, a system often consists of a variety of computing platforms networked together, providing access from many "clients" to many "servers." These platforms can range from ancient mainframes to the newest RISC workstations.

The Intel CISC architecture, ranging from the 8086 to the Pentium, has been around for a long time and works very well for client platforms and small-to-medium size servers, but it's not really up to handling the workload of a large server. It often takes a RISC architecture, such as Digital's Alpha chip or IBM's PowerPC microprocessor, to handle thousands upon thousands of client requests and gigabytes of storage at high speed. The best operating systems for client/server architectures should run not only on Intel Pentium processors but be portable to powerful RISC systems as well. As newer and faster hardware comes along, applications written for a good operating system can be easily "scaled-up" to take full advantage of it.

All of the computers in an enterprise can communicate and share data easily, and a huge variety of software tools can become available to end users thanks to powerful operating systems that support networked computing. This can mean vastly increased empowerment for end users, but it means extra work for systems administrators, who must keep the network running and the latest versions of the operating system and all the software applications talking to each other. With this flexibility, mainframes, super mini clusters, Macintoshes, Cray computers, etc., can be part of the same system.

When it comes to the client side of the equation, there's not much competition for the most popular operating system. Microsoft Windows is the winner going away. On the server side, however, there are several good operating systems vying for dominance. Among them are UNIX, OS/2, and Microsoft Windows NT. Each of these operating systems are supported by virtually all major tools and application vendors, so it's unlikely that any specific piece of software will be incompatible.

In addition to excellent support for network access, a good server operating system must be reliable, scaleable, and portable. Because a server is always running, ready to fulfill client requests, reliability is a top criterion for any server operating system. Here OS/2 gets especially high marks, but each of the three contenders also does well in this category. Unfortunately, as of this writing, OS/2 runs only on Intel processors and can't be scaled-up to handle huge client loads.

Windows NT doesn't have much of a track record yet but could become the ultimate in flexibility/portability, because it offers both POSIX (Portable Operating System Interface for Unix) and Windows compatibility and because virtually every major software vendor is porting tools to it. Windows NT also incorporates some of the better features of Digital's VMS and has the force of the mighty Microsoft juggernaut behind it.

UNIX has the advantage of salability, and it runs on virtually every platform in one version or another. UNIX definitely has stood the test of time; it's been around longer than most software developers working today. Network access also is well supported, and UNIX also has the advantage of familiarity, because more people know and have developed software using UNIX than either Windows NT or OS/2.

Thanks to a long chain of improving versions, MS-DOS still is a viable operating system for single-user systems, although its popularity is starting to wane. MS-DOS, mainframe systems such as IBM's MVS, mini-computer based VMS from Digital, and other venerable operating systems will slowly fade away and be replaced by systems with greater power and flexibility.

The client server paradigm

The essence of client/server computing is that any two computer programs or software tasks running within the system can communicate and share resources with each other, even if they are running on different platforms. Some of these platforms run programs that are designated as "servers," and as such they provide services (data, processing, etc.) to programs or applications designated as "clients" (Figure 10.3). For example, a "client" could be a user interface, and a "server" could be a database management system.

Client/server essentially means that a system can be distributed across many programs or tasks that might be executing on different computing platforms. It involves an operating system that supports networking, such as UNIX or Novell NetWare.

A well-planned client/server architecture can be a programmer's paradise, providing a variety of compilers and linkers on different servers, a DBMS or two on dedicated servers, online documentation on another, and a GUI builder or a fourth-generation language on yet another. Each server can run a different operating system, presenting a software developer with a plethora of the most advanced tools.

It's not uncommon for a complex and heavily used software system to outgrow its hardware, especially if massive amounts of data are stored and

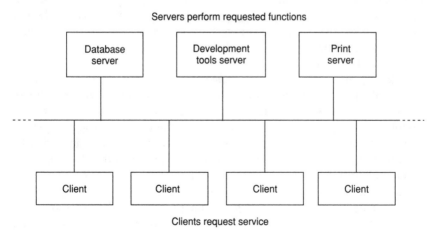

Figure 10.3 A client/server system.

accessed via complex queries. In the central mainframe paradigm, this could mean an extremely costly upgrade, or cutting back on the applications running on the system. Today, it often means transferring applications to a client-server environment.

Client/server hardware and software generally is less expensive than a typical mainframe system for comparable computing power and data storage. Within the client-server paradigm, an application such as a database can be distributed across many servers, with clients free to handle the user interface and other tasks. Because new clients and servers can be added relatively easily and inexpensively (especially when compared to upgrading a mainframe system), it's extremely difficult for an application to outgrow a well-planned client/server environment.

In addition to increased cost-effectiveness and virtually unlimited growth potential, the client/server paradigm offers the ability to connect islands of automation, easing downsizing pressures. For example, Apple Macintoshes, PCs, IBM mainframes, and DEC minicomputers scattered throughout an enterprise can be linked together such that they share information and processing power across many vendors and many platforms. This flexibility has the potential of giving end users, and especially developers, access to a huge variety of software tools and data. As of today, however, client/server computing has yet to live up to its promised potential.

In most enterprises today, client/server computing amounts to porting mainframe applications to less expensive and more expandable client/server hardware. End users often see little difference, except perhaps in increased downtime and decreased system administration support. Meanwhile, developers who approach client/server with essentially the same processes and tools that they used on the old mainframe are in for a rude awakening. Their new client/server environment is made up of a complex network and a variety of operating systems executing on clients and servers such as UNIX and Windows. Developers who have become accustomed to COBOL, DB2, and CISC now might have to face C++, distributed database servers, and a wide array of GUI builders.

Making a successful shift to client/server architecture involves the three R's: rethinking, retraining, and reengineering. Managers and developers must rethink their software development process and tools, with the goal of uniform data across platforms. Both developers and managers must be trained in the ins and outs of client/server oriented tools. Most importantly, a reengineering effort must be mounted to acquire and develop tools and common libraries of objects to facilitate client/server network access, data storage, and user interface.

Reengineering means examining existing processes and applications, and improving them with better methodologies and tools. Computers have long been used to speed up current business practices, but reengineering changes should result in better ways of doing business, driving changes into business policies and procedures. Reengineering efforts often result in downsizing from mainframe-based computing to a client-server environment.

Networks

One of the most dramatic advances in computing during the last 20 years has come in the proliferation of user-transparent networked systems. From inhouse local area networks to world-spanning wide area distributed systems, networks have made it possible to distribute data and computing power between platforms. To understand how networks fit in with the latest tools and processes, it's helpful to get a flavor for some of the popular inter-process communication strategies such as ORBs and RPCs.

The growth of networks and network operating systems, such as Novell NetWare, over the last 10 years has laid a foundation for the client/server paradigm. With the seamless integration of distributed systems now possible, a resource-sharing architecture can execute on top of the basic network layers to create an object-oriented client/server system (Figure 10.4).

Ideally, the layered machinations of getting from client to server and back again would be completely transparent to the user, with a call to a distributed service being as simple as a call to local library routine. The usual way that an application calls functions and procedures in associated libraries is that the application program makes a procedure call into a local library, and the function is performed locally. When an application is distributed across several network nodes (clients or servers), calling a function or procedure can be considerably more complex. One strategy is for libraries to reside on various servers, and the application to reside on a single client. The client then can access the libraries by means of network-access functions.

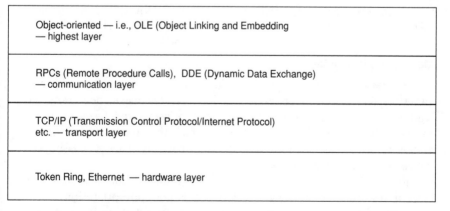

Figure 10.4 Network layers supporting a client/server system.

A much more efficient and flexible way combines the idea of making a simple procedure call and accessing an object on another node through the network. Known as a *remote procedure call*, or RPC, this method is supported by several operating systems, including Microsoft Windows NT. The RPC approach puts a matching set of call stubs and RPC runtime software between clients and servers, making it possible to make a remote call almost as easily as a local one. Because the remote-procedure call concept is supported to varying degrees on many different platforms, it's a great idea to become familiar with how RPCs are done on your specific target platform.

RPCs aren't the only method for gluing a distributed application together. Message queues, named pipes, and shared memory, along with several other approaches, are used on a variety of operating systems. In addition, there is a standardized object-oriented approach called the Common Object Request Broker Architecture (CORBA). This standard uses object request broker (ORB) objects instead of RPCs. Because each ORB is in itself an object that can broker services for other objects, and even other ORBs, it can be much more flexible than RPCs in a pure object-oriented environment.

Microsoft is becoming the IBM of the 90s, ruling the software world much as Big Blue did in the previous three decades. An indication of this is the fact that Microsoft Windows is far and away the most popular client operating system. Microsoft Windows NT also is making inroads into the server arena.

The CORBA standard hasn't fully caught on at Microsoft yet, however. Microsoft's Dynamic Data Exchange (DDE) architecture, which works closely with Microsoft's Object Linking and Embedding software (OLE), does not at this time fully support CORBA, although it is somewhat compatible.

If it's true that Microsoft is destined to rule the software world, eventually OLE will become the standard for all object-oriented data access, because it effectively is a set of data with all related processing on it, including across networks. OLE provides a top-layer of access that coordinates smoothly into the object paradigm. Even though OLE does not currently meet the CORBA standard, it provides a complete object-oriented view.

Moving to client/server

Client/server has become a common buzzword and, as such, has acquired a variety of different meanings. Some developers and managers define any network-based system or a mainframe with PCs connected to it as client/server. In reality, true client/server involves much more than hooking hardware together. It means that software tasks can transparently share processing and data across a variety of platforms.

The client/server model isn't the only option for developing an effective system; it's only one strategy and certainly is not appropriate for all systems. In many cases, a peer-to-peer network, a stand-alone PC, a minicomputer, or a mainframe still might be the perfect solution to users' needs.

A client/server system is needed primarily when a company wants to unify islands of automation such as marketing, accounting, engineering, graphic design, etc. Client/server also fills the void as mainframes disappear and can be a key to survival in downsizing, as people need faster access to information and a better variety of tools to help in getting jobs done with fewer workers.

The ultimate promise of distributed systems, such as client/server, is seamless integration throughout an enterprise, possibly using something like the CORBA standard to provide uniform, object-oriented access across a variety of platforms.

From the view of the client and the server, you get a set of services that are provided in an object-oriented way that allow the client and the server to find each other and to communicate with each other.

The client/server paradigm doesn't force an enterprise to dump it's existing software and hardware, either. A successful client/server system could include mainframes, minicomputers, micros, RISC-based workstations, and super computers.

In downsizing from mainframe to client/server, the best approach is to use off-the-shelf tools and environments that are designed and tested to work together. It also is crucial to start by moving small, nonmission-critical systems to the new environment and to bring in expert integrators to help with the transition of all mission-critical applications.

Don't Beta the Farm

To gain the greatest competitive advantage, some teams serve as beta test sites for a specific tool or vendor. While this is a good idea for a small pilot project, entrusting a mission-critical project to a beta release of any tool is a mistake. In today's complex development environments involving networks, database tools, GUI builders, etc., beta releases tend to proliferate.

Once one beta tool is adopted, others tend to follow. For example, a beta release of a compiler might offer some new language features, but it might be necessary to use a beta version of a database management tool to take full advantage of them. Frustration is much too mild a term to describe the byproduct of attempting to debug a system involving multiple beta tools, sometimes including beta versions of test tools!

Beta software eventually leads to a real product release; however, in today's environment, that might not be much better. The newly released version might not be compatible with the current versions of other tools, or it might be compatible only with older versions, preventing you from upgrading. This is complicated by the fact that new releases tend to come out every six months or so. With many tools involved, as often is the case in most client/server environments, the version treadmill can wear out even the best systems administrators.

In a multivendor, multiversion client/server environment, the systems administrator's job can be challenging to say the least. Today, systems administrators must be active partners in software development efforts, not hidden away in mainframe dungeons as were their predecessors. Systems administrators can be a primary source of information in the tool-selection process. They often understand better than anyone the compatibility, resource, and performance issues that are involved in getting a new project off the ground.

Tools and Process

There are two extremes when it comes to adopting new tools and environments. Some organizations make it a high priority to adopt the latest technology, hoping to gain an advantage over their competition. Others, realizing the expense and heartbreak involved in being the among the first to adopt a new tool, stick with the old stuff until it is hopelessly obsolete. Most organizations fall somewhere in between these two extremes.

The latest tools are no guarantee of success. Older technology supporting a good process will be infinitely more successful than the very latest tools coupled with a weak process. However, organizations married to old technology will fail to attract top software talent and eventually will be overtaken by the competition.

Some of the major factors contributing to the failure of new tools in a software development organization are:

- The lack of an effective, flexible process.
- The new tool doesn't fit in with existing tools.
- A lack of training.
- Lack of management support.
- The new tools don't support the process.

The main problem with processes and tools in any software development organization is that a tool won't be used effectively unless it supports the process and methodology in place on your team. If the organization doesn't have a good process and/or methodology in place, no tool will help you. Conversely, for a methodology to be fully effective, it must be supported by the right design tools.

This might seem like a "catch 22," but the way it should be done is to get a core process (including a development methodology) in place and working first, then carefully add tools for support. As the tools make the process more efficient, both tools and process can be expanded.

In adopting tools into a process, the following steps can be followed:

1. Through developer requests and research, identify the need for a tool.
2. Study the process to determine how the tool would fit in.
3. Determine the driving compatibilities with operating systems and in-use toolsets.
4. Get management buy-in for tool-search.
5. Conduct indepth literature searches of available tools.
6. Compile a list of features via interviews with developers.
7. Shorten the tool list to the 5 to 10 most promising.
8. Interview vendors and product users.
9. Conduct inhouse vendor-supported product testing.
10. Compile results of research, interviews, testing.
11. Evaluate results to determine the best candidate.
12. Bring in the 2 or 3 best candidates for inhouse prototyping.
13. Purchase a small number of copies of the best tool.
14. Modify the process as necessary to incorporate the tool.
15. Provide ongoing training and consulting as necessary to bring developers up to speed.
16. Use the tool on a small pilot project.
17. If all goes well, the tool is cleared for use on a large mission-critical project.

In the software-development trenches, the analysis and adoption of new tools and methods is seldom if ever done perfectly. The main reason for this is that a software tool is to a project a little like a prescription is to a seriously ill patient. The wrong drug, or an otherwise correct medication given at the wrong time or in the wrong dosage, can do great damage. Failing to try any cure, however, can doom the patient. In software development as in medical treatment, you can't afford to spend forever analyzing solutions. Budget and schedule constraints will force you to get a reasonably good tool in place quickly rather than holding out for a silver bullet.

Tools for the Bug-Tracking Example

Product research tools—such as Computer Select from Ziff Communications Company, the newsgroups on the Internet, or other online services—can be extremely valuable sources of the latest product information. If a company needed a software bug-tracking system like the one explained in chapter 9, the first step would be to conduct an online literature search for all available defect tracking tools. There are a number of commercially available anomaly tracking systems, one of which could form the basis for the bug-tracking system. Researching these tools could be the most important part of the project.

This research should turn up useful tools such as ProTeam from Scopus Technology Inc. or The Software Edge Inc's Defect Control System, which link to a configuration management/version control system such as PVCS from Intersolv. Tools like these could fit right into the bug-tracking system that was described in chapter 9, because the bug tracker must coordinate with the existing configuration management system.

No tool operates in a vacuum, so the defect-tracking tool that is selected must fit in with the other systems in the execution environment. To ensure compatibility, you'll need to evaluate the execution environments that are available inhouse or off-the-shelf and determine a compatible environment that would have the needed performance and hardware resources for the new tool.

The system can be implemented with several database servers, each containing a persistent data set. Each of the clients could provide a specific interface, supporting different views of the data, so an object-oriented DBMS such as ObjectStore could work well for the database servers. Because the bug-tracking system will need to grow as more customers use the company's software products and as new software products are developed, scaleability is extremely important.

UNIX could be an excellent choice for the server operating system because it is compatible with a huge variety of tools and has unmatched scaleability and portability. Microsoft Windows would be a good choice for the client platforms because of its ubiquity, as well as the plethora of fairly sophisticated GUI tools compatible with it.

If you find an off-the-shelf defect-tracking tool that fits the users' requirements perfectly, the effort involved will be primarily installation, training, and administration. If the programming effort is relatively small (involving fewer than 25 developers), an object-oriented CASE tool, such as Rational Rose, might be warranted, but the project probably could do well without one, depending upon the maturity of the process. To create the user interface, developers could use a visual-programming workbench or fourth-generation language such as PowerBuilder. For a large programming effort, a good CASE tool is required.

Summary

A good tool can be of maximum benefit only within a good process, and a good process can be greatly enhanced with good tools. Finding the right tools involves researching developers' needs and vendor offering, plus the expertise of a dedicated "toolsmithing" team.

CASE tools are far from a panacea, but good CASE support is essential for an effective process, especially when it comes to developing large mission-critical systems. Database management systems are an integral part of most mission-critical systems, and both relational and object-oriented systems offer advantages. Users' voracious appetites for ever-more-friendly graphical interfaces demand GUI builders, modern languages, and 4GLs, but none of these tools nor any others can make up for a lack of software process and integrated tool support.

Today's software execution environment involves much more than a simple scheduler and I/O handler. Handling asynchronous resource sharing across networks is the task for which modern networks and the client/server paradigm were designed, and several operating systems have what it takes to build an industrial-strength client/server environment. These include UNIX, OS/2, and Windows NT.

Multiple versions of software tools and environments from multiple vendors create compatibility problems and make client/server system administration extremely complex, especially when beta versions are involved.

Ideally, adopting a new software development tool will involve extensive research, analysis, training, and breaking the tool in on a small pilot project. Unfortunately, under real-world project pressures, this seldom happens.

Tools such as GUI builders and database management systems, as well as client/server operating environments, can increase developer productivity and software quality. In the grand scheme of things, however, the way that technology fits together and the way that it fits into a process has a much greater impact on productivity than does any specific tool or environment.

References

Bowman, Charles. 1994. "Objectifying Motif." *Software Development*. 2(4):55–61.

Brockschmidt, Kraig. 1993. *Inside OLE 2*. Redmond, Washington: Microsoft Press.

Brooks, Frederick P. 1972. *The Mythical Man-Month*. Reading, Massachusetts: Addison-Wesley.

DTC Staff. 1994. *Understanding New Technologies: Client/Server*. Distributed Technology Corporation.

Evans, Bergen. 1978. *Dictionary of Quotations*. New York: Avenel Books.

Gryphon, Robert. 1994. "The CASE for Client/Server." *Data Based Solution*. 12(8):72–80.

Gagnon, Gabrielle. 1994. "Building a Better App, SQL Style." Comparison of Gupta's SQLWindows 4.1, Knowledgeware's ObjectView 3.0, and Powersoft's PowerBuilder 3.0 database application development software. *PC Magazine*. 13(10):1–7.

Jicha, Henry. 1994. "Object Technology Explodes with Visual Programming." *Object Magazine*. 4(4):33–36.

Khoshafian, Setrag and Razmik Abnous. 1990. *Object Orientation: Concepts, Languages, Databases, User Interfaces*. New York: John Wiley and Sons.

Korzeniowski, Paul. 1994. "Client/Server Developers Give CASE Another Look." *Software Magazine*. 13(14):15–31.

Kruglinski, David J. 1993. *Inside Visual C++*. Redmond, Washington: Microsoft Press.

Linthicum, David. 1994. "Operating Systems for Database Servers." *DBMS*. 7(2):62–67.

Morse, Alan and George Reynolds. 1994. "Overcoming Current Growth Limits in UI Development." *Communications of the ACM*. 6(4):73–81.

Murphy, Thomas. 1993. "Looking at the World Through Cheap Sunglasses." *Computer Language*. 10(2):63–86.

Radding, Alan. 1994. "The Quiet NT Invasion." *InfoWorld*. 16(21):85–86.

Sarna, David E. Y. and George J. Febish. 1994. "The Case Against CASE." *Datamation*. 40(13):19–20.

Semich, J. William. 1994. "Can You Orchestrate Client/Server Computing?" *Datamation*. 40(16):36–43.

Semich, J. William. 1994. "Client/Server CASE: Oxymoron or Essential?" *Datamation*. 40(17):67–80.

Shammas, Namir C. 1994. *Using Visual C++*. Indianapolis, Indiana: Que Corporation.

Shelton, Tom. 1994. *LAN Times Encyclopedia of Networking*. Berkeley: Osborne McGraw-Hill.

Weissman, Ronald FE. 1994. "Unleashing the Power of Client/Server Computing." *Object Magazine*. 4(1):38–39.

Wolfe, Alexander. 1994. "Object Software Finally Comes to Life at Confab." *Electronic Engineering Times*. 808:1,15.

Yourdon, Edward. 1994. "C++: Whither or Wither?" *Ed Yourdon's Guerrilla Programmer*. 1(8):1–7.

Yourdon, Edward. 1993. *Decline and Fall of the American Programmer*. Englewood Cliffs, New Jersey: Prentice Hall.

Yourdon, Edward. 1994. "C++: Flying Monkeys, Old Goats, Young Turks, Software World, and Hong Kong." *Ed Yourdon's Guerrilla Programmer*. 1(4):1–8.

Quality—A Practical
Perspective

11

Guidelines for Software Quality

Software systems have become extremely complex over the years. This added complexity has resulted in higher development costs and an increase in the time that it takes to develop the system. As stated in *Ed Yourdon's Guerrilla Programmer* (Yourdon 1994), "consider the entire PC software industry's near-perfect record of *never* delivering a new software product on time." Companies are being forced to find better ways to manage the development of these complex software systems.

The software industry is on the verge of going through a revolution similar to the Industrial Revolution. During the Industrial Revolution, we went from making cars, for example, one at a time to mass production in which we invented assembly lines that allowed us to produce several cars at the same time. We were able to produce more cars in less time and at a reduced production cost.

The software revolution will be slightly different; instead of mass production, we will see massive savings in the development of software products. Another way to look at it is the Industrial Revolution focused on the production side of the process while the software revolution will focus on the development side. This will be accomplished not only through improved management of the development of software but also through better management of the process itself. We will see dramatic increases in the utilization of reusable components, development processes that have a built-in improvement mechanism, and an improvement in the development tools used to manage and develop software.

This revolutionary process already has begun in aerospace and Department of Defense (DoD) related fields and even in the commercial world. There has been a lot of focus on the evaluation of the development process as a whole and determining where a company stands relative to its ability to produce software-intensive products. The software industry continues to develop new and improved methodologies, which are incorporated into the tools of the trade, such as compilers and CASE tools. Everyone in the software industry is looking for a better mouse trap, and they are not limiting their view to the type of cheese to use in the trap; they are looking at the entire trap and the way it is produced.

One of the primary components of the software revolution is *software quality*. Although this often is used to mean the quality of the final product, we will take it one step further. In this chapter, we are expanding the definition to include the following items:

- The quality of the development process
- The quality associated with managing the development process
- The quality of the methods that are used to monitor product development (Software Quality Assurance)
- The quality of the final product itself

To identify ways to develop quality software, you must be able to quantify your present status. Over the past several years, there have been several new developments in the evaluation of a company's ability to develop reliable software. The list of assessment methods includes Trillium (developed by Bell and Northern Telecom), HealthCheck (developed by British Telecom), and ISO 9000, which is gaining acceptance in Europe as a major assessment method (ISO 9000-3 will focus on software development). Within the U.S., the most influential assessment method is the Process Maturity Model, which was developed by the Software Engineering Institute (SEI) at Carnegie-Mellon University. The Process Maturity Model also is known as the Capability Maturity Model (CMM).

Software Quality Assurance (SQA) is a key element in the Capability Maturity Model. SQA, or the Quality Monitoring Organization, should evolve as you continue to progress to a more mature state. Inspections and reviews also are a part of this improvement process, but they are dependent on the establishment of a sound development process.

Just as the Industrial Revolution took place over the course of 100 years, the software revolution will not happen overnight. It takes time to progress from one maturity level to another, and there is no way to circumvent the improvement process. As Yourdon (1993) points out, "For these [larger] organizations, it is reasonable to expect a period of 2 to 3 years between [process maturity] levels; that is, *a decade to go from level 1 to 5!*" One of the primary reasons for the slow progression is the overall cultural changes that must take place. Software organizations must allow time for the software developers to become comfortable with the new philosophy behind developing software. Other factors that account for the slow progression include: justifying and obtaining the monetary investment, establishing appropriate training and tools, etc.

The companies that complete the revolutionary process first will have a distinct advantage over those that continue to ignore it. The companies that accept and drive the revolutionary changes will be able to underbid (in both budget and schedule) those that do not. By the time the slower companies realize that they too should adopt measures to improve their development process, it might be too late.

This chapter will begin by examining SEI's Capability Maturity Model. We will look at the different maturity levels that are defined within this model and how to progress from level to level. We will provide an introductory view into this model. For a more in-depth description, we highly recommend reading *Managing the Software Process* by Watts S. Humphrey (1990).

We will continue by looking at SQA and its impact on the progression to a more improved state. This chapter will introduce inspections and reviews as another important aspect of managing software quality. We will examine the impacts that the software developers have on the success of the software organization. The chapter will conclude by looking at the cost and benefits associated with software quality.

SEI's Capability Maturity Model

As stated previously, to improve the development process, you must understand the current status of your process. You must know your strengths and weaknesses and identify the areas that need improvement. You need a method of quantifying your current and desired state. This is where SEI's Capability Maturity Model comes in.

The Capability Maturity Model was developed by Watts Humphrey and his colleagues at SEI (which is affiliated with Carnegie-Mellon University). SEI Capability Maturity Model was published first in 1988 in *IEEE Software* (Humphrey 1988). This model defines five levels of maturity. As shown in Figure 11.1, each level has specific characteristics associated with it.

The model also identifies what to focus on to move to a higher maturity level. Figure 11.2 shows what steps must be taken to move from one maturity level to the next. Although a company might have achieved some of the goals in a higher level, you cannot move up to the next level until *all* the requirements have been fulfilled.

The Assessment

When you are planning to take a trip, you do certain things to prepare for the journey. You obtain a map, determine where you are on the map, find

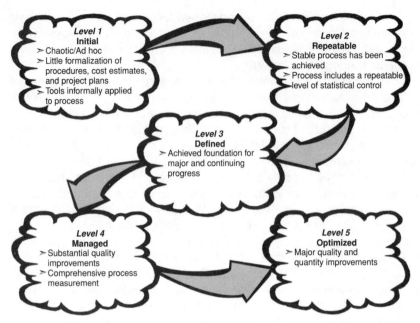

Figure 11.1   Characteristics of the process maturity levels.

your destination on the map, and determine the best route to take. In short, you need to know where you are, where you're going, and how to get there. If you leave any of these steps out, you might end up completely lost. If, for example, you try to go to the Super Bowl, you need to know where it will be held. If you try to get there without a map, chances are you won't make it. If you can't find your current location on the map, you won't be able to determine the best route to take. You probably won't be able to determine any route that will get you there.

Some of the same principles hold for improving the software development process. If you randomly select areas to improve, you might successfully identify the true problem areas and your efforts will be rewarded, but then again, you might not. Some of your efforts might interfere with other improvements that you are trying to make. Even the best educated guess might not identify the appropriate areas to focus on.

The best way to identify where to focus your efforts is first to identify your current status—your strengths and weaknesses, so to speak. You then must identify your goals—what you are trying to achieve. Last but not least, you must determine the best areas on which to focus and the order in which they should be accomplished to achieve your goals.

The Capability Maturity Model is like a road map that allows us to identify where we are, where we are going, and the best way to get there. It provides evaluation techniques to identify which of the five levels we are at currently. Combine this information with the characteristics of each successive level along with following the recommended steps to reach each level (Figure 11.2), and you have all the information that you need to chart a course to success. The ultimate goal is to reach level 5, but you must take it one step at a time. After all, it is very difficult to drive from Los Angeles to New York without making a few stops along the way. If nothing else, you'll need to get gas.

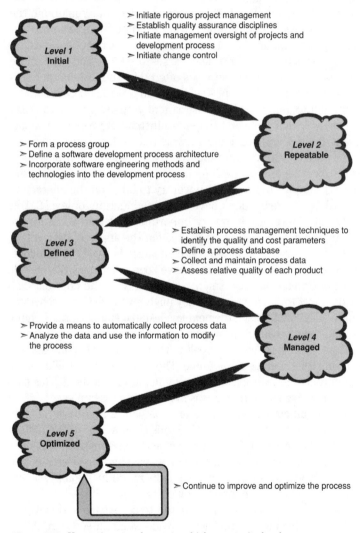

Figure 11.2 Key actions to advance to a higher maturity level.

An organization's current state or process maturity level is determined by a formal *assessment*. The assessment consists of a detailed questionnaire and field visits by qualified assessors to interview both managers and software developers. The results of the assessment indicate the organization's current state and provide recommendations of what to do to reach the next level. The assessment should be repeated after each level is achieved to verify the organization has fulfilled the requirements for the new level and to obtain new recommendations on how to reach the next higher level.

The Capability Maturity Model Assessment can be administered by yourself or an impartial entity (e.g., the SEI, etc.), assuming that they have had the appropriate SEI training. It is highly recommended that you obtain the services of a qualified assessor or attend the appropriate training before trying to perform an assessment. The SEI provides a wide array of courses, including training of assessors and lead assessors. To find out more information about the courses and services offered by the SEI contact customer relations at customer-relations@sei.cmu.edu or (402) 269-5800.

It often is difficult to administer the assessment yourself. It is all too easy to provide the answer that you want to believe instead of properly evaluating your current abilities and providing answers that reflect your true capabilities. If you evaluate yourself and incorrectly assess yourself at level 2 when you are truly at level 1, you will focus your efforts on addressing the changes required to move to level 3. You will try to build on the characteristics of level 2 when you really don't have a solid foundation for level 2. You will most likely fail. Therefore, it is very important to get an accurate assessment of your capabilities and place yourself at the appropriate level.

A problem that we have seen at several companies is the lack of follow-through after performing the assessment. I have seen companies that get all fired up about performing the assessment and identifying the changes that need to be made to get to the next level. They might even develop a schedule showing when they expect to reach the next level. Management stands behind it all the way until the assessment is over and the schedule is drawn, then . . . nothing. No follow-through to make it a reality. There is no push to implement the changes during the scheduled timeframe. The staff becomes disillusioned not only by the process assessment but also by management itself. This can leave a company in worse shape than it was in before the assessment.

This is not true of all companies. There are companies that have taken it seriously and currently are taking the right steps to move up to the higher levels. Bull HN, Hughes Aircraft, Schlumberger, and Texas Instruments have been very successful in implementing the necessary changes (Herbsleb, et al., 1994a). They already are seeing positive results in product quality, shortened schedules, and decreased nonrecurring costs.

As you can see, the successes are not limited to aerospace and DoD-related fields. They are having an impact on a wide range of software disciplines. The companies using SEI's Capability Maturity Model with success are involved in such domains as telecommunications, embedded real-time systems, information systems, and operating systems.

Even so, most companies still are at level 1. A few have reached level 2, and fewer still have reached level 3. As shown in Figure 11.3, the distribution of organizations by maturity level now is about 75% at level 1, 16% at level 2, 8% at level 3, 0% at level 4, and 0.5% at level 5 (Herbsleb, et al., 1994b). The only level 5 organization that SEI has information on is the highly publicized Motorola India site (Herbsleb 1994). Give these companies time, however, and they will succeed. They already have taken the first step; they have performed an assessment to determine their current state. One of them might be your prime competitor.

It is important to note that the percentages shown in Figure 11.3 represent the maturity levels achieved by *software organizations*. There have been several cases where individual projects have reached higher maturity levels. Yourdon (1993) identifies the example where "SEI concluded in September 1991 that the IBM site involved in software development for the U.S. space shuttle at NASA is indeed operating at level 5 [Bush 1991]".

Moving up the ladder takes time. It can take several years to move from one level to the next, and cheating is not allowed. You can't move from level 1 to level 3 without reaching level 2 first. It would be very difficult to collect and maintain process data (one of the key steps in moving from level 3 to level 4) prior to establishing a stable process (level 2 characteristic).

With that in mind, how do you recognize your current level? Before you can recognize a given level, you first must understand what the levels are

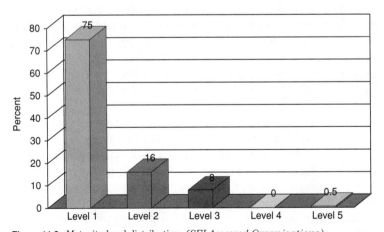

Figure 11.3 Maturity level distribution. *(SEI Assessed Organizations)*

and what characterizes them. As shown in Figure 11.1, the five maturity levels are as follows:

- Initial Process
- Repeatable Process
- Defined Process
- Managed Process
- Optimizing Process

The following section will look at the individual levels in more detail.

Level 1: The Initial Process

The Initial Process level is characterized by the chaotic or *ad hoc* nature of developing software. As Humphrey (1990) states, "At this stage the organization typically operates without formalized procedures, cost estimates, and project plans." The development tools that are used are not integrated with the development process (if any process exists). The tools that are used are not uniformly applied to the individual development groups. There might even be different tools used by different groups.

In a level-1 organization, the development process might be different among groups. There typically is no formal configuration management or change control mechanisms in place. Senior management is not exposed to the problems and issues facing the software organization. Because of the differences between individual groups, senior management has a difficult time understanding the scope of the actual problems that do exist; they might become confused trying to keep track of which project is using which process and which problems apply to which development groups.

With all this in mind, you probably can understand the difficulties a level-1 organization faces in trying to maintain a specific product. The lack of a development process or standards makes it extremely difficult to add new functionality or fix a problem with a given product. Even the original developer might find it difficult, after being away from it for some time, to work on the software system.

What happens when the project guru leaves the company? A lot of what went into the design of that system will walk out through the front door with him or her. The new person assigned to the project will require a steep, possibly unscalable learning curve just to get up to speed and become productive.

In some cases, companies decide to completely redevelop the system instead of adding the new functionality to the existing system. They feel that the lack of understanding of the current system will be harder to overcome than it would be to design it from scratch.

Another solution to the problem of dealing with software that is developed by a guru that is no longer with the company is to isolate the core of the system and protect it from any direct changes. Any new functionality or bug fix is accomplished by adding or changing the software that interfaces with it. Using this approach, a system can quickly degenerate into an unmaintainable mess.

A level-1 organization's typical solution to schedule problems is to throw more bodies at it and, if that doesn't work, bring in some expensive "sharpshooters." This really doesn't solve the short-term problem because even sharpshooters need a little time to become familiar with the target. The people that are making progress will need to stop and take the time to bring the new people up to speed. So whatever progress that is being made slows down or even stops until the new people become productive. You eventually will reach the point of diminishing returns. Assigning 20,000 developers to a project consisting of 10,000 lines of code is hardly productive and, for the reasons cited earlier, will result in delaying the scheduled completion of the project.

All in all, it doesn't sound like a productive environment. Keep in mind that this style of development, through the efforts of some very talented and dedicated developers and managers, has proven to be successful and profitable over the years. The problem is that the days where applications that could be developed by a handful of developers have all but come and gone. The complexity of today's systems, along with continued improvements to the existing systems, requires repeatability, maintainability, and all the other "-ilities" to decrease cost and shorten the time to delivery (or schedule). Customers are expecting more capability in less time than ever before. The company that can meet these needs and provide a good quality product will continue to be profitable through the turn of the century.

As shown in Figure 11.2, the level-1 organization must establish some basic project controls. You must initiate rigorous project management, establish quality assurance disciplines, initiate management oversight of projects and the development process, and initiate a change control mechanism.

An effective *project management system* will provide control over the company's software commitments. The project management system will define how to prepare the information that is required to develop a new system. It will define who is responsible for the different aspects of the estimate, how the project plans are to be created and monitored, and what the plans will contain.

The project plans will ensure that the company understands the magnitude of the new project. It will define the staffing, computing resource, and facility requirements (commonly referred to as *resource requirements*). It also will determine the schedule that is associated with the project, including project milestones that can be used to track the progress during the development of the system. The schedule also should include plans to perform a postmortem analysis so that the company can learn from the experience (what worked, what didn't work) while it still is fresh in the minds of those involved.

The company also must establish a *quality assurance organization* whose charter is to monitor the planning, development, implementation, and verification activities that are associated with the project. This organization should have an independent reporting chain to senior management and sufficient resources to do the job. As Watts Humphrey (1990) states, "This generally requires an [software quality assurance] organization of about 3% to 6% of the size of the software organization."

Senior management must oversee the activities of the software development and quality assurance organizations. "This includes review and approval of all major development plans prior to their official commitment" (Humphrey 1990).

Quarterly reviews should be used by senior management to monitor process compliance and to make necessary adjustments to project plans (e.g., adding resources), quality and schedule performance, cost trends, and quality and productivity goals for each individual project. This will help the company minimize over-commitments and budget problems.

The company must institute a *change control* mechanism. The system requirements must be relatively stable to ensure a good design. Even so, the system requirements seem to change continually throughout the life of the project. As the system becomes more thoroughly defined, issues arise and the overall result is a requirements change. The incorporation of these changes must be planned such that there is a minimal impact to the design, implementation, and testing phases of the project. If changes are incorporated in an *ad hoc* manner, the other phases of the project will suffer. Errors will be introduced unless a complete analysis of the impact of the change is performed.

Additional changes will be identified during the other phases of the project as well. Design and implementation issues can result in a change to the requirements, and the testing effort might uncover problems in the design. The incorporation of these changes must be controlled as well.

Some of these areas already might be sufficiently covered by the company's current software development policies. The specific areas that the company needs to focus on to reach level 2 will be identified by the assessment process.

Level 2: The Repeatable Process

You've reached level 2: The Repeatable Process. You have control over the way that the software organization establishes its plans and commitments. You have achieved a degree of statistical control through learning to make and meet your estimates and plans (Humphrey 1990). You have achieved a significant goal. It now is time to look ahead to the next level.

As Ed Yourdon (1994) states, "A level-2 organization has a repeatable process resulting from 'tribal folklore,' which has not been formally documented." The level-2 organization's strength is the result of their experience at doing similar work. There is a significant amount of risk associated with any new challenge. Developing a new product that is different from the types of projects that normally are developed by the organization and major organizational changes can prove disastrous to a level-2 organization.

As shown in Figure 11.2, the level-2 organization must form a process group, define a development process architecture, and incorporate software engineering methods and technologies.

Establishing a *process group* allows the company to prove its commitment to improvement and take some of the pressure off the individual development groups that are responsible for a specific project. The individual developers and the individual groups will accept process improvement more readily if they have visible proof that senior management stands behind it. This proof *must* continually be reinforced by communicating the status of the individual process improvement efforts to the software organization.

Some experienced developers/engineers should be given full-time assignments in the process group. Many companies try to fund the process improvement effort by forcing the individual development groups to supply resources and budget that initially was planned for developing their specific product. This not only puts a lot of pressure on the organization to cut back in some way, but the cutbacks also typically are in the area of software improvement efforts; progress in the area of software process improvement is slow at best. Providing a separately budgeted process group allows the development groups to focus their efforts on developing their product.

Other members should be involved in the process group on a part-time basis, where they also are involved in the development and software-quality organizations. This allows the development and software-quality organizations to have a voice in the process and keeps the lines of communication open.

Many "grass roots" improvement efforts are underway in the different development groups. The process group can help to combine these efforts and eliminate duplication of effort. The process group can publicize these efforts and expand them to an organization-wide effort. The individual groups can be recognized and they become a part of developing the process as a whole.

As Humphrey (1990) states, "The responsibilities of the process group include defining the development process, identifying technology needs and opportunities, advising the projects, and conducting quarterly management reviews of process status and performance." He goes on to recommend that "the process group should be about 1% to 3% of the size of the software organization."

The *software development architecture* or, as it sometimes is called, the *software development lifecycle* describes the required technical and management activities that are necessary to ensure proper execution of the development process. The company must establish an architecture that is compatible with the specific needs of the organization and with the technical nature of the work performed by the organization. The architecture progressively decomposes the development life cycle into individual tasks until each individual task can be performed by a single management unit. Each individual task defines a set of prerequisites, functional descriptions, verification procedures, and task completion specifications.

The incorporation of software methods and technologies into the development process requires that the company remain aware of new developments in the software industry. The software methods and technologies that should be introduced include a formal inspection process, formal design methods, library control systems, and comprehensive testing methods. Library control systems should address both reuse libraries and configuration management issues.

The process group must stay current on new methodologies and tool sets. Their findings must be communicated throughout the software organization. This evaluation should identify possible changes to the existing, organization-wide development process. Care must be taken to ensure that the new methodology or technology can be incorporated such that the development process still meets the needs of the individual development groups.

In many cases, a pilot project has been established to evaluate one or more of these methods/technologies. Pilot projects allow the company to experiment with new methodologies and technologies before making an organization-wide commitment. The company will be able to perform an evaluation based on comparing two similar projects where the differences are limited (for the most part) to the use of different software methods or technologies. The process group should be involved in the analysis of the results, and if successful, they can incorporate the methods and technologies into the organization-wide development process.

> I recently was involved in a pilot project to evaluate the use of object-oriented development methods on a real-time embedded system. When the results are completed and analyzed, the company will know if the object-oriented methods made a positive impact on the development of the system. I believe that using the object-oriented methodology resulted in a more maintainable product. The step from requirements analysis to preliminary design was easier to understand and did not require the "magic leap" that often is required when using the structured analysis and object-oriented design, or OOD (the company had already decided to use OOD).
>
> Rod Skoglund

Some of the advances that should be considered for incorporation are an object-oriented methodology, rapid prototyping, using a modern implementation language, CASE tools that allow part of the process to be automated, etc. The specific advances that are incorporated will depend on the organization and what works best for the company as a whole.

Level 3: The Defined Process

Your process improvement efforts have elevated your company to level 3: The Defined Process. You have successfully achieved yet another major goal. The individual developers and the individual development groups are putting a lot more faith in the process and the improvement effort. Your company has established the foundation for major and continuing progress.

As Ed Yourdon (1994) states, "Level 3 is where we see an organization with a documented, institutionalized software process, which includes configuration management, formal tracking of code/test errors, software reviews/inspections, etc."

Now that you're here, you might be surprised to find that it is difficult to nail down how effective the process really is. You do not have the means to quantitatively measure the impact of the process. It seems natural that this is where you should focus your efforts and that you should address these concerns now. After all, better management of the process is one of the keys to success.

As shown in Figure 11.2, the level-3 organization must establish process management techniques to identify the quality and cost parameters, define a process database, collect and maintain process data, and assess the relative quality of each product.

Establishing the process management techniques to identify the quality and cost parameters will allow the company to "quantify the relative costs and benefits of each major process activity, such as the cost and yield of error detection and correction methods" (Humphrey 1990). This will provide the data that is necessary to identify where the process is succeeding and where it needs to be improved.

A process database should be established to allow the data to be managed and maintained. The database must be readily accessible by the individual development groups, software quality assurance, and the process group. It should be used to analyze process quality and productivity improvements.

The company must provide the resources that are necessary to collect the data, maintain it, and advise the development groups on its use. Upon submission, the data must be carefully analyzed to ensure that it meets a minimal set of quality standards to maintain the credibility and reliability of the database.

The quality assurance organization is responsible for assessing the relative quality of each product. They are to inform management of any cases where quality targets are not being met. They should monitor the development process as it is applied to each individual project.

Level 4: The Managed Process

You now are at level 4: The Managed Process. Your company has made substantial quality improvements. "[Your software] organization has initiated comprehensive process measurements and analysis" (Humphrey 1990). The company is gathering and analyzing a lot of different data that is used to improve both the products and the process that is used to develop the products. However, given the enormous costs that are associated with gathering this data, you still are limited in how much you can collect and maintain.

You must be careful to identify metrics that can be uniformly defined and applied to the different projects. When the collection of data is not well defined, it might, in effect, be like comparing apples and oranges. If one group includes comments in their source code line count while another does not, comparisons of the two sets of data will be invalid and result in incorrect conclusions about the two projects.

Humphrey (1990) states, "Process data must not be used to compare projects or individuals." It must be limited to identifying areas in which process improvements can be made. If the data is used to judge projects or individuals, the reliability of the data will suffer.

As shown in Figure 11.2, the level-4 organization must provide a means to automatically collect process data and analyze the data. This information should be used to modify the process. Data that is collected manually often is error prone. This can be caused by different interpretations of what the data is and how it will be used. Automatically collected data is forced to be collected in the same way using the same criteria from project to project. Automation of the data gathering also will reduce the cost associated with its collection.

The collected data should be analyzed to identify problems in the process as well as ways to make the process more efficient. The results of the analysis should be used to modify the process to incorporate new solutions and continue to improve the process.

Level 5: The Optimizing Process

You've reached the ultimate goal: The Optimizing Process. Your company now is in a position to enjoy major quality and productivity benefits. As Humphrey (1990) states, "Up to this point, software development managers have focused largely on their products and typically will gather and analyze only data that directly relates to product improvement. In the Optimizing Process, the data is available to tune the process itself."

You might think that level 5 is when you can relax and reap the rewards of all this process improvement, but you will soon find that is not a wise idea. The improvement process requires a continuous effort to keep finding better and better ways to develop software. As shown in Figure 11.2, you must continue to improve and optimize the process.

Software Quality Assurance

The mere mention of Software Quality Assurance (SQA) can strike fear and disgust into the hearts of software developers. Software developers often view this side of software development as a nuisance at best—something to get through as quickly as you can while minimizing any impact to workload and the product. Ironically, SQA, when used appropriately, can help the developers achieve these goals.

The software developers working on software quality assurance assignments rarely are given the respect that they deserve. They often are brushed off with excuses such as "yes, we'll meet the standards, after we finish this delivery." More often than not, software organizations are scrambling to meet unrealistic budget and schedule constraints. Once again, SQA can help by providing metrics that will identify ways to become more efficient and improve budget and schedule estimating.

Establishing and using a Software Quality Assurance organization is one of the key steps for a level-1 organization to move up to a level 2 (see Figure 11.2). Due to the importance of this step and the previous misconceptions regarding SQA, we thought it would be useful to examine the fine art of SQA.

So why do we create software quality organizations? With so little respect for this discipline, how can it be effective? To completely understand the answers to these questions, we must look at what software quality is and some of the basic reasons behind our feelings regarding SQA.

Whether the software developers realize it or not, they are part of software quality assurance. Every time they review or inspect a document or write code in a way that meets the company's standard format, they are performing a part of software quality assurance. Even the way that we organize our review meetings and inspections is governed by software quality assurance.

If you ask 10 people to define quality, you probably will get ten different answers. For example, if you ask several people what determines the quality of a grocery store, you will get several different answers. One person might say that the quality is based on the freshness of their produce, while another person might say it depends on the length of the lines at the checkout stands. Another person might tie quality to the range of brands that are available or even the availability of sizes. As you can see, quality can mean different things to different people.

In software, as in most industries (including grocery retail), the ultimate goal of producing a quality product is to ensure that your customer is happy. When your customers are happy, they will feel more comfortable and confident about contracting with your company again. This translates to success. In addition, your reputation will help you win other contracts with new customers. Once again, this translates to success.

Keeping the customer happy is more than delivering a product that performs the tasks that he or she asked for; it also means being able to handle changes in the requirements and responding to problems in a timely manner. Customer requirements usually change over time. After a product is in the field for several years, the customer might want to add functionality or make other modifications to reflect changes in the way he or she does business themselves. You must be capable of incorporating these changes in a timely manner. Unless the new requirements are too extensive, you must be capable of incorporating the changes without completely redefining the system altogether.

Walkthroughs, Reviews, and Inspections

As Booch (1994) points out, "Perhaps the most important quantifiable measure of goodness is the defect-discovery rate." The best way to identify software defects is through the use of walkthroughs, reviews, and inspections.

Walkthroughs and reviews are important quality management tools. We will provide a brief description of walkthroughs and reviews and explain how they are used in the development process. Inspections play an even more important role in process improvement. We will provide a more detailed look at the inspection process and how it can be used effectively as a part of the software development process.

Walkthroughs

Walkthroughs allow the developers that are associated with a specific subsystem (one of the smaller pieces of the overall system) to present or "walk through" their design. It provides an opportunity to explore design alternatives and helps the other members of the team get a better understanding of the system as a whole.

Not only are walkthroughs an excellent learning tool, but they also help unify the project team. The team will work together more efficiently. Walkthroughs do not need to be a formal part of the development process, but they must be accounted for on the project development schedule.

Reviews

There are two types of reviews: management reviews and technical reviews. *Management reviews* provide a means for managers to track the development progress, identify problems, recommend solutions, and ensure that there is a proper allocation of resources. These reviews also give the project team a forum to raise issues that must be handled at a higher management level. These reviews form a part of the requirements that are associated with moving from a level-1 to a level-2 organization; they provide a means for management to oversee the project development. The frequency of these reviews are dependent on the needs of the company and the software organization.

Technical reviews are used to examine the project's planning documentation. This includes the development plan, SQA plan, verification and test plans, configuration management plans, etc. It ensures that the planning behind the project is sound and that all aspects of the project are accounted for.

Inspections

Inspections are an element of a formal process where an intermediate product—such as a requirements document, design document, code element, etc.—is examined for defects by the producer's peers. The inspections should ensure conformance with applicable specifications and standards, identify logical defects, and identify problems with the internal and external interfaces. Inspections must be an integral part of the development process and must cover all phases of the development life cycle.

Several formal inspection methods have been introduced over the years. One of the most famous was introduced by Michael Fagan (1976; 1986). *Fagan inspections*, or a slight variation of them, have been used successfully throughout the industry.

Establishing inspection procedures is a key step in progressing from a level-2 to a level-3 organization. The level-1 organization focuses its efforts on establishing some basic project controls. The level-2 organization is working on defining the process architecture and is establishing a process group to define the organization-wide development process.

The inspections are linked to the intermediate products that are produced during the different phases of the project. Therefore, the inspections are heavily dependent on a well-defined process architecture. The inspection procedures must be incorporated into the development process. Therefore, the process group must define these procedures and describe how inspections will fit into the overall development process.

There is a lot more to inspections than just the meeting itself. The following sections examine inspections in more detail.

Why we use inspections. Inspections allow the project to identify software defects early in the development cycle. The cost of fixing a defect increases when it is allowed to propagate through the different phases of the project. A design defect costs more to fix after the code is written, and it costs even more if it is not found until the testing phase. Fixing a design defect that was found during a design inspection involves correcting the design document. Fixing the design defect found during a code inspection requires correcting the design document and the code. Fixing the design defect found during the test phase requires writing and tracking a software problem report, correcting the design document and code, and rerunning the tests. As you can see, the sooner the defect is detected, the easier it is to correct.

Inspections tend to increase the quality of the product in several ways. The developers or producers of the intermediate products will try a little harder to ensure that they minimize the number of defects in the products that they produce. They know that their product will be inspected by their peers, and they want to do a good job.

After going through several inspections, the developer becomes aware of the types of defects that are identified and will put forth an extra effort to fix these types of defects *before* the actual inspection. This makes it harder for the inspectors to find defects, so they try harder to identify new types of defects. This cycle of events leads to a more experienced project team that has improved their development and inspecting skills. The final products produced by this team will be of a higher quality than those that are produced without the use of inspections.

The inspections might identify a common type of defect that can be categorized by the organization. The software organization can analyze the defect and incorporate the necessary steps to reduce that category of defect. The inspection process itself helps ensure that the developers are familiar with the other parts of the system (i.e., subsystems) that will ensure a smoother transition through the integration phase of the project. They will have a better understanding of the other subsystems that they interface with, and that understanding will be reflected in the subsystem they are designing.

Another very important aspect of inspections is that there *must* be a clear understanding of the purpose of the inspection. The purpose is to assist the developer or producer in improving his or her work and the quality of the project as a whole. The results of the inspection, in no way, should be used as a reflection of the developer's ability to produce a quality product.

If the developers view inspections as a personal attack or if they fear that management will use the results of the inspections to determine promotions or raises, they will be less likely to participate with an open mind. This tends to decrease the effectiveness of the inspection process. Put another way, inspections should be viewed as a review of the product, *not* a review of the originator of the product.

With this in mind, it would be counterproductive to have anyone other than the producer's peers involved in the inspection. The manager, software quality assurance, and the process group will need to have access to the results of the inspection, but the use of the data should be limited to identifying flaws in the development process and identifying common types of defects. Once again, the results of the inspections should *never* be used to evaluate the abilities of an individual developer.

Basic concepts behind inspections.   So far, we have talked a lot about inspections without describing what they are, the formalities behind them, or how to run them successfully. Let's start out by defining the basic principles behind the inspection process.

The inspection is a formal, structured process that uses a series of checklists and defined entrance and exit criteria. Even the role of each of the participants is well defined. The exact definition of these checklists, entrance and exit criteria, and the individual roles should be customized to fit the characteristics of the software organization.

The checklists should provide guidance to the inspectors and identify key items to watch out for. They should include specific items to aid in the discovery of any class or category of defect that has been identified as a problem during evaluation of the results of past inspections. Therefore, they should be a living document that can be modified as the inspection process evolves and matures through experience.

There should be a different checklist for each development phase of the project. Tables 11.1 through 11.4 provide example checklists for the requirements, design, code, and test phases of the project. These are only examples. The formal checklists that are used by any organization should be modified to meet the needs of the organization's development process. For example, the coding inspection checklist should take language-specific issues into account. In Ada, you might want to verify that the context clause does not contain extraneous dependencies. In Pascal, you might want to verify the correct usage of the "with" statement. In C, you might want to verify the appropriateness of the #include preprocessor statements.

TABLE 11.1   An Example of the Requirements Phase Inspection Checklist

1. Does the requirements document meet the company's documentation standards (header, footer, front page, table of contents, list of figures, etc.)?

2. For each individual requirement:
    a) Is it uniquely identifiable?
    b) Is it traceable to a system-level requirement?
    c) Is it clearly stated such that there is one and only one possible interpretation?
    d) Is it testable?

3. Do any of the requirements conflict with each other?

4. Are all of the system-level requirements addressed somewhere within the requirements document?

5. Are the requirements at the appropriate level of detail (see chapter 2)?

6. Are all references correct (system-level document, the company's documentation standards, etc.)?

TABLE 11.2 An Example of the Design Phase Inspection Checklist

1 Does the design document meet the company's documentation standards (header, footer, front page, table of contents, list of figures, etc.)?

2. Is the design stated in terms of the company's approved design representation standards (Object Message Diagrams, State Transition Diagrams, Class Dependency Diagrams, etc.)?

3. Are the internal and external interfaces clearly defined?

4. Are the internal and external interfaces consistent with each other?

5. For each individual design element:
   a) Is it uniquely identifiable?
   b) Is it traceable to a requirements document requirement?
   c) Is it clearly stated such that there is one and only one possible interpretation?
   d) Is it testable?

6. Do any of the requirements conflict with each other?

7. Are all the higher-level requirements addressed somewhere within the design cocument?

TABLE 11.3 An Example of the Coding Phase Inspection Checklist

1. Does the code meet the company's documentation standards, coding standards and style guide (header, indentation, etc.)?

2. For each coding element:
   a) Is it uniquely identifiable?
   b) Is it traceable to a design level element?
   c) Is it testable?

3. Are all of the design-level elements addressed somewhere within the code?

4. Are the internal and external interfaces clearly defined?

5. Are the internal and external interfaces consistent with each other?

6. Are there any logical errors within the code ("off by one" errors, etc.)?

7. Are the formal and actual parameters complete, and is each one required?

8. Are all the variables initialized properly?

9. Is any part of the code a possible candidate for reuse?

10. Is any part of the code already available from the reuse library?

11. Are comments used appropriately?

TABLE 11.4 An Example of the Testing Phase Inspection Checklist

1. Does each individual test meet the company's documentation standards (header, numbering, etc.)?

2. For each individual test case:
   a) Is it uniquely identifiable?
   b) Is it traceable to a system-level requirement (assuming requirements-based testing)?
   c) Are the expected results clearly defined?
   d) Is it repeatable?
   e) Are all the test equipment and setup requirements clearly defined?

3. Do any of the test cases overlap?

4. Are all of the system-level requirements fully tested (assuming requirements-based testing)?

In some cases, a company might want to define several checklists for each development phase. The individual inspectors are assigned a specific area that they are responsible for and are given a checklist to help them keep focused on that issue. The company might want one inspector to focus on conformance with the coding standards and style guide. Another inspector might be required to read the code backwards to help eliminate oversight of logical and typographical errors (I would not recommend requiring someone to read a document backwards, but it can be effective for a code inspection). Yet another might be responsible for ensuring proper higher-level requirement coverage. The inspectors are not limited to their assigned area of responsibility, but they are required to provide coverage of that aspect of the inspection.

The entrance criteria must define the minimum set of requirements that must be fulfilled before an inspection can take place. This ensures that the product to be inspected is truly ready for the inspection. Everyone's time won't be wasted inspecting an incomplete product. The exact requirements will vary depending on the product to be inspected. The entrance criteria for the inspection of the code for a given subsystem might require that the code compile successfully, that it is under configuration control (which should be true for any inspected product), that it includes the appropriate banner or header information, and so on. The entrance criteria for a design document might require that the document is run through a spell checker, that it is under configuration control, and so on.

Similarly, the exit criteria must define the minimum set of requirements that must be fulfilled before an inspection can be considered closed. Although this criteria might include some development of phase-specific items, there are some general requirements that will apply to all phases of the development. For example, the exit criteria must require that all the identified defects have been analyzed and resolved before the inspection can be closed.

The inspection team.   The members of the inspection team also are given a defined role in the inspection process. The specific people involved in an inspection, the inspection team, will vary from product to product. With the possible exception of the moderator and the scribe, the members of the team should be directly influenced by the product being inspected. The moderator also can be directly influenced by the product, but his or her role in the inspection process does not require it. Because of the other responsibilities of the scribe, you might find it difficult to log and present defects at the same time. The key roles of the inspection team include the following:

- Moderator
- Producers or Developers
- Inspectors
- Scribe or Recorder

The *moderator* is the leader for a given inspection. This can be a different person for each inspection. He or she is responsible for ensuring that the entrance criteria are met before the inspection package is sent out for review. He or she also is responsible for controlling the inspection meeting, keeping it running smoothly, and keeping the meeting focused on its objectives. This does not mean that they will "run" the meeting, but they are responsible for keeping the meeting focused on identifying, not resolving, defects and that the meeting does not get sidetracked or get off on a tangent. They also are responsible for ensuring that the exit criteria are met before filling out the paperwork that is associated with closing the inspection. In some cases, the moderator can be responsible for verifying that the individual inspectors are prepared before the meeting takes place. If they are not ready, the meeting is rescheduled for a time when they will be ready.

The *producers* or *developers* are responsible for producing the product (obviously) and for ensuring that the entrance criteria have been met before submitting it to the moderator. They also are responsible for putting the product under configuration control. When the moderator accepts the package, the producer is responsible for distributing the package to all of the members of the inspection team. This package should include, but is not limited to: the item being inspected, the appropriate checklists, and proof that the item is under configuration control. It is possible that there is more than one producer associated with a given product. In that case, they will share the responsibilities of the producer. After the inspection meeting, the producer is responsible for analyzing the defects and providing solutions for each one identified during the meeting. This typically is included in the exit criteria, which the producer is responsible for meeting.

The *inspectors* are responsible for inspecting the material *prior* to the inspection meeting. During the meeting, they should ensure that the defects that they found are logged by the scribe. If a follow-up inspection is required, they are responsible for ensuring proper incorporation of solutions to the defects that they identified, even if the defect also was found by other inspectors in the team. The moderator, producer, and scribe also can be inspectors, but this is not required. The inspectors should be people that are directly affected by the product. They can share common data, interface with the product, or share common resources.

One of the inspectors should be an SQA representative. This person will monitor the inspection to ensure that it conforms to the company's defined development process.

The *scribe* is responsible for filling out the defect log during the inspection. This log should include each defect that is identified during the inspection. Each entry (defect) should include sufficient information for the producer to analyze the defect. It also should identify the severity of the defect. If a document is being inspected, the log should identify the page and paragraph number (or a marked-up copy), a brief description of the defect, and the inspector that found the defect (in case the producer needs additional information during the analysis of the defect).

The look and feel of the defect log should be common throughout the organization. It should include a cover sheet that identifies all of the members of the inspection team, the amount of time spent by each team member on inspecting the product, and the signatures of all the participants (at the conclusion of the meeting). After the meeting, the scribe is responsible for getting any necessary signatures, then delivering the log to the moderator for filing. A copy should be given to the producers to allow them to analyze the data.

All of the data for a given inspection, along with a summary of the information, should be filed and submitted to SQA, management, and the process team. SQA will ensure that all of the inspection requirements from the development process are fulfilled. Management should use the data to identify common categories of defects, and the process team should use the data to identify ways to improve the organization-wide development process.

Training should play an important role in the inspection process. The moderator needs to be trained in how to be an effective meeting leader. The entire inspection team must learn all about the inspection process. They must understand the different roles of the team members and their individual responsibilities. They must understand the purpose of the inspection, as well as what the checklists are and how they are to be used. Classes, taught by well-trained instructors, will fill this need.

The inspection meeting.   The inspection meeting provides the opportunity for the inspectors to formally log the defects that they found during the inspecting. It often is referred to as a *defect logging session*. It should be no more than two hours in duration. If a product will take longer than two hours to log the defects, consider breaking it up into several separate inspections. If it does not make sense to break it up, hold several meetings, each of which is no more than two hours long. If the meeting becomes too long, it tends to become less effective.

The purpose of the meeting is to log defects. Analyzing any defect during the meeting must be avoided. More often than not, the analysis involves the producer and one or two of the inspectors. You are spending a lot of money for the other inspectors, the moderator, and the scribe to listen to the discussion. Their time could be better spent on meeting their individual project goals. It also tends to make the meeting drag.

The people who are not directly involved with the analysis discussion begin to feel like the inspection is a waste of their time. They become disillusioned with the inspection process as a whole. Although the discussion might be interesting, it should be postponed until after the meeting where the affected parties can meet and resolve the issue more efficiently. It is the moderator's responsibility to identify these situations and get the team back to logging defects.

There are several ways to run the meeting. One person, typically the producer, reads the product line by line. While this might work for code, it can become very slow when inspecting a document.

Another way to run the meeting is to begin at the beginning of the product and ask the inspectors to identify the first page in which they found a defect. The lowest number is the first defect that is logged. Continue through the product, defect by defect, until everyone has logged all the defects that they found.

Because all of the inspectors are responsible for inspecting the entire product, there is no need to go over pages where no defects were found. This tends to be quicker and allows you to focus on logging defects and not inspecting the product during the meeting.

At the conclusion of the meeting, the inspection team must determine whether a follow-up inspection is required. This should be based on the number and severity of the defects that were found. If a reinspection is required, the process starts all over again, except that, this time, the inspectors can focus on how the previously identified defects were resolved. They should ensure that they agree with the solution and that new defects have not been introduced.

The key is to keep the meeting short, sweet, and focused on meeting its objectives—logging defects.

Quality in the People

As Yourdon (1993) states, "Software quality is built into a software product, from the beginning, through the caliber of the people who create it, from the technology used to create it, and by means of a management discipline that oversees the process."

Software developers drive themselves to produce the best software that they can. They take pride in their work and their experience helps them achieve this goal. It is important to acknowledge this behavior and encourage the creativity that the software developers possess. This is not an easy task when you are asking them to conform to a set of guidelines and standards. Many people feel that this handcuffs the developers by not allowing them to design the code in their own way, giving it their signature, so to speak.

The truth of the matter is that the creativity that is incorporated in the design is independent of how we represent it on paper. It takes a creative mind to identify the classes and objects (assuming your using an object-oriented methodology) within a system. It takes a creative mind to define how the different objects will interact when responding to external system events and produce the required results. Whether you use OOCOBOL, Ada, C, or any other programming language, a creative mind is essential to the successful implementation of the design. It also takes a creative mind to identify the test cases that will verify the design and its implementation. Creativity is *not* limited by the development process. The development process allows the developer to focus creativity on the actual development and not on how it is represented on paper.

As stated previously, part of the software revolution involves going through a cultural change. Software developers, like people in general, are somewhat resistant to change; they tend to be more comfortable with conventional methods of development. They put more credibility in their direct experiences than they do in new methods. As more companies continue down the road of change, the software developers will put more faith in the new methods and concepts. Several companies have made excellent progress already (Herbsleb, et al., 1994a; 1994b).

The good news is that, as the revolution progresses through the industry, the software developers and the software industry as a whole will undergo the cultural changes that are part of the revolution process. This mainly will be due to the nomadic nature of the software developers themselves. A typical software developer will work for several companies throughout his or her career. As they move from company to company, they will bring valuable experience and ideas to the new company and will pick up more valuable experience and ideas from the new company. The cultural changes will move through the industry with the developers themselves.

The company has the ability to improve the quality of the people within its software organization. This is accomplished by providing the following support to the organizations:

- Provide the tools that will allow them to get the job done right.

- Provide and encourage training.

- Allow senior staff members to become mentors to those with less experience. This effort should be accounted for when evaluating their workload as well as their performance reviews.

- Provide a "dual ladder" that will allow promotions in either management or technical directions.

The quality of the people within the software organization will have a direct impact on the success of the organization. They are the key resource behind software development.

The Cost of Quality

Quality and process improvements do not come cheap. They require a substantial investment up front, and the benefits are difficult to quantify. You will have a difficult time justifying the need of such improvements. However, these improvements will not work without senior management buy-in. The software organization will be hesitant to participate unless there is visible senior management involvement and they show that they are committed to the improvement process. Once you can prove the benefits in terms of real dollars, senior management will have no trouble joining in and standing behind it.

Take inspections, for example. There are many costs involved in the inspection process: the inspectors' time inspecting the product, the moderator's time organizing the meeting, not to mention having a room full of developers involved in logging defects for two (or more) hours.

Inspections can be costly, both in budget dollars and schedule time. Time *must* be allocated for this effort. If it is not specifically identified on the project schedule as part of the tasks to be performed by the developers, they will be forced to work it in. The preparation for the inspections will suffer as the individual developers focus on their scheduled tasks.

We must keep it in perspective. Recall the example of a design defect that is not found until the testing phase of the project. The designer must spend time analyzing the problem and incorporating the changes into the design document. The coder must spend time analyzing the design changes and incorporating the necessary changes into the code. The tester must spend time writing and tracking the problem report and rerunning the test when the fix is incorporated. A new configuration and release of the design document and a new software build must be produced. This also tends to be a very costly effort.

Which is more expensive? Watts Humphrey (1990) provided the following list of success stories and states that, "[on] the positive side, there is an impressive and growing list of evidence that well-handled inspections pay enormous dividends in both quality and productivity":

- Yourdon (1979) and three experienced programmers found 25 defects during a 45-minute inspection of a 200 line PL/1 program. Five of these could not have been caught by testing. *This is typical of most developers' results with good inspections.*

- Freedman and Weinberg (1982) reported a decrease from 55% to 2% in errors associated with one-line maintenance changes immediately after inspections were introduced.

- In another example, Freedman and Weinberg (1982) state that the introduction of inspections in software maintenance reduced the number of production crashes by 77%.

- "Eleven COBOL programs were developed consecutively by the same people. After completion of the first five programs, inspections were instituted, and the error rates on the next six programs showed an average improvement of over five times" (Humphrey 1990).

- A large electronic switching system, developed by AT&T Bell Laboratories, was able to reduce the cost of finding errors by 10 times through the use of inspections (Fowler 1986).

- A dial-up central-switching system, which also was developed by AT&T Bell Laboratories, reported that inspections were 20 times more effective than testing in finding errors (Fowler 1986).

The list provided by Humphrey (1990) goes on and on. This is enough evidence that inspections are an effective way to improve the quality and productivity of software development. Keep in mind that inspections are just one of the elements associated with the process improvements that are part of the SEI Capability Maturity Model.

The SEI Capability Maturity Model also has been proven to be effective and has shown at least the possibility of a high return on investment. *The Benefits of CMM-Based Software Improvement: Initial Results* (SEI Technical Report CMU/SEI-94-TR-13, ESC-TR-94-013) by James Herbsleb, et al., (1994a) provides a good business case for investing in software process improvements. It summarizes the efforts of 13 companies that currently are using the Capability Maturity Model.

Five case studies are presented based on 5 of the 13 companies. The results are excellent. None of the companies were rated above level 3. The business value of using SEI's Capability Maturity Model (loosely referred to as the return on investment) ranged from 4.0 to 8.8 dollars returned for each dollar that was invested (Herbsleb, et al., 1994a; 1994b). These are impressive results. Herbsleb, et al., (1994a; 1994b) describe how the data was gathered and interpreted, as well as the caveats that shaped the way the data was interpreted. The initial analysis proves that the Capability Maturity Model can be used successfully to improve the software process.

Quality Improvement: Steps to Success

So how does a company ensure that they won't be left in the dust? We recommend the following steps described in this section to improve your software development process.

As mentioned earlier, the first step is to perform an assessment. Once the level is known, it can be determined where to focus your efforts and how to reach the next level. Take process improvement one step at a time, focusing your efforts and your goal toward reaching the next process maturity level.

The next step is to define a schedule showing when you will complete the steps and when you actually will reach the next level. Use the information and recommendations from the last assessment as your guide. You might want to show the next assessment on the schedule, at the time you expect to meet the requirements of the next level. The schedule must show intermediate goals (milestones) as well as the goal of reaching the next level.

A company might find that, after performing the assessment, they already have met some of the requirements for the next level. For example, the company that has performed the assessment and finds that it is at level 1 already might have a SQA organization in place. This should come out of the assessment and means that you have fewer things to accomplish to reach level 2. However, you cannot let these areas slide. You must stay on top of them to ensure that you eventually will meet the level 2 requirements.

Follow through and monitor your progress. If you see that you are not heading in the right direction, take the appropriate steps to get back on track.

Upon fulfilling all of the requirements for the next level, perform another assessment. If you still find that you are lacking in some area, focus on that area so that you can move on. If all the requirements are met, you've reached that level. You are ready to move on. If you have not reached level 5, return to the second step using the new assessment data and recommendations and set your sights a little higher. If you have reached level 5, continue to improve and optimize the process.

Before you begin this process, or shortly after starting, try to gather data from past projects that will be useful in quantifying the benefits of this process. You should include such things as: the percentage of the projects that ran late and by how much and the cost of the project, normalizing it where you can. Also include whatever else you feel would be useful.

Summary

The software revolution has begun. Companies from all software disciplines are looking for better ways to decrease costs, shorten delivery schedules, and still deliver a quality product. Improving the software development process is the key.

SEI's Capability Maturity Model is the map that we need to chart a course to an optimized development process. The model defines five levels of process maturity and what is required to move from one level to the next. Moving up the maturity ladder does not happen overnight. It must happen one step at a time. It also takes a visible commitment from management and a cultural change to get it started. The cultural change also has begun already. The developers themselves are looking for ways to improve their work. As the developers move from company to company, the changes will move as well, gaining momentum along the way.

The assessment identifies where the software organization is and what is required to reach the next level of maturity. The results of the assessment can be used to define a schedule that will take the company to the next maturity level. Following through on the schedule and monitoring your progress to keep the company on track will ensure success.

Software Quality Assurance, or the Quality Monitoring Organization, and the software inspection process are key process improvement elements that have proven successful in the past. Yet they are only a part of the changes we must go through to continue to improve.

This improvement process already is beginning to prove itself. Several companies from varying domains have achieved positive results. They will continue to move up the ladder, reach level 5, and prove to be difficult competition.

References

Booch, Grady. 1987. *Software Components With Ada: Structures, Tools, and Subsystems.* Menlo Park, California: The Benjamin/Cummings Publishing Company, Inc.

Booch, Grady. 1994. *Object-Oriented Analysis and Design with Applications.* Redwood City, California: The Benjamin/Cummings Publishing Company, Inc.

Bush, Marilyn. 1991. "Process Assessment in NASA." Proceedings of the 13th International Conference on Software Engineering, Austin, TX. *IEEE Computer Society Press.* 299–304.

Fagan, Michael E. 1986. "Advances in Software Inspection." *IEEE Transactions on Software Engineering.* SE-12(7).

Fagan, Michael E. 1976. "Design and Code Inspections to Reduce Errors in Program Development." *IBM System Journal.* 15(3).

Fowler, P. J. March–April 1986. "In-Process Inspections of Work Products at AT&T." *AT&T Technical Journal.*

Freedman, D. P. and G. M. Weinberg. 1982. *Handbook of Walkthroughs, Inspections, and Technical Reviews: Evaluating Programs, Projects, and Products.* 3rd edition. Boston, Massachusetts: Little, Brown.

Gilb, T. 1977. *Software Metrics*. Bromley, England: Winthrop Publishers.

Herbsleb, James. 1994. Personal correspondence with the author.

Herbsleb, James, Anita Carleton, James Rozum, Jane Siegel, and David Zubrow. August 1994a. "Benefits of CMM-Based Software Process Improvement: Initial Results." Pittsburgh, Pennsylvania: Software Engineering Institute, Carnegie-Mellon University. Technical Report CMU/SEI-94-TR-13, ESC-TR-94-013.

Herbsleb, James, Anita Carleton, James Rozum, Jane Siegel, and David Zubrow. September 1994b. "Software Process Improvement: State of the Payoff." *American Programmer*. 7(9):2–12.

Humphrey, Watts S. March 1988. "Characterizing the Software Process: A Maturity Framework." *IEEE Software*. 4(3):73–79.

Humphrey, Watts S. 1990. *Managing the Software Process*. Reading, Massachusetts: Addison-Wesley Publishing Company, Inc.

Seidewitz, Ed and Mike Stark. 1992. *Principles of Object-Oriented Software Development with Ada*. Rockville, Maryland: Millennium Systems, Inc.

Yourdon, Edward. 1979. *Structured Walkthroughs*. 2nd edition. Englewood Cliffs, New Jersey: Prentice-Hall.

Yourdon, Edward. 1993. *Decline & Fall of the American Programmer*. Englewood Cliffs, New Jersey: Yourdon Press.

Yourdon, Edward. July 1994. "Software Process Improvement." *Ed Yourdon's Guerrilla Programmer*. 1(7).

12

Configuration Management

Lehman's and Belady's (1985) "Second Law of Software Evolution" states that, unless steps are taken to maintain control of a software system, the entropy of the system will continually increase. When a system's entropy is increasing, the system becomes more chaotic; it becomes more and more difficult to correct errors and make enhancements. Humphrey (1990, 255) states, "Because increases in entropy mean increasing chaos, system structure thus progressively deteriorates unless efforts are made to preserve it."

This tendency toward chaos is caused by several natural and unavoidable circumstances. Errors found by the customer or during the testing phase must be corrected. New features are added to an existing system. Poor configuration management will allow different modifications to be made to the same product simultaneously, resulting in the overwriting and loss of the modifications that were completed first.

Although these circumstances occur naturally and, for the most part, are unavoidable, it does not mean that you can't manage the system such that the changes are controlled and the integrity of the system is maintained. This is where Configuration Management (CM) comes in.

This chapter begins by defining configuration management and its scope. We continue by defining the Software Configuration Management Plan. The importance of configuration control and managing changes to a system, which are the primary goals of configuration management, will be discussed. We will introduce the Project Configuration Manager and the Configuration Control Review Board and explain the important part that they play in configuration management. The chapter continues by defining the Change Request System, which provides a common format for submitting changes to a system. We discuss how to manage the different versions of the individual elements and work products that are associated with the system. The chapter concludes with a discussion of configuration management tools and the specifications of a good tool set.

What Is Configuration Management?

Configuration management defines the disciplines that identify and control the configuration of software, hardware (including support hardware), and tools used in all the phases of the development life cycle. These disciplines allow a systematic and traceable control of changes to the products that are associated with the different phases of development.

Configuration management coordinates the efforts of the project team. It allows the team to make changes to the work products in an organized manner. It also provides control over baseline and intermediate releases of the software, documents, and development tools.

Coordinating the efforts of many developers working on the same project is not an easy task. Once the requirements, design, and implementation phases are complete, the developers begin focusing on the testing phase. If a requirement or design problem is encountered, they will incorporate the changes in the code and, because of schedule constraints, plan to update the requirements and design documentation at a later date. The task of incorporating these changes in the documentation is rarely accounted for in the development schedule. If developers try to incorporate these changes, they will need to find time in an already aggressive schedule. When they do get the time to roll the changes into the requirements and design documentation, they are forced to remember all of the changes that were made and why they were necessary. The end result is out of date or incorrect documentation that does not accurately describe the delivered system.

A good configuration management system will keep track of the changes that are made to the products associated with the different phases of development.

Managing the different versions of the system can be a nightmare without some form of configuration management in place. Configuration management should be an integral part of the software development process.

Over time, a system will undergo a series of changes. Changes are made to the requirements, design, code, and test files and can occur during any phase of the project. The changes are implemented to fix a problem in the system. They are applied to the appropriate product and should be reflected in all of the later phases of development. We also implement changes to add capabilities that were not included in the original delivery of the system. Whatever the reason, changes are inevitable. However, the changes that are made to a system must be properly coordinated.

Two (or more) developers working on different parts of the system might need to modify a shared element (interface routines, I/O drivers, etc.). Assume that each of the developers copies the shared element at the same time and proceeds to make their individual changes. The first developer completes his or her changes and copies it back to the system library. The second developer then copies his or her updated version of the element back to the system library. The changes made by the first developer will be overwritten. The last person to copy the element back to the system library will overwrite the changes made by the other developer.

This situation can become even worse. Assume that the element is a code module and that a software build is made using the first developer's changes. The build is handed over to test where the correction is verified. The second developer submits his or her changes (overwriting the first developer's changes) and a new build is created. When the new build is tested, the first problem reappears. You now must back-track and determine when and why the problem went away and then returned.

Configuration management allows you to retrieve an earlier version of the module and compare it with the latest version to analyze the changes that were made. If you are not able to reproduce the earlier version, you are forced to fix the current version of the module. The chances of maintaining the integrity of the design are not good. You might even end up starting from scratch and reimplementing the design.

A good configuration management system should provide the following functions:

- Protected baselines for all the work products that are associated with the different phases of the development life cycle.

- A protected, chronicled description of the changes made to the individual work products.

- A means for work products to be checked out or "reserved" by one developer at a time. This will ensure that changes are made in an orderly manner.

- Allow developers to retrieve or "fetch" a read-only version of a work product. This is independent of the reserved status of the work product. It is important to note that changes *must* be made only to reserved copies of the work products.

- Provide private workspaces for the individual developers to modify and perform informal testing/verifying of the work products.

- Provide templates for new design, implementation, or test description elements.

- Provide a "replace" procedure that will allow a developer to check in a reserved work product. The replace procedure should ensure the following:

~The only person allowed to replace a work product is the person that reserved it.

~The new revision is in the correct format.

~The status of the work product is changed so that it can be reserved by another developer.

~The change history associated with the work product is updated to reflect the new change.

~The changes have been approved.

~The new revision is added to the baseline.

- Provide an "unreserve" procedure that will allow a developer to release the work product without making any changes. The work product will be the same as it was before the developer reserved it.

- Provide a method of removing a work product from the baseline. In some cases, a work product might become obsolete and does not need to be tracked with the current baseline.

Software configuration management plan

Developing a Software Configuration Management (SCM) Plan is the first step in establishing an effective configuration management system. The plan must provide the details of the configuration management system, including its objectives, responsibilities, tools that are used, and procedures that define how to use the system. The SCM Plan will provide a consistent, defined configuration management system that should be used by all the project groups within the software organization. Table 12.1 shows an example Table of Contents for a Software Configuration Management Plan.

The SCM Plan is linked to the software development process architecture. It must become a part of the organization-wide, software development process. These configuration management requirements also must be applied to all suppliers and subcontractors.

The Configuration Management Objectives and System Overview should provide an overview of the system and what it will accomplish. It should provide a brief explanation for why it is being used.

The Organization and Responsibilities section should define how the configuration management effort will be funded. It also should define the charter of the Configuration Control Review Board. This board is responsible for reviewing proposed changes and problem reports and for authorizing the changes that will be made to the project. We'll take a closer look at this board later in this chapter. The Configuration Control Review Board Members can be project dependent. If so, this item can be included by reference where the actual CCRB Members are identified by the individual project groups.

TABLE 12.1   An Example of the Software Configuration Management
Plan—Table of Contents

1. Overview
   * Configuration Management Objectives
   * Configuration Management System Overview

2. Organization and Responsibilities
   * Budget Responsibilities
   * Configuration Control Review Board (CCRB) Charter
   * Configuration Control Review Board (CCRB) Members
   * Organizational Responsibilities
     ~Software Configuration Management (if this is a separate organization)
     ~Software Quality Assurance
     ~System/Software Project Organization
     ~Configuration Management Audits

3. Methods
   * Baselines and their contents
   * Identification System
   * Change History
   * Configuration Management Support Tools

4. Procedures
   * Procedures Manual
     ~Configuration Management Procedures
     ~Configuration Management Support Tools User Manuals
   * Templates and Forms

The Organizational Responsibilities should be defined so that each organization clearly understands what parts of the configuration management system it is responsible for. It also should identify how these different organizations will interface and communicate with each other.

The Configuration Management Audits should be performed by the Software Quality Assurance organization to ensure that the configuration management system is implemented properly. The SCM Plan should define the general procedures for conducting audits as well as the frequency at which they should occur.

The Methods section defines the heart of the configuration management system. It defines the different baselines and their contents. This also provides a clear description of what work products will be under configuration control. It will even define the method of uniquely identifying the different releases of the work products.

This section will define how the change history that is associated with the different work products will be maintained and what it will contain at a minimum. The configuration management support tools also will be identified.

The Procedures section explains how to implement the configuration management system. It defines the configuration management procedures and the support tools user manuals (which can be included by reference to the vendors documentation). It also provides a copy of all the templates and forms that are associated with the configuration management system.

Configuration control

We maintain configuration control of the work products that are associated with the different phases of the development life cycle so that we can manage the different baselines and the changes that are incorporated in the baselines. To accomplish this, we must maintain control over the following items (Humphrey 1990):

- Operational concept
- Requirements
- Specifications
- Design documents
- Source code
- Object code
- Test plans
- Test cases, test configurations, and test results
- Maintenance and development tools
- User manuals
- Maintenance manuals
- Interface documents

The baselines that are associated with a given project are dependent on the software development architecture. Each baseline must be uniquely identifiable. In general, there is a set of eight baselines listed as follows:

- System Specification Baselines
- Software Requirements Baselines
- Design Baselines
- Unit/Module Level Baselines
- Integration or System Build Baselines
- Test Baselines
- Operational or Delivery Baselines
- Tool Baselines

The first *System Specification Baseline* is established when the system specification document is initially complete, agreed upon, and approved by you and your customer. This document defines the system level requirements and includes the operational concept. A new baseline is established for each complete set of approved system changes. You should avoid establishing a new baseline for each individual system requirements change. Instead, try to group the changes and establish major baselines that include several changes to the system-level requirements.

The first *Software Requirements Baseline* is established when the software requirements document is initially complete and approved via formal inspection. Each baseline includes a cross-reference or traceability matrix that maps each software requirement to their corresponding system-level requirements. A new baseline is established for each major, approved set of software requirements changes (typically associated with a new system specification baseline).

The first *Design Baseline* is established when the preliminary design is initially complete and approved via formal inspection. New baselines are established as the design progresses to the detailed design phase and in response to new software requirements baselines. As Humphrey (1990) states, "They [design baselines] include the design itself, all of the critical design relationships, and the rationale for all of the key design decisions." Again, each baseline must include a cross-reference or traceability matrix that maps each design element to their corresponding software requirements.

The *Unit/Module Level Baselines* are established for each unit or module when it is complete and approved via inspection. If the organization prefers, the unit or module baseline can be established *after* unit/module level testing is complete. It is important to establish baselines early to ensure that proper control is maintained. It is equally important to provide the developer with the freedom to work out the initial bugs prior to putting the unit or module under formal configuration control. This is a delicate line that must be clearly established and understood by the entire development team (even across the entire software organization). The software configuration management plan *must* clearly define when the unit or module is to be placed under configuration control.

The unit/module baselines include the source and object code. The software configuration management plan *must* provide a clear definition of what constitutes a unit or module. The unit/module also should contain a cross-reference or traceability matrix entry that maps the unit/module to the appropriate design elements. When the traceability matrix entries from all the units/modules are combined, you should be able to verify complete coverage of all the design elements.

The *Integration* or *System Build Baselines* are established after initial implementation and unit testing are complete. If the units/modules were not unit tested prior to placing them under configuration control, the integration or system build baselines are established after initial implementation only. In this case, unit testing will be performed as part of the integration testing or as a separate effort performed prior to integration testing.

The system build can include stubbed-out units/modules to allow integration testing of parts of the system that are complete while other parts still are under development. The stubbed-out units/modules *must* be under configuration control as part of the system build. Each integration or system build baseline *must* identify the exact versions of all the units/modules, including the stubbed units/modules that are included in the system build.

As more units/modules are complete, new integration or system build baselines are established. New integration or system build baselines also are established in response to changes to the units caused by design changes or incorporation of fixes to problems found during testing.

The first *Test Baseline* is established when the test plan is complete and approved via inspection. New test baselines are established as test files and test configurations are defined and targeted to a specific system build. The test files that are placed under configuration control can be individual test cases or groups of logically related test cases that are included in the same executable file. The tests and their respective test results must be maintained under configuration control. When a complete set of test results that are associated with a given system build is produced, a new test baseline is established. The existing test baseline can be used in the regression testing effort when a new system build is generated. Some of the tests in the baseline might change to address the changes that are incorporated in the new build (resulting in a new test baseline), but the unchanged tests also should be rerun as part of the regression testing.

The first *Operational* or *Delivery Baseline* is established when the first system is delivered to the customer. This baseline must include a description of the functionality that is included in the delivered system as well as a complete set of user and maintenance manuals. If the delivered system includes partial functionality, the customer must clearly understand the capabilities and limitations of the delivered system. New operational or delivery baselines are established with each new system that is delivered to the customer.

The *Tool Baselines* are established to control all of the development, maintenance, and test tools that are used throughout the development process. This will include design tools, configuration management tools, compilers, linkers, debuggers, etc. If a tool is provided by an outside vendor, you must ensure that they maintain configuration control of the tool. You also must track the specific version used by the appropriate baselines that use the tool to produce the work product.

If tools are developed by the organization, they must be placed under configuration control. If the tool is associated with another tool (i.e., a user interface tool that expands the capabilities of a vendors tool), the baseline for this user-defined tool must define all appropriate versions of the tools it must interface with.

Each element that is associated with a given baseline must define the key information that is required to reproduce it. For example, a test file must maintain the version of the software under test, test equipment configurations and IDs, test version ID, a list of test tools and their version numbers, etc. An individual unit/module must include a list of incorporated changes, compiler version number, linker version number, unit/module version ID, etc. Documentation must include the document version number, list of design tools and their version numbers, list of incorporated changes, and so on.

This is where the templates and forms come in. The developer should have a template or form that should be used to develop each work product. These templates should include all of the necessary information for that work product. Checklists can be developed and used by the developer to ensure that everything is included for that work product. These same checklists also can be used in the inspection process.

Traceability from system specification to the software requirements, design, test, and finally to the delivered system must be maintained. This is very useful when a requirements change must be incorporated into the system. It also is helpful in analyzing the scope of a specific change. You can get a better feel for how the change will flow through the different phases of the life cycle and the work involved in incorporating the change.

Managing changes

Changes to a system can be made at any time during the development life cycle. They can be made to incorporate new functionality, fix requirements, design, coding, or test errors. They càn be made to fix a problem that is found during inspection of an interfacing work product, during testing, or even by the customer after delivery of the system.

Some changes require immediate attention and must be incorporated into the next baseline release, while others can be planned for a future baseline release. Some changes affect a single work product, while others might impact the entire system. They can be as simple as correcting a spelling error and as complex as expanding the basic capabilities of the system (e.g., adding the maintenance of employee benefits information to an employee payroll system). These changes *must* be controlled, and the system integrity *must* be maintained.

To maintain control over the changes to the system, you must establish a *Project Configuration Manager* and a *Configuration Control Review Board* (CCRB). Their responsibilities must be clearly defined in the software configuration management plan.

The project configuration manager.

It is the responsibility of the process group to ensure that the spirit of the software configuration management plan and its objects are met by the software organization. It is the responsibility of each individual project team to provide a project configuration manager to manage the different configurations associated with that project.

The project configuration manager is responsible for the following tasks (Babich 1986):

- Develop, document, and distribute the SCM (Software Configuration Management) procedures. (This primarily is the responsibility of the process group, but it should be coordinated through the project configuration managers.)
- Establish the system baseline, including backup procedures.
- Ensure that no unauthorized changes are made to the baseline.
- Ensure that all baseline changes are recorded in sufficient detail so that they can be reproduced or backed out.
- Ensure that all baseline changes are regression tested.
- Provide the focal point for exception resolution.

The project configuration manager will have his or her hands full trying to keep up on these tasks, especially during system builds and the test phase of the project. They should not be overloaded with other tasks without making sure that they are able to keep up. The configuration management responsibilities must be the project configuration manager's highest priority.

The project configuration manager is the person who will understand and know how to use the configuration management tools and will be granted system level privileges to allow them to define and control access to the baselines. It might be a good idea to assign a backup person in case the project configuration manager is unavailable when a critical change must be incorporated.

> One of the development teams that I was a member of had a project configuration manager (although she was not officially given the title). Whenever anyone had a question about the configuration management process or tools (both vendor supplied and those developed by the company), the current configuration, or what changes were implemented in a given release, all they had to do was ask.
>
> She was responsible for setting up the working configurations as well as freezing the baseline configurations when we were ready to make a release. There was never any question about the system being under good configuration control. All changes were recorded and tracked with the appropriate documentation, including the documentation associated with each work product baseline release.
>
> This saved us all a lot of work and allowed us to focus on our own individual responsibilities. The configuration management was always under control.
>
> Rod Skoglund

Configuration Control Review Board (CCRB).

The project configuration manager's job is to maintain control of the baselines. You still need a mechanism in place to review and approve the changes. That is where the Configuration Control Review Board (CCRB) comes in.

The CCRB should be made up of members representing system development, software development, documentation, test, software quality assurance, and maintenance and the project configuration manager associated with the project. The manager of the project team typically is the chair person for the CCRB. The CCRB is responsible for ensuring that every baseline change is reviewed by all concerned parties and providing authorization to implement the change.

Regularly scheduled meetings are held to review new change requests and software problem reports and to approve new change requests or old change requests that have been more completely analyzed. The frequency of these meetings depends on the number of change requests and problem reports that are being generated. During the early stages of development, the meeting might be held once a month. During the later states (e.g., the testing phase), you might need to hold several meetings per week. The important thing is that the board keeps up on the changes that are requested.

When the change requests start coming in at a very fast rate, it's a great temptation to circumvent the review process. The CCRB members are overloaded with the responsibilities of the CCRB and their own individual tasks. Circumventing the CCRB usually ends up in a mangled mess. No one knows what changes have been incorporated or when a change is supposed to be incorporated. The time it takes to regain control will far exceed the time it takes to manage it properly from the start.

It is at these times that the CCRB can help the most. By analyzing and prioritizing the changes, everyone knows what is to be accomplished for the next release. The amount of work that is involved in incorporating the changes must be taken into consideration when the CCRB is determining what future baseline release each change will be incorporated into. As new changes are identified, analyzed, and prioritized, the CCRB can move the incorporation of a change to the next release and thereby make room for the incorporation of a more important change in the earlier release. The workload is not only prioritized, but it is spread across the current and all future releases.

The CCRB is not responsible for actually implementing the change. They review change requests and, based on help and recommendations from the project team, determine the priority and what release the fix should be incorporated in. They can assign the change request to a member of the project team for analysis to ensure that they fully understand the scope of the requested change. Once the priority and targeted release have been determined, the CCRB will assign the work to a member of the project team who then will be responsible for incorporating the necessary changes.

Once the assignee has completed the change, CCRB is called upon to review the changes that were made and close the request. The status of all requested changes must be maintained and readily available to all members of the CCRB, the project team, and software quality assurance. This can be accomplished electronically or by periodically sending out a summary report.

Change request system.

The CCRB will review a lot of change requests. The project team, as well as the customer, needs to have a formal method of submitting change requests. The CCRB will find it much simpler if all of the change requests used the same format. A Change Request System will help address these issues by providing a formal method of requesting changes to a system. A common template is used to provide a full description of the change, the reason for the change, and other applicable information associated with the request.

All change requests will be submitted using this form. The CCRB will become familiar with the form. They will be able to review the change requests much quicker because they will know exactly where to get the information they need during the review process. If a change request is incomplete, it can be sent back to the originator who can provide the missing information. Figure 12.1 shows an example of a Change Request Form.

The form can be used to request changes during any phase of the life cycle. The form is broken down into five sections: Originator, Configuration Control Review Board, Assignee, Status, and Process Improvement Information.

When someone wants to submit a change request, they start the process by filling out the Originator section and submitting it to the CCRB. The title should be a brief, one line description of the change. The origination date specifies the date that the change request was submitted. The project name identifies which project the change request is associated with. The originator must be identified because, as you will see later, they are part of the closure process.

The current configuration identifies the configuration in which the problem was exhibited or, if the change request is an enhancement, the latest configuration, which does not contain the requested functionality. The reason for change is used to distinguish between a request to expand on the current capabilities and a problem found during an inspection, testing, etc.

The description must provide a detailed description of the requested change. If the requested change is associated with adding a new capability, this section will provide a detailed description of the enhancement. If the requested change is required to fix a problem that was found during inspection or test, this section will provide a detailed description of the problem and any other information necessary to analyze and correct the problem. If it is easier to provide a marked up copy of the document, source code, etc., the originator can attach it to the change request and check the attachments line on the form.

CHANGE REQUEST

ORIGINATOR

Title: _____

Project Name: _____ Origination Date: _____

Originator: _____ Current Configuration: _____

Reason for Change: _____

Description: _____

_____

_____

_____

Attachments_____

CONFIGURATION CONTROL REVIEW BOARD

Change Request Number: _____ Priority:_____

Approved by:_____ Target Configuration:_____

Assignee: _____ Verification Assignee:_____

ASSIGNEE

Analysis/Solution: _____

_____

_____

_____

Estimated Time To Implement:_____ Actual Time To Implement:_____

List Of Affected Work Products: _____

_____

STATUS

Status: _____ Status Date:_____

Assignee: _____ Date:_____

Verification Assignee: _____ Date:_____

CCRB Representative: _____ Date:_____

Originator: _____ Date:_____

Quality Assurance: _____ Date:_____

Configuration Manager: _____ Date:_____

Closed In Configuration _____ Date:_____

PROCESS IMPROVEMENT INFORMATION

Type of Defect: _____ Introduction of Defect:_____

Figure 12.1 An example of a Change Request form.

When the originator has completed his or her part of the form, he or she will submit it to the CCRB. The CCRB will assign a Change Request Number and enter it in the change request tracking system. The change request tracking system is a tool that allows you to maintain the change requests and generate summary reports. The CCRB will distribute the change request to all CCRB members and disposition it at the next CCRB meeting. If the board feels that there was not enough information to evaluate and analyze the change request, they will return it to the originator along with a request for additional information. If they need help analyzing the change, they can assign the change request to a member of the project team along with a request for preliminary analysis.

When the board has established the priority and target configuration, they will identify the assignee (assuming that they have not already done so) and the verification assignee. A member of the board, typically the chair person or project configuration manager, will sign the change request on the "Approved by:" line and send a copy to the assignee and verification assignee. At this point, a copy is sent to the originator to keep them informed on the progress and status of their request.

If a preliminary analysis is requested, the assignee will analyze the change request and enter the results in the Analysis/Solution section. The analysis should identify the impact of the change and the consequences of not implementing the change. The assignee should provide an estimate of how much time it will take to implement the change (in person days) as well as a preliminary list of affected work products (Estimated Time To Implement and List Of Affected Work Products, respectively). The affected work products can include any of the system or design documentation, source and object code, test procedures, etc. Once the preliminary analysis is complete, the change request is returned to the CCRB.

When the change request is approved by the CCRB, the assignee will schedule the work such that it will be complete for the target configuration. The specific solution will be described in the Analysis/Solution section, and the actual time that it took to implement the change will be recorded (Actual Time To Implement). Any preliminary analysis information that previously was entered must be preserved. A complete list of affected work products also must be provided by the assignee.

When the assignee has completed implementing the change, he or she will sign the Status section and send a copy to the verification assignee. The verification assignee is responsible for ensuring that the solution was correct and that it was implemented properly. It is his or her job to verify that the changed work products are under configuration control. If everything is in order, the verification assignee will sign the Status section and send a copy to the CCRB.

The CCRB representative, typically the chair person, will ensure that everything is filled out properly and sign the Status section and send a copy to the originator. If the originator agrees with the implemented change, they will sign the Status section and return the change request to the CCRB. A quality assurance representative and the project configuration manager (typically members of the CCRB) will review and sign the change request.

The Status section is updated incrementally throughout the life of the change request. The status will transition from "open" through "in preliminary analysis" (when appropriate), "approved," "implemented," "verified," and finally to "closed." The status date will reflect the last time that the status was updated. Whenever a signature is added to the status section, the date it was added also is recorded. When the change request is closed, the actual configuration in which the change was or will be implemented will be recorded and the date this entry was entered is recorded.

The last section, Process Improvement Information, is used to categorize the change and what stage of development the problem or enhancement was introduced (Type of Defect and Introduction of Defect, respectively). This information will be useful in identifying common types of defects that occur as well as problems in the overall development process.

Version Management

Any given work product can have several changes implemented as you go from one baseline configuration to another. Each change that is implemented creates a new version of the work product. These versions must be under configuration control so that, if needed, they can be reproduced at a later date.

For example, a system build baseline is made up of several source and object code elements (the work products). A defect is found during the testing of the system build. The defect is analyzed and the necessary corrections are implemented, creating a new version of the affected elements. Assume that all of these new versions are version 2. As the testing continues (on the original, configured source code), another defect is found. This defect also is analyzed and the necessary corrections are implemented, creating still newer versions of the elements (version 3). A new system build baseline is established using the latest versions of the source and object code elements and possibly adding new elements to the build. The testing of the new baseline finds that the second defect still exists, only now it is worse. You must be able to back the changes out without losing the changes that corrected the first defect. You must be able to reproduce version 2 so that you can implement the proper changes to fix the second defect mentioned above.

Configuration Management Tools

Configuration management requires that you maintain a large amount of information on all of the work products that are associated with the project. The data that is recorded and maintained includes the change history, current status of all the change requests, and who is responsible for changing and approving the changes associated with each work product. You must be able to produce summary reports of what changes are open, closed, approved, etc., for all the baselines. You need to know what changes were implemented, when they were implemented, who implemented them, and the configuration in which they were implemented. You also must record the decisions of the CCRB.

You must be able to reproduce earlier versions and configurations so that you can determine when a defect was introduced and what it will take to correct the defect. You also must be able to reproduce the results of a specific test.

You must be able to have different configuration at different stages of development. For example, you will have one configuration, with partial functionality, delivered to the customer and another configuration, with some additional functionality, that currently is being tested. You will have another that still is under development. You might have a defect reported (via change request) by the customer and another defect reported by the test team (also via change request), where these defects are associated with different baselines.

You must be able to control when changes are made and who is allowed to make them, and you need to be able to ensure that changes are made by one person at a time.

This would be impossible for even the smallest of projects without some form of automation. You need tools to manage the different versions of the work products as well as the different baselines associated with the project.

There are many configuration management system tools available for almost any development environment. Whenever possible, you should use vendor-supplied tools so that you are not responsible for the maintenance that is associated with them. If you produce the tool yourself, you will need to provide a full staff to develop, test, and maintain it. You will need to provide customer support and be able to manage the different configurations of the tool itself.

If you produce a tool that will be used in conjunction with a vendor supplied tool, you will need to modify the tool to address all of the changes in an upgraded version of the vendor-supplied tool. Once again, you must provide the development, test, and customer-support personnel.

In either case, you must continue to provide support for the inhouse-developed tools throughout the entire life cycle of all the projects that will use the tool set. On the other hand, if you use vendor-supplied tools, without any inhouse-developed tools, you can focus your efforts on the development of your own projects. The development, test, and customer support that is associated with the tool is the responsibility of the vendor. The vendors that supply tools that interface with the configuration management system tools are responsible for implementing the necessary changes to remain compatible with any new versions of the configuration management tools.

At the heart of any configuration management system is the system library. The system library is where the versions of the work products, including the source and object code, are stored. All of the baselines that are associated with the project are defined within the system library. The system library maintains the documents, source and object code, and the test files (where each file contains one or more test case). The system library provides the mechanism to reserve and replace the different work products and allows only authorized changes to be made. It is capable of storing, cataloging, and retrieving the various system configurations, test drivers, and the executable software that is associated with a given configuration. The primary functions of the system library are as follows:

- Retrieving elements (work products) by name, date of creation, developer, type of element, or development status.

- Building a work product release.

- Maintaining the change history for each work product and its individual elements.

- Reproducing an earlier version of a work product.

- Managing access to the work products and their individual elements.

- Maintaining status information associated with the individual elements as well as the complete work products.

- Collecting any desired statistical and accounting information. Report generation capabilities will summarize this information.

The tool set and the system library also must fulfill the requirements of the change request management system. This requires managing changes to the work products and their individual elements, storing and tracking change requests and their status information, and providing report generation capabilities to determine the current status of a work product.

In some cases, the change requests are handled electronically. The entire change request is entered into the system as soon as it is received from the originator. As each responsible party completes his or her section by entering the system and entering the data, he or she also provides an electronic signature, which is dated automatically. Even the status can be generated automatically based on the data and signatures that are present.

All of the tools that are associated with the project also must be under configuration control. Whether this is handled by the tool vendor or your own company, you must be able to manage the different versions and baseline releases of the tools.

The individual development groups should use a common set of tools. That is, the tool set should be defined for the entire software organization. Even so, not every group will be ready to move to a new release of a tool at the same time. One group might change over right away, while another might wait until they make their next baseline release. Even if they all wait until the next baseline release, their individual schedules will be different, so they will change over at different times. Therefore, you must be able to manage and use different releases of the tool set.

Summary

Configuration management allows you to maintain control over the development of a system. It provides the disciplines that allow a systematic and traceable control of changes to the products that are associated with the different phases of development. It allows you to coordinate the efforts of the project team and will ensure that changes are implemented in an organized manner.

The Software Configuration Management Plan is the first step in establishing an effective configuration management system. It provides the details of the configuration management system including its objectives, responsibilities, tools that are used, and procedures that define how to use the system.

There are eight basic baselines that are associated with a system. These are dependent on the organization-wide process, which defines the process architecture and the work products that are produced. It is important to establish baselines early to ensure that proper control is maintained. It is equally important to provide the developer the freedom to work out the initial bugs prior to putting the element under formal configuration control. This is a delicate line that must be clearly established and understood by the entire development team (even across the entire software organization).

Managing the changes to a system involves analyzing the requested change, approving the change, and identifying the target configuration. A Project Configuration Manager and the Configuration Control Review Board (CCRB) are established to manage the different configurations and dispositioning the requested changes. Managing the changes requires a change request system that can track the status of all the requested changes and identifies all of the changes that were incorporated into a given configuration. The change request system provides a common template for submitting change requests and simplify the CCRB's job.

Each baseline is composed of one or more elements. Each element can have several changes incorporated before a new baseline is established. A new version of the element is produced each time a specific change is incorporated. Therefore, an element can have several version changes between baselines. Managing the individual versions and ensuring that any previous version can be reproduced makes sure that you can back any change out of the system, assuming that the change was improperly incorporated.

Configuration management tools automate the configuration management process. Without these tools, it would be next to impossible to establish an effective configuration management system for even the smallest of projects. Whenever possible, you should avoid developing the tools or even a tool that interfaces with a vendor-supplied tool so that you can focus on developing your own systems.

The system library is the heart and soul of the configuration management system. It is the system library that controls the access to any given work product. It allows you to manage the different versions and coordinates the changes to the work products and their individual elements.

Configuration management requires a lot of effort and resources, but it is all very worth it in the end. Without it, you can spend a lot of time reimplementing changes that were lost when two or more developers work on the same project. You will avoid the problems of trying to identify and incorporate changes that were found by the customer (on a delivered system) and, at the same time, changes found during the test effort (on a different build of the system). Configuration management allows you to determine the priority of a requested change, relative to other requested changes, and determine when the change should be incorporated. You can spread the work load of incorporating changes across the different scheduled deliveries of the system in an intelligent manner.

References

Babich, W. A. 1986. *Software Configuration Management, Coordination for Team Productivity*. Reading, Massachusetts: Addison-Wesley Publishing Company, Inc.

Booch, Grady. 1994. *Object-Oriented Analysis and Design with Applications*. Redwood City, California: The Benjamin/Cummings Publishing Company, Inc.

Humphrey, Watts S. 1990. *Managing the Software Process*. Reading, Massachusetts: Addison-Wesley Publishing Company, Inc.

Lehman, M. M., and L. A. Belady. 1985. *Program Evolution, Processes of Software Change*. New York, New York: Academic Press.

Nix, Kevin. December 1994. "Make CM Work for You, not Against You." *Software Development*. 2 (12): 61–65.

13

Automated Testing

Testing mission-critical software is a complex and frustrating task. Just when you squash one pesky bug, others will boldly crop up. In ferreting out and fixing logic errors, the automated testing tools that you use can be your best friends, provided your process (or lack thereof) doesn't get in the way.

In this chapter, we'll discuss testing processes and look at how automated tools fit into them. Some of the considerations for how and what tools are used are the processes and tools already in place, the level of testing needed, the state of the requirements specification, the maturity of the software development organization, and the development paradigm (i.e., structured or object-oriented).

The Testing Process

Manual testing efforts tend to find the bulk of errors toward the end of the release effort or during beta testing, where they're more expensive to fix. Automated testing tools can catch errors earlier in the development process, where they're easier and cheaper to fix and have less impact on the customer.

No matter how advanced your testing tools are, they will work only as well as your process works. If your company has no active SQA organization, no configuration management, and no specified requirements, there's little chance that even the best tools can help. On the other hand, if your process is well-organized and actually is working to improve quality, automated tools can offer a dramatic improvement.

Test planning

In a good software development process, test planning and design should parallel the steps needed to produce the working code. Your test plan should start where the rest of the process begins: during the generation of requirements. Even though a lot of details aren't known early on, some system-level tests can be designed.

While it's good to start planning tests early in the process, it's not advisable to commit test implementation resources before the requirements are sufficiently mature. Many early requirements are incorrect, and tests written in detail based on these can lead to huge maintenance problems. Test implementation should lag behind requirements definition but probably not by more than one document iteration.

After the first semi-solid requirements specification is completed, test development should begin in earnest. At this point, you'll start to determine which modules will need white-box testing, what test data will need to be generated, how regression testing will be done, and what level of coverage analysis is necessary. In addition, a good test plan will specify the resources necessary to carry out the testing effort, including software tools, training, personnel, and hardware. All of this should be seriously attempted early in the process in spite of the fact that there could be substantial rework ahead.

Regression testing

As stated in the IEEE Standard Glossary of Software Engineering Terminology, "Regression Testing is the selective retesting [of software] to detect faults introduced during modification of a system or system component, to verify that modifications have not caused unintended adverse effects, or to verify that a modified system or system component still meets specified requirements." (IEEE 1990) In other words, regression testing answers the oft-asked question "Does it still work after I fixed it?"

A major section in any test plan must detail regression testing, including when and how test suites will be run, what tools will be used, who will be responsible for the test suite, how developers will be notified of errors found, coordination of bug fixes, testing standards, etc. The type of tests to be run for each class also must be determined.

Incremental development virtually mandates automated regression testing. In the OO spiral development model, classes are added, deleted, and changed frequently during the testing process. To complete each increment, all changed classes and all classes coupled with them must pass a complete suite of regression tests.

There's some good news in all of this, though. Good testing tools can help you implement your process (if you have one). Traditionally, test cases are developed on paper during the implementation and testing phase of a project. Automated testing tools can help implement a test plan or matrix developed during the analysis/requirements phase. This not only ensures the testability of requirements, but creates a document trail to support retesting of future versions of the software, helping to identify tests that must change when a requirement is changed.

Stress testing

One facet of testing is determining that a program fulfills the requirements that are defined for it. Equally important is "pushing the envelope" to make sure that a program works as it should even under extreme conditions. This type of "stress testing" generally falls into two categories: limit verification and iterative testing.

Limit verification tests how well a program handles input values outside of a defined legal range. For example, if a program were required to handle all printable alphanumeric characters, a stress test might input control characters or escape sequences to verify that the program executes correctly in spite of exotic data.

A module or subsystem might appear to run just fine when it is called once, but repeated calls can cause problems over time. This is especially true of modules that allocate and deallocate memory, update the screen, or access servers via a network. Memory leaks or screen updates that are "off by a pixel," for example, often are revealed only after many iterations. The ability to run the same test in a loop from 1 to N times therefore can be crucial. The ability to fire off a large number of repeated asynchronous events to test a client-server system under high stress also is very valuable.

Unit testing

Organizations committed to producing quality software historically have relied on coverage testing for each function, module, or class in the object-oriented paradigm. This practice, called *unit testing*, is effective but also is extremely time-consuming and labor-intensive. With the test analysis tools made available in recent years and with the popularity of software inspections (Price, Ragland, and Daich 1993), exhaustive unit testing is slowly being replaced on many projects by a combination of black-box and white-box testing. However, there is no substitute for full-path coverage unit testing in the most critical units in the system.

The criticality of failures within units can be divided into five levels:

- Potential Safety Impact—These failures could cause injury or death, significant property loss, or environmental damage. Also known as "CNN-level" errors because failures of this magnitude could be covered on the network news.

- Major Financial Impact—These errors cause loss of production, disappearance of electronic funds, loss of important information, incorrect payments, etc. They also are known as "CEO-level" errors due to the fact that these often get the attention of top management.

- Loss of Access—This level encompasses all errors that result in losing an accurate view into stored data. The data still is there, but users have trouble getting to it.

- Reduced Functionality—When these errors occur, users temporarily are unable to use the system to perform some noncritical functions.

- Nuisance Problems and Cosmetic Defects

Note that, if errors in the third, fourth, and fifth categories occur often enough, they might constitute a level 1 or 2 error.

In an effective limited-unit-testing approach, inspections of source code against requirements must find the majority of the coding errors. In concert with the inspection process, a test analysis tool can examine a suite of tests and the source code or object code of the software under test to determine how many of the program statements were exercised. Tests then need to be written only to exercise execution paths not hit by the system test suite.

This approach still has some major drawbacks, however. Test analysis tools cannot yet reliably handle multitasking or dynamically allocated data structures in the source code and sometimes report errors related to infeasible paths. In addition, enough system-level requirements might never be known to provide adequate, timely code coverage because so many requirements, such as error handling, usually are not hammered out until deep into the software life cycle.

There are different levels of code coverage, however, as can be illustrated using the example in Figure 13.1. In this example, A, B, D, E, F, and G are blocks of code, and C1, C2, C3, and C4 are Boolean conditions such as "X > Y."

The code that corresponds to this diagram is as follows:

```
A
if C1 and C2 then
    B
else
    begin
        D
        while C3 and C4
            do E
        F
    end
G
```

Depending upon how critical the module under test is, one or a combination of the following strategies can be used:

- "Minimal Path," or "Statement," testing covers paths ABG and ADEFG.

- "Basis Path" testing covers ABG, ADFG, ADEFG, and ADEEFG.

- "Condition Coverage" or "Branch" testing covers all possible combinations of conditions in each decision statement (Table 13.1).

Depending upon how critical the module of class is, different types of code-coverage strategies can be used. Even with automated tools, exhaustive white-box testing is time-consuming. To ensure quality, however, these tests must be performed for the most crucial components of the system.

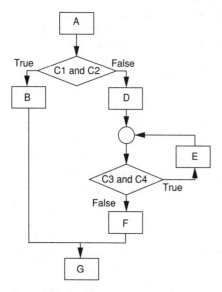

Figure 13.1 A path-coverage example.

TABLE 13.1 All Possible Combinations of Conditions

C1	C2	C3	C4
FALSE	FALSE	FALSE	FALSE
FALSE	TRUE	FALSE	TRUE
TRUE	FALSE	TRUE	FALSE
TRUE	TRUE	TRUE	TRUE

Developmental testing

In many organizations, a wall stands between testing and development. Code and requirements are tossed over the wall to the testing group, and test results sent back to the development team are the only permissible communication. To produce a quality mission-critical system on schedule, testing must become an integral part of the development effort. In the spiral development model, initial test cases can be embedded in the requirements to ensure their testability. The design of test cases should be done in parallel with the system design, and the implementation of automated tests should essentially mirror the coding effort.

In an object-oriented system, the complex interactions between objects make it mandatory to test a class in concert with related classes as soon as possible, even if some classes must be simulated (hopefully some classes also will be included from a reusable library). Progressive integration of new classes should be coupled with a bottom-up testing approach (see Yourdon, 1994) in which objects are first tested individually, then in logical groups. This should be followed by testing larger subsystems and finally the entire system. Failure to systematically and incrementally integrate classes not only can cripple an incremental-development (spiral) process but also will lead to a huge explosion late in the project timeline.

Only automated tools can provide the turn-around necessary to really make the spiral life cycle work. Developers should be able to make fixes, then rerun a suite of tests to make sure everything still works without missing a beat. Results can be compared automatically and other developers notified via e-mail if their code is not compatible with the repair or enhancement.

No system is ever fully debugged; however, after enough errors have been found and corrected that the frequency and severity of errors reaches a tolerable level (or you run out of time or money), you need to take the system out of the testing/development "bed" and let customers subject it to real-world usage ("beta testing"). When you do this, it's wise to let the program continue testing itself and reporting errors.

Designing testability into software is the key. Some of the testing-related capabilities that need to be present in good software are the ability to get or set the state of any object, as well as saving and viewing "logs" of information such as input/output events, errors, and network traffic. In addition, a high level of error-recovery capability needs to be built into the system. Built-in error logging and recovery is discussed further in chapter 14.

If sufficient detail is paid to testability issues, the system can be tested in a much more parallel manner. For example, a GUI-based front end can be tested with the same inputs that verify and validate a back-end database server.

Obstacles to Automated Testing

In most programs, there are chunks of code that are especially difficult to test. These include interrupt handlers, exception handlers, conditions (such as February 29th) that are relatively rare occurrences and critical sections relating to multitasking. To thoroughly test this kind of code, it often is necessary to manually set up pretest conditions or set values dynamically via a debugger. Due to schedule constraints and to fully automate the running of regression tests, it might be necessary to make some difficult trade-offs in the level of path coverage. While 100% statement coverage on all regression tests is a good goal, it might be necessary to settle for covering every statement in the initial release, but running only automated tests in regression testing.

Testing Tools

Automated testing tools can provide the greatest return-on-investment of nearly all software tools. This fact is well understood by the Japanese software industry: "A survey of 200 Japanese software development groups ranked software test tools as having the highest productivity return on investment, ahead of standard methodology, CASE, any software-development tool, and reviews and inspections" (Bezier 1990, 449).

Unfortunately, American software developers are bogged down with reinventing the testing wheel. The reason for this is that, on most projects, testing tools often are the last to be considered and must fit in with the already-specified development tools (some created inhouse). After all the other tools are in place, the budget and schedule often are stretched, leaving little of either for bringing testing tools online. As Morin (1993, 107) explains:

> Although some commercial packages for bug tracking and regression testing are available, most companies write their own. This might have to do with local conditions (assumed or real), deficiencies in the commercial offerings, or cost factors. Regardless, the result is that many programmers currently are busy writing and maintaining private versions of these software systems. What's worse, these systems really aren't solving the problems at hand.

Because up to 50% of the effort in developing and maintaining software can be burned up in testing, doing things the pick-and-shovel way can cost a fortune in both time and money when it comes to validating and verifying a large mission-critical system (Daich and Price 1992 and Bezier 1990).

In spite of this, you'll find chain gangs of testers working in almost every company involved in software development. These employees laboriously generate test cases by hand, write or modify drivers to test a function, or fix a home-grown test tool. All of this is wasted, error-prone effort when you consider that there are hundreds of off-the-shelf test tools, with more being made available all the time.

There's little excuse for not knowing about these tools because virtually anyone can subscribe to the free bi-yearly reports offered by the Software Technology Support Center. The STSC is a government organization responsible for cataloging and reviewing thousands of commercially available software tools, as well as providing process and methodology information. Although STSC publications should not be taken as the final authority on how well a particular tool might meet the specific needs of your project, the information provided can give you a good head start on your tool research.

The plethora of available testing tools can be roughly divided into six categories.

Requirements analysis and design testers

These tools aid in defining a testing approach based on requirements and design information. They can help prove the testability of requirements and can assist in determining whether or not the tests cover the requirements.

Knowing what code has been completely tested and what has been missed can be extremely useful information for another reason. Due to schedule pressures, tests might need to be prioritized based on the importance of requirements. Management then can decide to ship the product even if some of the code has not been thoroughly tested against less-critical requirements.

Regression testing tools

Software is constantly upgraded and fixed by highly pressured maintenance teams who often don't understand a program well enough to adequately retest it. It's no wonder that the Software Engineering Institute cites a lack of regression testing as the second most common weakness in any software process; the most common is a lack of training (Humphrey 1990). A major reason for this weakness is that regression testing is often tedious and time-consuming. Fortunately, there are some off-the-shelf tools to make things easier.

With a good regression testing tool, you can use the keyboard and mouse as you expect a user would, and the tool automatically will produce a repeatable suite of tests. You also can use the high-level script language that is available with the best test tools to modify capture-generated tests or to write your own. When the test runs, the user interface will be driven by the tool to act as if a user were using the mouse and keyboard. The tool also can automatically compare results with expected results and report the outcome of the comparison. Results also can be saved for comparison with outputs produced during the execution of subsequent test cases. Better tools of this variety also can combine scripts, manage script files, allow for in-file comments, and run in batch-mode in the wee hours of the morning.

A good example of this kind of tool is WinRunner from Mercury Interactive Corp. WinRunner has Windows event-capturing capabilities, as well as a scripting language that supports not only regression testing but also stress testing and test reuse via procedure definition (see Figure 13.2).

Test-reuse tools

A software shop needs to have a good process (at least SEI level 2) to get much benefit from test-reuse tools (see chapter 11). Probably the most advanced of all testing tools, these tools fully integrate testing into the design and requirements analysis process. Using these tools, test suites, code, design, and even requirements can be parameterized and reused from project to project. As each project is completed, metrics provided and used would further improve the process.

A WinRunner-style test scripting language, a test browser, and a configuration management tool can give an organization a good start toward reusable tests. Basic utility scripts can be written and configured into a library. These components then can be browsed and used to create unit tests, which also can be configured in a library along with the code they test. Unit tests then can be combined and reworked into integration tests.

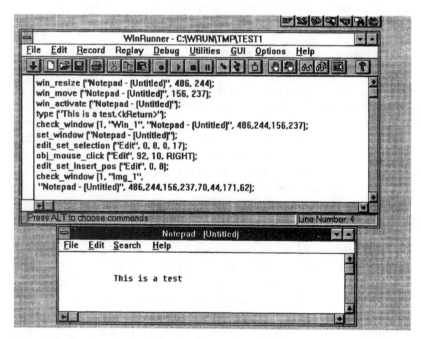

Figure 13.2 Testing a simple application (Notepad) with WinRunner.

Test generators

Test generators create test cases from requirements. With this type of tool, laboring for months to come up with sets of test cases to fully exercise a piece of software could be a thing of the past. There's a big catch, however. You need good requirements, and those requirements must be encoded in a specific format (i.e., output from an integrated CASE Tool).

Requirements-based test case generators exist to build test cases by random, algorithmic, or heuristic means. Randomly built test cases form a statistically random distribution of possible test inputs. Algorithmically built test cases include boundary values, cause-effect scenarios, and functional analysis test cases. Heuristically built test cases include tests based on faults discovered during previous testing (Poston 1992).

Using a requirements-based test case generator has the added advantage of automatically tracing test cases to requirements, an otherwise tedious task. This type of tool also produces nonredundant test cases, thus increasing testing efficiency (Poston 1994).

The ability to automatically generate tests and run batches of tests overnight can be a great blessing. It also can be a curse. Some automatically generated tests must be reworked manually before they will work in a specific environment. As the code changes, these must be maintained by hand. As the number of test scripts grows into the hundreds or even thousands, maintenance can involve a huge amount of work and can be a nightmare without effective configuration management.

Test analyzers

Due to the high reliability demanded of mission critical systems, each function, class, or logical group (i.e., "read_item"/"write_item") of functions at the lowest level will need to undergo the most detailed ("white-box") testing. This means that each logical path in the code must be exercised and the results compared against a predicted value (hopefully determined from the requirements). This can be an extremely time-consuming task, as most software testers know. Fortunately, if you're using C, C++, or Ada, tools are available to either automatically generate test cases to cover all decisions and logical paths within the code or to verify how much coverage a test suite actually provides (Price, Ragland, and Daich 1993). Test analyzers also can produce test metrics detailing the error-frequency within units, among other things. To be effective, however, code-coverage analysis must be combined with a good set of requirements-based tests.

One flavor of this type of tool, called a "static path/data flow analyzer" (Price, Ragland, and Daich 1993), can generate test cases directly from source code. While this is a useful supplement to requirements-based testing, it only answers the question "Did we build the product right?" Using only these tools, the more important question "Did we build the right product?" would never be answered.

Test analyzers are a rapidly improving type of test tool that is becoming more widely available. An increasing number of compilers now offer advanced code-analysis, and maintenance and reverse engineering efforts rely heavily on this technology. As stated by Price, Ragland, and Daich (1993), "As systems continue to become more complex and schedules become tighter, test analysis and test planning will rely more and more on equally sophisticated static analysis tools to meet the demands of quality checking."

A good share of all software development tools that end up in dusty boxes on developers' shelves rather than as part of a development process are test coverage analysis tools. A truly useful tool should have the following capabilities:

- Any good test analysis tool must facilitate different types of coverage, such as paths, statements, and conditions.

- Most analysis tools are not user-friendly. They force users to cross-reference between listings and complex reports. A truly useful tool will produce results in the form of easy-to-read annotated program listings.

- Most code-analysis tools produce metrics of software complexity. These metrics generally apply only to structured modules, where the complexity can be isolated to specific functions. Methods in object-oriented code generally are very simple, with few branches. The complexity in object technology is in the interaction between objects, so it's important that a good test analyzer provides meaningful object-oriented metrics, such as the depth of inheritance trees (DIT) or the coupling between objects (CBO).

- The best test analyzers can handle multitasking software. Whatever form of concurrent execution is supported on the target platform (threads, tasks, processes, etc.) must be supported.

- It's difficult to test most software, especially when it comes to error handling, without some type of simulation. Situations that normally would not occur in correctly functioning components such as disk drives, keyboards, monitors, scanners, etc., must be simulated in software to facilitate complete testing. A truly useful test analysis tool will support function simulation.

- To be useful for verifying object-oriented software, dynamic analysis tools (i.e., debuggers) should support multiple threads of control. The tool also should understand class and object semantics, such as class and instance variables, and the inheritance tree associated with an object.

Complete CAST (Computer Aided Software Testing) Tools

As explained in the "Test Preparation, Execution, and Analysis Tools Report 1992," some ambitious tool makers have attempted to create a complete testing environment that does everything from helping to write a requirements-based test plan to producing test metrics. These tools usually work as part of a corresponding CASE tool. So far, no one has produced a workable "grand unified testing tool," although some are coming close. What's available today is more of a "Swiss army knife" approach: some good tools that work with each other, but no seamless unification between test analysis, capture/replay, requirements, design, and code.

Object Technology and Automated Testing

After testing and fixing bugs in one class, it's a good possibility that bugs might be created in other dependent classes as a result of the fixes made. Dependencies between classes might be either the result of an inheritance class/subclass hierarchy or of one class using methods and instance variables from another. The following is a simple scenario.

You send software quality assurance version 1.1 of a class "A" (Figure 13.3). After testing it, 12 tests pass and 2 fail, so you fix the bugs, and version 1.2 is tested. When no tests fail in version 1.2, everything seems fine.

There's a big problem lurking here, however. You're testing only the fixes to your class, not the dependent classes. Often when a new bug is fixed, one or more additional bugs are introduced into the system. This phenomenon is sometimes called the *ripple effect* or the "fix one, get one free" phenomenon. Those new bugs might not be caught for a while, and that's why regression testing is essential.

If automated regression testing tools and test coverage analyzers were part of your process, you would have created version 1.1, and SQA would run tests for it along with test suites for the dependent classes. Then you and your fellow developers that are responsible for any classes in which tests failed would be contacted, make the appropriate fixes, and send version 1.2 to SQA. SQA then would run tests for the complete system including the fixes that you made. If all went well, version 1.2 would be ready for release.

The safest approach to regression testing is simply to rerun all tests for the system after each change is made. That way, if there is a failure, you know which change caused it. In developing a large system, however, this approach can cause a project to grind to a halt.

If an object-oriented approach is used, there is an alternative to this. An object-oriented system is made up of independent objects that interact with each other only through well-defined interfaces, using an analysis tool to determine the depth and area of inheritance and the coupling between classes. Each class then (theoretically, at least) can be regression-tested

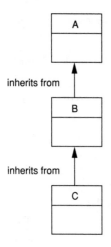

inherits from

inherits from

Figure 13.3 Class dependencies.

with only classes dependent upon it. With this approach, you probably won't have to retest the whole system each time tests fail, and the results of regression testing can be made available to developers in record time.

Requirements-Based Testing

Because a high-quality product is essentially defined as one that fulfills the customers' requirements (Crosby 1979), it makes sense that most test cases should be based on specific requirements. There obviously will be tests designed to verify code coverage, and there will be a number of tests to validate implementation components not included in the requirements.

Tools that assist in the generation of test cases based on requirements assume a good requirements specification. To get to the next level of automated test-generation and reuse, good requirements management is critical.

The strictest definition of requirements-based testing dictates that each test be derived entirely from a requirement. In practice, this seldom works because few requirements specifications can, or should, be written at a low enough level of detail. A more realistic approach is to develop tests to verify all requirements against the code in as much detail as feasible.

Schulmeyer (1990, 118) provides guidelines for adequate test coverage of requirements:

> 1) Every specified requirement is covered by at least one test case. 2) Test cases have been selected for both "average" and "boundary" conditions such as minimum and maximum values. 3) "Stress" cases have been selected such as out-of- bounds values, and 4) test cases that exercise combinations of different functions are included.

To understand how code can be tested against requirements, consider the following tests, based on the two examples introduced in chapter 2:

Trace anchor STRS0001. The SPR/SRR system shall be open only to users with a valid password.

Tests. Attempt to access the system without a valid password. Attempt to access the system with a valid password.

Trace anchor STRS0004. It shall be possible for many SRRs to correspond to the same STR, and many STRs can be fixed by a single SRR.

Tests. Enter an STR and several SRRs corresponding to it. Query the database to verify that the STR and SRRs are correctly related.

Enter several STRs and one SRR that corresponds to all of them. Query the database to verify that the STRs and the SRR are correctly related.

To test the automated parking garage software, a simulator is required. Assuming a simulation capability is available, the following tests can be run:

Trace anchor APG0001. The parking garage shall be open only to drivers with valid parking-debit cards (PDCs).

Tests. Attempt to enter using a PDC for which there is insufficient money (for a day's parking) in the corresponding account. If the entrance gate does not open, the test is successful.

Attempt to enter using a magnetically encoded card that does not have a corresponding account. If the entrance gate does not open, the test is successful.

Attempt to enter using a magnetically encoded card that has a corresponding account containing sufficient funds or a day of parking. If the entrance gate opens, the test is successful.

Note: The preceding three test cases must be run with parking spaces available in the garage.

Trace anchor APG0002. A unique, encoded number on each PDC shall correspond to a unique account number for each card holder. The account number shall be printed on each daily management report.

Test. For a representative sample of PDCs, access the database and print a customer report. If the test is successful, only one account will be printed for each number.

Trace anchor APG0008. The number of available parking spaces shall be tracked constantly, incrementing by one for each car that enters, and decrementing by one for each car that leaves. The number of available spaces shall be displayed on a sign outside the parking garage.

Test. With one parking space left in the garage, one car will enter, and no cars will be allowed to leave until the test is completed. If the test is successful, the parking-status sign will be lit with the words "LOT FULL."

Summary

The level of verification needed for high-quality mission-critical systems can't be achieved without both a good testing process and good automated testing tools. Test planning is part of a good process, and an existing process can be improved through the integration of the right testing tools. There are essentially six categories of available automated testing tools: requirements analysis and design testers, regression testing tools, test-reuse tools, test generators, test analyzers, and complete CAST tools. If an object-oriented methodology is part of your process, good encapsulation can keep bugs from propagating and increase testing efficiency. Object technology, however, has its own unique testing problems. Being able to develop tests to provide complete path coverage, perform regression testing, and use other tools are parts of the solutions, but no test plan will work without good, testable requirements.

References

Bezier, Boris. 1990. *Software testing techniques, second edition*. New York: Van Nostrand Reinhold.

Binder, Robert V. 1994. "Design for Testability." *Communications of the ACM*. 37(9) 87–101.

Crosby, P. 1979. *Quality is free*. New York: McGraw-Hill.

Daich, Gregory and Price, Gordon. 1992. *Test preparation, execution, and analysis tools report 1992*. Hill Air Force Base, Utah: Software Technology Support Center.

Dichter, Carl. 1993. Surviving software testing. *UNIX Review*. Feb. 1993 v11 n2 p28(7).

Farley, Kevin J. 1993. "Programs up to the Test." *Data Based Adviser*. April 1993 v11 n4 p83(9).

Humphrey, Watts. 1990. *Software process maturity*. Proceedings of the Case World Conference. Andover, MA: Digital Consulting. October 1990.

IEEE. 1990. IEEE standard glossary of software engineering terminology. *IEEE Standard* 610.12 1990.

Jorgensen, Paul G. and Carl Erickson. 1994. "Object-Oriented Integration Testing." *Communications of the ACM*. 37(9)30–38.

Marks, David. 1992. *Testing very big systems*. New York: McGraw-Hill.

Marsh, Vivien. 1994. "Testing the GUI." *DBMS*. 7(12)52–60.

McGregor, John D. and Timothy D. Korson. 1994. "Integrated Object-Oriented Testing and Development Processes." *Communications of the ACM*. 37(9)59–77.

Meyers, Glen J. 1979. *The Art of Software Testing*. New York: John Wiley and Sons.

Morin, Richard. 1993. "Distributed Quality Assurance." *UNIX Review*. Sept. 1993 v11 n9 p107(2).

Parrington, Norman and Mark Roper. 1989. *Understanding software testing*. New York: John Wiley and Sons.

Poston, Robert. 1992. "A complete toolkit for the software tester." *Crosstalk*. October 1992.

Poston, Robert N. 1994. "Automated Testing from Object Models." *Communications of the ACM*. 37(9)87–101.

Price, Gordon, Bryce Ragland, and Gregory Daich. 1993. *Source Code Static Analysis Report 1993, Volumes 1 and 2*. Hill Air Force Base, Utah: Software Technology Support Center.

Schulmeyer, Gordon. 1990. *Zero-Defect Software*. New York: McGraw-Hill.

Silver, Bill. 1993. *The Computer Conference Analysis Newsletter*. Dec. 9, 1993 n333 p11(1).

Yourdon, Edward. 1994. *Object-Oriented Systems Design: An Integrated Approach*. Englewood Cliffs, New Jersey: Prentice Hall.

14

Exception Handling: When Bad Things Happen to Good Software

Even when things go wrong, a mission-critical system needs to keep on running. It certainly is not acceptable to die a silent death or simply display a generic error message. A flight-control system, for example, must remain functional despite incorrect input, bad memory, device errors, power glitches, or coding errors. Even the best pilot would panic if his controls locked up and all that appeared on his cockpit display was "Internal Error." If things are not entirely right with the system, problems must be detected and some action needs to be taken to keep the system alive.

It's no secret that error handling is a weak link in most mission-critical software development efforts—object-oriented projects included. Object-oriented approaches tend to address error handling less adequately than do other methodologies. This is due in part to the fact that most object-oriented practitioners assume a system consisting of encapsulated objects isn't subject to the same error-handling problems that plague structured systems. In addition, most object-oriented teams need all their energy just to get up to speed in the basics of the new paradigm, and they can design only a minimal system in the face of an unrealistic schedule.

To make matters worse, error-handling methods are not taught adequately to new software developers, and few books address the topic at all. Those who have learned intelligent error-handling strategies (especially in the object-oriented paradigm) have done so through hard-won experience.

The fact that error handling tends to be, at best, an afterthought doesn't help the situation either. Most methodologies (structured or object-oriented) don't mention error handling or, at best, recommend it be considered only after the rest of the system has been essentially designed. In practice, it usually is not addressed until deep into implementation.

In spite of all of this, most mission-critical systems eventually have some built-in error-handling capability, as untimely, inefficient, and ineffective as it may be. In the most rudimentary cases, error handling consists of conditional statements scattered throughout the code with little rhyme or reason.

The Old-Fashioned Way

It used to be that, if you wanted to make your software bulletproof, there wasn't much help available. Your only choice was to write line after line of difficult-to-test-and-maintain code to detect and handle errors, such as the following:

```
if value > UPPER_LIMIT return
UPPER_LIMIT_EXCEEDED
    else if value < LOWER_LIMIT return LOWER_LIMIT_EXCEEDED
```

In many mission-critical systems, this error-handling code is inserted into the middle of virtually every algorithm. This undesigned error-handling code can make up over ⅓ of a piece of a mission-critical system, driving complexity into the design (Rafnel 1993). Things are even worse for programmers in the maintenance phase, who spend up to 90% of their time on code written to take care of situations that typically occur only 1% of the time (Goodman 1994).

Traditionally in mission-critical systems, each function determines and returns its own error status, and calling functions must act accordingly. Through this approach, interfaces can become cluttered with error-flags, and an added level of complexity is driven into algorithms throughout a system. This is made even worse when a module must keep track of multiple error states. Other schemes include setting and checking global status variables and using a common set of error routines to assert and handle exceptions.

It is possible to simply use longjump() and setjump() or go to a label where something might be done to remedy the error. However, this approach does not "unwind" through the stack and leaves the machine in an unknown state. This is bound to lead to disaster, considering the complex objects that can end up on mission-critical system stacks. When it comes to reusable component libraries, this approach has another major shortcoming. Because the designer of a library component can detect errors but has no knowledge of how a user might want to handle them, a component would have to know about the user's program to jump to a meaningful label.

To produce a quality software product, error handling must be approached in a similar fashion to all other features of the software being developed. Error contexts need to be determined via scenarios, requirements must be written, then objects need to be modeled and designed. As the system as a whole is designed and implemented, strict encapsulation standards must be followed. In addition, the interface that is designed for each object must detail the error-handling methods used. This leads to more efficient, verifiable, and maintainable software, because the effects of errors can be isolated to a specific class. This facilitates debugging, because the effects of a bug (for example, a memory-allocation problem) often are not visible until long after the error occurred.

Objective Anomalies

The impact of object technology on error handling generally is positive. Error classes fit well into inheritance hierarchies, and a class can contain polymorphic functions (see chapter 9) and data to facilitate error detection and handling. These aspects, along with the exception handling features available in some object-oriented languages, make the object-oriented paradigm well suited for error-handling subsystems.

The object paradigm is not necessarily compatible with error handling. In the requirements phase, careful consideration of error handling can lead to a more complete object-oriented system specification. Encapsulation, including protected data access and strong typing, can limit the spread of "ripple effect" errors beyond the borders of the initially affected object. However, poorly defined error handling threatens the encapsulation of object-oriented systems because only the user of a component knows how to handle the error that was detected in the component. This can violate some of the rules of encapsulation because the user might have to know something about how the component is implemented to recover from the error.

Error handling can either weaken or strengthen a software product. If error handling is pursued in an *ad hoc* manner or is treated as an afterthought, it can destroy many of the advantages for which object-oriented systems are known. On the other hand, if it is designed into objects and created from well-designed classes, error handling can improve nearly every aspect of software development.

Object technology offers some important error-handling advantages. Languages like Ada $9x$ and C++, operating environments like Windows NT, and object-oriented database management systems offer an alternative to checking and setting states in the midst of complex functions.

Exception Handling

With reliability being a major requirement for most mission-critical systems, it would seem that the best mission-critical system building blocks (languages, operating environments, component libraries, database management systems, etc.) should have features facilitating graceful error recovery.

Exception handling is built into Ada and C++ compilers, as well as into operating systems such as Microsoft Windows NT and in component libraries such as the Microsoft Foundation Classes. These exception handling features make it possible to develop software that concentrates on the 90% case, allowing you to ignore the anomalies until they occur (Goodman 1994). This makes it possible not only to develop more maintainable and reliable software but also to develop it more efficiently as well.

Generally, exception handling takes the form described in the following sections.

Declare an exception. In addition to providing the ability to define new exceptions, some systems also provide built-in exceptions to handle common anomalies. Predefined exceptions generally fit into the following categories:

- Constraint errors—Subscript out of range, etc.
- Memory errors—Not enough memory left on the heap, etc.
- Numeric errors—Divide by 0, overflow, underflow, etc.
- Program errors—The program structure is flawed (i.e., a function is exited other than via a return statement).
- Concurrency errors—Tasks aren't communicating directly, or a task dies prematurely.
- Timing errors—Time values are outside a specified range.
- I/O errors—These are raised if there are problems with format, files, devices, or types.
- Network errors—Communication problems between clients and servers.

Define the block of code to be checked. Within this block, exceptions will be "thrown" or "raised" when errors occur.

Define exception behavior. This is the code to be executed when an exception is thrown or raised. Several effective actions are:

- Retry the block of code (especially effective for I/O errors).
- Roll back to previous good state.
- Execute a different block of code.
- Log the error and display a message.

For example, this is how the Windows NT exception-handling feature looks:

```
__try
{
// Check the code in this block for errors, raise an exception if
errors occur
        RaiseException(...);
}
__except (exception filter)
{
  //     Do this when errors occur
}
```

Where the exception filter enumerates the exceptions to be handled.

Making Exceptions for Ada and C++

The Ada approach to error handling starts by assuming that programmers are, by nature, a bit shortsighted and sloppy, especially when a large group of them are working together on a project. C++ assumes that programmers know what they are doing and tries to stay out of their way unless asked to step in and help. Unlike C++, Ada assumes that there will be run-time errors and automatically makes provisions for detecting and handling the most common of them. Even if these exceptions are not handled in a program, Ada will display helpful information when they occur, such as a number of the erroneous line in the program and a list of the sections in the Ada Language Reference Manual that pertain to the error. All of this can lead to run-time overhead. Ada therefore includes a pragma (preprocessor request) called "suppress," which turns off all automatic run-time checking. Because the implementation of this pragma is compiler dependent, refer to your compiler manual for details.

Once we find an exception, we want to do more than simply display a relevant error message if we can. We really would like to do something in the exception handler to recover from the error so that the program can continue to run. This could be a retry of the block of code that failed (i.e., user input is involved), trying alternate memory or an alternate device, or restarting the system. The exception features in both Ada and C++ allow not only for detection of the error but correction as well. A user-defined Ada exception consists of a declaration of the exception, one or more raisings of the exception, and one or more handlers for the exception, as in the following simple example:

```
package Exception_Demo is
    Bad_Input : exception; -- can be declared like any data object.
    procedure Anything(x : in integer);
end Exception_Demo;
```

```
package body Exception_Demo is
    procedure Anything (x : in integer) is
    begin
      if x > 10 then
        raise Bad_Input; -- sends control to nearest exception block,
                          -- backing through the call chain.
      end if;
    end Anything;
end Exception_Demo;

with Exception_Demo;
procedure Main is
begin
   Exception_Demo.Anything(11); -- This call to Anything will cause an
                                -- exception to be raised.
     Exception                  -- begin exception block
       when Exception_Demo.Bad_Input =>
         put ("Bad Input!");    -- Almost any statements can
         Input_Error_Recovery;  -- make up a handler.
      when others =>            -- Catches anything not already caught.
         put ("Another Error detected");
         Clean_Up_Resources;
         raise;                 -- Sends it on to the caller
                                -- because we can't handle it here.
end Main;
```

Note that `raise` without an argument reraises the current exception. If no handler for a raised exception is found in the call chain, the program dies and an error message indicating that there was an unhandled exception is displayed. If an exception is raised when the exception name is not in our scope, it can be handled only with a `when others =>` statement.

As explained in the C++ language standard, exceptions consist of three parts: throw (the same as a raise in Ada), catch (like a handler in an Ada exception block), and try, which defines the scope of the code to be checked for exceptions. A throw essentially acts like a jump with a parameter and transfers control to a corresponding catch. The catch tells what to do when the exception is thrown. A catch can appear only after a try block or after another catch. The try block consists of all the code to which the catches after the block and the corresponding throws inside the block apply.

Here's what a simple C++ exception looks like:

```
main() {
    try {                      // try block
      anything(11);
    }
    catch (Ex& Ex_catch) {     // exception handler
        cout << Ex_catch.Input_Error_Recovery() << endl;
    }
    catch (...) {  // means "catch anything not already caught"
        cout << Clean_Up_Resources() << endl;
        throw;                 // sends it on to the caller
                               // because we can't handle it here.
    }
}
```

Throw and catch each take a single operator of any type (in this case, class Ex). An exception gets thrown like this:

```
void
anything(int x) {
        if (x > 10)
            throw Ex("Bad Input!");

};
```

When the throw is executed, control will be passed up to the nearest exception handler in the call chain that can deal with the exception.

Because C++ exception handlers accept a parameter, we have the opportunity to define a class that has member functions to help deal with the exception:

```
class Ex {
    //...
public:
    Ex(const char*):
    const char* Input_Error_Recovery();
};
```

Note that, if an exception is thrown and never finds a handler, the built-in function `terminate()` will be called. `terminate()` executes the last function given as an argument to `set_terminate()`.

From the preceding examples, it should be obvious that the syntax and function of both Ada and C++ are very much the same. Their recommended usage is similar as well. In general, both C++ and Ada exceptions should be used only for events that are not expected in the normal flow of execution. For example, an exception should not be used to indicate the last element in a list or the end of a file. Exceptions should be reserved to indicate bad input, device errors, memory errors, etc. Ada and C++ exception handlers should be placed in the calling function or Ada procedure, just up the call chain from where a corresponding exception might be raised or thrown.

In addition to the similarities, there also are important differences. Because C++ supports inheritance, a hierarchy of related classes can be defined and used as exception parameters. This would work well for a category of related errors, such as those pertaining to numeric or I/O operations. The concept of a *try block* is relatively foreign to Ada, as is the concept of passing an exception parameter. C++ has no built-in exceptions and precious little automatic run-time checking.

Exceptions almost always involve more overhead than straight-line code, but any kind of good error handling will involve more overhead than a "don't care" approach. Compared to other methods, exceptions can be very efficient, depending upon the kind of optimization that your compiler does.

You would be well advised to check your compiler manuals before using a lot of exception handling, because some compilers produce a huge amount of code to handle an exception.

Exceptions in Ada form the basis for extensive run-time checking, and are uniformly supported on all compilers. C++ exceptions add a customized run-time checking capability that is sorely needed in the language. As of this writing, however, there are several different flavors of exception handling supported on C++ compilers that are not supported on all C++ compilers.

The Good Old Stuff

If a major error occurs during execution, the best approach often is to roll back to a previous good state. In some systems, this is best accomplished by saving a consistent set of critical data periodically and rolling back to the saved data when an error occurs. This approach is called *checkpointing* and often is used in embedded real-time systems, as well as in other high-criticality software. This approach is effective but far from perfect because the overhead for frequent checkpointing can be high, especially as a huge set of data must be saved. In addition, saving and restoring a set of data doesn't guarantee that execution can continue, especially if the problem involves incorrect input.

One error-handling approach attempts to prevent errors from actually occurring by defining wrapping operations within *transactions*. The idea is to build up a buffer of executable functions during a transaction, then actually execute or *commit* them at the end of the transaction if all goes well. If there is an error, the commitment is aborted and the potential error never occurs. This automatically resets the system back to a previous good state (Rafnel 1993).

This approach is directly supported by many database management systems and can be quite effective in keeping errors out of persistent data storage. There can be significant overhead involved in trying to prevent errors through transactions, and unfortunately, the approach doesn't work for all types of systems.

In general, transactions look like this:

```
begin Transaction One
   .... Executable statements
   if there_is_a_problem then
      abort_transaction
   end if
 ... more executable statements
commit Transaction One
```

Note that, when the `abort_transaction` is executed, all of the changes that would have been made to data elements in the system during this transaction will be abandoned and effectively undone. The system then will return to a previous good state.

When it comes to using transactions, the best advice is to wrap only the most critical data updates in small transactions. This will involve far less overhead that encasing huge blocks of code in one transaction, and it will make it far easier to abandon changes when things go wrong.

Error Logging

Whether or not an error can be corrected when it is detected at run time, it's a good idea to log errors in persistent memory. A circular queue is an ideal data structure for this. The type of information that should be stored for each error that was detected varies with the type of system being implemented, but it generally includes the following:

- An identifier for the function that generated the error.
- The state that caused the error.
- An alphanumeric code identifying the recommended correction.
- An alphanumeric code identifying the severity of the error (refer to chapter 13 for more information or error severity).
- An identifier for the error.
- A reference to the appropriate error-message string.
- The current state of the processor and other hardware components.

Off-the-Shelf

Off-the-shelf solutions range in complexity from overloading existing memory allocation functions to detect memory leaks to a full range of run-time error handling—including stack, heap, range, and numeric checking.

Examples of available run-time error-checking packages are: SmartHeap from MicroQuill Software Publishing, Inc., Sentinel from AIB Software Corp. (Freeman-Benson 1993), Bounds Checker from Nu-Mega Technologies Inc. (Knoblaugh 1993), and Purify from Pure Software Inc. (Nelson 1993). An off-the-shelf package might be suitable for inhouse debugging or for including in a beta release to assist in testing by customers.

Off-the-shelf solutions can't perform all of the error handling needed on a mission-critical system, but they can be an important component of a comprehensive error-handling strategy. If you're using a language that doesn't have built-in run-time error checking, such as C or C++, it's vital that an off-the-shelf error-handling package be included throughout the development process. Because there often is a performance penalty for extensive run-time error checking, error-checking packages often are included for testing but not in the final product.

Built-In Testing

If hardware (or in some cases, system software) reliability constantly needs to be ensured (as often is the case in embedded, real-time systems) or simply needs to provide extra error checking to assure reliability, tests can be built into the software itself. During times when the processor otherwise would be idle (in "background mode"), these tests are run to assure hardware components—such as memory, disk storage, network access, and I/O capabilities—are working well.

As these components are checked, a log of related data often is kept. When the system crashes, this log, as well as other error-logging structures in the system, serve the same purpose as a flight data recorder in an airplane. In both cases, the recorded data is analyzed to determine the cause of the crash.

Built-in testing, sometimes called "BITE" or "BIT," can be designed to run not only in background mode but at startup only or on demand. The initial BITE, which is run at startup, checks the initial state of the hardware. On-demand BITE can be run during program execution to determine the state of the system. If a problem is detected—such as a nonfunctional I/O port, some bad memory chips, or a bug in a low-level utility function—the system can take appropriate action depending on severity.

In spite of the problems BITE detects, the system might be able to continue to run in a degraded mode, without the functionality provided by specific components. In the worst of cases, it might be necessary to halt the system and display the error logs.

Ambitious built-in testing can add great complexity, so this approach should be used sparingly in all but the most critical embedded systems. In addition, it is impossible to exhaustively monitor a system from the inside without affecting the performance and reliability of the system. Built-in testing also can be extremely difficult to test, as can error handling in general.

Error-Handling Strategies

A successful error-handling strategy in a mission-critical system must include facilities for detecting and logging anomalies, as well as strategies for error recovery. It also must include strategies for recovery, such as checkpointing transactions, retrying blocks of code, etc. In most systems, a wise mix of several different detection and correction methods must be used. Depending upon the criticality of the system as a whole, schedule pressure, project budget, customer requirements, and the type of system (embedded real-time, information processing, etc.), error-handling strategies ranging from very aggressive to minimally aggressive can be adopted.

A moderately aggressive strategy, for example, might specify that built-in testing be provided for those objects that deal most directly with hardware components and that the most crucial database updates be wrapped in transactions. Specific exception handlers might be provided for errors only of the highest severity, and only high or moderately high severity errors will be logged.

The minimum level of error handling acceptable in a mission-critical system must include logging and specific exception handlers for the most severe errors, as well as boundary checking and memory-allocation error detection. In addition, all errors must be handled in some manner, even if by a default handler, so that the user is never left with a frozen system and no clues about the cause. Ideally, each error must be handled within its scope to avoid losing information and provide a reasonable chance at recovery.

Armed with object technology, the tools of structured exception handling, third-party libraries and tools, and the other methods described in this chapter, software developers can create mission-critical systems that are not only more reliable but also more reusable and maintainable as well.

Summary

To ensure reliability in a mission-critical system, error-handling capabilities must be considered during the requirements analysis and design process. Object technology can have a positive impact on error handling because encapsulation can help restrict the spread of "tramp errors," inheritance and polymorphism can provide class hierarchies of error handlers, and some object-oriented languages have well-designed error-handling features. Off-the-shelf error-handling software is available, as are error-handling library components. Error-recovery strategies include retrying the error, trying an alternate path and rolling back to a previous good state.

Transactions that allow changes to be abandoned and the system to revert to a previous good state and built-in testing that periodically checks for error states throughout the system are examples of aggressive error-handling strategies. Error logging is a capability that must be included in any mission-critical system. Error logs can provide invaluable bug-detection information.

Detecting and correcting run-time errors and exceptional cases can constitute a huge programming problem in a mission-critical system. Fortunately, there are built-in language features, off-the-shelf error-checking software operating system features, library components, and some effective strategies to help get error handling under control. Using these tools, programmers are freed from designing the nuts and bolts of error handling, and can focus on designing a system the customer wants.

References

Barnes, J. G. P. 1991. *Programming in Ada plus language reference manual.* Wokingham, England: Addison-Wesley, 1991.

Freeman-Benson, Bjorn N. 1993. "Sentinel." *Unix Review.* Sept. 1993 v11 n9 p58(1).

Goodman, Kevin. 1994. "Clearer, more comprehensive error processing with Win32 structured exception handling." *Microsoft Systems Journal.* Jan. 1994 v9 n1 p29(10).

Johnson, Jay. "Handling Exceptions in Ada and C++." *Embedded Systems Programming.* 6(12)42–45.

Keffer, Thomas. 1993. "Creating C++ Libraries." *UNIX Review.* July 1993 v11 n7 p46(7).

Knoblaugh, Rich. 1993. "Fortify your programs with Bounds-Checker for Windows." *PC Magazine.* Sept. 28, 1993 v12 n16 p77(1).

Murray, James. 1993 *C++ strategies and tactics.* Reading, Massachusetts: Addison-Wesley, 1993.

Nelson, Taed. 1993 "Finding run-time memory errors: a sophisticated tool for the thorniest of bugs." *Dr. Dobbs Journal.* Nov. 1993 v18 n12 p34(7).

Rafnel, Bruce A. 1993. "A transaction approach to error handling." *Hewlett-Packard Journal.* June 1993 v44 v3 p71(7).

Reed, David R. 1993. "Exceptions (pragmatic features with a new language feature)." *C++ Report.* October 1993 p39(6).

Stevens, Al. 1993. "C++ exception handling." *Dr. Dobbs Journal.* Sept. 1993 v18 n9 p105(5).

Stroustrup, Bjarane. 1991. *The C++ Programming Language.* Reading, Massachusetts: Addison-Wesley, 1991.

A Sample Formal Process

Chapter 2 was devoted to a thorough discussion of high-powered processes. Attributes of a good process were discussed as were the warning signs that process might be in trouble. Additionally, it was emphasized that there is no perfect process, no silver bullet. Having made that assertion, however, it would be beneficial to present for the reader a sample formal process or a kind of process template. This would be useful in the following situations, for example:

- A small shop has been operating informally in the past and now is suffering "growing pains" due to rapid expansion. The last project got out of control due to the informality of the development environment, and they need to get some formalization of process in place.

- An organization started a project with little or no formal processes in place but now is running into problems due to the lack of formalization. To make matters worse, there is very little inhouse process expertise.

- An organization had had varied success with formal processes in the past but wants to firm up the "weak areas" with specific improvements to the process.

Obtain Project Management Support

It is not by coincidence that this aspect of formal process should be the starting point. This is because it is the most important aspect of process. Project management support must be obtained at the initial stages of a program and maintained throughout the project. This support must be manifested through active involvement in the process definition and modification efforts. Get a key member of upper management to be a process "sponsor" that must be involved (as an observer) in the step-by-step implementation of process.

Gather the Process Experience and Analyze Available Process Skills

Among the initial project staff, determine who has formal process experience and interest. In addition to putting together a process team, consider bringing on external process consultants. Bringing on external consultants might be difficult, especially for organizations that have a history of disdain for external consultation.

Prior process experience might abound on the project. This experience, however, might be that which was garnered during process "failures." These individuals might not have adequate knowledge and training of formal process but might think that they do. There are several software process assessment methods that can be used as a basis for implementation of software process on a project. (See Table A.1.) For a more detailed explanation of each of these assessment methods, refer to the glossary.

Empower the Process Team

Empowerment is a term that is used frequently but often misapplied. A process team must be established early on in the project. It must be empowered to make decisions, and these decisions must be supported by upper management and implemented by the project. As described in chapter 1, it is inevitable that, when difficulties arise, sections of the project will want to forgo elements of the process.

One of the first tasks of the process team should be ensuring that they have a method for not only putting the process in place but also providing the mechanism for modifying the process. This occurs mostly through the mere existence of the process team. This team must ensure that there is an adequate method for input into the process definition effort and feedback to the group to be able to support rapid modifications to the process, if desired.

TABLE A.1 Assessment Methods

Origin	Name	Focus	Proj. size
SEI	CMM	PCD, PI	Large
BT	SAM	PCD	Large
Bell, NT	Trillium	PCD, PI	Large
HP	SQPA	PI	Medium
COMPITA	STD	PI	Small
ESPIRIT	Bootstrap	PI	Medium
ISO	SPICE	PCD, PI	All

The key to effective process is that it is just that, a "process." It must be able to be modified and fit the needs of the organization, the people involved, and the customer.

Refrain from "Wheel Reinvention"

Use as many tools and procedures that already are in place which make sense. If there is a CASE tool that has limited scope but is well understood and minimally meets your needs, then by all means try to incorporate it into the process. When developing format standards for documents, use industry standards and tools that already are in place. For example, many projects will spend an extraordinary amount of time and effort coming to agreement on the appropriate coding standards. The same is true for most languages. There are industry-accepted coding standards available (and supporting tools) that can and should be used.

Make an Appropriate Life-Cycle Choice

The waterfall life cycle will be around for a very long time. We have discussed spiral and other concurrent life-cycle methods in this book. In general, these life cycles will address the concurrent nature of software development better than a strict waterfall approach. Like any other aspect of the development process, just using something new will not guarantee success. It must be used appropriately.

If this project is part of an organization that has always implemented a strict waterfall life-cycle approach, then perhaps using a modified waterfall approach might be best, at first. For example, even if the project has a single deliverable product to the customer, partitioning the requirements into phased releases using some early prototyping might be all that the project can handle for its first attempt at concurrent phase development.

Choose an Appropriate Method

A major thread of this book has been the benefits of the use of object-oriented methods and techniques. Like any other aspect of software process, the development team must be able to implement the method that is chosen. If an organization is not able to implement functional methodologies well, it's likely that they're not going to be able to implement any other methodology (including object-oriented methodologies) well.

Document Format

Establish the least complicated document format that can be accommodated into user requirements. Do not allow document maintenance to drive the program. The documents must be usable to the developers and the customer.

Requirements documents

Make certain that maintenance of the requirements documents is possible in "real-time." Requirements will change. Count on it. Requirements documentation is useless if changes to the documents cannot be updated in such a way as to make them useful. If a diagramming tool is used for requirements representation, especially if the requirements are organized in a "functional manner," refrain from attempting to link this requirements representation with an implied design structure. There is no necessary link between requirements representation and implementation. Simply put, don't overdo it.

Design documentation

As with requirements documentation, design documentation must be easily modifiable. With the widespread use of CASE tools, it is customary to fall into the trap of having a false sense of security because all of the diagrams "balanced." Most CASE tools have internal consistency checks that must balance before the design is correct. As a result, unfortunately, all too often more attention is paid to getting the model to balance instead of ensuring that the model provides a basis for the implementation that satisfies the requirements.

Code

Compliance with coding standards should be accomplished through the use of formatting tools, tailorable language-sensitive editors (LSEs), "pretty-printers," or more sophisticated coding standards compliance tools. The common look and feel that coding standards enforce will enhance productivity at reviews.

User documentation (user manuals)

If there is user documentation to be delivered, do not wait until the end of the project to begin generating it. For many projects, there is a distinct aversion to begin the user manuals too early. There is a fear that the system will change enough before the final version is delivered that most preliminary work will be premature and result in wasted effort. There is one area of the development, however, that desperately needs access to user documentation and that is testing.

It usually is not too difficult to put together preliminary user documentation using screen dumps and brief functional descriptions. There will be some resources expended, but it usually will be well worth the effort to the testers. Very often testers are brought in who have little or no knowledge of the product. Any kind of user documentation, preliminary as it might be, will be extremely helpful.

Tool Choice

Ensure that the tools that are acquired are necessary and comply with the rest of the software process that is being implemented for the project. Make sure that the tools don't drive the process, but also make sure that all process decisions are supportable by available tools.

Make absolutely certain that all tool development choices are scrutinized carefully. Is the tool necessary? If it is necessary, has it already been written? Are we trying to do too much with this toolset? Do the tools fit well with our process?

Risk Management

Although risk management generally is considered to be a project management issue, when putting together an appropriate process, appropriate attention to high-risk areas is critical. For example, it might have been determined that an object-oriented method might work well for the application that is being developed. If there is little OO experience on the project, then without OO mentors and an aggressive commitment to training, project risk will be high.

Every aspect of the process (and project) needs to be thoroughly analyzed for potential risk areas. If an aspect of the proposed process imposes undue risk, then that aspect needs to be modified or eliminated.

Staff Requirements Analysis and Design Activities

It will be natural to increase the staffing on the project as more activities begin to occur. Early on in the project when most of the requirements analysis and design occur, the most senior analysts and designers should be utilized. No amount of "coding magic" will cure most analysis and design errors. If your organization is such that the analysis and design are performed by disjoint entities, do your best to change it. If this organization structure cannot be changed, then at least get the software designers involved in the analysis phase as much as possible and continue to have the analysts actively involved in the design as much as possible.

Training and Mentoring

Ensure that a training program is in place (and has been funded) for all aspects of the program. Make sure that there is adequate tool, method, and process training. There are two other aspects of training that go largely un-heeded on most projects: timing of the training and ongoing "mentoring" programs to follow up on the formal training.

Timeliness of the training is critical. Appropriate training that is too late has its obvious drawbacks. The training also can be too early. For example, if some new testing tools have been developed, it probably is not appropri-ate to start training early on in the project. For the training to be effective, what is learned from the training must be used.

Another aspect of training that is practically ignored in all but a select few projects is that of training follow-up or mentoring. There must be des-ignated experts that can be consulted, each in a specific area: language, CASE tool, document format, process, debugging, testing, etc. One of the reasons given for not implementing this element of the process is that it can overburden a few select individuals. This certainly is possible, but there is no reason that these experts cannot offload this expertise to newly trained experts.

Another aspect of this "mentoring" approach is implementing online question and answer "forums" for technical questions. It is extremely rare that someone has a question that someone else does not also have. There is not a method more conducive to learning than seeing the question asked and answered and having ancillary discussions about the topic in question. The "expert" also saves time because the question is asked and answered once.

Reviews

When setting up the details of the formal software process for your project, ensure that an adequate level of inspections and reviews occurs. Reviews and inspections can take on varying degrees of formality. Whatever level of formality is decided upon, ensure that these reviews occur and are at-tended by all those required. It goes without saying that groups that inter-face with elements that are being developed must attend those reviews. Action items of the reviews must be documented and followed up on for the disposition of those action items.

It is critical that the reviews be handled as a means to improve the prod-uct and not to embarrass or even to critique the skills of the developer. Questions of style certainly will surface during the reviews. The reviews should be focused on exactly what is being reviewed. Other discussions should be taken offline. It sometimes is difficult to do this. Often, one will be tempted to say, "Well, I know that this is off of the topic of this review, but since we have everyone here . . . ." Often these discussions cause the origi-nal review topic to never get covered fully. There are several formal review or inspection formalisms that are worthwhile investigating and adopting.

Although reviews should be scheduled to critique all products of all phases of the development, extra scrutiny and review time should be scheduled for requirements and high-level design reviews.

Summary

The previous discussion is a kind of process template. All of this should exist to some degree in your formal process. Again, the details will be specific to your organization.

Glossary

Ada Reference to the language that originally was developed for the DoD and initially released in 1985 for use in most new military systems. Ada has been widely accepted as an object-based language.

Ada 9X Latest release of the Ada language. This version is to be released in the 1994–1995 time frame, thus the 9X appellation. This version will include constructs to better support object-oriented development activities among other "improvements."

Capability Maturity Model (CMM) A process assessment method that was developed by the Software Engineering Institute (SEI) at Carnegie-Mellon University. The model developed by the SEI is used to determine the relative level at which a given software organization or project is able to develop "good" software using "good" processes.

CASE Computer Aided Software Engineering. An often-used term that usually refers to tools used in this arena.

CEO-level error A runtime error serious enough to gain the attention of upper-level management.

client/server A "server" is a software entity that provides data or processing, and a "client" is a software entity that consumes data or processing provided by a server. Specific machines also can be designated as servers that provide processing and data, and others as clients that use the processing and data provided by the servers.

CNN-level error A runtime error so serious that it can result in unwanted media coverage.

concurrent programs Programs in which there are several processes or tasks that are executed simultaneously (also known as *parallel programs*).

empowerment Concept by which individuals or teams are able to make decisions without always having to obtain management approval.

encapsulation Both data and functionality integrated into a class, object, or package.

exception handling When an error occurs during the execution of a program, the error can be "thrown" to a "handler" where steps can be taken to recover from the error. Exception handling features are available in several different programming languages, including C++ and Ada.

inheritance A class can be composed of data definitions and functionality from other classes. Inheritance facilitates this by means of a family tree of classes, with each class inheriting capabilities from its ancestors.

MIP   Millions of instructions per second. A metric that is used to measure processor performance.

object oriented   That concept that describes or has to do with that modern aspect of software development methods that attempts to model the software solution more in terms of the way that the problem being modelled exists in the "real world." This is in contrast to more historical software development methods such as functional decomposition or data-flow models.

object-oriented programming   Developing software based on functionality and related data definitions combined into units called "classes" or "objects."

object-oriented requirements analysis (OORA)   The application of object-oriented techniques to activities that typically are denoted as analysis or requirements analysis.

parallel programs   Programs in which there are several processes or tasks that are executed simultaneously (also known as *concurrent programs*).

parametric polymorphism   Fill-in-the-blank programming in which placeholders for data types and processing are provided in class definitions. Actual values then can be substituted for the placeholders, resulting in different executable objects based on a single definition.

polymorphism   Changing the functionality of an object at runtime, based on the classes to which the object corresponds.

process (software process)   An organized, documented set of methods that are used for software development activities.

prototyping   A software development construct by which a subset of the final deliverable product is developed very early in the software life cycle. A prototype typically is used as a "proof of concept" mechanism.

regression testing   Rerunning tests to make sure that a program still works after modifications are made.

rendezvous   The event that occurs when two tasks combine into a single thread of execution and possibly exchange information, at which point the two tasks are said to be synchronized.

requirements   Capabilities that a system must have to be useful to its intended customers.

requirements analysis   Organizing and prioritizing requirements in such a way as to lead to a successful design.

requirements specification   A document detailing all of the functions a system must perform to be useful to a customer.

SEI   Software Engineering Institute. A part of Carnegie-Mellon Institute, funded by DARPA, that is chartered with investigating methods and proposing models to improve software process activities.

sequential process   A process or task in which there is a series of operations where each operation is completed before the next one is executed.

software development environment   A set of integrated software consisting of an operating system, a software development framework, a database management system, a network, and tools for testing and configuration management.

software development framework   A set of integrated software tools, often including a compiler and linker, a GUI builder, debugger, class library, class browser, and online help.

stress testing   Simulating extreme conditions to determine the robustness of a program.

teaming   The method by which individuals working on a software project gather together for a fixed period of time to solve a finite problem or a set of problems.

thread of control   The series of operations within a process or task.

TQM   Total Quality Management. A management philosophy under which operational decisions are made at the lowest possible level. The intent is to empower individuals to make decisions that typically, in the past, were made by management even though staff at lower levels were capable of making these decisions.

Index

ABOUT THE AUTHORS

JAY JOHNSON started developing software before the beginning of the PC revolution and now is a senior software engineer at Honeywell. His articles appear regularly in various computer magazines, and he has given a number of lectures on various software-development topics.

ROD SKOGLUND is an independent consultant and currently is developing software systems at Honeywell. Over the years, he has developed software systems for Motorola, Sundstrand, and Boeing. Rod's experience spans all phases of the software development life cycle.

JOE WISNIEWSKI (MSEE) has been a lead software developer for the last 10 years. He owns his own software consulting services company in Phoenix, Arizona. The company specializes in all phases of software development and training.